Los Angeles

" "When it comes to information on regional history, what to see and do, and shopping, these guides are exhaustive."

—*USAir Magazine*

"Usable, sophisticated restaurant coverage, with an emphasis on good value."

—Andy Birsh, *Gourmet Magazine* columnist

"Valuable because of their comprehensiveness."

—*Minneapolis Star-Tribune*

"Fodor's always delivers high quality...thoughtfully presented...thorough."

—*Houston Post*

"An excellent choice for those who want everything under one cover."

—*Washington Post* "

Fodor's Travel Publications, Inc.
New York • Toronto • London • Sydney • Auckland

Fodor's Los Angeles

Editor: Alison B. Stern

Contributors: Steven Amsterdam, Robert Andrews, Robert Blake, William P. Brown, Bruce David Colen, Seira de la Croix, Echo Garrett, Janice Wald Henderson, Mary Jane Horton, Jane E. Lasky, Lynne Lussier, Ellen Melinkoff, Mary Ellen Schultz, Marshall T. Schwartzman, Dinah Spritzer, Aaron Sugarman, Bobbi Zane, Terri Zitnick

Creative Director: Fabrizio La Rocca

Cartographer: David Lindroth

Cover Photograph: Alan Becker/Image Bank

Text Design: Between the Covers

Copyright

Copyright © 1995 by Fodor's Travel Publications, Inc.

Fodor's is a registered trademark of Fodor's Travel Publications, Inc.

All rights reserved under International and Pan-American Copyright Conventions. Published in the United States by Fodor's Travel Publications, Inc., a subsidiary of Random House, Inc., New York, and simultaneously in Canada by Random House of Canada Limited, Toronto. Distributed by Random House, Inc., New York.

No maps, illustrations, or other portions of this book may be reproduced in any form without written permission from the publishers.

ISBN 0–679–03039–5

Special Sales

Fodor's Travel Publications are available at special discounts for bulk purchases for sales promotions or premiums. Special editions, including personalized covers, excerpts of existing guides, and corporate imprints, can be created in large quantities for special needs. For more information, contact your local bookseller or write to Special Markets, Fodor's Travel Publications, 201 East 50th Street, New York, NY 10022. Inquiries from Canada should be directed to your local Canadian bookseller or sent to Random House of Canada, Ltd., Marketing Department, 1265 Aerowood Drive, Mississauga, Ontario L4W 1B9. Inquiries from the United Kingdom should be sent to Fodor's Travel Publications, 20 Vauxhall Bridge Road, London, England SW1V 2SA.

MANUFACTURED IN THE UNITED STATES OF AMERICA

10 9 8 7 6 5 4 3 2 1

CONTENTS

On the Road with Fodor's v

About the Writers v
What's New v
How to Use This Book vi
Please Write to Us vi

The Gold Guide xv

Important Contacts A to Z xv
Smart Travel Tips A to Z xxvii

1 Destination: Los Angeles 1

Los Angeles: A Lot of Something for Everyone 2
What's Where 4
Fodor's Choice 5

2 Exploring Los Angeles 7

Tour 1: Downtown Los Angeles 9
Tour 2: Hollywood 14
Tour 3: Wilshire Boulevard 19
Tour 4: The Westside 24
Tour 5: Santa Monica, Venice, Pacific Palisades, and Malibu 27
Tour 6: Palos Verdes, San Pedro, and Long Beach 33
Tour 7: Highland Park, Pasadena, and San Marino 38
The San Fernando Valley 43
Other Places of Interest 45
Off the Beaten Track 46
Sightseeing Checklists 47

3 Shopping 53

4 Sports and Fitness 65

Spectator Sports 66
Participant Sports 67
Beaches 73

5 Dining 77

6 Lodging 97

7 The Arts and Nightlife 117

8 Excursions from Los Angeles 132

Big Bear/Lake Arrowhead 133
Catalina Island 137
Riverside 141
Temecula 143

9 Orange County 145

10	Los Angeles for Children	178
11	Portrait of Los Angeles	190
	Index	193

Maps

Los Angeles *xviii–ix*
Southern California *x–xi*
World Time Zones *xii–xiii*
Los Angeles Freeways *xiv*
Tour 1: Downtown Los Angeles *10*
Tour 2: Hollywood *15*
Tour 3: Wilshire Boulevard *20*
Tour 4: Westside *25*
Tour 5: Santa Monica and Venice *30*
Tour 6: Palos Verdes, San Pedro, and Long Beach *35*
Tour 7: Highland Park, Pasadena, San Marino *39*
Melrose Avenue Shopping *55*
Beverly Hills Shopping *61*
Los Angeles Area Beaches *74*
Los Angeles Dining *79*
Downtown Los Angeles Dining *81*
Beverly Hills and Hollywood Dining *82–83*
Coastal Los Angeles Dining *85*
San Fernando Valley Dining *87*
Los Angeles Lodging *99*
Downtown Los Angeles Lodging *100*
Beverly Hills and Hollywood Lodging *104–105*
Coastal Los Angeles Lodging *111*
San Fernando and San Gabriel Valleys Lodging *115*
Excursions from Los Angeles *134*
Big Bear Lake *135*
Catalina Island *139*
Orange County *148–149*
Orange County Dining and Lodging *162–163*

ON THE ROAD WITH FODOR'S

A GOOD TRAVEL GUIDE is like a wonderful traveling companion. It's charming, it's brimming with sound recommendations and solid ideas, it pulls no punches in describing lodging and dining establishments, and it's consistently full of fascinating facts that make you view what you've traveled to see in a rich new light. In the creation of Los Angeles '96, we at Fodor's have gone to great lengths to provide you with the very best of all possible traveling companions— and to make your trip the best of all possible vacations.

About Our Writers

The information in these pages is a collaboration of a couple of extraordinary writers.

Jane E. Lasky and William P. Brown are a pair of die-hard Angelenos who have an insatiable grasp on what this city has to give. Together, they have explored and written about the City of Angels for 15 years.

Jane E. Lasky, dubbed "Draculina" (because she always wears black), is a transplanted New Yorker who jets all over the world, working in television and print journalism. Among other credits she writes a syndicated travel column through Chronicle Features in San Francisco, now in its ninth year. Her passion, outside of media, is collecting 1940s and '50s memorabilia, including a vintage machine-age home, circa 1947.

William P. Brown is one of those rare creatures thriving in the California Southland: a native. His uniqueness is played out in the many ventures he's pursued in the past 20 years. Those who know Bill recognise him as a versatile person—a veritable "career accumulator." He owns and runs a successful dance studio (where he also teaches jazz) and has built a journalism career as well, researching and writing for numerous magazines and half a dozen travel guidebooks. Landscaping and modeling are two other careers Bill pursues.

Brown and Lasky met in a dance class in 1981 and have been collaborating ever since.

In her previous life as an editor at Fodor's, **Alison B. Stern** worked on destinations from Portugal to the Pacific Northwest, from Branson to Great Britain. She's now a freelance editor with a special place in her heart for Fodor's.

What's New

Big things are happening at Fodor's—and in Los Angeles.

A New Design

If this is not the first Fodor's guide you've purchased, you'll immediately notice our new look. More readable and easier-to-use than ever? We think so—and we hope you do, too.

New Takes on Hotels and Restaurants

As she's done every year, Jane Laskey has thoroughly updated the Dining and Lodging chapters to bring you the latest on what's cooking in some of the hippest new kitchens in L.A. and the scoop on renovations and management changes at some of your favorite hotels.

Let Us Do Your Booking

Our writers have scoured Los Angeles to come up with an extensive and well-balanced list of the best B&Bs, inns, and hotels, both small and large, new and old. But you don't have to beat the bushes to come up with a reservation. Now we've teamed up with an established hotel-booking service to make it easy for you to secure a room at the property of your choice. It's fast, it's free, and confirmation is guaranteed. If your first choice is booked, the operators can line up your second right away. Just call 1–800/FODORS–1 or 1–800/363–6771 (0800/89–1030 in Great Britain; 0014–800/12–8271 in Australia; 1–800/55–9101 in Ireland).

Travel Updates

In addition, just before your trip, you may want to order a Fodor's Worldview Travel Update. From local publications all over Los Angeles, the lively, cosmopolitan editors at Worldview gather information on concerts, plays, opera, dance performances, gallery and museum shows, sports competitions, and other special events that coincide with your visit. See the order blank at the back of this book, call 800/799–9609, or fax 800/799–9619.

And in Los Angeles

Los Angeles has always been a newsworthy city, but this has been especially true during the past five years. The eyes of the world have focused on this city while it endured the ravages of riots and fires and the devastation of the Northridge earthquake.

In 1995, a more-outrageous-than-usual event took place: the **double murder trial of L.A. resident O.J. Simpson.** For months, TV sets throughout the world were tuned to what became the country's new addiction. Of course, when tourists arrived here, O.J. and the late Nicole Brown's homes were among the first sights to see. However, rubbernecking soon ended when neighbors of this famous pair demanded that the police reroute the barrage of invaders who were intruding on the privacy of the residential area.

Determined to prove that there are better ways to spend time in sunshine city, **community efforts have been made to lure visitors Downtown.** Hollywood Boulevard, for example, has undergone megachanges to diminish its bad rap as a seedy place. In fact, some of the glamour of Hollywood's heyday is slowly being restored: The streets are on a continual cleanup program; more than 100 trees have been planted; and new lampposts shaped like massive movie kliegs have gone up around the strip. Also, high in the hills, the four-story-tall Hollywood sign had its youth restored with a face-lift in 1995.

Across town, atop the Santa Monica Mountains, finishing touches on the $400 million **Getty Center Museum** are taking place in preparation for the museum's 1997 opening, when one of the world's most renowned art collections will be unveiled.

Among the city's other improvements are several attractions at local theme parks. **Six Flags Magic Mountain,** in Valencia, opened Hurricane Harbor, a water extravaganza. Across the San Fernando Valley at **Universal Studios,** the multimillion-dollar Waterworld: A Live Sea War Spectacular promises

to be one of the most ambitious (and wettest) stunt shows ever. The attraction, scheduled to open by 1996, includes a sea-plane crash that stops just two feet short of the audience.

Catalina Island is now closer than ever, thanks to Catalina Express. The new, state-of-the-art high-speed cruising boats can get you to Avalon Harbor in less than one hour.

Disneyland has also been busy, with the opening of the treacherous Indiana Jones Adventure. It delivers action and thrills to the participant, who chooses which route to take, so guests will never experience the same ride twice. There's another Disney project, too, but this one is in downtown L.A. It's the building of the avant garde Frank Gehry–designed **Disney Concert Hall,** which will be the future home of the Los Angeles Philharmonic in 1997.

How to Use This Book

Organization

Up front is **The Gold Guide,** comprising two sections on gold-colored paper chock-full of information about traveling in general and specifically at your destination. Both are in alphabetical order by topic. **Important Contacts A to Z** gives you addresses and telephone numbers of organizations and companies that offer detailed information and publications, plus information about arriving and departing from your destination. **Smart Travel Tips A to Z** gives you specific tips on how to get the most out of your travels as well as information on how to accomplish what you need to in your destination.

Stars

Stars in the margin are used to denote highly recommended sights, attractions, hotels, and restaurants.

Credit Cards

The following abbreviations are used: **AE,** American Express; **D,** Discover; **DC,** Diners Club; **MC,** MasterCard; and **V,** Visa.

Please Write to Us

Everyone who has worked on Los Angeles has worked hard to make the text accurate. All prices and opening times are based on information supplied to us at press time, and the publisher cannot accept responsibility for any errors that may have occurred. The passage of time will bring changes, so it's always a good idea to call ahead and confirm information when it matters—particularly if you're making a detour to visit specific sights or attractions. When making reservations at a hotel or inn, be sure to mention if you have a disability or are traveling with children, if you prefer a private bath or a certain type of bed, or if you have specific dietary needs or any other concerns.

Were the restaurants we recommended as described? Did our hotel picks exceed your expectations? Did you find a museum we recommended a waste of time? Positive and negative, we would love your feedback. If you have complaints, we'll look into them and revise our entries when the facts warrant it. If there's a special place you've happened upon that we haven't included, we'll pass the information along to the writers so they can check it out. So please send us a letter or post card (we're at 201 East 50th Street, New York, New York 10022.) We'll look forward to hearing from you. And in the meantime, have a wonderful trip!

Karen Cure
Editorial Director

Los Angeles

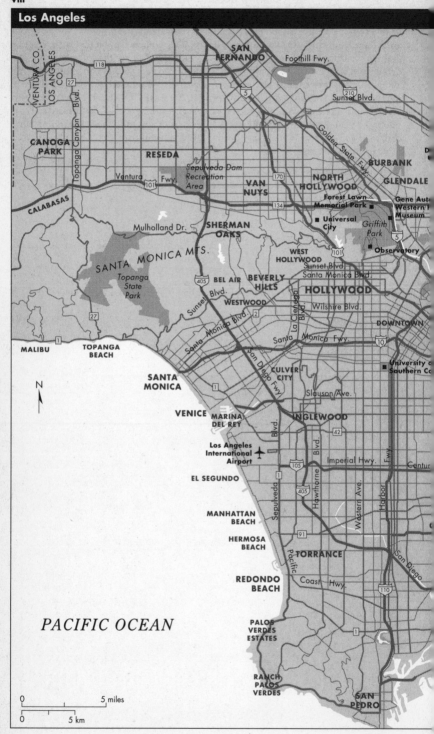

SAN FERNANDO
Foothill Fwy.
118
Sunset Blvd.
210
5
Golden State Fwy.
VENTURA CO.
LOS ANGELES CO.
Topanga Canyon Blvd.
27
CANOGA PARK
RESEDA
Ventura Fwy.
Sepulveda Dam Recreation Area
VAN NUYS
170
NORTH HOLLYWOOD
BURBANK
GLENDALE
101
134
Forest Lawn Memorial Park
Gene Aut Western Museum
CALABASAS
Universal City
Griffith Park
Mulholland Dr.
SHERMAN OAKS
SANTA MONICA MTS.
Topanga State Park
WEST HOLLYWOOD
101
Observatory
5
405
BEL AIR
BEVERLY HILLS
Sunset Blvd.
Santa Monica Blvd.
HOLLYWOOD
27
Sunset Blvd.
WESTWOOD
2
Wilshire Blvd.
DOWNTOWN
La Cienega Blvd.
1
MALIBU
TOPANGA BEACH
Santa Monica Blvd.
Santa Monica Fwy.
San Diego Fwy.
10
SANTA MONICA
CULVER CITY
University o Southern Co
VENICE
Slauson Ave.
MARINA DEL REY
INGLEWOOD
42
Los Angeles International Airport
105
Imperial Hwy.
Centur
EL SEGUNDO
405
Sepulveda Blvd.
Hawthorne Blvd.
Western Ave.
Harbor Fwy.
MANHATTAN BEACH
1
HERMOSA BEACH
91
San Diego
REDONDO BEACH
Pacific Coast Hwy.
TORRANCE
110
PACIFIC OCEAN
PALOS VERDES ESTATES
N
RANCH PALOS VERDES
SAN PEDRO
0   5 miles
0   5 km

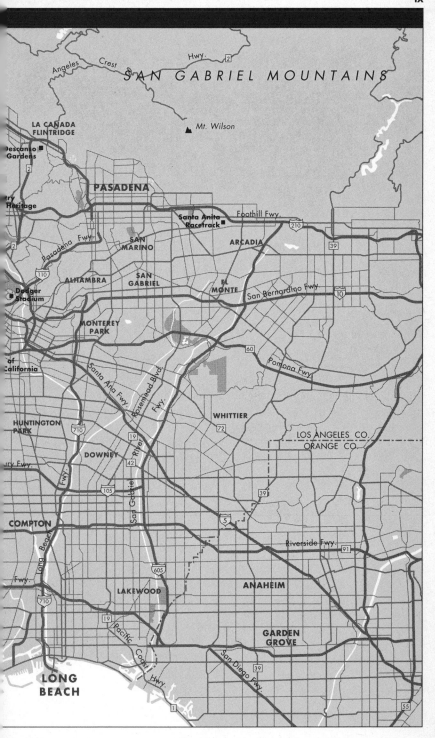

Southern California

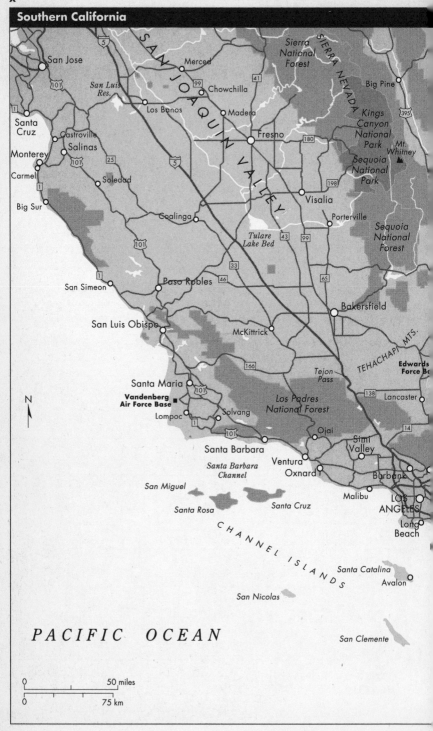

PACIFIC OCEAN

50 miles
0
0   75 km

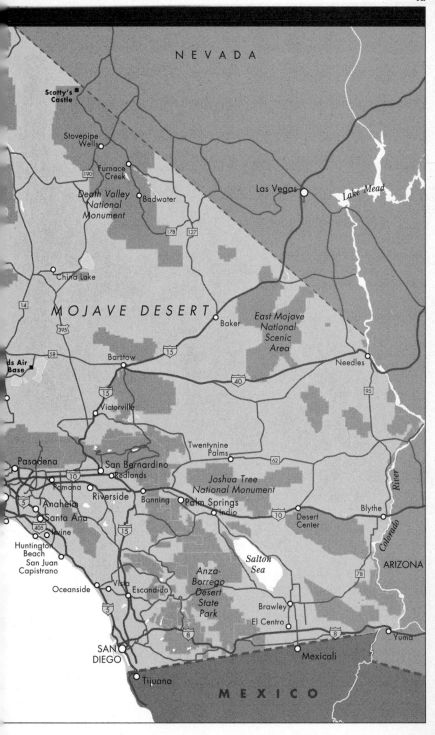

NEVADA

Scotty's
Castle

Stovepipe
Wells

190 Furnace
Creek

Death Valley
National
Monument

Badwater

Las Vegas

Lake Mead

178 127

China Lake

14

MOJAVE DESERT

395

Baker

East Mojave
National
Scenic
Area

58

ds Air
Base

Barstow

15

Needles

40

95

15

Victorville

Twentynine
Palms

Pasadena

San Bernardino

Redlands

62

Joshua Tree
National Monument

Colorado River

10

Pomona

Riverside

Banning

Palm Springs

Indio

10

Desert
Center

Blythe

5

Anaheim

Santa Ana

405

Irvine

15

Huntington
Beach

San Juan
Capistrano

Salton
Sea

ARIZONA

Oceanside

Vista

Escondido

Anza-
Borrego
Desert
State
Park

78

Brawley

El Centro

8

8

Yuma

SAN
DIEGO

Tijuana

Mexicali

MEXICO

World Time Zones

Numbers below vertical bands relate each zone to Greenwich Mean Time (0 hrs.).
Local times frequently differ from these general indications,
as indicated by light-face numbers on map.

Algiers, **29**

Anchorage, **3**

Athens, **41**

Auckland, **1**

Baghdad, **46**

Bangkok, **50**

Beijing, **54**

Berlin, **34**

Bogotá, **19**

Budapest, **37**

Buenos Aires, **24**

Caracas, **22**

Chicago, **9**

Copenhagen, **33**

Dallas, **10**

Delhi, **48**

Denver, **8**

Djakarta, **53**

Dublin, **26**

Edmonton, **7**

Hong Kong, **56**

Honolulu, **2**

Istanbul, **40**

Jerusalem, **42**

Johannesburg, **44**

Lima, **20**

Lisbon, **28**

London
(Greenwich), **27**

Los Angeles, **6**

Madrid, **38**

Manila, **57**

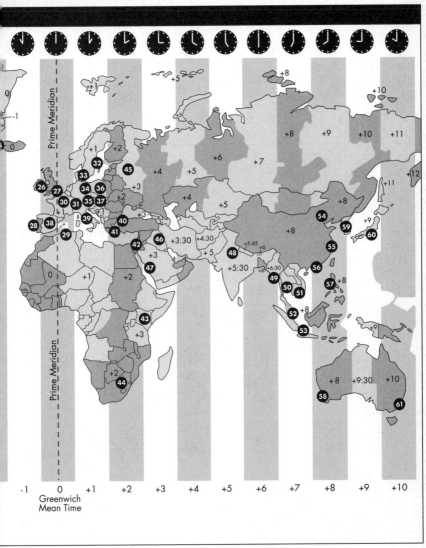

Mecca, **47**
Mexico City, **12**
Miami, **18**
Montréal, **15**
Moscow, **45**
Nairobi, **43**
New Orleans, **11**
New York City, **16**

Ottawa, **14**
Paris, **30**
Perth, **58**
Reykjavík, **25**
Rio de Janeiro, **23**
Rome, **39**
Saigon (Ho Chi Minh City), **51**

San Francisco, **5**
Santiago, **21**
Seoul, **59**
Shanghai, **55**
Singapore, **52**
Stockholm, **32**
Sydney, **61**
Tokyo, **60**

Toronto, **13**
Vancouver, **4**
Vienna, **35**
Warsaw, **36**
Washington, D.C., **17**
Yangon, **49**
Zürich, **31**

Los Angeles Freeways

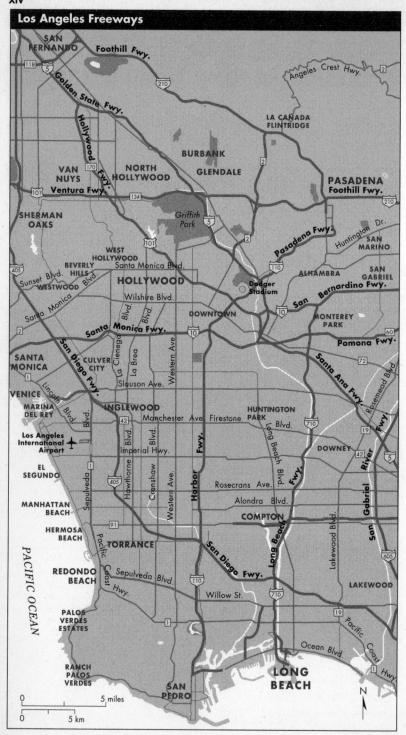

SAN FERNANDO

Foothill Fwy.

Golden State Fwy.

Angeles Crest Hwy.

LA CAÑADA FLINTRIDGE

Hollywood Fwy.

BURBANK

GLENDALE

PASADENA
Foothill Fwy.

VAN NUYS

NORTH HOLLYWOOD

Ventura Fwy.

Griffith Park

Pasadena Fwy.

Huntington Dr.

SAN MARINO

SHERMAN OAKS

WEST HOLLYWOOD

BEVERLY HILLS

Santa Monica Blvd.

HOLLYWOOD

ALHAMBRA

SAN GABRIEL

San Bernardino Fwy.

Sunset Blvd.

WESTWOOD

Santa Monica Blvd.

Wilshire Blvd.

Dodger Stadium

DOWNTOWN

MONTEREY PARK

Santa Monica

Santa Monica Fwy.

Pomona Fwy.

SANTA MONICA

San Diego Fwy.

CULVER CITY

La Cienega Blvd.

La Brea Blvd.

Western Ave.

Santa Ana Fwy.

Rosemead Blvd.

VENICE

MARINA DEL REY

Lincoln Blvd.

INGLEWOOD

Manchester Ave.

Firestone

HUNTINGTON PARK

Long Beach Blvd.

DOWNEY

River Fwy.

Los Angeles International Airport

Imperial Hwy.

Crenshaw Blvd.

Western Ave.

Harbor Fwy.

Rosecrans Ave.

San Gabriel

EL SEGUNDO

Sepulveda

Hawthorne Blvd.

Alondra Blvd.

MANHATTAN BEACH

COMPTON

Lakewood Blvd.

HERMOSA BEACH

Pacific Coast Hwy.

TORRANCE

Long Beach Fwy.

LAKEWOOD

REDONDO BEACH

Sepulveda Blvd.

San Diego Fwy.

Willow St.

PALOS VERDES ESTATES

Pacific Coast Hwy.

PACIFIC OCEAN

Ocean Blvd.

RANCH PALOS VERDES

SAN PEDRO

LONG BEACH

N

0   5 miles

0   5 km

IMPORTANT CONTACTS A TO Z

An Alphabetical Listing of Publications, Organizations, and Companies That Will Help You Before, During, and After Your Trip

No single travel resource can give you every detail about every topic that might interest or concern you at the various stages of your journey—when you're planning your trip, while you're on the road, and after you get back home. The following organizations, books, and brochures will supplement the information in *Fodor's Los Angeles '96*. For related information, including both basic tips on visiting Los Angeles and background information on many of the topics below, study Smart Travel Tips A to Z, the section that follows Important Contacts A to Z.

A

AIR TRAVEL

The major gateways to Los Angeles are:

Los Angeles International Airport (☎ 310/646–5252), commonly called LAX. Departures are from the upper level and arrivals on the lower level. LAX is serviced by more than 85 major airlines and is the third largest airport in the world in terms of passenger traffic.

Ontario International Airport (☎ 909/988–2700), about 35 miles east of Los Angeles, serves the San Bernardino–Riverside area.

Flights are offered by Alaska Airlines, American, America West, Continental, Delta, Northwest, Reno Air, SkyWest, Southwest, TWA, United, United Express, and USAir Express. Ground transportation possibilities include SuperShuttle, Inland Express (☎ 909/626–6599), and Southern California Coach (☎ 714/978–6415).

Long Beach Airport (☎ 310/570–2600), at the southern tip of Los Angeles County, is served by America West, and Sunjet International airlines.

Burbank/Glendale/Pasadena Airport (☎ 818/840–8847) serves the San Fernando Valley with commuter and some longer flights. Alaska Airlines, American, America West, SkyWest, Southwest, and United Airlines are represented.

John Wayne Airport (☎ 714/252–5006), in Orange County, is served by Alaska, American, American West, Continental, Delta, Northwest, Reno Air, Southwest, TWA, United, and USAir airlines. Airport Coach (☎ 800/772–5299) provides ground transportation.

CARRIERS

Carriers serving Los Angeles include **Air Canada** (☎ 800/776–3000), **America West** (☎ 800/235–9292), **American** (☎ 800/433–7300), **British Airways** (☎ 800/247–9297), **Continental** (☎ 800/525–0280), **Delta** (☎ 800/221–1212), **Japan Air Lines** (☎ 800/525–3663), **Northwest** (☎ 800/225–2525), **Southwest** (☎ 800/435–9792), **TWA** (☎ 800/221–2000), **United** (☎ 800/241–6522), and **USAir** (☎ 800/428–4322).

LOW-COST CARRIERS

For inexpensive, no-frills flights to Los Angeles, contact **Private Jet** (☎ 404/231–7571 or 800/546–7571); **Reno Air** (☎ 800/736–6247); and **Southwest Airlines** (☎ 800/444–5660), based in Salt Lake City and serving California.

COMPLAINTS

To register complaints about charter and scheduled airlines, contact the U.S. Department of Transportation's **Office of Consumer Affairs** (400 7th St. NW, Washington, DC 20590, ☎ 202/366–2220 or 800/322–7873).

CONSOLIDATORS

Established consolidators selling to the public include **TFI Tours International** (34 W. 32nd St., New York, NY

THE GOLD GUIDE / IMPORTANT CONTACTS

10001, ☎ 212/736–1140 or 800/745–8000).

PUBLICATIONS

For general information about charter carriers, ask for the Office of Consumer Affairs' brochure **"Plane Talk: Public Charter Flights."** The Department of Transportation also publishes a 58-page booklet, **"Fly Rights"** ($1.75; Consumer Information Center, Dept. 133-B, Pueblo, CO 81009).

For other tips and hints, consult the Consumers Union's monthly **"Consumer Reports Travel Letter"** ($39 a year; Box 53629, Boulder, CO 80322, ☎ 800/234–1970) and the newsletter **"Travel Smart"** ($37 a year; 40 Beechdale Rd., Dobbs Ferry, NY 10522, ☎ 800/327–3633); *The Official Frequent Flyer Guidebook,* by Randy Petersen ($14.99 plus $3 shipping; 4715-C Town Center Dr., Colorado Springs, CO 80916, ☎ 719/597–8899 or 800/487–8893); *Airfare Secrets Exposed,* by Sharon Tyler and Matthew Wonder (Universal Information Publishing; $16.95 plus $3.75 shipping from Sandcastle Publishing, Box 3070-A, South Pasadena, CA 91031, ☎ 213/255–3616 or 800/655–0053); and *202 Tips Even the Best Business Travelers May Not Know,* by Christopher McGinnis ($10 plus $3 shipping; Irwin Professional Publishing, 1333 Burr Ridge Pkwy., Burr Ridge, IL 60521,

☎ 708/789–4000 or 800/634–3966).

AIRPORT TRANSFERS

A taxi ride to downtown from LAX can take 20 minutes—if there is no traffic. But in Los Angeles, that's a big if. Visitors should request the flat fee ($24 at press time) to downtown or choose from the several ground transportation companies that offer set rates.

SuperShuttle (☎ 310/782–6600) offers direct service between the airport and hotels. The trip to or from downtown hotels costs about $12. The seven-passenger vans operate 24 hours a day. In the airport, ☎ 310/782–6600 or use the SuperShuttle courtesy phone in the luggage area; the van should arrive within 15 minutes. **Shuttle One** (9100 S. Sepulveda Blvd., No. 128, ☎ 310/670–6666) features door-to-door service and low rates ($10 per person from LAX to hotels in the Disneyland/Anaheim area). **Airport Coach** (☎ 714/938–8900 or 800/772–5299) provides regular service between LAX and the Pasadena and Anaheim areas.

The following limo companies charge a flat rate for airport service, ranging from $65 to $95: **Jackson Limousine** (☎ 213/734–9955), **A-1 West Coast Limousine** (☎ 213/756–5466), and **Dav-El Livery** (☎ 310/550–0070). Many of the cars have bars, stereos, televisions, and cellular phones.

Flyaway Service (☎ 818/994–5554) offers round-trip transportation between LAX and the central San Fernando Valley for $6. For the western San Fernando Valley and Ventura area, contact the **Great American Stage Lines** (☎ 800/287–8659). They charge $10–$20 one way.

MTA (☎ 213/626-4455) also offers limited airport service to all areas of greater LA; bus lines depart from bus docks directly across the street from airport parking lot C. Prices vary from $1.25 to $3.10; some routes require transfers. The best line to take to downtown is the direct express line 439, which costs $1.50 and takes 45–50 minutes.

B

BETTER BUSINESS BUREAU

Contact the Los Angeles **Better Business Bureau** (3400 W. 6th St., Suite 403, 90020–2538, ☎ 900/225–5222; 95¢/minute). For other local contacts, consult the **Council of Better Business Bureaus** (4200 Wilson Blvd., Arlington, VA 22203, ☎ 703/276–0100).

BUS TRAVEL

The Los Angeles **Greyhound Lines** terminal (☎ 800/231–2222) is at 208 East 6th Street, on the corner of Los Angeles Street.

WITHIN LOS ANGELES

A bus ride on the **Metropolitan Transit**

Authority (MTA) (☎ 213/626–4455) costs $1.10, with 25¢ for each transfer.

DASH (Downtown Area Short Hop) minibuses travel around the downtown area, stopping every two blocks or so. There are five different routes. You pay 25¢ every time you get on, no matter how far you go. DASH (☎ 213/626–4455) runs weekdays 6:30 AM–6 PM, Saturday 10 AM–5 PM.

C

CAR RENTAL

In Los Angeles, it's not a question of whether wheels are a hindrance or a convenience: They're a necessity. More than 35 major companies and dozens of local rental companies serve a steady demand for cars at Los Angeles International Airport and various city locations.

Major car-rental companies represented in Los Angeles include **Alamo** (☎ 800/327–9633, 0800/272–2000 in the U.K.); **Avis** (☎ 800/331–1212, 800/879–2847 in Canada); **Budget** (☎ 800/527–0700, 0800/181–181 in the U.K.); **Dollar** (known as Eurodollar outside North America, ☎ 800/800–4000 in the U.S. and Canada, 0181/952–6565 in the U.K.); **Hertz** (☎ 800/654–3131, 800/263–0600 in Canada, 0181/679–1799 in the U.K.); and **National** (☎ 800/227–7368, 0181/950–5050 in the U.K., where it is known as Europcar). Also try local renter **Ugly Duck-**

ling (☎ 800/843–3825), which usually has good prices. Rates in Los Angeles begin at $25 a day and $170 a week for an economy car with unlimited mileage.

If expense is no object, **Luxury Line** (300 S. La Cienega, Beverly Hills 90048, ☎ 310/657–2800) can rent you everything from Toyota Tercels to Rolls-Royces, Jaguars, and Ferraris. Ironically, the Marina del Rey branch of **Budget** (☎ 310/821–8200) also rents upscale vehicles, like Jaguars, Mercedes, BMWs, and Miata or Corvette convertibles.

CHILDREN AND TRAVEL

BABY-SITTING

Sitters Unlimited has franchises in Los Angeles County, Huntington Beach, and Long Beach (☎ 310/596–0550), and Irvine, Tustin, and Santa Ana (☎ 714/251–1948).

FLYING

Look into **"Flying With Baby"** ($5.95 plus $1 shipping; Third Street Press, Box 261250, Littleton, CO 80126, ☎ 303/595–5959), cowritten by a flight attendant. **"Kids and Teens in Flight,"** free from the U.S. Department of Transportation's Office of Consumer Affairs, offers tips for children flying alone. Every two years the February issue of *Family Travel Times* (*see* Know-How, *below*) details children's services on three dozen airlines.

KNOW-HOW

Family Travel Times, published 10 times a year by Travel with Your Children (TWYCH, 45 W. 18th St., New York, NY 10011, ☎ 212/206–0688; annual subscription $55), covers destinations, types of vacations, and modes of travel.

The *Family Travel Guides* catalogue ($1 postage; ☎ 510/527–5849) lists about 200 books and articles on family travel. Also check *Take Your Baby and Go! A Guide for Traveling with Babies, Toddlers and Young Children,* by Sheri Andrews, Judy Bordeaux, and Vivian Vasquez ($5.95 plus $1.50 shipping; Bear Creek Publications, 2507 Minor Ave., Seattle, WA 98102, ☎ 206/322–7604 or 800/326–6566). *100 Best Family Resorts in North America,* by Jane Wilford with Janet Tice ($12.95), and the two-volume *50 Great Family Vacations in Western North America,* by Candyce Stapen ($18.95 per volume), both from Globe Pequot Press (plus $3 for shipping; Box 833, 6 Business Park Rd., Old Saybrook, CT 06475, ☎ 203/395–0440 or 800/243–0495, 800/962–0973 in CT), help plan your trip with children, from toddlers to teens.

LOCAL INFORMATION

Consult the lively by-parents, for-parents *Where Should We Take the Kids? California*

($17; Fodor's Travel Publications, ☎ 800/533-6478 and in bookstores).

L.A. Parent (Box 3204, Burbank 91504, ☎ 818/846-0400) is a monthly newspaper filled with events listings and resources; it is available free at such places as libraries, supermarkets, museums, and toy stores. For a small fee, you can have an issue sent to you before your trip.

Places to Go with Children in Southern California, by Stephanie Kegan, is published by Chronicle Books; $9.95. **The Parents' Guide to L.A.** (Mani Flattery Publications, c/o SCB Distributors, 15612 S. New Century Dr., Gardena, CA 90248, ☎ 310/532-9400; $19.95 plus $4-$5 shipping) has more than 500 pages listing shopping, goods, recreation, and entertainment for kids.

LODGING

At the **Sheraton Grande** (333 S. Figueroa Ave., Los Angeles, CA 90071, ☎ 213/617-1133 or 800/325—3535), children under 18 stay free, and the **Sheraton Universal Hotel,** on the lot of Universal Studios (333 Universal Terrace Pkwy., Universal City, CA 91608, ☎ 818/980-1212 or 800/325-3535) offers special packages, including free parking and tickets to Universal Studios.

Some area hotels, especially those in the vicinity of Disneyland, have children's programs: The **Anaheim Hilton**

(777 Convention Way, Anaheim, CA 92802, ☎ 714/750-4321 or 800/445-8667) has a free summer day-care center with several counselors, videos, and sometimes even teen stars who make guest appearances.

TOUR OPERATORS

Contact **Grandtravel** (6900 Wisconsin Ave., Suite 706, Chevy Chase, MD 20815, ☎ 301/986-0790 or 800/247-7651), which has tours for people traveling with grandchildren aged 7-17.

CUSTOMS

CANADIANS

Contact **Revenue Canada** (2265 St. Laurent Blvd. S, Ottawa, Ontario, K1G 4K3, ☎ 613/993-0534) for a copy of the free brochure **"I Declare/Je Déclare"** and for details on duties that exceed the standard duty-free limit.

U.K. CITIZENS

HM Customs and Excise (Dorset House, Stamford St., London SE1 9NG, ☎ 0171/202-4227) can answer questions about U.K. customs regulations and publishes **"A Guide for Travellers,"** detailing standard procedures and import rules.

D

FOR TRAVELERS WITH DISABILITIES

COMPLAINTS

To register complaints under the provisions of the Americans with Disabilities Act, contact the U.S. Department of Justice's **Public Access**

Section (Box 66738, Washington, DC 20035, ☎ 202/514-0301, TDD 202/514-0383, FAX 202/307-1198).

ORGANIZATIONS

FOR TRAVELERS WITH HEARING IMPAIRMENTS➤ Contact the **American Academy of Otolaryngology** (1 Prince St., Alexandria, VA 22314, ☎ 703/836-4444, FAX 703/683-5100, TTY 703/519-1585).

FOR TRAVELERS WITH MOBILITY IMPAIRMENTS➤ Contact the **Information Center for Individuals with Disabilities** (Fort Point Pl., 27-43 Wormwood St., Boston, MA 02210, ☎ 617/727-5540, 800/462-5015 in MA, TTY 617/345-9743); **Mobility International USA** (Box 10767, Eugene, OR 97440, ☎ and TTY 503/343-1284, FAX 503/343-6812), the U.S. branch of an international organization based in Belgium (*see below*) that has affiliates in 30 countries; **MossRehab Hospital Travel Information Service** (1200 W. Tabor Rd., Philadelphia, PA 19141, ☎ 215/456-9603, TTY 215/456-9602); the **Society for the Advancement of Travel for the Handicapped** (SATH, 347 5th Ave., Suite 610, New York, NY 10016, ☎ 212/447-7284, FAX 212/725-8253); the **Travel Industry and Disabled Exchange** (TIDE, 5435 Donna Ave., Tarzana, CA 91356, ☎ 818/344-3640, FAX 818/344-0078); and **Travelin' Talk** (Box 3534, Clarksville, TN 37043,

☎ 615/552–6670, FAX 615/552–1182).

FOR TRAVELERS WITH VISION IMPAIRMENTS➤ Contact the **American Council of the Blind** (1155 15th St. NW, Suite 720, Washington, DC 20005, ☎ 202/467–5081, FAX 202/467–5085) or the **American Foundation for the Blind** (15 W. 16th St., New York, NY 10011, ☎ 212/620–2000, TTY 212/620–2158).

IN THE U.K.

Contact the **Royal Association for Disability and Rehabilitation** (RADAR, 12 City Forum, 250 City Rd., London EC1V 8AF, ☎ 0171/250–3222) or **Mobility International** (Rue de Manchester 25, B1070 Brussels, Belgium, ☎ 00–322–410–6297), an international clearinghouse of travel information for people with disabilities.

PUBLICATIONS

Several free publications are available from the U.S. Information Center (Box 100, Pueblo, CO 81009, ☎ 719/948–3334): **"New Horizons for the Air Traveler with a Disability"** (address to Dept. 355A), describing legally mandated changes; the pocket-size **"Fly Smart"** (Dept. 575B), good on flight safety; and the Airport Operators Council's worldwide **"Access Travel: Airports"** (Dept. 575A).

Fodor's **Great American Vacations for Travelers with Disabilities** ($18; available in bookstores, or call 800/533–6478)

details accessible attractions, restaurants, and hotels in U.S. destinations. The 500-page **Travelin' Talk Directory** ($35; Box 3534, Clarksville, TN 37043, ☎ 615/552–6670) lists people and organizations who help travelers with disabilities. For specialist travel agents worldwide, consult the **Directory of Travel Agencies for the Disabled** ($19.95 plus $2 shipping; Twin Peaks Press, Box 129, Vancouver, WA 98666, ☎ 206/694–2462 or 800/637–2256). The Sierra Club publishes **Easy Access to National Parks** ($16 plus $3 shipping; 730 Polk St., San Francisco, CA 94109, ☎ 415/776–2211 or 800/935–1056).

"Round the Town with Ease" is distributed by the Junior League of Los Angeles (Farmers Market, 3rd and Fairfax Sts., Gate 12, Los Angeles, CA 90036, ☎ 213/937–5566; free to travelers with disabilities, $2 for all mail order requests). The **"Los Angeles Visitors Guide"** and the **"Los Angeles Lodging Guide,"** both published by the Los Angeles Convention and Visitors Bureau (*see* Visitor Information, *above*), use symbols to indicate attractions and accommodations with facilities for travelers with disabilities.

TRAVEL AGENCIES AND TOUR OPERATORS

The Americans with Disabilities Act requires that travel firms serve

the needs of all travelers. However, some agencies and operators specialize in making group and individual arrangements for travelers with disabilities, among them **Access Adventures** (206 Chestnut Ridge Rd., Rochester, NY 14624, ☎ 716/889–9096), run by a former physical-rehab counselor; **Tailored Tours** (Box 797687, Dallas, TX 75379, ☎ 214/612–1168 or 800/628–8542); **Travel Trends** (2 Allan Plaza, 4922–51 Ave., Box 3581, Leduc, Alberta, T9E 6X2, ☎ 403/986–9000), which has group tours and is especially good for cruises. In addition, many general-interest operators and agencies (*see* Tour Operators, *below*) can arrange vacations for travelers with disabilities.

FOR TRAVELERS WITH HEARING IMPAIRMENTS➤ One agency is **International Express** (7319-B Baltimore Ave., College Park, MD 20740, ☎ TDD 301/699–8836, FAX 301/699–8836), which arranges group and independent trips.

FOR TRAVELERS WITH MOBILITY IMPAIRMENTS➤ A number of operators specialize in working with travelers with mobility impairments: **Hinsdale Travel Service** (201 E. Ogden Ave., Suite 100, Hinsdale, IL 60521, ☎ 708/325–1335 or 800/303–5521), a travel agency that will give you access to the services of wheel chair traveler Janice Perkins, and **Wheelchair**

THE GOLD GUIDE / IMPORTANT CONTACTS

Journeys (16979 Redmond Way, Redmond, WA 98052, ☎ 206/885–2210), which can handle arrangements worldwide.

FOR TRAVELERS WITH DEVELOPMENTAL DISABILITIES➤ Contact the nonprofit **New Directions** (5276 Hollister Ave., Suite 207, Santa Barbara, CA 93111, ☎ 805/967–2841).

DISCOUNTS

Options include **Entertainment Travel Editions** (fee $28–$53, depending on destination; Box 1068, Trumbull, CT 06611, ☎ 800/445–4137); **Great American Traveler** ($49.95 annually; Box 27965, Salt Lake City, UT 84127, ☎ 800/548–2812); **Moment's Notice Discount Travel Club** ($25 annually, single or family; 163 Amsterdam Ave., Suite 137, New York, NY 10023, ☎ 212/486–0500); **Privilege Card** ($74.95 annually; 3391 Peachtree Rd. NE, Suite 110, Atlanta, GA 30326, ☎ 404/262–0222 or 800/236-9732); **Travelers Advantage** ($49 annually, single or family; CUC Travel Service, 49 Music Sq. W, Nashville, TN 37203, ☎ 800/548–1116 or 800/648–4037); and **Worldwide Discount Travel Club** ($50 annually for family, $40 single; 1674 Meridian Ave., Miami Beach, FL 33139, ☎ 305/534–2082).

E
EMERGENCIES

Dial 911 for **police** and **ambulance** in an emergency.

COMMUNITY SERVICES

You can call **Community Services** (☎ 800/339–6993) 24 hours.

DOCTORS

The **Los Angeles Medical Association Physicians Referral Service** (☎ 213/483–6122) is open weekdays 8:45–4:45. Most larger hospitals in Los Angeles have 24-hour emergency rooms. Two are **Cedar-Sinai Medical Center** (8700 Beverly Blvd., ☎ 310/855–5000) and **Queen of Angels Hollywood Presbyterian Medical Center** (1300 N. Vermont Ave., ☎ 213/413–3000).

24-HOUR PHARMACIES

The **Kaiser Bellflower Pharmacy** (9400 E. Rosecrans Ave., Bellflower, ☎ 310/461–4213) is open around the clock. The **Horton and Converse** pharmacies (6625 Van Nuys Blvd., Van Nuys, ☎ 818/782–6251; 11600 Wilshire Blvd., W. Los Angeles, ☎ 310/478–0801) are open until 2 AM.

G
GAY AND LESBIAN TRAVEL

ORGANIZATION

The **International Gay Travel Association** (Box 4974, Key West, FL 33041, ☎ 800/448–8550), a consortium of 800 businesses, can supply names of travel agents and tour operators.

PUBLICATIONS

The premier international travel magazine for gays and lesbians is **Our World** ($35 for 10 issues; 1104 N. Nova Rd., Suite 251, Daytona Beach, FL 32117, ☎ 904/441–5367). The 16-page monthly **"Out & About"** ($49 for 10 issues; ☎ 212/645–6922 or 800/929–2268) covers gay-friendly resorts, hotels, cruise lines, and airlines.

TOUR OPERATORS

Cruises and resort vacations are handled by **R.S.V.P. Travel Productions** (2800 University Ave. SE, Minneapolis, MN 55414, ☎ 800/328–RSVP) for gays. For mixed gay and lesbian travel, **Toto Tours** (1326 W. Albion, Suite 3W, Chicago, IL 60626, ☎ 312/274–8686 or 800/565–1241) have group tours worldwide.

TRAVEL AGENCIES

The largest agencies serving gay travelers are **Advance Travel** (10700 Northwest Freeway, Suite 160, Houston, TX 77092, ☎ 713/682–2002 or 800/695–0880), **Islanders/Kennedy Travel** (183 W. 10th St., New York, NY 10014, ☎ 212/242–3222 or 800/988–1181), **Now Voyager** (4406 18th St., San Francisco, CA 94114, ☎ 415/626–1169 or 800/255–6951), and **Yellowbrick Road** (1500 W. Balmoral Ave., Chicago, IL 60640, ☎ 312/561–1800 or 800/642–2488). **Skylink Women's Travel** (746 Ashland Ave., Santa Monica, CA 90405, ☎

310/452–0506 or 800/225-5759) works with lesbians.

I

INSURANCE

Travel insurance covering baggage, health, and trip cancellation or interruptions is available from **Access America** (Box 90315, Richmond, VA 23286, ☎ 804/285–3300 or 800/284–8300); **Carefree Travel Insurance** (Box 9366, 100 Garden City Plaza, Garden City, NY 11530, ☎ 516/294–0220 or 800/323–3149); **Near** (Box 1339, Calumet City, IL 60409, ☎ 708/868–6700 or 800/654–6700); **Tele-Trip** (Mutual of Omaha Plaza, Box 31716, Omaha, NE 68131, ☎ 800/228–9792); **Travel Insured International** (Box 280568, East Hartford, CT 06128-0568, ☎ 203/528–7663 or 800/243–3174); **Travel Guard International** (1145 Clark St., Stevens Point, WI 54481, ☎ 715/345–0505 or 800/826–1300); and **Wallach & Company** (107 W. Federal St., Box 480, Middleburg, VA 22117, ☎ 703/687–3166 or 800/237–6615).

IN THE U.K.

The **Association of British Insurers** (51 Gresham St., London EC2V 7HQ, ☎ 0171/600–3333; 30 Gordon St., Glasgow G1 3PU, ☎ 0141/226–3905; Scottish Provident Bldg., Donegall Sq. W, Belfast BT1 6JE, ☎ 01232/249176; and other locations) gives advice by phone and publishes the free "Holi-day Insurance," which sets out typical policy provisions and costs.

L

LIMOUSINES

Limousines come equipped with everything from a full bar and telephone to a hot tub and a double bed. Reputable companies include **Dav-El Livery** (☎ 310/550–0070), **First Class** (☎ 310/476–1960), and **Le Monde Limousine** (☎ 310/474–6622 or 818/887–7878).

LODGING

APARTMENT AND VILLA RENTAL

Among the companies to contact are **Home-tours International** (Box 11503, Knoxville, TN 37939, ☎ 615/588–8722 or 800/367–4668), **Vacation Home Rentals Worldwide** (235 Kensington Ave., Norwood, NJ 07648, ☎ 201/767–9393 or 800/633–3284), and **Villas and Apartments Abroad** (420 Madison Ave., Suite 1105, New York, NY 10017, ☎ 212/759–1025 or 800/433–3020). Members of the travel club **Hideaways International** ($99 annually; 767 Islington St., Portsmouth, NH 03801, ☎ 603/430–4433 or 800/843–4433) receive two annual guides plus quarterly newsletters, and arrange rentals among themselves.

HOME EXCHANGE

Principal clearinghouses include **Intervac International** ($65 annually; Box 590504, San Francisco, CA 94159, ☎ 415/435–3497), which has three annual directories, and **Loan-a-Home** ($35–$45 annually; 2 Park La., Apt. 6E, Mount Vernon, NY 10552-3443, ☎ 914/664–7640), which specializes in long-term exchanges.

M

MONEY MATTERS

ATMS

For specific **Cirrus** locations in the United States and Canada, call 800/424–7787. For U.S. **Plus** locations, call 800/843–7587 and enter the area code and first three digits of the number you're calling from (or of the calling area where you want an ATM).

WIRING FUNDS

Funds can be wired via **American Express MoneyGram** (☎ 800/926–9400 from the U.S. and Canada for locations and information) or **Western Union** (☎ 800/325–6000 for agent locations or to send using MasterCard or Visa, 800/321–2923 in Canada).

P

PASSPORTS
AND VISAS

U.K. CITIZENS

For fees, documentation requirements, and to get an emergency passport, call the **London passport office** (☎ 0171/271–3000). For visa information, call the **U.S. Embassy Visa Information Line** (☎ 0891/200–290; calls cost 49p per minute or 39p per minute cheap rate) or write the **U.S. Embassy Visa Branch** (5 Upper Grosvenor St., London W1A 2JB). If you live in Northern Ireland, write the **U.S. Consulate General** (Queen's House, Queen St., Belfast BTI 6EO).

PHOTO HELP

The **Kodak Information Center** (☎ 800/242–2424) answers consumer questions about film and photography.

R

RAIL TRAVEL

Los Angeles can be reached by **Amtrak** (☎ 800/872–7245). The *Coast Starlight,* a superliner, travels along the spectacular California coast. It offers service from Seattle–Portland and Oakland–San Francisco down to Los Angeles. The *Sunset Limited* goes to Los Angeles from New Orleans, the *Texas Eagle* from San Antonio, and the *Southwest Chief* and the *Desert Wind* from Chicago.

Union Station (800 N. Alameda St.) in Los Angeles is one of the grande dames of railroad stations.

WITHIN LOS ANGELES

The **Metrorail Blue Line** runs daily, 5 AM–10 PM, from downtown Los Angeles (corner of Flower and 7th Sts.) to Long Beach (corner of 1st St. and Long Beach Ave.), with 18 stops en route, most of them in Long Beach. The fare is $1.10 one way.

S

SENIOR CITIZENS

EDUCATIONAL TRAVEL

The nonprofit **Elderhostel** (75 Federal St., 3rd Floor, Boston, MA 02110, ☎ 617/426–7788), for people 60 and older, has offered inexpensive study programs since 1975. The nearly 2,000 courses cover everything from marine science to Greek myths and cowboy poetry. Fees for programs in the United States and Canada, which usually last one week, run about $300, not including transportation.

ORGANIZATIONS

Contact the **American Association of Retired Persons** (AARP, 601 E St. NW, Washington, DC 20049, ☎ 202/434–2277; $8 per person or couple annually). Its Purchase Privilege Program gets members discounts on lodging, car rentals, and sightseeing, and the AARP Motoring Plan furnishes domestic trip-routing information and emergency road-service aid for an annual fee of $39.95 per person or couple ($59.95 for a premium version).

For other discounts on lodgings, car rentals, and other travel products, along with magazines and newsletters, contact the **National Council of Senior Citizens** (membership $12 annually; 1331 F St. NW, Washington, DC 20004, ☎ 202/347–8800) and **Mature Outlook** (subscription $9.95 annually; 6001 N. Clark St., Chicago, IL 60660, ☎ 312/465–6466 or 800/336–6330).

PUBLICATIONS

The 50+ Traveler's Guidebook: Where to Go, Where to Stay, What to Do, by Anita Williams and Merrimac Dillon ($12.95; St. Martin's Press, 175 5th Ave., New York, NY 10010, ☎ 212/674–5151 or 800/288–2131), offers many useful tips. **"The Mature Traveler"** ($29.95; Box 50400, Reno, NV 89513, ☎ 702/786–7419), a monthly newsletter, covers travel deals.

SIGHTSEEING

Los Angeles is so spread out and has such a wealth of sightseeing possibilities that an orientation bus tour may prove useful. The cost is between $25 and $40. All tours are fully narrated by a driver-guide. Reservations must be made in advance. Many hotels can book them for you.

L.A. Tours and Sightseeing (6333 W. 3rd St., at the Farmers' Market, ☎ 213/937–3361 or 800/286–8752) has a $38 tour covering various parts of the city, including downtown, Hollywood, and Beverly Hills. The company also operates tours to Disneyland, Universal Studios, Magic Mountain, beaches, and stars' homes.

Tourcoach Charter and Tours (6922 Hollywood Blvd., Hollywood 90028, ☎ 213/463–3333) picks up passengers from area hotels as well as around the corner from Mann's Chinese Theater (6925 Hollywood Blvd.). Sights such as Universal Studios, Sea World, Knott's Berry Farm, Stars' Homes, Disneyland, and other attractions are on this popular tour company's agenda. Price range is from $26 to $68.

A more personalized look at the city can be had by planning a tour with **Casablanca Tours** (Roosevelt Hotel, 7000 Hollywood Blvd., Cabana 4, Hollywood 90028, ☎ 213/461–0156), which offers a four-hour insider's look at Hollywood and Beverly Hills. Tours are in minibuses with a maximum of 14 people, and prices are equivalent to the large bus tours—about $33.

PERSONAL GUIDES

Elegant Tours for the Discriminating (☎ 310/472–4090) is a personalized sightseeing and shopping service for the Beverly Hills area. Joan Mansfield offers her extensive knowledge of Rodeo Drive to one, two, or three people at a time. Lunch is included.

L.A. Nighthawks (Box 10224, Beverly Hills 90213, ☎ 310/392–1500) will arrange your nightlife for you. For a rather hefty price, you'll get a limousine, a guide (who ensures you're in a safe environment at all times), and immediate entry into L.A.'s hottest nightspots.

SPECIAL-INTEREST TOURS

Advantage Tours and Charters (Box 1192, Beverly Hills 90213, ☎ 310/823–0321 or 213/933–1475) specializes in touring area museums, both large and small.

Grave Line Tours (Box 931694, Hollywood 90093, ☎ 213/469–4149) is a clever, off-the-beaten-track tour that digs up the dirt on notorious suicides and visits the scenes of various murders, scandals, and other crimes via a luxuriously renovated hearse. Tours, which begin daily at 9:30 AM and last 2½ hours (a 12:30 tour will be scheduled if the morning one is full, and sometimes a 3:30 PM tour leaves as well), are offered Tuesday–Sunday and cost $40 per person.

Hollywood Fantasy Tours (6731 Hollywood Blvd., Hollywood 90028, ☎ 213/469–8184 or 800/782–7287) has one tour that takes you through Beverly Hills, down Rodeo Drive, around Bel Air, and up and down the colorful Sunset Strip, then on to exclusive Holmby Hills. If you're only interested in Hollywood, ask about a tour of that area. Cost is $14–$25 per person, depending on the tour.

Visitors who want something dramatically different should check with Marlene Gordon of **The Next Stage** (Box 35269, Los Angeles 90035, ☎ 213/939–2688). This innovative

tour company takes 4–46 people, on buses or vans, in search of ethnic L.A., Victorian L.A., Underground L.A. (in which all the places visited are underground), as well as the Insomniac's Tour and Wacky L.A.

LA Today Custom Tours (14964 Camarosa Dr., Pacific Palisades 90272, ☎ 310/454–5730) has a wide selection of offbeat tours, some of which tie in with seasonal and cultural events, such as theater, museum exhibits, and the Rose Bowl. Groups range from 8 to 800, and prices are from $6 to $85. The least expensive is a two-hour walking tour of downtown Los Angeles architecture that costs $6.

WALKING TOURS

Walking is something that Angelenos don't do much of, except perhaps in Westwood and Beverly Hills and in parks throughout the city. But there is no better way to see things close up.

A very pleasant self-guided walking tour of **Palisades Park** is detailed in a brochure available at the park's Visitors Center (1400 Ocean Blvd., Santa Monica). Many television shows and movies have been filmed on this narrow strip of parkland on a bluff overlooking the Pacific. The 26-acre retreat is always bustling with walkers, skaters, Frisbee-throwers, readers, and sunbathers.

The **Los Angeles Conservancy** (☎ 213/623–

THE GOLD GUIDE / IMPORTANT CONTACTS

CITY) offers low-cost walking tours of the downtown area. Each Saturday at 10 AM one of six different tours leaves from the Olive Street entrance of the Biltmore Hotel. Cost is $5 per person. Make reservations because group size is limited.

STUDENTS

GROUPS

A major tour operator is **Contiki Holidays** (300 Plaza Alicante, Suite 900, Garden Grove, CA 92640, ☎ 714/740–0808 or 800/466–0610).

HOSTELING

Contact **Hostelling International–American Youth Hostels** (733 15th St. NW, Suite 840, Washington, DC 20005, ☎ 202/783–6161) in the United States, **Hostelling International–Canada** (205 Catherine St., Suite 400, Ottawa, Ontario K2P 1C3, ☎ 613/237–7884) in Canada, and the **Youth Hostel Association of England and Wales** (Trevelyan House, 8 St. Stephen's Hill, St. Albans, Hertfordshire AL1 2DY, ☎ 01727/855215 and 01727/845047) in the United Kingdom. Membership ($25 in the U.S., C$26.75 in Canada, and £9 in the U.K.) gets you access to 5,000 hostels worldwide that charge $7–$20 nightly per person.

I.D. CARDS

To get discounts on transportation and admissions, get the **International Student Identity Card** (ISIC) if you're a bona fide

student or the **International Youth Card** (IYC) if you're under 26. In the United States, the ISIC and IYC cards cost $16 each and include basic travel accident and illness coverage, plus a toll-free travel hot line. Apply through the Council on International Educational Exchange (*see* Organizations, *below*). Cards are available for $15 each in Canada from Travel Cuts (187 College St., Toronto, Ontario M5T 1P7, ☎ 416/979–2406 or 800/667–2887) and in the United Kingdom for £5 each at student unions and student travel companies.

ORGANIZATIONS

A major contact is the **Council on International Educational Exchange** (CIEE, 205 E. 42nd St., 16th Floor, New York, NY 10017, ☎ 212/661–1450) with locations in Boston (729 Boylston St., Boston, MA 02116, ☎ 617/266–1926), Miami (9100 S. Dadeland Blvd., Miami, FL 33156, ☎ 305/670–9261), Los Angeles (1093 Broxton Ave., Los Angeles, CA 90024, ☎ 310/208–3551), 43 college towns nationwide, and the United Kingdom (28A Poland St., London W1V 3DB, ☎ 0171/437–7767). Twice a year, it publishes *Student Travels* magazine. The CIEE's Council Travel Service offers domestic air passes for bargain travel within the United States and is the exclusive U.S. agent for several student-discount cards.

Campus Connections (325 Chestnut St., Suite 1101, Philadelphia, PA 19106, ☎ 215/625–8585 or 800/428–3235) specializes in discounted accommodations and airfares for students. The **Educational Travel Centre** (438 N. Frances St., Madison, WI 53703, ☎ 608/256–5551) offers rail passes and low-cost airline tickets, mostly for flights departing from Chicago.

In Canada, also contact **Travel Cuts** (*see above*).

PUBLICATIONS

See the *Berkeley Guide to California* ($17.50; Fodor's Travel Publications, 800/533–6478 or from bookstores).

SUBWAYS

The **Metro Red Line,** opened in January 1993, runs 4.4 miles through downtown, from Union Station to MacArthur Park, making five stops. The fare is $1.10.

T

TAXIS

You probably won't be able to hail a cab on the street in Los Angeles. Instead, you should phone one of the many taxi companies. The metered rate is $1.60 per mile. Two of the more reputable companies are **Independent Cab Co.** (☎ 213/385–8294 or 310/569–8214) and **United Independent Taxi** (☎ 213/653–5050).

TOUR OPERATORS

Among the companies selling tours and packages to Los Angeles, the following have a proven reputation, are nationally known, and have plenty of options to choose from.

GROUP TOURS

For deluxe escorted tours to Los Angeles, contact **Maupintour** (Box 807, Lawrence, KS 66044, ☎ 913/843–1211 or 800/255–4266) and **Tauck Tours** (11 Wilton Rd., Westport, CT 06880, ☎ 203/226–6911 or 800/468–2825). Another operator falling between deluxe and first-class is **Globus** (5301 South Federal Circle, Littleton, CO 80123-2980, ☎ 303/797–2800 or 800/221–0090). In the first-class and tourist range, try **Collette Tours** (162 Middle Street, Pawtucket, RI 02860, ☎ 401/728–3805 or 800/832–4656), **Domenico Tours** (750 Broadway, Bayonne, NJ 07002, ☎ 201/823–8687 or 800/554–8687), and **Mayflower Tours** (1225 Warren Ave., Downers Grove, IL 60515, ☎ 708/960–3430 or 800/323–7604). For budget and tourist class programs, try **Cosmos** (*see* Globus, *above*).

PACKAGES

Independent vacation packages are available from major tour operators and airlines. Contact **Airlines Fly AAway Vacations** (☎ 800/321–2121); **Certified Vacations** (Box 1525, Ft. Lauderdale, FL 33302, ☎ 305/522–1414 or 800/233-7260); **Continental Airlines' Grand Destinations** (☎ 800/634–5555); **Delta Dream Vacations**

(☎ 800/872–7786); **Kingdom Tours** (300 Market St., Kingston, PA 18704, ☎ 717/283–4241 or 800/872–8857); **SuperCities** (139 Main St., Cambridge, MA 02142, ☎ 617/621–0099 or 800/333–1234); **United Vacations** (☎ 800/328–6877); and **USAir Vacations** (☎ 800/455–0123). **Funjet Vacations,** based in Milwaukee, Wisconsin, and **Gogo Tours,** based in Ramsey, New Jersey, sell packages to Los Angeles only through travel agents. For rail packages, contact **Amtrak** (☎ 800/872–7245).

FROM THE U.K.➤ Tour operators offering packages to the Los Angeles area include **British Airways Holidays** (Astral Towers, Betts Way, London Rd., Crawley, West Sussex RH10 2XA, ☎ 01293/518–0222); **Jetsave** (Sussex House, London Rd., East Grinstead, W. Sussex RH19 1LD, ☎ 01342/312033); **Key to America** (1–3 Station Rd., Ashford, Middlesex TW15 2UW, ☎ 01784/248777); **Kuoni Travel Ltd.** (Kuoni House, Dorking, Surrey RH5 4AZ, ☎ 01306/742222); **Premier Holidays** (Premier Travel Center, Westbrook, Milton Rd., Cambridge CB4 1YG, ☎ 01223/355977); and **Trailfinders** (42–50 Earl's Court Rd., London W8 6FT, ☎ 0171/937–5400; 58 Deansgate, Manchester M3 2FF, ☎ 0161/839–6969).

THEME TRIPS

SPORTS➤ Rose Bowl packages including

accommodations and transportation are available from **Spectacular Sports Specials** (5813 Citrus Blvd., New Orleans, LA 70123, ☎ 504/734–9511 or 800/451–5772) and **Dan Chavez's Sports Empire** (Box 6169 Lakewood, CA 90714-6169, ☎ 310/809–6930 or 800/255–5258).

TRAIN TOURS➤ Contact Amtrak (*see* Packages, *above*).

ORGANIZATIONS

The **National Tour Association** (546 E. Main St., Lexington, KY 40508, ☎ 606/226–4444 or 800/682–8886) and **United States Tour Operators Association** (USTOA, 211 E. 51st St., Suite 12B, New York, NY 10022, ☎ 212/750–7371) can provide lists of member operators and information on booking tours.

PUBLICATIONS

Consult the brochure **"Worldwide Tour & Vacation Package Finder"** from the National Tour Association (*see above*) and the Better Business Bureau's **"Tips on Travel Packages"** (publication No. 24-195, $2; 4200 Wilson Blvd., Arlington, VA 22203).

For names of reputable agencies in your area, contact the **American Society of Travel Agents** (1101 King St., Suite 200, Alexandria, VA 22314, ☎ 703/739–2782).

THE GOLD GUIDE / IMPORTANT CONTACTS

V

VISITOR INFORMATION

The **Los Angeles Convention and Visitors Bureau** (633 W. 5th St., Suite 6000, 90071, ☎ 213/624–7300) will provide you with extensive free information about the region. **"Destination Los Angeles,"** a packet of annually updated lists of entertainment and special events with lodging and dining suggestions, costs $2. Los Angeles also maintains a 24-hour toll-free multilingual line for information about community services (☎ 213/689–8822 or 800/339–6993).

In addition, there are visitor centers and chambers of commerce in many of the communities in the Los Angeles area, including **Beverly Hills** (239 S. Beverly Dr., 90212, ☎ 310/271–8174 or 800/345–2210); **Channel Islands** (3810 W. Channel Islands Blvd., Suite 6, 93035, ☎ 800/994–4852); **Glendale** (200 S. Louise St., Box 112, 91209, ☎ 818/240–7870); **Hollywood** (7000 Hollywood Blvd., Suite 1, 90028, ☎ 213/469–8311); **Hollywood Visitors Center** (6541 Hollywood Blvd., ☎ 213/689–8822; open Mon.–Sat. 9–5); **Long Beach Area Convention and Visitors Council** (1 World Trade Ctr., Suite 300, 90831, ☎ 310/436–3645); **Oxnard** (715 S. A St., 93030, ☎ 800/2-OXNARD); **Pasadena** (171 S. Los Robles Ave., 91101, ☎ 818/795–9311); **Santa Monica Visitors Center** (1400 Ocean Ave., Palisades Park, ☎ 310/393–7593; open daily 10–4); and **West Hollywood** (8687 Melrose Ave. 90069, ☎ 310/289–2525).

The **California Division of Tourism** (801 K St., Suite 1600, Sacramento, CA 95814, ☎ 916/322–2882 or 800/462–2543) can answer many questions about travel in the state. You can also order a free, detailed, 162-page book, *Golden California Visitor's Guide,* which includes an informative section on the Los Angeles area (☎ 800/862–2543). The **Visitor Information Center** (685 S. Figueroa St., ☎ 213/689–8822) is open Monday–Saturday 8:30–5.

In the United Kingdom, also contact the **United States Travel and Tourism Administration** (Box 1EN, London W1A 1EN, ☎ 0171/495–4466). For a free USA pack, write the USTTA at Box 170, Ashford, Kent TN24 0ZX). Enclose stamps worth £1.50.

W

WEATHER

For current conditions and forecasts, plus the local time and helpful travel tips, call the **Weather Channel Connection** (☎ 900/932–8437; 95¢ per minute) from a touch-tone phone.

You can also call the Los Angeles **Surf and Weather Report** (☎ 310/578–0478).

SMART TRAVEL TIPS A TO Z

Basic Information on Traveling in Los Angeles and Savvy Tips to Make Your Trip a Breeze

The more you travel, the more you know about how to make trips run like clockwork. To help make your travels hassle-free, Fodor's editors have rounded up dozens of tips from our contributors and travel experts all over the world, as well as basic information on visiting Los Angeles. For names of organizations to contact and publications that can give you more information, *see* Important Contacts A to Z, *above.*

A
AIR TRAVEL

If time is an issue, **always look for nonstop flights,** which require no change of plane and make no stops. If possible, **avoid connecting flights,** which stop at least once and can involve a change of plane, although the flight number remains the same; if the first leg is late, the second waits.

CUTTING COSTS

The Sunday travel section of most newspapers is a good source of deals.

MAJOR AIRLINES➤ The least-expensive airfares from the major airlines are priced for round-trip travel and are subject to restrictions. You must usually **book in advance and buy the ticket within 24 hours** to get cheaper fares, and you

may have to **stay over a Saturday night.** The lowest fare is subject to availability, and only a small percentage of the plane's total seats are sold at that price. It's good to **call a number of airlines—and when you are quoted a good price, book it on the spot**—the same fare on the same flight may not be available the next day. Airlines generally allow you to change your return date for a $25–$50 fee, but most low-fare tickets are nonrefundable. However, if you don't use it, you can apply the cost toward the purchase price of a new ticket, again for a small charge.

CONSOLIDATORS➤ Consolidators, who buy tickets at reduced rates from scheduled airlines, sell them at prices below the lowest available from the airlines directly—usually without advance restrictions. Sometimes you can even get your money back if you need to return the ticket. Carefully read the fine print detailing penalties for changes and cancellations. If you doubt the reliability of a consolidator, **confirm your reservation with the airline.**

ALOFT

AIRLINE FOOD➤ If you hate airline food, **ask for special meals when booking.** These can be vegetarian, low choles-

terol, or kosher, for example; commonly prepared to order in smaller quantities than standard catered fare, they can be tastier.

JET LAG➤ To avoid this syndrome, which occurs when travel disrupts your body's natural cycles, try to maintain a normal routine. At night, **get some sleep.** By day, move about the cabin to **stretch your legs, eat light meals, and drink water—not alcohol.**

SMOKING➤ Smoking is banned on all flights within the U.S. of less than six hours' duration and on all Canadian flights; the ban also applies to domestic segments of international flights aboard U.S. and foreign carriers. Delta has banned smoking system-wide.

C
CAMERAS, CAMCORDERS, AND COMPUTERS

LAPTOPS

Before you depart, **check your portable computer's battery,** because you may be asked at security to turn on the computer to prove that it is what it appears to be. At the airport, you may prefer to **request a manual inspection,** although security X-rays do not harm hard-disk or floppy-disk storage.

THE GOLD GUIDE / SMART TRAVEL TIPS

PHOTOGRAPHY

If your camera is new or if you haven't used it for a while, **shoot and develop a few rolls of film** before you leave. Always **store film in a cool, dry place**—never in the car's glove compartment or on the shelf under the rear window.

Every pass through an X-ray machine increases film's chance of clouding. To protect it, carry it in a clear plastic bag and **ask for hand inspection at security.** Such requests are virtually always honored at U.S. airports. Don't depend on a lead-lined bag to protect film in checked luggage—the airline may increase the radiation to see what's inside.

VIDEO

Before your trip, **test your camcorder, invest in a skylight filter to protect the lens, and charge the batteries.** (Airport security personnel may ask you to turn on the camcorder to prove that it's what it appears to be.)

Videotape is not damaged by X-rays, but it may be harmed by the magnetic field of a walk-through metal detector, so **ask that videotapes be hand-checked.**

CHILDREN AND TRAVEL

BABY-SITTING

For recommended local sitters, **check with your hotel desk.**

DRIVING

If you are renting a car, **arrange for a car seat when you reserve.** Sometimes they're free.

FLYING

On domestic flights, children under 2 not occupying a seat travel free, and older children currently travel on the "lowest applicable" adult fare.

BAGGAGE➤ In general, the adult baggage allowance applies for children paying half or more of the adult fare.

SAFETY SEATS➤ According to the FAA, it's a good idea to **use safety seats aloft.** Airline policy varies. U.S. carriers allow FAA-approved models, but airlines usually require that you buy a ticket, even if your child would otherwise ride free, because the seats must be strapped into regular passenger seats.

FACILITIES➤ When making your reservation, **ask for children's meals and a freestanding bassinet** if you need them; the latter are available only to those with seats at the bulkhead, where there's enough legroom. If you don't need the bassinet, **think twice before requesting bulkhead seats**—the only storage for in-flight necessities is in the inconveniently distant overhead bins.

LODGING

Most hotels allow children under a certain age to stay in their parents' room at no extra charge, while others charge them as extra adults; be sure to **ask about the cut-off age.** Some hotels make nominal charges for cribs and $5–$10 charges for extra beds.

CUSTOMS AND DUTIES

IN LOS ANGELES

Visitors aged 21 or over may import the following into the United States: 200 cigarettes, or 50 cigars, or 2 kilograms of tobacco; 1 U.S. liter of alcohol; gifts with a total value of $100. Restricted items include meat products, seeds, plants, and fruits. Never carry illegal drugs.

BACK HOME

IN CANADA➤ Once per calendar year, when you've been out of Canada for at least seven days, you may bring in C$300 worth of goods duty-free. If you've been away less than seven days but more than 48 hours, the duty-free exemption drops to C$100 but can be claimed any number of times (as can a C$20 duty-free exemption for absences of 24 hours or more). You cannot combine the yearly and 48-hour exemptions, use the C$300 exemption only partially (to save the balance for a later trip), or pool exemptions with family members. Goods claimed under the C$300 exemption may follow you by mail; those claimed under the lesser exemptions must accompany you.

Alcohol and tobacco products may be included in the yearly and 48-hour exemptions but not in the 24-hour exemption. If you meet the age requirements of the province through which you reenter Canada, you may bring in, duty-free, 1.14 liters (40 imperial ounces) of wine or liquor *or* 24 12-ounce cans or bottles of beer or ale. If you are 16 or older, you may bring in, duty-free, 200 cigarettes, 50 cigars or cigarillos, and 400 tobacco sticks or 400 grams of manufactured tobacco. Alcohol and tobacco must accompany you on your return.

An unlimited number of gifts valued up to C$60 each may be mailed to Canada duty-free. These do not count as part of your exemption. Label the package "Unsolicited Gift—Value under $60." Alcohol and tobacco are excluded.

IN THE U.K.➤ From countries outside the EU, including the United States, you may import duty-free 200 cigarettes, 100 cigarillos, 50 cigars or 250 grams of tobacco; 1 liter of spirits or 2 liters of fortified or sparkling wine; 2 liters of still table wine; 60 milliliters of perfume; 250 milliliters of toilet water; plus £136 worth of other goods, including gifts and souvenirs.

D
DIVERS' ALERT

Scuba divers take note: **Do not fly within 24 hours of scuba diving.**

DRIVING

Los Angeles is at the western terminus of I–10, a major east–west interstate highway that runs all the way east to Florida. I–15, angling down from Las Vegas, swings through the

eastern communities around San Bernardino before heading on down to San Diego. I–5, which runs north–south through California, leads up to San Francisco and down to San Diego. A tangle of freeways converge in the Los Angeles area**where?**; *see* Getting Around Los Angeles, *below,* for a freeway map that should help you negotiate around the L.A. sprawl.

A car is a must in Los Angeles; the freeway map below **ditto** should help you to get around the maze. If you plan to drive extensively, consider buying a *Thomas Guide,* which contains detailed maps of the entire county. Despite what you've heard, traffic is not always a major problem, especially if you avoid rush hours (7–9 AM and 3–7 PM). Seat belts must be worn by all passengers at all times.

FOR TRAVELERS
WITH DISABILITIES

California is a national leader in making attractions and facilities accessible to travelers with disabilities. Since 1982, the state building code has required that all construction for public use include access for people with disabilities. State laws more than a decade old provide special privileges, such as license plates allowing special parking spaces, unlimited parking in time-limited spaces, and free parking in metered

spaces. ID from states other than California is honored.

When discussing accessibility with an operator or reservationist, **ask hard questions.** Are there any stairs, inside *or* out? Are there grab bars next to the toilet *and* in the shower/tub? How wide is the doorway to the room? To the bathroom? For the most extensive facilities, meeting the latest legal specifications, **opt for newer facilities,** which more often have been designed with access in mind. Older properties or ships must usually be retrofitted and may offer more limited facilities as a result. Be sure to **discuss your needs before booking.**

DISCOUNT CLUBS

Travel clubs offer members unsold space on airplanes, cruise ships, and package tours at as much as 50% below regular prices. Membership may include a regular bulletin or access to a toll-free hot line giving details of available trips departing from three or four days to several months in the future. Most also offer 50% discounts off hotel rack rates. Before booking with a club, **make sure the hotel or other supplier isn't offering a better deal.**

I
INSURANCE

BAGGAGE

Airline liability for your baggage is limited to $1,250 per person on domestic flights. On international flights, the airlines' liability is $9.07 per pound or $20 per kilogram for checked baggage (roughly $640 per 70-pound bag) and $400 per passenger for unchecked baggage. However, this excludes valuable items such as jewelry and cameras that are listed in your ticket's fine print. You can buy additional insurance from the airline at check-in, but first **see if your home-owner's policy covers lost luggage.**

FLIGHT

You should **think twice before buying flight insurance.** Often purchased as a last-minute impulse at the airport, it pays a lump sum when a plane crashes, either to a beneficiary if the insured dies or sometimes to a surviving passenger who loses eyesight or a limb. Supplementing the airlines' coverage described in the limits-of-liability paragraphs on your ticket, it's expensive and basically unnecessary. Charging an airline ticket to a major credit card often automatically entitles you to coverage and may also embrace travel by bus, train, and ship.

HEALTH

FOR U.K. TRAVELERS➤ According to the Association of British Insurers, a trade association representing 450 insurance companies, it's wise to **buy extra medical coverage when you visit the United States.** You can buy an annual travel-insurance policy valid for most

vacations during the year in which it's purchased. If you go this route, make sure it covers you if you have a preexisting medical condition or are pregnant.

TRIP

Without insurance, you will lose all or most of your money if you must cancel your trip due to illness or any other reason. Especially if your airline ticket, cruise, or package tour is nonrefundable and cannot be changed, it's essential that you **buy trip-cancellation-and-interruption insurance.** When considering how much coverage you need, look for a policy that will cover the cost of your trip plus the nondiscounted price of a one-way airline ticket should you need to return home early. Read the fine print carefully, especially sections defining "family member" and "preexisting medical conditions." Also **consider default or bankruptcy insurance,** which protects you against a supplier's failure to deliver. However, such policies often do not cover default by a travel agency, tour operator, airline, or cruise line if you bought your tour and the coverage directly from the firm in question.

L
LODGING

APARTMENT AND VILLA RENTALS

If you want a home base that's roomy enough for a family and comes with cooking

facilities, **consider a furnished rental.** It's generally cost-wise, too, although not always—some rentals are luxury properties (economical only when your party is large). Home-exchange directories list rentals—often second homes owned by prospective house swappers—and some services search for a house or apartment for you (even a castle if that's your fancy) and handle the paperwork. Some send an illustrated catalogue and others send photographs of specific properties, sometimes at a charge; up-front registration fees may apply.

HOME EXCHANGE

If you would like to find a house, an apartment, or other vacation property to exchange for your own while on vacation, **become a member of a home-exchange organization,** which will send you its annual directories listing available exchanges and will include your own listing in at least one of them. Arrangements for the actual exchange are made by the two parties to it, not by the organization.

M
MONEY AND EXPENSES

ATMS

Also **ask whether your card's PIN must be reprogrammed** for use in Los Angeles. Four digits are commonly used overseas. Note that Discover is accepted only in the United States.

On cash advances you are charged interest from the day you receive the money from ATMs as well as from tellers. Transaction fees for ATM withdrawals outside your home turf may be higher than for withdrawals at home.

TRAVELER'S CHECKS

Whether or not to buy traveler's checks depends on where you are headed; **take cash to rural areas and small towns, traveler's checks to cities.** The most widely recognized are American Express, Citicorp, Thomas Cook, and Visa, which are sold by major commercial banks for 1%–3% of the checks' face value—it pays to **shop around.**

Both American Express and Thomas Cook issue checks that can be countersigned and used by you or your traveling companion. You can cash them in banks without paying a fee (which can be as much as 20%) and use them as readily as cash in many hotels, restaurants, and shops.

WIRING MONEY

You don't have to be a cardholder to send or receive funds through MoneyGram℠ from American Express. Just go to a MoneyGram agent, located in retail and convenience stores and in American Express Travel Offices. Pay up to $1,000 with cash or a credit card, anything over that in cash. The money can be picked up within 10 minutes in cash or check

at the nearest Money-Gram agent. There's no limit, and the recipient need only present photo identification. The cost, which includes a free long-distance phone call, from 3% to 10%, depending on the amount sent, the destination, and how you pay.

Money sent from the United States or Canada will be available for pickup at agent locations in 100 countries within 15 minutes. Once the money is in the system, it can be picked up at any one of 25,000 locations. Fees range from 4% to 10%, depending on the amount you send.

P
PACKAGES
AND TOURS

A package or tour to Los Angeles can make your vacation less expensive and more convenient. Firms that sell tours and packages purchase airline seats, hotel rooms, and rental cars in bulk and pass some of the savings on to you. In addition, the best operators have local representatives to help you out at your destination.

A GOOD DEAL?

The more your package or tour includes, the better you can predict the ultimate cost of your vacation. Make sure you know exactly what is included, and **beware of hidden costs.** Are taxes, tips, and service charges included? Transfers and baggage handling? Entertainment and

excursions? These can add up.

Most packages and tours are rated deluxe, first-class superior, first class, tourist, and budget. The key difference is usually accommodations. If the package or tour you are considering is priced lower than in your wildest dreams, **be skeptical.** Also, **make sure your travel agent knows the hotels** and other services. Ask about location, room size, beds, and whether it has a pool, room service, or programs for children, if you care about these. Has your agent been there or sent others you can contact?

BUYER BEWARE

Each year consumers are stranded or lose their money when operators go out of business—even very large ones with excellent reputations. If you can't afford a loss, take the time to **check out the operator**—find out how long the company has been in business, and ask several agents about its reputation. Next, **don't book unless the firm has a consumer-protection program.** Members of the United States Tour Operators Association and the National Tour Association are required to set aside funds exclusively to cover your payments and travel arrangements in case of default. Nonmember operators may instead carry insurance; look for the details in the operator's brochure—and the name of an underwriter with a solid reputation. Note: When it comes to tour operators, **don't trust escrow accounts.** Although there are laws governing those of charter-flight operators, no governmental body prevents tour operators from raiding the till.

Next, **contact your local Better Business Bureau and the attorney general's office** in both your own state and the operator's; have any complaints been filed? Last, **pay with a major credit card.** Then you can cancel payment, provided that you can document your complaint. Always **consider trip-cancellation insurance** (*see* Insurance, *above*).

BIG VS. SMALL➤ An operator that handles several hundred thousand travelers annually can use its purchasing power to give you a good price. Its high volume may also indicate financial stability. But some small companies provide more personalized service; because they tend to specialize, they may also be experts on an area.

USING AN AGENT

Travel agents are an excellent resource. In fact, large operators accept bookings only through travel agents. But it's good to **collect brochures from several agencies,** because some agents' suggestions may be skewed by promotional relationships with tour and package firms that reward them for volume sales. If you have a special interest, **find an agent with**

expertise in that area; the American Society of Travel Agents can give you leads in the United States. (Don't rely solely on your agent, though; agents may be unaware of small niche operators, and some special-interest travel companies only sell direct).

SINGLE TRAVELERS

Prices are usually quoted per person, based on two sharing a room. If you are traveling solo, you may be required to pay the full double occupancy rate. Some operators eliminate this surcharge if you agree to be matched up with a roommate of the same sex, even if one is not found by departure time.

The most important rule to bear in mind in packing for a southern California vacation is to prepare for temperature changes. An hour's drive can take you up or down many degrees, and there can be a marked drop in temperature from daytime to nighttime. Clothes that can be layered are your best insurance—take along a sweater or jacket but also bring some shorts and cool cottons. Always tuck in a bathing suit; most lodgings have a pool, a spa, or a sauna.

While casual dressing is a hallmark of the California lifestyle, men will need a jacket and tie for many good restaurants in the evening, and women will be more

comfortable in something dressier than the regulation sightseeing garb of cotton dresses, walking shorts, or jeans and T-shirts.

Be sure you take comfortable walking shoes. Even if you're not much of a walker at home, you're bound to find many occasions on a southern California vacation when you'll want to hoof it, and nothing ruins the pleasures of sightseeing like sore feet.

Bring an extra pair of eyeglasses or contact lenses in your carry-on luggage, and if you have a health problem, **pack enough medication** to last the trip. In case your bags go astray, **don't put prescription drugs or valuables in luggage to be checked.**

LUGGAGE

REGULATIONS➤ Free airline baggage allowances depend on the airline, the route, and the class of your ticket; ask in advance. In general, on domestic flights you are entitled to check two bags—neither exceeding 62 inches, or 158 centimeters (length + width + height), or weighing more than 70 pounds (32 kilograms). A third piece may be brought aboard; its total dimensions are generally limited to less than 45 inches (114 centimeters), so it will fit easily under the seat in front of you or in the overhead compartment. In the United States, the Federal Aviation Administration gives airlines broad latitude to limit carry-on allowances and tailor them to different aircraft and operational conditions. Charges for excess, oversize, or overweight pieces vary.

SAFEGUARDING YOUR LUGGAGE➤ Before leaving home, **itemize your bags' contents** and their worth, and label them with your name, address, and phone number. (If you use your home address, cover it so potential thieves can't see it.) Inside your bag, **pack a copy of your itinerary.** At check-in, **make sure that your bag is correctly tagged** with the airport's three-letter destination code. If your bags arrive damaged or not at all, file a written report with the airline before you leave the airport.

PASSPORTS AND VISAS

If you don't already have one, **get a passport.** While traveling, **keep one photocopy of the data page** separate from your wallet and leave another copy with someone at home. If you lose your passport, promptly call the nearest embassy or consulate and the local police; having the data page can speed replacement.

CANADIANS

No passport is necessary to enter the United States.

U.K. CITIZENS

British citizens need a valid passport. If you are staying fewer than 90 days and traveling on a vacation, with a return or onward ticket,

you will probably not need a visa. However, you will need to fill out the Visa Waiver Form, 1-94W, supplied by the airline.

R
RENTING A CAR

CUTTING COSTS

To get the best deal, **book through a travel agent and shop around.** When pricing cars, **ask where the rental lot is located.** Some off-airport locations offer lower rates—even though their lots are only minutes away from the terminal via complimentary shuttle. You may also want to **price local car-rental companies,** whose rates may be lower still, although service and maintenance standards may not be up to those of a national firm. Also **ask your travel agent about a company's customer-service record.** How has it responded to late plane arrivals and vehicle mishaps? Are there often lines at the rental counter, and, if you're traveling during a holiday period, does a confirmed reservation guarantee you a car?

INSURANCE

When you drive a rented car, you are generally responsible for any damage or personal injury that you cause as well as damage to the vehicle. Before you rent, **see what coverage you already have** by means of your personal auto-insurance policy and credit cards. For about $14 a day, rental companies sell insurance, known as a

collision damage waiver (CDW), that eliminates your liability for damage to the car; it's always optional and should never be automatically added to your bill. California, New York, and Illinois have outlawed the sale of CDW altogether.

SURCHARGES

Before picking up the car in one city and leaving it in another, **ask about drop-off charges or one-way service fees,** which can be substantial. Note, too, that some rental agencies charge extra if you return the car before the time specified on your contract. To avoid a hefty refueling fee, **fill the tank just before you turn in the car.**

FOR U.K. CITIZENS

In the United States, you must be 21 to rent a car; rates may be higher for those under 25. Extra costs cover child seats, compulsory for children under 5 (about $3 per day), and additional drivers (about $1.50 per day). To pick up your reserved car you will need the reservation voucher, a passport, a U.K. driver's license, and a travel policy covering each driver.

S
SENIOR-CITIZEN DISCOUNTS

To qualify for age-related discounts, **mention your senior-citizen status up front** when booking hotel reservations, not when checking out, and before you're seated in

SMART TRAVEL TIPS / THE GOLD GUIDE

restaurants, not when paying your bill. Note that discounts may be limited to certain menus, days, or hours. When renting a car, **ask about promotional car-rental discounts**—they can net lower costs than your senior-citizen discount.

STUDENTS ON THE ROAD

To save money, **look into deals available through student-oriented travel agencies.** To qualify, you'll need to have a bona fide student I.D. card. Members of international student groups also are eligible. *See* Students *in* Important Contacts A to Z, *above.*

T
TELEPHONES

LONG-DISTANCE

The long-distance services of AT&T, MCI, and Sprint make calling home relatively convenient and let you avoid hotel surcharges; typically, you dial an 800 number in the United States and a local number abroad).

W
WHEN TO GO

Almost any time of the year is the right time to go to Los Angeles; the climate is mild and pleasant year-round. There is, however, a rainy season from November through March (the heaviest downpours are usually January). Summers are virtually rainless but usually see the famous Los Angeles smog at its worst, and this can cause problems for people with respiratory ailments.

CLIMATE

Seasons in Los Angeles and southern California are not as defined as in other temperate areas of the world. The Pacific Ocean is the primary moderating influence. In addition, mountains along the north and east sides of the Los Angeles coastal basin act as buffers against the extreme summer heat and winter cold of the desert and plateau regions.

Mild sea breezes and winds from the interior can mix to produce a variety of weather conditions; an unusual aspect of the Los Angeles climate is the pronounced difference in temperature, humidity, cloudiness, fog, rain, and sunshine over short distances.

The following are average daily maximum and minimum temperatures for Los Angeles.

Climate in Los Angeles

Jan.	64F	18C	May	69F	21C	Sept.	75F	24C
	44	7		53	12		60	16
Feb.	64F	18C	June	71F	22C	Oct.	73F	23C
	46	8		57	14		55	13
Mar.	66F	19C	July	75F	24C	Nov.	71F	22C
	48	9		60	16		48	9
Apr.	66F	19C	Aug.	75F	24C	Dec.	66F	19C
	51	11		62	17		46	8

1 Destination: Los Angeles

LOS ANGELES: A LOT OF SOMETHING FOR EVERYONE

YOU'RE PREPARING FOR YOUR TRIP to Los Angeles. You're psyching up with Beach Boys CDs, and some Hollywood epics on the laser-disc player. You've pulled out your Hawaiian shirts and tennis shorts. You've studied the menu at Taco Bell. You're even doing a crash regimen at your local tanning salon and aerobics studio so you won't *look* so much like a tourist when you hit the coast.

Well, relax. *Everybody's* a tourist in LaLa Land. Even the stars are starstruck (as evidenced by the celebrities watching the other celebrities at Spago). Los Angeles is a city of ephemerals, of transience, and above all, of illusion. Nothing here is quite real, and that's the reality of it all. That air of anything-can-happen—as it often does— is what motivates thousands to move to and millions to vacation in this promised land each year. Visitors don't just come from the East or Midwest, mind you, but from the Far East, Down Under, Europe, and South America. It's this influx of cultures that's been the lifeblood of Los Angeles since its Hispanic beginning.

We cannot predict what *your* Los Angeles will be like. You can laze on a beach or soak up some of the world's greatest art collections. You can tour the movie studios and stars' homes or take the kids to Disneyland, Magic Mountain, or Knott's Berry Farm. You can shop luxurious Beverly Hills' Rodeo Drive or browse for hipper novelties on boutique-lined Melrose Avenue. The possibilities are endless—rent a boat to Catalina Island, watch the floats in Pasadena's Rose Parade, or dine on tacos, sushi, or pizza with goat cheese.

No matter how fast-forward Los Angeles seems to spin, the heart of the city— or at least its stomach—is still deep in the 1950s. Sure, the lighter, nouvelle-inspired California cuisine has made a big splash (no one here has ever been ridiculed as a "health-food nut" for preferring a healthier diet), but nothing is more quintessen-

tially Californian than Johnny Rockets (a chrome-and-fluorescent burger paradise on Melrose) or Pink's (a beloved greasy spoon of a chili-dog dive on La Brea).

None of this was imagined when Spanish settlers founded their Pueblo de la Reina de Los Angeles in 1781. In fact, no one predicted a golden future for desert-dry southern California until well after San Francisco and northern California had gotten a head start with their own gold rush. The dusty outpost of Los Angeles eventually had oil and oranges, but the golden key to its success came on the silver screen: the movies. Although, if the early pioneers of Hollywood—religiously conservative fruit farmers—had gotten their way, their town's name would never have become synonymous with cinema and entertainment.

The same sunshine that draws today's visitors and new residents drew Cecil B. DeMille and Jesse Lasky in 1913 while they were searching for a place to make movies besides New York City. Lesser filmmakers had been shooting reels for the nickelodeons of the day in Hollywood, but DeMille and Lasky were the first to make a feature-length movie here. It took another 14 years to break through the sound barrier in cinema, but the silent-film era made Hollywood's name synonymous with fantasy, glamour, and, as the first citizens would snicker in disgust, with sin.

Outrageous partying, extravagant homes, eccentric clothing, and money, money, money have been symbols of life in Los Angeles ever since. Even the more conservative oil, aerospace, computer, banking, and import/export industries on the booming Pacific Rim have enjoyed the prosperity that leads inevitably to fun living. The economic downturn has hit California hard, but while some people are still waiting for prosperity to return, others—notably those in the entertainment business—never felt it at all. Even without piles of bucks, many people have found a kindred spirit in Los Angeles for their colorful lifestyles, be they spiritually, socially, or sexually unusual.

Tolerance reigns; live and let live—which explains why you, too, will fit in.

When you arrive in Los Angeles, turn your car radio to 94.7 FM. "Ninety-four-seven, the Way-ee-yave," as this station's identifiers croon it, plays New Age, mellow modern, and a synthesizer blend of soft jazz, gentle rock, and cosmic chords not easily found anywhere else on your dial. The mix makes for the perfect freeway-driving soundtrack. It's Muzak for tomorrow's world—the '60s recycled into the '90s; the tempo of Tinseltown, laid back and out there.

If cosmic music sounds corny to you, there are classical, contemporary, blues, soul, and rock stations here—and, believe us, with "drive time" what it is in Los Angeles, you'll have plenty of time to find them. Disc jockey Jay Thomas plays the latest dance, rock, and pop hits on KPWR 106 FM, better known as The Power, and jazz and blues can be heard on KLON, 88.1 FM, featuring such artists as Wynton Marsalis and Ray Charles. For the latest traffic update, tune in KFWB, 98 AM, the 24-hour news station ("You give us 22 minutes, we'll give you the world") that offers traffic updates every 10 minutes. Dr. David Viscott has a radio show on KABC AM Talkradio, weekdays from 1 to 3 PM, offering free psychiatric help to callers.

No matter what you turn on and what turns you on while you drive the infamous freeways, these asphalt ribbons are your passage to the far-flung pleasures of Los Angeles. Getting there *can* be half the fun, outside of rush-crush hours (7–9 AM and 3–7 PM), but when the freeway bogs down with bumper-to-bumper Japanese imports, minipickups, and sleek Mercedes, blame Detroit. It was the U.S. automakers and oil companies that, earlier in this century, lobbied successfully to replace an electric mass transit system in southern California with a diesel bus system. Free-spirited Californians drove blithely on, indulging their independence until one day, sometime in the mid-1950s, the smog got thick enough to kill. Mandatory emission controls have helped clear up that problem. Nevertheless, check the papers daily to ascertain the air quality.

No city has embraced the romance of the automobile as has Los Angeles. Cars are not only essential transportation but essential fashion accessories. They announce the wealth, politics, and taste of their drivers. Vanity license plates, a California innovation, condense the meaning of one's life into seven letters (MUZKBIZ). Sunroofs, ski racks, and cardboard windshield visors sell better here than anywhere else. You are what you drive—a thought worth remembering when you rent a car. Yes, Lamborghinis are available, even by the hour.

The distance between places in Los Angeles explains why the ethnic enclaves have not merged, regardless of the melting-pot appearance of the city. Especially since the rioting in the spring of 1992, which—among other things—brought to the surface much long-simmering tension between various ethnic groups, it is impossible to gloss over the disparities of race, economics, and social mobility between neighborhoods. Nonetheless, at its best, and most notable for visitors, is the rich cultural and culinary diversity this mix of peoples creates.

There's something about a shiny, better world that beckons so many diverse people to Los Angeles. For some, a better world is self-enhancing—the building of the body beautiful, a personal fortune, or the hottest hot rod. Others try to better their world through the arts, politics, or spiritual exploration. For some it is enough just to surf and sun.

Set off from the rest of the continent by mountains and desert, and from the rest of the world by an ocean, this incredible corner of creation has evolved its own identity that conjures envy, fascination, ridicule, and scorn—often all at once. Those from purportedly more sophisticated cities note what Los Angeles lacks. Others from more provincial towns raise an eyebrow at what it has. But 12.5 million people visit the city annually, and three-quarters of them come back for more. Indeed, you cannot do Los Angeles in a day or a week or even two. This second largest city in America holds too many choices between its canyons and its coast to be exhausted in one trip; it will exhaust you first.

WHAT'S WHERE

Downtown Los Angeles

Although this misplaced menage of skyscrapers often plays second fiddle to some of L.A.'s more glamorous tourist areas, its multicultural pockets, museums, and historic buildings make it worth a couple of quarters on the DASH (Downtown Area Short Hop) transit system. Chinatown, Little Tokyo, and Olvera Street (with tiled walks, strolling mariachis, and great Mexican food) exemplify the rich cultural diversity of the city, while Victorian, Art Deco, and Beaux Arts buildings (in various stages of preservation) on and around Broadway are snippets of L.A.'s architectural past.

Highland Park, Pasadena, San Morino

Los Angeles' suburbs are blessed with stunning architecture from late 1800 Victorian and Craftsman homes to prefab minimalls. While Pasadena and San Morino flash their stately mansions, Highland Park holds on to its modest, early 1900 California bungalow classics, many of them in a sad state of disrepair.

Hollywood

Hollywood has changed since the golden days of big-screen legends, but its name still conjures images of paparazzi stealing shots of beautiful celebs making their screen debuts. Currently under revitalization, flashy Hollywood Boulevard has buried historical treasures among souvenir shops, office buildings, and renewed facades. Still, the Walk of Fame, Mann's Chinese Theater, Hollywood Bowl, El Capitan Theater, and the Capitol Records Building are among the highlights on many tourists' lists, and for those visitors with keen imaginations, Hollywood's romantic past life still pulses.

Orange County

Disneyland, in Anaheim, is probably the best-known attraction in this neck of the woods, but other deserving attractions see much tourist traffic as well, including Knott's Berry Farm in nearby Buena Park and UCLA, Irvine campus. Looking to join the ranks of laid-back, sun-worshipping Californians? Coastal Orange County provides countless pleasures and personalities with a multitude of beach and harbor towns. Huntington Beach, Newport Harbor, the Balboa Peninsula, and Laguna Beach each define a different kind of lifestyle, from surfdom to sailing and ritzy to arty.

Palos Verdes, San Pedro, and Long Beach

This stretch of coastline is L.A.'s modest resort area—simple, pretty peninsula towns, with plenty of hotels and decent attractions, but not too many supermodels or politics. These hamlets are a good distance from hustle and bustle, stars, and star-gazers, making them low-key, safe beach destinations for the family.

San Fernando Valley

Referred to as "The Valley," this expansive area has metamorphosized from what was once orange groves and ranches into a well-populated solidly middle-class community with some of L.A.'s most lucrative attractions, including Burbank and Universal Studios.

Santa Monica, Venice, Pacific Palisades, and Malibu

No matter how far up Pacific Coast Highway you drive, you're assured dramatic views. Locals flex their muscles, in-line skate, and perform along Venice's boardwalk, while Santa Monica and Pacific Palisades draw vacationing families. Malibu is where the rich-and-famous hide away in their "Colony."

The Westside

La Brea Avenue west to the ocean is one of the ritziest areas in L.A., were the beautiful, wealthy people go to dine, shop, and mingle. Melrose Avenue is the place for up-to-the-minute fashion reports, especially if you need a little something to wear to a party in Beverly Hills. If your name didn't make it on any guest list, at least take a drive along bustling Sunset Strip (Sunset Boulevard) to the "Hills" to see its palatial homes and sanitized landscapes. A walk down Rodeo Drive is another lesson in trendiness.

Wilshire Boulevard

Running west from Downtown, through Beverly Hills and Santa Monica, and to the Pacific, Wilshire Boulevard encapsulates all the flavors of Los Angeles, from the city's poorer neighborhoods to some of the priciest real estate in the country. There's a lot to see here in a day, including Koreatown, Westwood (UCLA's college scene), Art Deco beauties, the Farmers Market, and plenty of museums, parks, and good food.

FODOR'S CHOICE

Museums

★ **Gene Autry Western Heritage Museum.** Griffith Park is the setting for this rambling museum showcasing artifacts of the Old West.

★ **J. Paul Getty Museum.** Malibu's treasure trove, housed in a replica of an Italian villa, stands perched high above the Pacific.

★ **Museum of Contemporary Art.** The works of today's mainstream artists are represented in this striking seven-story structure designed by Japanese architect Arata Isozaki.

★ **The Museum of Tolerance.** Bigotry, racism, and the many genocides in the history of our planet are explored in a fascinating interactive setting.

★ **Natural History Museum of Los Angeles.** Dinosaurs, birds, insects, and artifacts fill the more than 35 halls in Exposition Park.

Parks and Gardens

★ **Descanso Gardens.** Walk through one of Los Angeles' most peaceful environments, canopied by native oaks.

★ **Griffith Park.** Crowned by a pristine Art Deco observatory, this piece of hilly terrain is the largest municipal park in the nation.

★ **Huntington Library and Botanical Garden.** View Gainsborough's Blue Boy and the Gutenberg Bible before basking in the sun.

★ **The Regent Beverly Wilshire.** At the foot of Rodeo Drive stands this majestic hotel where Julia Roberts slept in the film *Pretty Woman.*

★ **Will Rodgers State Park.** Polo is played in this shady park across the highway from a sunny, white sand beach.

Hotels

★ **Hotel Bel Air.** In addition to an atmosphere of elegance, there's a lovely garden setting that hallmarks this rarefied retreat that's especially popular with the rich and famous. $$$$

★ **The New Otani Hotel and Gardens.** This high rise is where visitors get the luxurious Japanese treatment—indoors and outside—in the heart of downtown. $$$$–$$$

★ **The Beverly Hills Ritz.** This low-rise accommodation is small and friendly. $$$

★ **The Inn at 657.** One of L.A.'s few bed-and breakfasts is an oasis near bustling downtown. $

Restaurants

★ **Rex II Ristorante.** This lavishly restored Art Deco building, formerly a haberdashery, serves downtown's most celebrated Italian fare. $$$$

★ **L'Orangerie.** The epitome of classic French food in L.A. delivered reliably. $$$$–$$$

★ **Restaurant Katsu.** This is the ultimate sushi scene, one of America's best Japanese restaurants. $$$

★ **Nicola.** Larry Nicola's hip downtown bistro is big with business people during the day and theater goers at night. $$$–$$

★ **Spago.** Possibly the world's most celebrated pizza parlor, this Sunset Strip landmark showcases super chef Wolfgang Puck's culinary prowess. $$$–$$

★ **Cha Cha Cha.** Funky decor and spiced-up dishes at this downscale eatery make you feel like you're in the Caribbean, instead of L.A. $$–$

★ **Louise's Trattoria.** One of a local chain, this fun-loving pizza and pasta place draws in hungry folks from the happening Derby Room jazz club. $$–$

★ **Canter's.** L.A.'s most authentic deli is a round-the-clock meeting place with very friendly employees and generous, savory fare. $

★ **El Cholo.** This authentic Mexican restaurant serves the best Margaritas in town. $

2 Exploring Los Angeles

By Ellen
Melinkoff

Updated and
revised by Jane
E. Lasky and
William P.
Brown

BECAUSE LOS ANGELES IS SUCH A SPREAD-OUT METROPOLIS, seeing the sights—from the Huntington Library in San Marino to the *Queen Mary* in Long Beach—requires a decidedly organized itinerary. Be prepared to put miles on the car. It's best to view Los Angeles as a collection of destinations, each to be explored separately, and not to jump willy-nilly from place to place.

In this guide, we've divided up the major sightseeing areas of Los Angeles into eight major tours: Downtown; Hollywood; Wilshire Boulevard, a major boulevard that slices through a fascinating cross section of the city; the posh and trendy Westside neighborhoods; the beachside towns of Santa Monica, Venice, Pacific Palisades, and Malibu; the often overlooked coastal towns of Palos Verdes, San Pedro, and Long Beach; the well-to-do northern inland suburbs of Highland Park, Pasadena, and San Marino; and the San Fernando Valley.

After the eight exploring tours, the rest of Los Angeles's most noteworthy attractions have been organized into four miscellaneous sections. Other Places of Interest includes sights outside the map areas but definitely worth visiting. Off the Beaten Track highlights a few unusual, lesser-known sights. Sightseeing Checklists is a comprehensive alphabetical list of sights in various categories, including those covered in the exploring tours. For example, every noteworthy museum in Los Angeles is listed in the Museums checklist; the Huntington Library, Art Gallery, and Botanical garden is mentioned there, but cross-referenced to the Highland Park, Pasadena, and San Marino tour, where it is more fully described.

Orientation

First, a brief orientation lesson, using LAX (Los Angeles International Airport) as a starting point. Head north from LAX and you'll soon reach the coastal area of Santa Monica, from which two major thoroughfares run due east into downtown. Sunset Boulevard winds around the upscale residential areas of Bel-Air and Beverly Hills before hitting the notorious commercial stretch known as the Sunset Strip. Sunset then passes through Hollywood and ends downtown near Chinatown and Dodger Stadium. The other major street, south of Sunset, is Wilshire Boulevard, which takes you from Santa Monica through Westwood, UCLA's college town, past Beverly Hills' famous shopping district, through the financial Wilshire district, and into the city center.

For a good overall view of the layout, head up to the Griffith Park Observatory, which is a bit east of Hollywood proper. Standing on the terraces there (where James Dean, Natalie Wood, and Sal Mineo stood in the movie *Rebel Without a Cause*), you're well above this massive city, and suddenly the various parts start to make sense. To the south are Long Beach and Orange County. To the left, a few miles southeast, is downtown, and below to the right is Hollywood (look for the whimsical Capital Records Building, which resembles a stack of old 45s). About 6 miles southwest of that, you'll notice the twin towers of ABC, marking Century City, and on a clear day you can see the Pacific Ocean in the distance. Directly to your right, the Hollywood Hills run west past the HOLLYWOOD sign through Beverly Hills, Bel-Air, and on to the coastline, where the hills become the Santa Monica Mountains, rising above the ritzy shoreline community of Malibu. Over the hill behind Griffith Park lie the San Fernando and San Gabriel valleys.

TOUR 1: DOWNTOWN LOS ANGELES

Numbers in the margin correspond to points of interest on the Tour 1: Downtown Los Angeles map.

All those jokes about Los Angeles being a city without a downtown are simply no longer true. This may have been true a few decades ago when Angelenos ruthlessly turned their backs on the city center and hightailed it to the suburbs. There *had* been a downtown, once, when Los Angeles was very young, and now the city core is enjoying a resurgence of attention from urban planners, real-estate developers, and downtown office workers who have discovered the advantages of living close to work.

Downtown Los Angeles can be explored on foot, or better yet, on DASH—Downtown Area Short Hop (*see below*). The natives might disagree, but these are the same natives who haven't been downtown since they took out a marriage license at city hall 30 years ago (unless they got hitched a second or third time as is often the case in LaLa Land); don't follow their lead. During the day, downtown is relatively safe (though be on your guard when you look around, just as you should be in any major city center).

Getting around to the major sites in downtown Los Angeles is actually quite simple, thanks to DASH. This minibus service travels in a loop past most of the attractions listed here, stopping every two blocks or so. Every ride costs 25¢, so if you hop on and off to see attractions, it will cost you every time. But the cost is worth it, since you can travel quickly and be assured of finding your way. DASH (☎ 213/626–4455) runs weekdays and Saturday 5 AM–10 PM. To follow the tour outlined below, get on Line A or B at ARCO Plaza (505 S. Flower St., between 5th and 6th Sts.).

❶ Hidden directly under the twin ARCO towers, ARCO Plaza is a subterranean shopping mall that's jam-packed with office workers during the week, nearly deserted on weekends. The **Los Angeles Convention and Visitors Bureau** is nearby. It offers free information about attractions as well as advice on public transportation. *685 S. Figueroa St., between 7th St. and Wilshire Blvd.,* ☎ *213/689–8822.* ⊙ *Mon.–Sat. 8:30–5.*

❷ Just north of ARCO, the **Westin Bonaventure Hotel and Suites** (404 S. Figueroa St., ☎ 213/624–1000) is unique in the L.A. skyline: five shimmering cylinders in the sky, without a 90° angle in sight. Designed by John Portman in 1974, the building looks like science-fiction fantasy. Nonguests can use only one elevator, which rises through the roof of the lobby to soar through the air outside to the revolving restaurant and bar on the 35th floor.

❸ The **Museum of Contemporary Art** houses a permanent collection of international scope, representing art from 1940 to the present. Included are works by Mark Rothko, Franz Kline, and Susan Rothenberg. The red sandstone building was designed by renowned Japanese architect Arata Isozaki and opened in 1986. Pyramidal skylights add a striking geometry to the seven-level, 98,000-square-foot building. Don't miss the gift shop or the lively Milanese-style café. *250 S. Grand Ave.,* ☎ *213/626–6222.* ☛ *$6 adults, $4 senior citizens and children, children under 12 free; free Thurs. 5–8.* ⊙ *Tues., Wed., Fri., Sat., and Sun. 11–5, Thurs. 11–8. Closed Mon.*

❹ Walk north to the **Music Center,** which has been the cultural center for Los Angeles since it opened in 1969. In spring, it's the site of the Academy Awards presentation: Limousines arrive at the Hope Street

Tour 1: Downtown Los Angeles

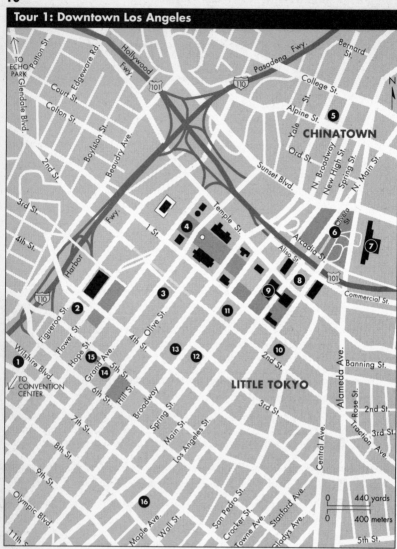

Biltmore Hotel, **14**
Bradbury
Building, **12**
Central Library, **15**
Chinatown, **5**
El Pueblo de Los
Angeles Historical
Monument, **6**
Garment District, **16**
Grand Central
Market, **13**
Little Tokyo, **10**
Los Angeles
Children's
Museum, **8**

Los Angeles City
Hall, **9**
Los Angeles *Times*
Complex, **11**
Los Angeles Visitor
and Convention
Bureau, **1**
Museum of
Contemporary Art, **3**
Music Center, **4**
Union Station, **7**
Westin Bonaventure
Hotel, **2**

drive-through and celebrities are whisked through the crowds to the Dorothy Chandler Pavilion, the largest and grandest of the three theaters. It was named after the widow of the publisher of the *Los Angeles Times,* who was instrumental in fund-raising efforts to build the complex. The round building in the middle, the Mark Taper Forum, is a smaller theater. Most of its offerings are of an experimental nature, many of them on a pre-Broadway run. The Ahmanson, at the north end, is the venue for many musical comedies. The plaza has a fountain and sculpture by Jacques Lipchitz. *1st St. and Grand Ave.,* ☎ *213/972–7211. Free 45-min tours offered Tues.–Sat. 10–1:30. Schedule subject to change; call 213/972–7483 for reservations.*

❺ L.A.'s **Chinatown** runs a pale second to San Francisco's Chinatown but still offers visitors an authentic slice of life, beyond the tourist hokum. The neighborhood is bordered by Yale, Bernard, and Ord streets and Alameda Avenue. The main drag is North Broadway, where, every February, giant dragons snake down the center of the pavement during Chinese New Year celebrations. More than 15,000 Chinese and Southeast Asians actually live in the Chinatown area, but many thousands more regularly frequent the markets (filled with exotic foods unfamiliar to most Western eyes) and restaurants (dim-sum parlors are currently the most popular).

❻ **El Pueblo de Los Angeles Historical Monument** preserves the "birthplace" of Los Angeles (no one knows exactly where the original 1781 settlement was), the oldest downtown buildings, and some of the only remaining pre-1900 buildings in the city. The historical area covers 44 acres, bounded by Alameda, Arcadia, Spring, and Macy streets.

★ **Olvera Street** is the heart of the park and one of the most popular tourist sites in Los Angeles. With its tile walkways, piñatas, mariachis, and authentic Mexican food, Olvera Street should not be dismissed as merely some gringo approximation of the real thing. Mexican-American families come here in droves, especially on weekends—to them it feels like the old country.

Begin your walk of the area at the **Plaza,** on Olvera Street between Main and Los Angeles streets, a wonderful Mexican-style park shaded by a huge Moreton Bay fig tree. There are plenty of benches and walkways for strolling. On weekends there are often mariachis and folkloric dance groups here. Two annual events are particularly worth seeing here: the Blessing of the Animals, at 2 PM on the Saturday before Easter, when residents bring their pets (not just dogs and cats but horses, pigs, cows, birds, hamsters) to be blessed by a priest, and Las Posadas, every night December 16–24, when merchants and visitors parade up and down the street, led by children dressed as angels, to commemorate Mary and Joseph's search for shelter on Christmas Eve.

Head north up Olvera Street proper. Mid-block is the park's **visitors center,** housed in Sepulveda House (622 N. Main St., ☎ 213/628–1274; ☉ Mon.–Sat. 10–3). The Eastlake Victorian was built in 1887 as a hotel and boardinghouse. **Pelanconi House** (17 Olvera St.), built in 1855, was the first brick building in Los Angeles and has been home to La Golondrina restaurant for 60 years. During the 1930s, famed Mexican muralist David Alfaro Siquieros was commissioned to paint a mural on the south wall of the **Italian Hall** building (650 N. Main St.). The patrons were not prepared for—and certainly not pleased by—this anti-imperialist mural depicting the oppressed workers of Latin America held in check by a menacing American eagle. It was promptly whitewashed into oblivion, and it remains under the paint to this day.

While preservationists from the Getty Conservation Trust work on ways of restoring the mural, copies can be seen at the visitors center.

Walk down the east side of Olvera Street to mid-block, passing the only remaining sign of Zanja Ditch (mother ditch), which supplied water to the area in the earliest years. **Avila Adobe** (E–10 Olvera St., open Mon.–Sat. 10–3), built in 1818, is generally considered the oldest building still standing in Los Angeles. This graceful, simple adobe is designed with the traditional interior courtyard and is furnished in the style of the 1840s.

On weekends, the restaurants are packed, and there is usually music in the plaza and along the street. Two Mexican holidays, Cinco de Mayo (May 5) and Independence Day (September 16), also draw huge crowds—and long lines for the restaurants. To see Olvera Street at its quietest and perhaps loveliest, visit on a late weekday afternoon. The long shadows heighten the romantic feeling of the street, and there are only a few strollers and diners milling about.

South of the plaza is an area that has undergone renovation but remains, for the most part, only an ambitious idea. Although these magnificent old buildings remain closed, awaiting some commercial plan (à la Ghirardelli Square in San Francisco) that never seems to come to fruition, docent-led tours explore the area in depth. Tours depart Tuesday–Saturday 10–1, on the hour, from the **Old Firehouse** (south side of plaza, ☎ 213/628–1274), an 1884 building that contains early fire-fighting equipment and old photographs. Buildings seen on tours include the Merced Theater, Masonic Temple, Pico House, and Garnier Block—all ornate examples of the late 19th-century style. Under the Merced, Masonic Temple, and Garnier Block are passageways once used by Chinese immigrants.

TIME OUT   The dining choices on Olvera Street range from fast-food stands to comfortable, sit-down restaurants. The most authentic Mexican food is at **La Luz del Dia** (107 Paseo de la Plaza, ☎ 213/628–7495). Here they serve traditional favorites, such as *chile rellenos* and pickled cactus, as well as handmade tortillas patted out in a practiced rhythm by the women behind the counter. **La Golondrina** (☎ 213/628–4349) and **El Paseo** (☎ 213/626–1361) restaurants, across from each other in mid-block, have delightful patios and extensive menus.

❼ **Union Station** (800 N. Alameda St.), directly east of Olvera Street across Alameda, is one of those quintessential Californian buildings that seemed to define Los Angeles to moviegoers all over the country in the 1940s. Built in 1939, its Spanish Mission style is a subtle combination of Streamline Moderne and Moorish. The majestic scale of the waiting room alone is worth the walk over. The place is so evocative of its heyday that you'll half expect to see Carole Lombard, Groucho Marx, or Barbara Stanwyck step onto the platform from a train and sashay through.

❽ **Los Angeles Children's Museum** was the first of several strictly-for-kids museums now open in the city. All the exhibits here are hands-on, from Sticky City (where kids get to pillow fight with abandon in a huge pillow-filled room) to a TV studio (where they can put on their own news shows) to The Cave (where hologram dinosaurs lurk, seeming almost real). *310 N. Main St.,* ☎ *213/687–8800.* ☞ *$5, children under 2 free.* ☺ *Weekends 10–5; also Tues.–Fri. 11:30–5 during summer vacation.*

❾ **Los Angeles City Hall** is another often-photographed building, well-known from its many appearances on *Dragnet, Superman,* and other television shows. Opened in 1928, the 27-story city hall remained the only building to break the 13-story height limit (earthquakes, you know) until 1957. There is a 45-minute tour and ride to the top-floor observation deck. Although some more recent buildings (e.g., the Bonaventure) offer higher views, city hall has a certain landmark panache. *200 N. Spring St.,* ☎ *213/485–4423. Tours by reservation only, weekdays at 10 and 11.*

⑩ Little Tokyo is the original ethnic neighborhood for Los Angeles's Japanese community. Most have deserted the downtown center for suburban areas such as Gardena and West Los Angeles, but Little Tokyo remains a cultural focal point. Nisei Week ("Nisei" is the name for second-generation Japanese) is celebrated here every August with traditional drums, dancing, a carnival, and a huge parade. Bounded by 1st, San Pedro, 3rd, and Los Angeles streets, Little Tokyo has dozens of sushi bars, tempura restaurants, trinket shops, and even a restaurant that serves nothing but eel. The Japanese American Cultural and Community Center (244 S. San Pedro St., ☎ 213/628–2725) presents such events as Kabuki theater straight from Japan.

⑪ The **Los Angeles *Times* complex** is made up of several supposedly architecturally harmonious buildings. Actually, the various styles from many eras looks pretty much like a hodgepodge. *202 W. 1st St.,* ☎ *213/237–5000. 2 public tours given weekdays after 2 and on Sat. morning (tour times vary): 35-min tour of old plant and 45-min tour of new plant; reservations required. Free parking at 213 S. Spring St.*

Broadway between 1st and 9th is one of Los Angeles's busiest shopping streets. The shops and sidewalk vendors cater primarily to the Hispanic population with bridal shops, immigration lawyers, and cheap stereo equipment. Be on your guard, as pickpockets and homeless people can approach you on the street, but this can be an exhilarating slice-of-life walk, past the florid old movie theaters like the Orpheum (842 S. Broadway) and the Million Dollar (310 S. Broadway) and the **⑫** perennially classy **Bradbury Building** (304 S. Broadway, ☎ 213/626–1893), a marvelous specimen of Victorian-era commercial architecture at the southeast corner of 3rd Street and Broadway. Once the site of turn-of-the-century sweatshops, it now houses somewhat more genteel law offices. The interior courtyard, with its glass skylight and open balconies and elevator, really is picture perfect and, naturally, a popular movie locale. The building is only open Monday through Saturday 9–5; its owners prefer that you not wander too far past the lobby.

⑬ Grand Central Market (317 S. Broadway, ☎ 213/624–2378) is the most bustling market in the city and a testimony to the city's diversity. It's open Monday–Saturday 9–6, Sunday 10–5. This block-long marketplace of colorful and exotic produce, herbs, and meat draws a faithful clientele from the Latino community, senior citizens on a budget, and Westside matrons for whom money is no object. Even if you don't plan to buy anything, Grand Central Market is a delightful place in which to browse: The butcher shops display everything from lambs' heads and bulls' testicles to pigs' tails; the produce stalls are piled high with locally grown avocados and the ripest, reddest tomatoes; and the herb stalls promise remedies for all your ills.

⑭ The **Biltmore Hotel** (506 S. Grand Ave.), built in 1923, rivals Union Station for sheer architectural majesty in the Spanish-Revival tradition. The public areas have been restored, with the magnificent hand-painted wood beams brought back to their former glory.

⑮ Around the corner on 5th Street, the city's **Central Library** reopened in 1993, after a six-year hiatus resulting from major fires. At twice its former size, it's now the third-largest public library facility in the nation. The original Goodhue building still stands, completely restored to its 1926 splendor, with shimmering Egyptian-style bas-reliefs around its roofline. Go inside, through wooden doors that resemble an old Spanish-era mission, to see Dean Cornwell's murals depicting the history of California. A 1½-acre outdoor garden within the library complex has a restaurant. *630 W. 5th St.,* ☎ *213/228–7000.* ☛ *Free.* ⊙ *Mon. and Thurs.–Sat., 10–5:30; Tues. and Wed. noon–8; Sun. 1–5.*

⑯ The **Garment District** (700–800 blocks of Los Angeles St.) is an enclave of jobbers and wholesalers that sell off the leftovers from Los Angeles's considerable garment industry production. The **Cooper Building** (860 S. Los Angeles St.) is the heart of the district and houses several of what local bargain hunters consider to be the best pickings.

TOUR 2: HOLLYWOOD

Numbers in the margin correspond to points of interest on the Tour 2: Hollywood map.

"Hollywood" once meant movie stars and glamour. The big film studios were here, starlets lived in sorority-like buildings in the center of town, and movies premiered beneath the glare of klieg lights at the Chinese and the Pantages theaters.

Those days are long gone. Paramount is the only original major studio still physically located in Hollywood, and though some celebrities may live in the Hollywood Hills, there certainly aren't any in the "flats." In short, Hollywood is no longer "Hollywood." These days it is, even to its supporters, little more than a seedy town—though it's finally undergoing a large dose of urban renewal (some projects are, in fact, already completed). So why visit? Because the legends of the golden age of the movies are heavy in the air. Because this is where the glamour of Hollywood originated and where those who made it so worked and lived. Judy Garland lived here and so did Marilyn Monroe and Lana Turner. It is a tribute to Hollywood's powerful hold on the imagination that visitors can look past the junky shops and the lost souls who walk the streets to get a sense of the town's glittering past. Besides, no visit to Los Angeles is truly complete without a walk down Hollywood Boulevard.

❶ Begin your tour simply by looking to the HOLLYWOOD sign in the Hollywood Hills that line the northern border of the town. Even on the smoggiest days, the sign is visible for miles. It is on Mt. Lee, north of Beachwood Canyon, which is approximately 1 mile east of Hollywood and Vine. The 50-foot-tall letters, originally spelling out "Hollywoodland," were erected in 1923 as a promotional scheme for a real-estate development. The "land" was taken down in 1949, and the remaining sign has become one of Los Angeles's best-known landmarks. Pranksters are constantly altering it, albeit temporarily, to say things like Hollyweed (in the 1970s, to commemorate the lenient marijuana laws), UCLA (during a football playoff game with local rival USC), and Perotwood (during the 1992 presidential election).

❷ **Hollywood and Vine** was once considered the heart of Hollywood. The mere mention of this intersection still inspires images of a street corner bustling with movie stars, starlets, and moguls passing by, on foot or in snazzy convertibles. But these days, Hollywood and Vine is far

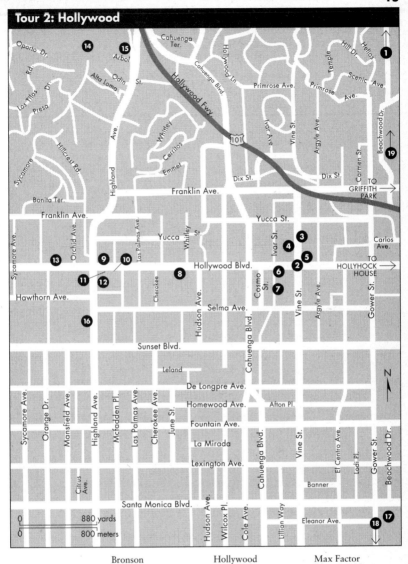

Tour 2: Hollywood

Bronson
Caves, **19**

Capitol Records
Building, **3**

Frederick's of
Hollywood, **8**

Hollywood
Bowl, **14**

Hollywood
Farmer's
Market, **7**

Hollywood
Guinness World
of Records
Museum, **10**

Hollywood High
School, **16**

Hollywood
Memorial
Cemetery, **17**

Hollywood sign, **1**

Hollywood Studio
Museum, **15**

Hollywood and
Vine, **2**

Hollywood Walk
of Fame, **6**

Hollywood Wax
Museum, **9**

Mann's Chinese
Theater, **13**

Max Factor
Museum, **12**

The Palace, **4**

Pantages
Theater, **5**

Paramount
Studios, **18**

Ripley's Believe
It or Not, **11**

from the action, and pedestrian traffic is, well, pedestrian. No stars, no starlets, no moguls. The Brown Derby restaurant that once stood near the southeast corner is long gone, and the intersection these days is little more than a place for visitors to get their bearings.

3 **Capitol Records Building** (1756 N. Vine St., 1 block north of Hollywood Blvd.) opened in 1956, is the very picture of '50s chic. When Capitol decided to build its new headquarters here, two of the record company's big talents of the day (singer Nat King Cole and songwriter Johnny Mercer) suggested that it be done in the shape of a stack of records. It was, and compared to much of what's gone up in L.A. since then, this building doesn't seem so odd. On its south wall, look at L.A. artist Richard Wyatt's mural *Hollywood Jazz, 1945–1972,* immortalizing such musical greats as Duke Ellington, Billie Holiday, Ella Fitzgerald, and Miles Davis. Murals play as important a role in Hollywood as billboards do along the Sunset Strip, so keep an eye out for others on several buildings in the immediate area. By the way, note the blinking light at the top of the Capital Records Building; those who don't know Morse code will be interested to learn that the rooftop glow spells out Hollywood in this silent language.

4 **The Palace** (1735 N. Vine St., ☎ 213/467–4571), just across the street from the Capitol Building, was opened in 1927 as the Hollywood Playhouse. It has hosted many shows over the years, from Ken Murray's *Blackouts* to Ralph Edwards's *This Is Your Life.* It is now the site of popular rock concerts and late-night weekend dancing.

5 When the **Pantages Theater,** at 6233 Hollywood Boulevard, just east of Vine, opened in 1930, it was the very pinnacle of movie-theater opulence. From 1949 to 1959, it was the site of the Academy Awards and today hosts large-scale Broadway musicals.

6 The **Hollywood Walk of Fame** is at every turn along the sidewalks as you make your way through downtown. The name of one or another movie star legend is embossed in brass, each at the center of a pink star embedded in a dark gray terrazzo circle. The first eight stars were unveiled in 1960 at the northwest corner of Highland Avenue and Hollywood Boulevard: Olive Borden, Ronald Colman, Louise Fazenda, Preston Foster, Burt Lancaster, Edward Sedgwick, Ernest Torrence, and Joanne Woodward (some of these names have stood the test of time better than others!). In the 36 years since, more than 2,000 others have been added. But this kind of immortality doesn't come cheap—the personality in question (or more likely his or her movie studio or record company) must pay $5,000 for the honor. Walk a few blocks and you'll quickly find that not all the names are familiar. To aid in the identification, celebrities are classified by one of five logos: a motion picture camera, a radio microphone, a television set, a record, or theatrical masks. Here's a guide to a few of the more famous stars: Marlon Brando at 1765 Vine, Charlie Chaplin at 6751 Hollywood, W. C. Fields at 7004 Hollywood, Clark Gable at 1608 Vine, Marilyn Monroe at 6774 Hollywood, Rudolph Valentino at 6164 Hollywood, Michael Jackson at 6927 Hollywood, and John Wayne at 1541 Vine.

Every Sunday, a couple of blocks in this part of town are transformed into a festive street fair. Traffic is diverted so that no vehicle passes through

★ **7** the **Hollywood Farmer's Market,** situated on Ivar Street, between Hollywood Boulevard and Selma Avenue. Instead, some 20,000 people show up to sample ethnic foods and listen to lively musical entertainment as they peruse stalls packed with fruits, vegetables, crafts, and antiques. The Ivar Theater sponsors an outdoor coffee shop, where celebrities are often spotted. After decades of sporting a gaudy lavender paint job, the

8 exterior of **Frederick's of Hollywood** (6608 Hollywood Blvd., ☎ 213/466–8506) has been restored to its original understated Art Deco look, gray with pink awnings. Fear not, however, that the place has suddenly gone tasteful: Inside is all the risqué and trashy lingerie that made this place famous. There is also a bra museum that features the undergarments of living and no-longer-living Hollywood legends. This is a popular tourist spot, if only for a good giggle.

TIME OUT At **Me & Me** (6687 Hollywood Blvd., ☎ 213/464–8448), you can munch on what just may be the city's best falafels. Or, if you're looking for a more formal meal, look in at **Musso & Franks** (6667 Hollywood Blvd., ☎ 213/467–5123), a Hollywood mainstay, especially popular with writers who like to dine at the restaurant's long oak bar as they work on scripts or novels. (F. Scott Fitzgerald and Raymond Chandler both frequented this restaurant, back in Hollywood's glamour days.) For dessert, head up the street to **C. C. Brown's** (7007 Hollywood Blvd., ☎ 213/464–9726), home of the original hot-fudge sundae and reportedly the family-owned soda fountain where Judy Garland once waitressed.

9 **Hollywood Wax Museum** offers visitors sights that real life no longer can (Mary Pickford, Elvis Presley, and Clark Gable) and a few that even real life never did (Rambo and Conan). Recently added living legends on display include actors Kevin Costner and Patrick Swayze. A short film on Academy Award winners is shown daily. *6767 Hollywood Blvd.,* ☎ *213/462–8860.* ☛ *$8.95 adults, $7.50 senior citizens, $6.95 children, under 6 free if with adult.* ☉ *Sun.–Thurs. 10 AM–midnight, Fri.–Sat. 10 AM–2 AM.*

10 The **Hollywood Guinness World of Records Museum,** across the street from the Hollywood Wax Museum, is a testament to just how far some people will go to achieve record-book immortality. Visitors can tap into a computer system that reveals who holds what record. Also on view are videos documenting various feats, as well as life-size replicas—like the one of Robert Wardlow, the world's tallest man, who stood 8 feet, 11¼ inches. *6764 Hollywood Blvd., ☎ 213/463–6433.* ☛ *$8.95 adults, $7.50 senior citizens, $6.95 children, under 12 free.* ☉ *Sun.–Thurs. 10–midnight, Fri.–Sat. 10–2 AM.*

11 **Ripley's Believe It or Not** is for people who like to gawk at freaks of nature and strange illusions. This wacky museum contains more than 300 weird exhibits, such as the skeleton of a two-headed baby, a shrunken head from Ecuador, and a life-size portrait of John Wayne made of dryer lint. *6780 Hollywood Blvd., ☎ 213/466–6335.* ☛ *$8.95 adults, $7.95 senior citizens, $5.95 children.* ☉ *Sun.–Thurs. 10 AM–11 PM, Fri. and Sat., 10 AM–midnight.*

12 The **Max Factor Museum** lets civilians in on the beauty secrets of screen idols from flicks filmed as far back as the turn of the century. *1666 N. Highland Ave., ☎ 213/463–6668.* ☛ *Free.* ☉ *Mon.–Sat. 10 AM–4 PM.*

★ **13** Angelenos no longer call **Mann's Chinese Theater** (6925 Hollywood Blvd., ☎ 213/464–8111) "Grauman's Chinese," and the new owners seem finally to have a firm hold on the place in the public's eye. The architecture is a fantasy of Chinese pagodas and temples as only Hollywood could turn out. Although you'll have to buy a movie ticket to appreciate the interior trappings, the courtyard is open for browsing, where you'll see the famous cement hand- and footprints. The tradition is said to have begun at the theater's opening in 1927, with the premiere of Cecil B. DeMille's *King of Kings,* when actress Norma Talmadge accidentally stepped into the wet cement. Now more than 160 celebrities have added their footprints or handprints, along with a few oddball prints like the one of Jimmy Durante's nose. Space has pretty much run out now, though there's always room to squeeze in another superstar, should Hollywood conjure one up.

⑭ Summer evening concerts at the **Hollywood Bowl** have been a tradition since 1922, although the band shell has been replaced several times. The musical fare ranges from pop to jazz to classical; the L.A. Philharmonic has its summer season here. The 17,000-plus seating capacity ranges from boxes (where local society matrons put on incredibly fancy alfresco preconcert meals for their friends) to concrete bleachers in the rear. Some people actually prefer the back rows for their romantic appeal. *2301 N. Highland Ave., ☎ 213/850–2000. Grounds open daily sunrise–sunset. Call for schedule.*

⑮ The **Hollywood Studio Museum** sits in the Hollywood Bowl parking lot, east of Highland Boulevard. The building, recently moved to this site, was once called the Lasky–DeMille Barn; in it Cecil B. DeMille produced the first feature-length film, *The Squaw Man.* In 1927, the barn became Paramount Pictures, with the original company of Jesse Lasky, Cecil B. DeMille, and Samuel Goldwyn. The museum contains a re-creation of DeMille's office, original artifacts, and a screening room showing vintage film footage of Hollywood and its legends. A great gift shop sells such quality vintage memorabilia as autographs, photographs, and books. *2100 N. Highland Ave., ☎ 213/874–2276.* ☛ *$4 adults, $3 senior citizens and children, children under 6 free. Free parking. ☯ Weekends 10–4.*

⑯ Such stars as Carol Burnett, Linda Evans, Rick Nelson, and Lana Turner attended **Hollywood High School** (1521 N. Highland Ave.). Today the student body is as diverse as Los Angeles itself, with every ethnic group represented.

⑰ Many of Hollywood's stars, from the silent-screen era on, are buried in **Hollywood Memorial Cemetery.** Walk from the entrance to the lake area and you'll find the crypt of Cecil B. DeMille and the graves of Nelson Eddy and Douglas Fairbanks, Sr. Inside the Cathedral Mausoleum is Rudolph Valentino's crypt (where fans, the press, and the famous Lady in Black turn up every August 23, the anniversary of his death). Other stars interred in this section are Peter Lorre and Eleanor Powell. In the Abbey of Palms Mausoleum, Norma Talmadge and Clifton Webb are buried. *6000 Santa Monica Blvd., ☎ 213/469–1181. ☯ Daily 8–5.*

⑱ Take Gower Street south to Melrose Avenue, turn right, and on the right-hand side you'll see the main gate of **Paramount Studios** (5555 Melrose Ave.), the only original, major movie studio still in Hollywood. Since it opened here in 1926, Paramount has produced more than 3,000 films. Stars, such as Mae West, Mary Pickford, and John Barrymore, were under contract here; more recent Paramount hits include *The Firm* and *Wayne's World.* The studio occupies two large city blocks, including the now-defunct Desilu Studios, and its three arched entrances are familiar landmarks from such films as the 1950 classic *Sunset Boulevard* (which showed the entrance at Marathon and Bronson avenues). You can explore the studio lot on two-hour guided walking tours or by joining the audience for tapings of TV shows. *For tours or tapings, check in at 860 N. Gower St., ☎ 213/956–5575.* ☛ *$15. Tours held weekdays, on the hr, 9–2. Children under 10 not admitted.*

⑲ A bit farther east and north of Bronson Avenue (where the thoroughfare's name becomes Canyon Drive), you'll discover **Bronson Caves,**

up in the hills at the end of this long street. You may have déjà vu if you visit, as this is the setting for such memorable celluloid treats as the bat cave in television's version of *Batman,* many of the gunfights seen on the small screen in *Bonanza,* and a remote (and scary) setting in old science-fiction films, such as *Invasion of the Bodysnatchers* and *It Conquered the Earth.*

TOUR 3: WILSHIRE BOULEVARD

Numbers in the margin correspond to points of interest on the Tour 3: Wilshire Boulevard map.

Wilshire Boulevard begins in the heart of downtown Los Angeles and runs west, through Beverly Hills and Santa Monica, ending at the cliffs above the Pacific Ocean. In 16 miles it moves through fairly poor neighborhoods populated by recent immigrants, through solidly middle-class enclaves, and through a corridor of the highest priced high-rise condos in the city. Along the way, and all within a few blocks of each other, are many of Los Angeles's top architectural sites, museums, and shops.

This linear tour can be started at any point along Wilshire Boulevard, but to savor the cross-section view of Los Angeles that this street provides, take the Bullocks-west-to-the-sea approach. If you have only limited time, it would be better to skip Koreatown and Larchmont and pare down the museum time than to do only one stretch. All these sites are on Wilshire or within a few blocks north or south.

"One" Wilshire, at the precise start of the boulevard in downtown Los Angeles, is just another anonymous office building. Begin, instead, a few miles westward, past the Harbor Freeway. As Wilshire Boulevard moves from its downtown genesis, it quickly passes through neighborhoods now populated by recent immigrants from Central America. Around the turn of the century, however, this area was home to many of the city's wealthy citizens, as the faded Victorian houses on the side streets attest.

As the population crept westward, the distance to downtown shops began to seem insurmountable and the first suburban department-store ❶ branch, **Bullocks Wilshire** (3050 Wilshire Blvd.), was opened in 1929. The store closed in 1993, but this giant tribute to early Art Deco has been purchased by the Southwestern University of Law, which is adapting the building to accommodate its law library and as office and classroom spaces. The exterior is often now used as a background for films. Notice the behind-the-store parking lot—quite an innovation in 1929 and the first accommodation a large Los Angeles store made to the automobile age. On the ceiling of the porte cochere, a mural depicts the history of transportation.

❷ **Koreatown** begins almost at Bullocks Wilshire's back door. Koreans are one of the latest and largest groups in this ethnically diverse city. Arriving from the old country with generally more money than most immigrant groups do, Koreans nevertheless face the trauma of adjusting to a new language, new alphabet, and new customs. Settling in the area south of Wilshire Boulevard, along Olympic Boulevard between Vermont and Western avenues, the Korean community has slowly grown into a cohesive neighborhood with active community groups and newspapers. The area is teeming with Asian restaurants (not just Korean but also Japanese and Chinese). Many of the signs in this area are in Korean only. For a glimpse of the typical offerings of Korean shops,

20

Tour 3: Wilshire Boulevard

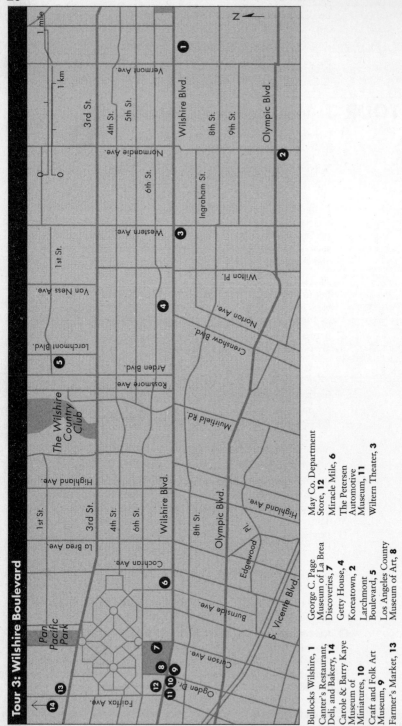

Bullocks Wilshire, **1**
Canter's Restaurant, Deli, and Bakery, **14**
Carole & Barry Kaye Museum of Miniatures, **10**
Craft and Folk Art Museum, **9**
Farmer's Market, **13**

George C. Page Museum of La Brea Discoveries, **7**
Getty House, **4**
Koreatown, **2**
Larchmont Boulevard, **5**
Los Angeles County Museum of Art, **8**

May Co. Department Store, **12**
Miracle Mile, **6**
The Petersen Automotive Museum, **11**
Wiltern Theater, **3**

browse the large **Koreatown Plaza** mall, on the corner of Western and San Marino avenues.

❸ At the southeast corner of Wilshire and Western Avenue sits the **Wiltern Theater** (3780 Wilshire Blvd.), part of the magnificent Wiltern Center and one of the city's best examples of full-out Art Deco architecture. The 1930s zigzag design was restored to its splendid turquoise hue. Inside, the theater is full of opulent detail at every turn. Originally a movie theater, the Wiltern is now a multiuse arts complex.

Continuing west on Wilshire, the residential real-estate values start to make a sharp climb. In the past, the mayor of Los Angeles had his of-
❹ ficial home in **Getty House** (605 S. Irving Blvd., 1 block north of Wilshire), a white-brick, half-timber residence that was donated to the city by the Getty family. This area, known as Hancock Park, is one of the city's most genteel neighborhoods, remaining in vogue since its de-velopment in the 1920s. Many of L.A.'s old-money families live here in English Tudor homes with East Coast landscaping schemes that defy the local climate and history.

Hancock Park has its own little shopping street about ½ mile farther
❺ north: **Larchmont Boulevard.** Named after the New York suburb, Larchmont is a very un–Los Angeles shopping district, a bit of small-town America in the middle of the metropolitan sprawl. The tree-lined street has 45-degree-angle parking and a cozy, everybody-knows-ev-erybody feeling. Many celebrities live in the area and can be seen dart-ing in and out of the boutiques, health-food store, and the old-time five-and-dime. There are also several chic restaurants here.

Drop back down to Wilshire Boulevard again and continue westward.
❻ **Miracle Mile,** the strip of Wilshire Boulevard between La Brea and Fair-fax avenues, was so dubbed in the 1930s as a promotional gimmick to attract shoppers to the new stores. The area went into something of a decline in the '50s and '60s, but is now enjoying a comeback, as Los Angeles's Art Deco architecture has come to be appreciated, pre-served, and restored. Exemplary buildings like the **El Rey Theater** (5519 Wilshire Blvd., ☎ 213/936–6400) stand out as examples of period de-sign (in spite of the fact that it now houses a nightclub). In **Callender's Restaurant** (corner of Wilshire and Curson), murals and old pho-tographs effectively depict life on the Miracle Mile in its heyday.

Across Curson Avenue is **Hancock Park,** an actual park, not to be con-fused with Hancock Park, the residential neighborhood. This park is home to the city's world-famous fossil source, the **La Brea Tar Pits.** De-spite the fact that *la brea* already means "tar" in Spanish and to say "La Brea Tar Pits" is redundant, the name remains firm in local minds. About 35,000 years ago, deposits of oil rose to the Earth's surface, col-lected in shallow pools, and coagulated into sticky asphalt. In the early 20th century, geologists discovered that the sticky goo contained the largest collection of Pleistocene fossils ever found at one location: more than 200 varieties of birds, mammals, plants, reptiles, and in-sects. More than 100 tons of fossil bones have been removed in more than 70 years of excavations. Statues of mammoths in the big pit near the corner of Wilshire and Curson depict how many of them were en-tombed: Edging down to a pond of water to drink, animals were caught in the tar and unable to extricate themselves. There are several pits scattered around Hancock Park; construction in the area has often had to accommodate these oozing pits, and in nearby streets and along sidewalks, little bits of tar occasionally ooze up, unstoppable.

❼ The **George C. Page Museum of La Brea Discoveries,** a satellite of the Natural History Museum of Los Angeles County, is situated at the tar pits and set, bunkerlike, half underground. A bas-relief around four sides depicts life in the Pleistocene era, and the museum has more than 1 million Ice Age fossils. Exhibits include reconstructed, life-size skeletons of mammoths, wolves, sloths, eagles, and condors. In l994 there was a new, permanent installation of a robotic saber-toothed cat attacking a woolly mammal. The glass-enclosed Paleontological Laboratory permits observation of the ongoing cleaning, identification, and cataloging of fossils excavated from the nearby asphalt deposits. *The La Brea Story* and *A Whopping Small Dinosaur* are short documentary films shown every 15–30 minutes. A hologram magically puts flesh on "La Brea Woman," and an interactive tar mechanism shows visitors just how hard it would be to free oneself from the sticky mess. *5801 Wilshire Blvd.,* ☎ *213/936–2230.* ☛ *$6 adults, $3.50 senior citizens and students, $2 children 5–10; free every 1st Tues. of the month.* ☉ *Tues.–Sun. 10–5.*

❽ The **Los Angeles County Museum of Art,** just west of Hancock Park, is the largest museum complex in Los Angeles, comprising five buildings surrounding a grand central court. The Times Mirror Central Court provides both a visual and symbolic focus for the museum complex. The Ahmanson Building, built around a central atrium, houses the museum's collection of paintings, sculpture, costumes and textiles, and decorative arts from a wide range of cultures and periods. Highlights include a unique assemblage of glass from Roman times to the 19th century, the renowned Gilbert collection of mosaics and monumental silver, one of the nation's largest holdings of costumes and textiles, and an Indian and Southeast Asian art collection considered to be one of the most comprehensive in the world.

The Hammer Building features major special loan exhibitions as well as galleries for prints, drawings, and photographs. The Anderson Building features 20th-century painting and sculpture as well as special exhibitions. The museum's collection of Japanese sculpture, paintings, ceramics, and lacquerware, including the internationally renowned Shin'enkan collection of Japanese paintings and a collection of extraordinary netsuke, is on view in the Japanese Pavilion. The Contemporary Sculpture Garden comprises nine large-scale outdoor sculptures. The B. Gerald Cantor Sculpture Garden features bronzes by Auguste Rodin, Émile-Antoine Bourdelle, and George Kolbe. *5905 Wilshire Blvd.,* ☎ *213/857–6000; ticket information, 213/857–6010.* ☛ *$6 adults, $4 senior citizens and students, $1 children 6–17;* ☛ *Free every 2nd Wed. of the month.* ☉ *Tues.–Thurs. 10–5, Fri. 10–9, Sat.–Sun. 11–6.*

The County Museum, Page Museum, and indeed all of Hancock Park itself are brimming with visitors on warm weekends. Although crowded, it can be the most exciting time to visit the area. Mimes and itinerant musicians ply their trades. Street vendors sell fast-food treats, and there are impromptu soccer games on the lawns. To study the art, though, make a quieter weekday visit.

❾ The **Craft and Folk Art Museum,** across Wilshire Boulevard from Hancock Park, is worth checking out, for the museum offers consistently fascinating exhibits of both contemporary crafts and folk crafts from around the world. The museum's collections include Japanese, Mexican, American, and East Indian folk art, textiles, and masks. Six to eight major exhibitions are planned each year. In the past, sunglasses, jewelry, and architecture have been featured. The International Festival of Masks, one of the more popular celebrations, is held in Hancock Park annually the last weekend in October. *5800 Wilshire Blvd.,* ☎ *213/937–5544.* ☛ *$4 adults, $2.50 senior citizens and students, children under 12 free.* ☯ *Tues.–Sun. 11–5, Fri. 11–8.*

⑩ Up the street is the **Carole & Barry Kaye Museum of Miniatures,** where a world of pint-size exhibits are showcased. You'll see landmarks, such as the Hollywood Bowl and the chateau Fountainebleau, as well as important local architecture like an original Greene and Greene California craftsman house in ¹⁄₁₂th scale. The most notable exhibits include the First Ladies (as far back as Martha Washington) dolled up in their inaugural ball gowns and a rendition of a turn-of-the-century soda fountain with silver spoons the size of eyelashes and a cherry as small as a fly's eye. *5900 Wilshire Blvd.,* ☎ *213/937–6464.* ☛ *$7.50 adults, $6.50 senior citizens, $5 youths 13–21, $3 children 3–12.* ☯ *Tues.–Sat. 10–5, Sun. 11–5.*

⑪ Farther west, **The Petersen Automotive Museum** proves that, in L.A., you are what you drive. Cars of the stars are part of this museum that debuted in 1994, where you'll even have the opportunity to view Fred's rockmobile from *The Flintstones* flick. If two wheels entice you more than four, you need not seek out the harsh Harley crowd to get your fill: This museum has an entire gallery devoted to the motorcycle. A history of the automobile is also among the permanent collections, with rare French luxury cars from the '30s and '40s on view, as well as race cars created in Southern California. There's a great gift shop for the automotive enthusiast, and a research library for everything you ever wanted to know about, you guessed it, the car. *6060 Wilshire Blvd.,* ☎ *213/930–2277.* ☛ *$7 adults, $5 senior citizens and students; $3 children 5–12.* ☯ *Sat.–Thurs. 10–6, Fri. 10–9.*

⑫ Continue west on Wilshire a few blocks to the corner of Fairfax Avenue. On the northeast corner is the former **May Co. department store,** another 1930s landmark, with a distinctive curved corner done in gold tile. The building is now owned by the L.A. County Museum of Art, which plans to use it for a future expansion.

⑬ Head north on Fairfax a few blocks to the **Farmer's Market,** a favorite L.A. attraction since 1934. Along with the 120 shops, salons, stores, and produce stalls, there are 30 restaurants (some of which offer alfresco dining under umbrellas), serving an interesting variety of international and domestic fare. Although originally it was exactly what the name implies—a farmer's market—these days you will find not only food and produce, but gifts, clothing, beauty shops, and even a shoe repair. Because it is next door to the CBS Television Studios, you never know whom you will run into, as TV celebrities shop and dine here often. *6333 W. 3rd St.,* ☎ *213/933–9211.* ☯ *Mon.–Sat. 9–6:30, Sun. 10–5.* ☯ *Later in summer.*

TIME OUT Kokomo (on 3rd St. side of market, ☎ 213/933–0773) is not only the best eatery inside the Farmer's Market, it's got some of the best new-wave diner food anywhere in L.A. Lively, entertaining service is almost always included in the reasonable prices. For those in a hurry, Kokomo A Go Go, its take-out store, is adjacent.

North of the market, Fairfax is the center of Los Angeles's Jewish life. The shops and stands from Beverly Boulevard north are enlivened with friendly conversations between shopkeepers and regular customers. ⑭ **Canter's Restaurant, Deli, and Bakery** (419 N. Fairfax, ☎ 213/651–

2030) is a traditional hangout during the day, and a haven for rockers in the wee hours, after all of L.A.'s bars shut down at 2 AM.

TOUR 4: THE WESTSIDE

Numbers in the margin correspond to points of interest on the Tour 4: Westside map.

The Westside of Los Angeles—which to residents means from La Brea Avenue westward to the ocean—is where the rents are the most expensive, the real-estate prices sky-high, the restaurants (and the restaurateurs) the most famous, and the shops the most chic. It's the best of the good life, Southern-California style, and to really savor (and understand) the Southland, spend a few leisurely days or half days exploring this area. Short on such traditional tourist attractions as amusement parks, historic sites, and museums, it more than makes up for those gaps with great shopping districts, exciting walking streets, outdoor cafés, and a lively nightlife.

The Westside can be best enjoyed in at least three outings, allowing plenty of time for browsing and dining. Attractions 1 through 4 are in the West Hollywood area; 5 through 9 in Beverly Hills; and 10 through 12 in Westwood. But the Westside is also small enough that you could pick four or five of these sites to visit in a single day, depending on your interests.

West Hollywood

Once an almost forgotten parcel of county land surrounded by the city of L.A. and Beverly Hills, West Hollywood became an official city in 1984. The West Hollywood attitude—trendy, stylish, and with plenty of disposable income—spills over beyond the official city borders.

★ ❶ **Melrose Avenue** provides plenty of fodder for people-watching: post-punk fashion plates, people in spiked hairdos, earrings and tatoos on every conceivable body part, and outlandish ensembles. It's where panache meets paparazzi, and Beverly Hills chic meets Hollywood hip. The busiest stretch of Melrose is between Fairfax and La Brea avenues. Here you'll find one-of-a-kind boutiques and small, chic restaurants for more than a dozen blocks. Park on a side street (and read the parking signs carefully: Parking regulations around here are vigorously enforced and a rich vein for the city's coffers) and begin walking. On the 7400 block are **Tempest** and **Notorious,** boutiques with the latest of California's trendsetting designers' clothes for women, along with **Mondial,** for men, and **Roppongi,** which supplies the sought-after Melrose look. In the other direction—in more ways than one—**Wasteland** (7428) is a great find for vintage clothing as well as resale items brought in by locals every day. **Melrose Place Antique Market** (7002 Melrose) is a collection of small items, vintage in nature, high in appeal. (*See* Chapter 3, Shopping, for more store recommendations.)

❷ That hulking monolith dominating the corner of La Cienega and Beverly boulevards is none other than the **Beverly Center** (8500 Beverly Blvd., ☎ 310/854–0070). Designed as an all-in-one stop for shopping, dining, and movies, it has been a boon to Westsiders—except for those who live so close as to suffer the consequences of the heavy traffic. Parking is on the second through fifth floors; shops on the sixth, seventh, and eighth floors; and movies and restaurants on the eighth floor. The street level features a variety of restaurants, the most popular being the **Hard Rock Cafe** (look for the vintage green Cadillac in the roof). In the center proper are two major department stores, **Bullocks** and the

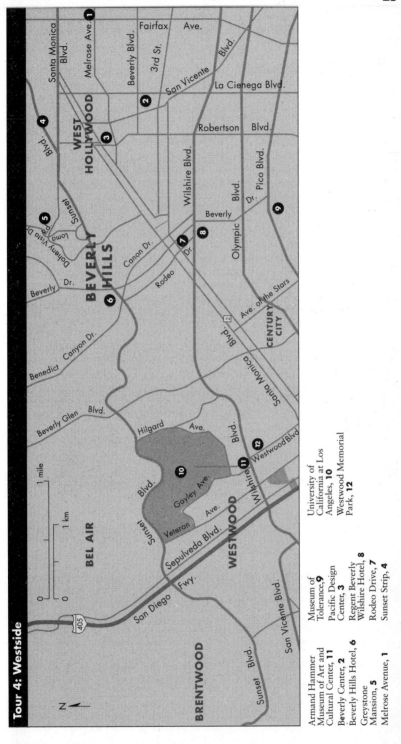

Tour 4: Westside

Fairfax Ave.
Santa Monica Blvd.
Melrose Ave.
Beverly Blvd.
3rd St.
San Vicente Blvd.
La Cienega Blvd.
WEST HOLLYWOOD
Robertson Blvd.
Sunset Blvd.
Loma
Doheny Vista Dr.
Rd.
BEVERLY HILLS
Wilshire Blvd.
Canon Dr.
Rodeo
Beverly Dr.
Beverly Dr.
Pico Blvd.
Olympic Blvd.
Benedict Canyon Dr.
Ave. of the Stars
CENTURY CITY
Beverly Glen Blvd.
Hilgard Ave.
Blvd.
Santa Monica Blvd.
Westwood Blvd.
Wilshire
BEL AIR
Gayley Ave.
Sunset Blvd.
Veteran Ave.
Sepulveda Blvd.
WESTWOOD
San Diego Fwy.
405
San Vicente Blvd.
BRENTWOOD
Sunset Blvd.
N
1 mile
1 km

Armand Hammer Museum of Art and Cultural Center, **11**
Beverly Center, **2**
Beverly Hills Hotel, **6**
Greystone Mansion, **5**
Melrose Avenue, **1**
Museum of Tolerance, **9**
Pacific Design Center, **3**
Regent Beverly Wilshire Hotel, **8**
Rodeo Drive, **7**
Sunset Strip, **4**
University of California at Los Angeles, **10**
Westwood Memorial Park, **12**

Broadway, as well as dozens of upscale clothing boutiques, a 14-screen movie theater, and a wide variety of restaurants (California Pizza Kitchen, Panda Express, Vie de France, plus Mrs. Field's Cookies and Häagen Daz ice-cream outlets). **Sam Goody,** whose 15,000 square feet make it the world's largest enclosed music store, features a glass-walled, and spectacular, view of Hollywood. The **Warner Bros. Studio Store,** popular with both adults and kids, is crammed with movie and cartoon memorabilia and apparel.

❸ West Hollywood is the center of Los Angeles's thriving interior decorating business. The **Pacific Design Center** (8687 Melrose Ave., ☎ 310/657–0800) is known to residents as the "Blue Whale." The blue-glass building, designed by Cesar Pelli in 1975, houses to-the-trade-only showrooms filled with the most tempting furnishings, wall coverings, and accessories. In 1988 the center added a second building by Pelli, this one clad in green glass. The building is open to the public (Mon.–Fri. 9–5), who are allowed to browse in many of the more than 200 showrooms or opt for a free group tour at 10 AM. Note: Purchases can be made only through design professionals (a referral system is available). The **Murray Feldman Gallery,** featuring various art, design, and cultural exhibitions, sits on the adjacent 2-acre land-scaped public plaza (⊙ Tues.–Sat. noon–6).

❹ **Sunset Strip** was famous in the '50s, as in the TV show *77 Sunset Strip,* but it was popular as far back as the 1930s, when nightclubs like Ciro's and Mocambo were in their heyday and movie stars frequented the Strip as an after-work gathering spot. This winding, hilly stretch is a visual delight, enjoyed both by car (a convertible would be perfect) or on foot. Drive it once to enjoy the hustle-bustle, the vanity boards (huge bill-boards touting new movies, new records, new stars), and the dazzling shops. Then pick a section and explore a few blocks on foot. The Sunset Plaza area is especially nice for walking, a stretch of expensive shops and outdoor cafés (including the nouvelle Chinese favorite, **Chin Chin**) that are packed for lunch and on warm evenings. At Horn Street, **Tower Records** (a behemoth of a CD store with two satellite shops across the street), **Book Soup** (L.A.'s literary bookstore), and Wolfgang Puck's famous restaurant **Spago** (a half block up the hill on Horn) make satisfying browsing, especially in the evening.

Beverly Hills

The glitz of Sunset Strip ends abruptly at Doheny Drive, where Sunset Boulevard enters the world-famous and glamorous Beverly Hills. Suddenly the sidewalk street life gives way to expansive, perfectly manicured lawns and palatial homes.

❺ Doheny Drive is named for oilman Edward Doheny, the original owner of the **Greystone Mansion,** built in 1927. This Tudor-style mansion, now owned by the city of Beverly Hills, sits on 18½ landscaped acres and has been used in such films as *The Witches of Eastwick* and *Indecent Proposal.* The gardens are open for self-guided tours, and peeking (only) through the windows is permitted. Picnics are permitted in specified areas during hours of operation and, sporadically, concerts are held in the mansion's courtyard on summer afternoons. *905 Loma Vista Dr.,* ☎ *310/550–4796.* ☛ *Free.* ⊙ *Daily 10–5 in fall and winter, 10–6 in spring and fall.*

❻ West of Sunset Strip a mile or so is the **Beverly Hills Hotel** (9641 Sunset Blvd.), whose Spanish Colonial Revival architecture and soft pastel exterior have earned it the name "the Pink Palace." The legendary landmark, which reopened in 1995 after a multimillion-dollar renovation, is considered to be the first citizen of Beverly Hills—it opened two years prior to the time the city incorporated.

It is on this stretch of Sunset, especially during the day, that you'll see hawkers peddling maps to stars' homes. Are the maps reliable? Well, that's a matter of debate. Stars do move around, so it's difficult to keep any map up to date. But the fun is in looking at some of these magnificent homes, regardless of whether or not they're owned by a star at the moment.

Beverly Hills was incorporated as a city early in the century and has been thriving ever since. As a vibrant city within the larger city, it has retained and enhanced its reputation for wealth and luxury, an assessment with which you will surely agree as you drive along any of its main thoroughfares; Sunset or Wilshire boulevards or Santa Monica Boulevard (which is actually two parallel streets at this point: "Santa Monica" is the northern one; "Little Santa Monica," the southern).

Within a few square blocks in the center of Beverly Hills are some of the most exotic, to say nothing of high-priced, stores in Southern California. Here you can find such items as a $200 pair of socks wrapped in gold leaf and stores that take customers only by appointment. A fun
★ ⑦ way to spend an afternoon is to stroll famed **Rodeo Drive** between Santa Monica and Wilshire boulevards. Some of the Rodeo (pronounced ro-*day*-o) shops may be familiar to you since they supply clothing for major network television shows and their names often appear among the credits. Others, such as Gucci, have a worldwide reputation. Fortunately, browsing is free (and fun), no matter how expensive the store is. Several nearby restaurants have outside patios where you can sit and sip a drink while watching the fashionable shoppers saunter by. At the southern end of this thoroughfare is Via Rodeo, a curvy cobblestone street that somewhat emulates the picture-perfect layout of Disneyland's main drag, though the boutiques that thrive here are definitely for adults—with money.

⑧ The **Regent Beverly Wilshire Hotel** (9500 Wilshire Blvd., ☎ 310/275–5200) anchors the south end of Rodeo Drive, at Wilshire. Opened in 1928, and vigorously expanded and renovated since, the hotel is often home to visiting royalty and celebrities; it's where the millionaire businessman played by Richard Gere ensconced himself with the hooker played by Julia Roberts in the movie *Pretty Woman*. The lobby is quite small for a hotel of this size and offers little opportunity to meander; you might stop for a drink or meal in one of the hotel's restaurants.

A sobering but moving experience in the midst of all this glamour, the
⑨ **Museum of Tolerance,** which opened adjacent to the Simon Weisenthal Center in 1993, deserves a thoughtful visit. Using lots of state-of-the-art interactive technology, the museum challenges visitors to confront bigotry and racism. One of the most affecting sections of this museum covers the Holocaust—each visitor is issued a "passport" bearing the name of a child whose life was dramatically changed by the German Nazi rule and by World War II, and ultimately the museumgoer learns the fate of that child. Anne Frank artifacts are part of the museum's permanent collection. Expect to spend at least three hours to see the whole museum. *9786 W. Pico Blvd., ☎ 310/553–8403. ☛ $8 adults, $6 senior citizens, $5 students, $3 children 3–12. ☉ Sun. 10:30–5, Mon.–Thurs. 10–4, Fri. 10–1. Reservations advised.*

Westwood

⑩ Westward from Beverly Hills, Sunset continues to wind past palatial estates and passes by the **University of California at Los Angeles.** Nestled in the Westwood section of the city and bound by Le Conte Avenue, Sunset Boulevard, and Hilgard Avenue, the parklike UCLA campus is an inviting place for visitors to stroll. The most spectacular buildings are the original ones, Royce Hall and the library, both in Romanesque style. (Royce Hall is closed indefinitely due to earthquake damage.) In the heart of the north campus is the Franklin Murphy Sculpture Garden, with works by Henry Moore and Gaston Lachaise dotting the landscaping. For a gardening buff, UCLA is a treasure of unusual and well-labeled plants. The Mildred Mathias Botanic Garden is in the southeast section of the campus and is accessible from Tiverton Avenue. Sports fans will enjoy the Morgan Center Hall of Fame (west of Campus bookstore), where memorabilia and trophies of the athletic departments are on display. Maps and information are available at drive-by kiosks at major entrances, even on weekends, and free 90-minute, walking tours of the campus are given on weekdays. The campus has several indoor and outdoor cafés, plus bookstores that sell the very popular UCLA Bruins paraphernalia. *Tours (☎ 310/206–8147) weekdays at 10:30 AM and 1:30 PM. Call for reservations. Meet at 10945 LeConte St., Room 1417, on south edge of campus, facing Westwood.*

Directly south of the campus is Westwood, once a quiet college town and now one of the busiest places in the city on weekend evenings—so busy that during the summer, many streets are closed to car traffic and visitors must park at the Federal Building (Wilshire Blvd. and Veteran Ave.) and shuttle over. However you arrive, Westwood remains a delightful village filled with clever boutiques, trendy restaurants, movie theaters, and colorful street life.

⑪ **Armand Hammer Museum of Art and Cultural Center** is small compared to other museums in Los Angeles, but the permanent collection here includes thousands of works by Honoré Daumier. The Hammer regularly features special blockbuster displays that cannot be seen elsewhere, such as the 1992 exhibit "Catherine the Great: Treasures of Imperial Russia." *10899 Wilshire Blvd., ☎ 310/443–7000. ☛ $4.50 adults, $3 senior citizens, children under 18 free; free every Thurs. 6–9. ⊙ Tues., Wed., Fri., Sat. 11–7, Thurs. 11–9, Sun. 11–5. Parking fee $2.75.*

The Westwood stretch of Wilshire Boulevard is a corridor of cheek-by-jowl office buildings whose varying architectural styles can be jarring, to say the least. Tucked behind one of these behemoths is
⑫ **Westwood Memorial Park** (1218 Glendon Ave.). In this very unlikely place for a cemetery is one of the most famous graves in the city. Marilyn Monroe is buried in a simply marked wall crypt. For 25 years after her death, her former husband Joe DiMaggio had six red roses placed on her crypt three times a week. Also buried here is Natalie Wood.

TOUR 5: SANTA MONICA, VENICE, PACIFIC PALISADES, AND MALIBU

Numbers in the margin correspond to points of interest on the Tour 5: Santa Monica and Venice map.

The towns that hug the coastline of Santa Monica Bay reflect the wide diversity of Los Angeles, from the rich-as-can-be Malibu to the yuppie/seedy mix of Venice. The emphasis is on being out in the sunshine, always within sight of the Pacific. You would do well to visit the area in two excursions: Santa Monica to Venice in one day and Pacific Palisades to Malibu in another.

Santa Monica

Santa Monica is a tidy little city, about 2 miles square, where expatriate Brits tend to settle (there's an English music hall and several pubs here), attracted perhaps by the cool, foggy climate. The sense of order is reflected in the economic-geographic stratification: The most northern section has broad streets lined with superb, older homes. As you drive south, real estate prices drop $50,000 or so every block or two. The middle class lives in the middle and the working class, to the south, along the Venice border.

★ ❶ Begin exploring at **Santa Monica Pier,** located at the foot of Colorado Avenue and easily accessible for beachgoers as well as drive-around visitors. Cafés, gift shops, a psychic adviser, bumper-car rides, and arcades line the truncated pier, which was severely damaged in a storm a few years ago. The 46-horse carousel, built in 1922, has seen action in many movie and television shows, most notably the Paul Newman/Robert Redford film *The Sting.* ☎ *310/458–8900. Rides: 50¢ adults, 25¢ children. Carousel open in summer, Tues.–Sun. 10–9; in winter, weekends 10–5.*

❷ **Palisades Park** is a ribbon of green that runs along the top of the cliffs from Colorado Avenue to just north of San Vicente Boulevard. The flat walkways are usually filled with casual strollers as well as joggers who like to work out with a spectacular view of the Pacific as company. It is especially enjoyable at sunset.

The **Santa Monica Visitor Information Center,** in the park at Santa Monica Boulevard, offers bus schedules, directions, and information on Santa Monica–area attractions. ☎310/393–7593. ⊘ *Daily 10–4.*

Santa Monica has grown into a major center for the L.A. art community, and the **Santa Monica Museum of Art** is poised to boost that reputation. Designed by Frank Gehry, the well-known architect who's also a resident of Santa Monica, the museum presents the works of performance and video artists and exhibits works of lesser-known painters and sculptors. *2437 Main St.,* ☎ *310/399–0433.* ☛ *Suggested $4 donation for adults, $2 artists, senior citizens, and students.* ⊘ *Wed. and Thurs. 11–6, Fri.–Sat. 11–10, Sun. 11–6.*

❹ The **California Heritage Museum,** housed in an 1894-vintage, late-Victorian home once owned by the founder of Santa Monica, was moved to its present site on trendy Main Street in the late 1970s. Three rooms have been fully restored: the dining room in the style of 1890 to 1910; the living room, 1910–1920; and the kitchen, 1920–1930. The second-floor galleries feature photography and historical exhibits as well as shows by contemporary California artists. *2612 Main St.,* ☎ *310/392–8537.* ☛ *$2 adults, children under 12 free.* ⊘ *Wed.–Sat. 11–4, Sun. noon–4.*

The museum faces a companion home, another Victorian delight moved to the site; it's now occupied by a catering company, **Monica's.** These two dowagers anchor the northwest corner of the funky **Main Street area** of Santa Monica. Several blocks of old brick buildings here have undergone a rejuvenation (and considerable rent increases) and now house galleries, bars, cafés, omelet parlors, and boutiques. It's a delightful area to walk around, though with its proximity to the beach,

Tour 5: Santa Monica And Venice

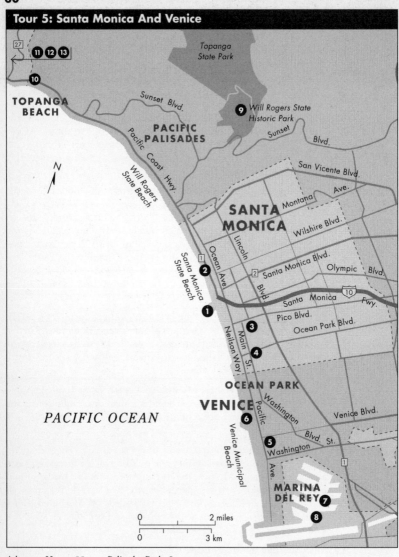

Adamson House, **11**

Burton Chase Park, **7**

California Heritage Museum, **4**

Canals, **5**

Fisherman s Village, **8**

J. Paul Getty Museum, **10**

Malibu Lagoon State Park, **12**

Palisades Park, **2**

Pepperdine University, **13**

Santa Monica Museum of Art, **3**

Santa Monica Pier, **1**

Venice Boardwalk, **6**

Will Rogers State Historic Park, **9**

parking can be tight on summer weekends. Best bets are the city pay lots behind the Main Street shops, between Main and Neilsen Way.

Venice

Venice was a turn-of-the-century fantasy that never quite came true. Abbot Kinney, a wealthy Los Angeles businessman, envisioned this little piece of real estate, which then seemed so far from downtown, as a romantic replica of Venice, Italy. He developed an incredible 16 miles of canals, floated gondolas on them, and built scaled-down versions of the Doge's Palace and other Venetian landmarks. The name remains, but the connection with Old World Venice is as flimsy as ever. Kinney's project was plagued by ongoing engineering problems and disasters and drifted into disrepair, to be restored only in the early 1990s.

⑤ Three small **canals** and bridges remain and can be viewed from the southeast corner of Pacific Avenue and Venice Boulevard. But long gone are the amusement park, swank seaside hotels, and gondoliers.

By the late 1960s, however, actors, artists, musicians, hippies, and anyone who wanted to live near the beach but couldn't afford to, were attracted by the low rents in Venice, and the place quickly became SoHo-by-the-Sea. The trade-off was that the area was pretty rundown, and the remaining canals were stagnant and fairly smelly, but as the area's appeal grew, and a more upscale crowd started moving in, these drawbacks were rectified. Venice's locals today are a grudgingly thrown-together mix of aging hippies, yuppies with the disposable income to spend on inflated rents, senior citizens who have lived here for decades, and the homeless.

Venice has the liveliest waterfront walkway in Los Angeles, known as
⑥ both Ocean Front Walk and the **Venice Boardwalk.** It begins at Washington Street and runs north. There is plenty of action year-round: Bicyclists zip along and bikini-clad roller and in-line skaters attract crowds as they put on impromptu demonstrations, vying for attention with the unusual breeds of dogs that locals love to prance along the walkway. A local bodybuilding club works out on the adjacent beach, and it's nearly impossible not to stop to ogle at the pecs as these strongmen lift weights.

At the south end of the boardwalk, along Washington Street, near the Venice Pier, in-line skates, roller skates, and bicycles (some with baby seats) are available for rent.

TIME OUT The boardwalk is lined with fast-food stands, and food can then be carried a few feet to the beach for a picnic. But for a somewhat more relaxing meal, stand in line for a table at **Sidewalk Cafe** (1401 Ocean Front Walk, ☎ 310/399–5547). Wait for a patio table, where you can watch the free spirits on parade.

Marina del Rey

Just south of Venice is a quick shift of values. Forget about Venice—Italy or California—Marina del Rey is a modern and more successful, if less romantic, dream. It is the largest man-made boat harbor in the world, with a commercial area catering to the whims of boat owners and boat groupies. The stretch between Admiralty Way and Mindinao Way has some of the area's best restaurants—expensive but worth it. Most of the better hotel chains, such as the Ritz-Carlton, also have properties here.

For boatless visitors, the best place from which to view the marina is
⑦ **Burton Chase Park,** at the end of Mindinao Way. Situated at the tip of

a jetty and surrounded on three sides by water and moored boats, this 6-acre patch of green offers a cool and breezy spot from which to watch boats move in and out of the channel, and it's great for picnicking.

8 **Fisherman's Village** is a collection of cute Cape Cod clapboards housing shops and restaurants (open daily 8 AM–9 PM). It's not much of a draw unless you stop in for a meal or a snack or take one of the 45-minute marina cruises offered by **Hornblower Dining Outs** that depart from the village dock. *13755 Fiji Way,* ☎ *310/301–6000. Tickets: $7 adults, $4 senior citizens and children. Cruises leave June–Aug., weekdays 12–3 every hr; year-round, weekends 11–5.*

Pacific Palisades
From Santa Monica, head north on Pacific Coast Highway toward Malibu, a pleasant drive in daytime or evening. The narrow-but-expensive beachfront houses were home to movie stars in the 1930s.

9 Spend a few hours at **Will Rogers State Historic Park** in Pacific Palisades and you may understand what endeared America to this cowboy/humorist in the 1920s and 1930s. The two-story ranch house on Rogers's 187-acre estate is a folksy blend of Navajo rugs and Mission-style furniture. Rogers's only extravagance was raising the roof several feet (he waited till his wife was in Europe to do it) to accommodate his penchant for practicing his lasso technique indoors. The nearby museum features Rogers memorabilia. Short films show his roping technique and his homey words of wisdom. Rogers was a polo enthusiast, and in the 1930s, his front-yard polo field attracted such friends as Douglas Fairbanks for weekend games. The tradition continues, with free games scheduled when the weather's good. The park's broad lawns are excellent for picnicking, and there's hiking on miles of eucalyptus-lined trails. *1501 Will Rogers State Park Rd., Pacific Palisades,* ☎ *310/454–8212.* ☞ *Free; parking $5. Call for polo schedule.*

Malibu
★ **10** You'll want to plan in advance to visit the **J. Paul Getty Museum,** which contains one of the country's finest collections of Greek and Roman antiquities. The oil millionaire began collecting art in the 1930s, concentrating on three distinct areas: Greek and Roman antiquities, Baroque and Renaissance paintings, and 18th-century decorative arts. In 1946 he purchased a large Spanish-style home on 65 acres in a canyon just north of Santa Monica to house the collection. By the late 1960s, the museum could no longer accommodate the rapidly expanding collection, and Getty decided to build this new building, which was completed in 1974. It's a re-creation of the Villa dei Papiri, a luxurious 1st-century Roman villa that stood on the slopes of Mt. Vesuvius overlooking the Bay of Naples, prior to the volcano's eruption in AD 79. The villa is thought to have once belonged to Lucius Calpurnius Piso, the father-in-law of Julius Caesar. The two-level, 38-gallery building and its extensive gardens (which include trees, flowers, shrubs, and herbs that might have grown 2,000 years ago at the villa) provide an appropriate and harmonious setting for Getty's classical antiquities. Note that in late 1997, everything except the classical antiquities will be moved to a new J. Paul Getty Center in Brentwood; now might be a good time to see the whole collection while it's still in one spot.

The main level houses sculpture, mosaics, and vases. Of particular interest are the 4th-century Attic stelae (funerary monuments) and Greek and Roman portraits. The decorative arts collection on the upper level features furniture, carpets, tapestries, clocks, chandeliers, and small decorative items made for the French, German, and Italian nobility, with a wealth of royal French treasures (Louis XIV to Napoléon). Richly colored brocaded walls set off the paintings and furniture to great advantage. All major schools of Western art from the late 13th century to the late 19th century are represented in the painting collection, which emphasizes Renaissance and Baroque art and includes works by Rembrandt, Rubens, de la Tour, Van Dyck, Gainsborough, and Boucher. Recent acquisitions include Old Master drawings, medieval and Renaissance illuminated manuscripts, works by Picasso, Van Gogh's *Irises,* and a select collection of Impressionist paintings including some by Claude Monet. The only catch in visiting this museum is that parking is limited and reservations are necessary; they should be made one week in advance. The only other way in if you're not on a tour—handy if you've arrived too late to reserve a parking slot—is to take MTA Bus 434 from Santa Monica. The driver will give you an entrance pass. You can also take the bus from Santa Monica that runs along Pacific Coast Highway (and doesn't require reservations). *17985 Pacific Coast Hwy.,* ☎ *310/458–2003.* ☛ *Free.* ☉ *Tues.–Sun. 10–5.*

TIME OUT   One of the best located restaurants in Malibu is **Pierview** (22718 Pacific Coast Hwy., ☎ 310/456–6962), set right on the ocean just south of the pier. The menu ranges from sandwiches and pizzas to Mexican food, including shark fajitas. Try to get outdoor seating if the weather's warm.

⓫   **Adamson House** is the former home of the Rindge family, which owned much of the Malibu Rancho in the early part of the 20th century. Malibu was quite isolated then, with all visitors and supplies arriving by boat at the nearby Malibu Pier (and it can still be isolated these days when rock slides close the highway). The Moorish-Spanish home, built in 1928, has been opened to the public and may be the only chance most visitors get to be inside a grand Malibu home. The Rindges led an enviable Malibu lifestyle, decades before it was trendy. The house is right on the beach (high chain-link fences keep out curious beachgoers). The family owned the famous Malibu Tile Company, and their home is predictably encrusted with magnificent tile work in rich blues, greens, yellows, and oranges. Even an outside dog shower, near the servants' door, is a tiled delight. Docent-led tours help visitors to envision family life here as well as to learn about the history of Malibu and its real estate (you can't have one without the other). *23200 Pacific Coast Hwy.,* ☎ *310/456–8432.* ☛ *$2 adults, $1 children.* ☉ *Wed.–Sat. 11–3. Parking (fee).*

⓬   Adjacent to Adamson House is **Malibu Lagoon State Park** (23200 Pacific Coast Hwy.), a haven for native and migratory birds. Visitors must stay on the boardwalks so that the egrets, blue herons, avocets, and gulls can enjoy the marshy area. The signs that give opening and closing hours refer only to the parking lot; the lagoon itself is open 24 hours and is particularly enjoyable in the early morning and at sunset. Luckily, street-side parking is available then (but not at midday).

⓭   **Pepperdine University** (24255 Pacific Coast Hwy.) looks exactly like a California school should. Designed by William Pereira, this picture-perfect campus is set on a bluff above the Pacific.

TOUR 6: PALOS VERDES, SAN PEDRO, AND LONG BEACH

Numbers in the margin correspond to points of interest on the Tour 6: Palos Verdes, San Pedro, and Long Beach map.

Few residents take advantage of Long Beach's attractions. If they had taken a day to see the *Queen Mary* when their in-laws visited from back East, they were duly astounded to discover Long Beach's impressive skyline, the string of hotels along Ocean Boulevard, the revitalized downtown area, and the city's close proximity to the rest of L.A. and Orange County. How could this entire city, the fifth largest in the state, have been right here and they never really knew about it?

Palos Verdes

Palos Verdes Peninsula is a hilly haven for horse lovers and other gentrified folks, many of them executive transplants from east of the Mississippi. The real estate in these small peninsula towns, ranging from expensive to very expensive, is zoned for stables, and you'll often see riders along the streets (they have the right of way).

❶ South Coast Botanic Garden began life ignominiously—as a garbage dump-cum-landfill. It's hard to believe that as recently as 1960, truckloads of waste (3½ million tons) were being deposited here. With the intensive ministerings of the experts from the L.A. County Arboreta Department, the dump soon boasted lush gardens with plants from every continent except Antarctica, with all the plants eventually organized into color groups. Self-guided walking tours take visitors past flower and herb gardens, rare cacti, and a lake with ducks. Picnicking is limited to a lawn area outside the gates. *26300 S. Crenshaw Blvd., Rancho Palos Verdes,* ☎ *310/544–6815.* ☛ *$5 adults, $1 senior citizens and children 5–12.* ☼ *Daily 9–4:30.*

The drive on Palos Verdes Drive around the water's edge takes you high above the cliffs. An aerial shot of this area was used in the opening of television's *Knots Landing.*

❷ Wayfarers Chapel (5755 Palos Verdes Dr. S, Rancho Palos Verdes, ☎ 310/377–1650) was designed by architect Lloyd Wright, son of Frank Lloyd Wright, in 1949. He planned this modern glass church to blend in with an encircling redwood forest. The redwoods are gone (they couldn't stand the rigors of urban encroachment), but another forest has taken their place, lush with ferns and azaleas, adding up to a breathtaking combination of ocean, vegetation, and an architectural wonder. This "natural church" is a popular wedding site, so avoid visiting on weekends.

San Pedro

San Pedro shares the peninsula with the Palos Verdes towns, but little else. Here, the cliffs give way to a hospitable harbor. The 1950s-vintage executive homes give way to tidy 1920s-era white clapboards, and horses give way to boats. San Pedro (locals steadfastly ignore the correct Spanish pronunciation—it's "San Peedro" to them) is an old seaport community with a strong Mediterranean and Eastern European flavor. There are enticing Greek and Yugoslavian markets and restaurants throughout the town.

❸ Cabrillo Marine Aquarium is a gem of a small museum dedicated to the marine life that flourishes off the Southern California coast. It's set in a modern Frank Gehry–designed building right on the beach and is popular with school groups because its exhibits are especially instructive as well as fun. The 35 saltwater aquariums include a shark tank, and a see-through tidal tank gives visitors a chance to see the long view of a wave. On the back patio, docents supervise as visitors reach into a shallow tank to touch starfish and sea anemones. *3720 Stephen White Dr.,* ☎ *310/548–7562.* ☛ *Free; parking $6.50.* ☼ *Tues.–Fri. noon–5, weekends 10–5.*

Tour 6: Palos Verdes, San Pedro, and Long Beach

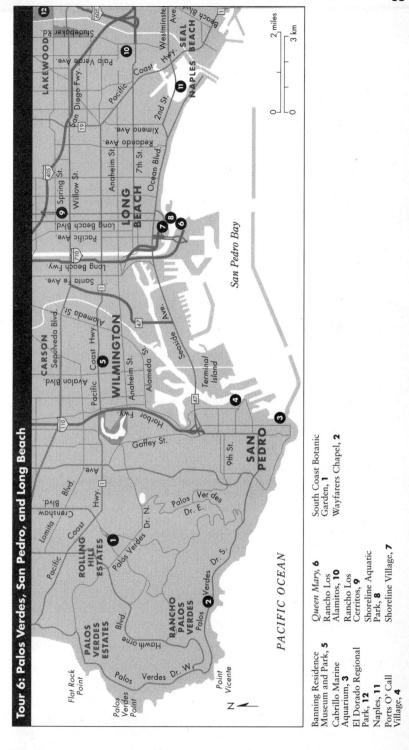

Banning Residence Museum and Park, **5**
Cabrillo Marine Aquarium, **3**
El Dorado Regional Park, **12**
Naples, **11**
Ports O' Call Village, **4**

Queen Mary, **6**
Rancho Los Alamitos, **10**
Rancho Los Cerritos, **9**
Shoreline Aquatic Park, **8**
Shoreline Village, **7**

South Coast Botanic Garden, **1**
Wayfarers Chapel, **2**

PACIFIC OCEAN

San Pedro Bay

2 miles
3 km

If you're lucky enough to visit at low tide, take time to explore the tide pool on nearby Cabrillo Beach (staff can direct you).

❹ Ports O' Call Village is a commercial rendition of a New England shipping village, an older version of Fisherman's Village in Marina del Rey, with shops, restaurants, and fast-food windows. Two companies run 1- to 1½-hour harbor cruises ($10 adults, $5 children) and whale-watching cruises, January–April ($15 adults, $5–$8 children). Cruises depart from the village dock; call 310/831–1073 for schedules.

Wilmington

To preserve transportation and shipping interests for the city of Los Angeles, Wilmington was annexed in the late 19th century. A narrow strip of land, mostly less than ½ mile wide, it follows the Harbor Freeway from downtown south to the port. **Banning Residence Museum and Park** is a pleasant, low-key stop here. General Phineas Banning, an early entrepreneur in Los Angeles, is credited with developing the harbor into a viable economic entity and naming the area Wilmington (he was from Delaware). Part of his estate has been preserved in a 20-acre park that offers excellent picnicking possibilities. A 100-year-old wisteria, near the arbor, blooms in the spring. The interior of the house can be seen on docent-led tours. *401 E. M St., Wilmington,* ☎ *310/548–7777.* ☛ *To house: $2. House tours Tues.–Thurs. 12:30–2:30, Sat. and Sun. 12:30–3:30, on ½ hr.*

Long Beach

Long Beach began as a seaside resort in the 19th century and during the early part of the 20th century was a popular destination for Midwesterners and Dust Bowlers in search of a better life. They built street after street of modest wood homes.

★ ❻ The first glimpse of the **Queen Mary**—the largest passenger ship ever built, now sitting snugly in Long Beach Harbor—is disarming. What seemed like sure folly when Long Beach officials bought her in 1964 put the city on the proverbial map. The 50,000-ton *Queen Mary* was launched in 1934, a floating treasure of Art Deco splendor. It took a crew of 1,100 to minister to the needs of its 1,900 demanding passengers. Allow a generous half day to explore this most luxurious of luxury liners, admiring the extensive wood paneling, the gleaming nickel- and silver-plate handrails, and the hand-cut glass. Tours through the ship are available, and guests are invited to browse the 12 decks and witness close up the bridge, staterooms, officers' quarters, and engine rooms. There are several restaurants and shops on board. *Pier J,* ☎ *310/435–3511.* ☛ *$10 adults, $8 senior citizens, $6 children under 11. Guided 1-hr tour ($3 extra adults and senior citizens, $1 children).* ☉ *Daily 10–6.*

❼ Shoreline Village is the most successful of the pseudo–New England harbors here. Its setting, between downtown Long Beach and the *Queen Mary,* is reason enough to stroll here, day or evening (when visitors can enjoy the lights of the ship twinkling in the distance). In addition to gift shops and restaurants, there's a 1906 carousel with bobbing giraffes, camels, and horses. *Corner of Shoreline Dr. and Pine Ave.,* ☎ *310/435–2668. Carousel* ☛ *$1 adults, children under 40″ free with adult.* ☉ *May–Sept., daily 10AM–11PM; Oct.–Apr., 10–10.*

TIME OUT   Housed in a working lighthouse, the aptly named **Parker's Lighthouse** (435 Shoreline Village Dr. in Shoreline Village, ☎ 213/432–6500) does double duty: It's the best place to enjoy a view of the *Queen Mary* and surrounding harbor, and it offers the best seafood in this part of town.

❽ **Shoreline Aquatic Park** (205 Marina Dr.) is literally set in the middle of Long Beach Harbor and is a much-sought-after resting place for RVers. Kite flyers also love it, because the winds are wonderful here. Casual passersby can enjoy a short walk, where the modern skyline, quaint Shoreline Village, the *Queen Mary,* and the ocean all vie for attention. The park's lagoon is off-limits for swimming, but aquacycles and kayaks can be rented during the summer months. Contact **Long Beach Water Sports** (730 E. 4th St., ☎ 310/432–0187) for information on sea kayaking lessons, rentals, and outings.

❾ **Rancho Los Cerritos** is a charming Monterey-style adobe built by the Don Juan Temple family in 1844. Monterey-style homes can be easily recognized by two features: They are always two-story and have a narrow balcony across the front. It's easy to imagine Zorro, that swashbuckling fictional hero of the rancho era, jumping from the balcony onto a waiting horse and making his escape. The 10 rooms have been furnished in the style of the period and are open for viewing. The gardens here were designed in the 1930s by well-known landscape architect Ralph Cornell. *4600 Virginia Rd., ☎ 310/570–1755.* ☛ *Free.* ☉ *Wed.–Sun. 1–5. Self-guided tours on weekdays. Free 50-min guided tours on weekends hourly 1–4.*

❿ **Rancho Los Alamitos** is said to be the oldest one-story domestic building still standing in the county. It was built in 1806, when the Spanish flag still flew over California. There's a blacksmith shop in the barn. *6400 E. Bixby Hill Rd., ☎ 310/431–3541.* ☛ *Free.* ☉ *Wed.–Sun. 1–5. Free 90-min tours leave every ½ hr until 4.*

⓫ The **Naples** section of Long Beach is known for its pleasant and well-maintained canals. Canals in *Naples,* you ask? Yes, this is a misnomer. But better misnamed and successful than aptly named and a bust. The developer who came up with the Naples canal idea learned from the mistakes and bad luck that did in Venice, just up the coast, and built the canals to take full advantage of the tidal flow that would keep them clean. Naples is actually three small islands in man-made Alamitos Bay. It is best experienced on foot—park near Bayshore Drive and 2nd Street and walk across the bridge, where you can begin meandering the quaint streets with Italian names. This well-restored neighborhood boasts eclectic architecture: vintage Victorians, Craftsman bungalows, and Mission Revivals. You may spy a real gondola or two on the canals. You can hire them for a ride but not on the spur of the moment. **Gondola Getaway** offers one-hour rides, usually touted for romantic couples, although the gondolas can accommodate up to four people. *5437 E.Ocean Blvd., ☎ 310/433–9595. Rides: $55 per couple, $10 for each additional person. Reservations essential, at least 1 to 2 wks in advance. Cruises operate 4 PM–midnight.*

⓬ **El Dorado Regional Park** (7550 E. Spring St.) hosted the 1984 Olympic Games archery competition and remains popular with local archery enthusiasts. Most visitors, however, come to this huge, 800-acre park for the broad, shady lawns, walking trails, and lakes. Several small lakes are picturesquely set among cottonwoods and pine trees. This is a wonderful picnicking spot. Fishing is permitted in all the lakes (stocked with catfish, carp, and trout), but the northernmost one is favored by local anglers. Pedal boats are available by the hour (one hour of pedaling is plenty for most people). The Nature Center is a bird and native plant sanctuary.

TOUR 7: HIGHLAND PARK, PASADENA, AND SAN MARINO

Numbers in the margin correspond to points of interest on the Tour 7: Highland Park, Pasadena, San Marino map.

The suburbs north of downtown Los Angeles have much of the richest architectural heritage in Southern California as well as several fine museums. To take advantage of the afternoon-only hours of several sites, the Highland Park part of this tour is best scheduled in the afternoon. Pasadena could take a full day, more if you want to savor the museums' collections.

To reach this area, drive north on the Pasadena Freeway (110), which follows the curves of the arroyo (creek bed) that leads north from downtown. It was the main road north during the early days of Los Angeles, when horses and buggies made their way through the chaparral-covered countryside to the small town of Pasadena. In 1942, the road became the Arroyo Seco Parkway, the first freeway in Los Angeles, later renamed the Pasadena Freeway. It remains a pleasant drive in non–rush-hour traffic, with the freeway lined with old sycamores and winding up the arroyo like a New York parkway.

Highland Park

Midway between downtown Los Angeles and Pasadena, Highland Park was a genteel suburb in the late 1800s, where the Anglo population tried to keep an Eastern feeling alive in their architecture in spite of the decidedly Southwest landscape. The streets on both sides of the freeway are filled with faded beauties, classic old clapboards that have gone into decline in the past half century.

1 **Heritage Square** is the ambitious attempt by the Los Angeles Cultural Heritage Board to save from the wrecking ball some of the city's architectural gems of the 1865–1914 period. During the past 20 years four residences, a depot, a church, and a carriage barn have been moved to this small park from all over the city. The most breathtaking building here is **Hale House,** built in 1885. The almost-garish colors of both the interior and exterior are not the whim of some aging hippie painter, but rather a faithful re-creation of the palette that was actually in fashion in the late 1800s. The **Palms Depot,** built in 1886, was moved to the site from the Westside of L.A. The night the building was moved, down city streets and up freeways, is documented in photomurals on the depot's walls. Docents dress in period costume. *3800 Homer St., off Ave. 43 exit,* ☎ *818/449–0193.* ☛ *$5 adults, $4 senior citizens and children 13–17, $2 children 6–12.* ☉ *Sat., Sun., and most holidays noon–4* PM. *Tours every 45 min or so.*

2 **El Alisal** was the home of eccentric Easterner-turned-Westerner-with-a-vengeance Charles Lummis. This Harvard graduate was captivated by Native American culture (he founded the Southwest Museum, *see below*), often living the lifestyle of the natives, much to the shock of the staid Angelenos of the time. His home, built from 1898 to 1910, is constructed of boulders from the arroyo itself, a romantic notion until recent earthquakes made the safety of such homes questionable. The art-nouveau fireplace was designed by Gutzon Borglum, the sculptor of Mt. Rushmore. *200 E. Ave. 43 (entrance on Carlota Blvd.),* ☎ *213/222–0546.* ☛ *Free.* ☉ *Fri.–Sun. noon–4.*

3 You can spot the **Southwest Museum** from the freeway—it's the huge Mission Revival building standing halfway up Mt. Washington. Inside

El Alisal, **2**

Gamble House, **5**

Heritage Square, **1**

Huntington Library,
Art Gallery, and
Botanical Gardens, **12**

Kidspace, **10**

The Norton Simon
Museum, **7**

Old Town Pasadena, **8**

The Pacific Asia
Museum, **9**

Pasadena Historical
Society, **6**

Ritz-Carlton,
Huntington Hotel, **11**

The Rose
Bowl, **4**

The Southwest
Museum, **3**

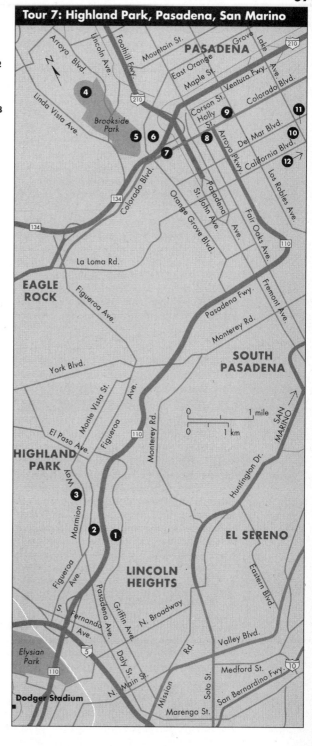

Tour 7: Highland Park, Pasadena, San Marino

is an extensive collection of Native American art and artifacts, with special emphasis on the people of the Plains, Northwest Coast, Southwest U.S., and Northern Mexico. The basket collection is outstanding. *234 Museum Dr., off Ave. 43 exit, ☎ 213/221–2163. ☛ $5 adults, $3 senior citizens and students, $2 children 7–18. ☉ Tues.–Sun. 11–5.*

TIME OUT Just blocks down the street in either direction from the Southwest Museum you'll discover authentic Mexican food that is downright cheap. The first, **Señor Fish** (5111 Figueroa St., ☎ 213/257–2498), looks like a taco stand—but don't pass it up. Its intriguing selections include octopus tostada, scallop burritos, and refreshing ceviche. A few minutes' walk in the other direction, you'll come across **La Abeja** (3700 Figueroa St., ☎ 213/221–0474), a Mexican café that's been around for two dozen years. The word inexpensive takes on new meaning at this hangout, known for its salsas and steak picado with chili.

Pasadena

Although now fully absorbed into the general Los Angeles sprawl, Pasadena was once a separate and distinctly defined—and refined—city. Its varied architecture, augmented by lush landscaping, is the most spectacular in Southern California. Visitors with only a few hours to spend should consider at least driving past the Gamble House, through Old Town, and then on to the grand old neighborhood of the Huntington Library, spending most of their time there.

❹ The **Rose Bowl** (991 Rosemont Ave.) is set at the bottom of a wide area of the arroyo in an older wealthy neighborhood that must endure the periodic onslaught of thousands of cars and party-minded football fans. The stadium is closed except for games and special events such as the monthly Rose Bowl Swap Meet. Held the second Sunday of the month, it is considered the granddaddy of West Coast swap meets.

❺ **Gamble House,** built by Charles and Henry Greene in 1908, is the most spectacular example of Craftsman-style bungalow architecture. The term "bungalow" can be misleading, since the Gamble House is a huge two-story home. To wealthy Easterners such as the Gambles, this type of vacation home seemed informal compared with their accustomed mansions. What makes visitors swoon here is the incredible amount of hand craftsmanship: the hand-shaped teak interiors, the Greene-designed furniture, the Louis Tiffany glass door. The dark exterior has broad eaves, with many sleeping porches on the second floor. It's on a private road, which is not well marked; take Orange Grove Boulevard to the 300 block to find Westmoreland Place. *4 Westmoreland Pl., ☎ 818/793–3334. ☛ $4 adults, $3 senior citizens, $2 students, children under 13 free. ☉ Thurs.–Sun. noon–3. 1-hr tours every 15–20 min.*

❻ The **Pasadena Historical Society** is housed in Fenyes Mansion. The 1905 building still holds the original furniture and paintings on the main and second floors; in the basement, the focus is on Pasadena's history. There are also 4 acres of well-landscaped gardens. *470 W. Walnut St., ☎ 818/577–1660. ☛ $4 adults, $3 senior citizens and students, children under 12 free. ☉ Thurs.–Sun. 1–4. 1-hr docent-led tours.*

❼ The **Norton Simon Museum** will be familiar to television viewers of the Rose Parade: The sleek, modern building makes a stunning background for the passing floats. Like the more famous Getty Museum, the Norton Simon is a tribute to the art acumen of an extremely wealthy businessman. In 1974, Simon reorganized the failing Pasadena Museum of Modern Art and assembled one of the world's finest collections, richest in its Rembrandts, Goyas, Degas, and Picassos—and dotted with Rodin sculptures throughout. Rembrandt's development can be traced in three oils—*The Bearded Man in the Wide Brimmed Hat, Self Portrait,* and *Titus.* The most dramatic Goyas are two oils—*St. Jerome* and the portrait of *Dona Francisca Vicenta Chollet y Caballero.* Down the walnut-and-steel staircase is the Degas gallery. Picasso's renowned *Woman with Book* highlights a comprehensive collection of his paintings, drawings, and sculptures. The museum's collections of Impressionist (van Gogh, Matisse, Cézanne, Monet, Renoir, et al.) and Cubist (Braque, Gris) work is extensive. Older works include Southeast Asian artwork from 100 BC and bronze, stone, and ivory sculptures from India, Cambodia, Thailand, and Nepal. The museum also has a wealth of Early Renaissance, Baroque, and Rococo artwork: Church works by Raphael, Guariento, de Paolo, Filippino Lippi, and Lucas Cranach give way to robust Rubens maidens and Dutch landscapes, still lifes, and portraits by Frans Hals, Jacob van Ruisdael, and Jan Steen, and a magical Tiepolo ceiling highlights the Rococo period. *411 W. Colorado Blvd.,* ☎ *818/449–6840.* ✎ *$4 adults, $2 senior citizens and students, children under 12 free.* ☉ *Thurs.–Sun. noon–6.*

⑧ A half mile east of the museum is **Old Town Pasadena,** which once fell into seedy decay, but in the 1990s, the area was revitalized as a blend of restored brick buildings with a yuppie overlay. Rejuvenated buildings include bistros, elegant restaurants, and boutiques. On Raymond Street, the Hotel Green, now the Castle Apartments, dominates the area. Once a posh resort hotel, the Green is now a faded Moorish fantasy of domes, turrets, and balconies reminiscent of the Alhambra but with, true to its name, a greenish tint. Holly Street, between Fair Oaks and Arroyo, is home to several shops offering an excellent selection of vintage '50s objects, jewelry, and clothes; it's an area that's best explored on foot. Old Town is bisected by Colorado Boulevard, which, west of Old Town, rises onto the **Colorado Street Bridge,** a raised section of roadway on graceful arches built in 1912 and restored in 1993. On New Year's Day throngs of people line Colorado Boulevard to watch the Rose Parade.

TIME OUT If browsing the Holly Street shops leaves you both nostalgic and hungry, walk down to Fair Oaks Avenue to seek out the **Market City Cafe** (33 S. Fair Oaks Ave., ☎ 818/568-0203), which you'll recognize by the life-size black-and-white cow in the window. Imaginative Italian fare, including a self-serve antipasto bar, brick-oven pizzas, and charbroiled fish, is served both indoors and alfresco.

⑨ The **Pacific Asia Museum** is the gaudiest Chinese-style building in Los Angeles outside of Chinatown. Designed in the style of a northern Chinese imperial palace with a central courtyard, it is devoted entirely to the arts and crafts of Asia and the Pacific Islands. Most of the objects are on loan from private collections and other museums, and there are usually changing special exhibits that focus on the objects of one country. *46 N. Los Robles Dr.,* ☎ *818/449–2742.* ✎ *$3 adults, $1.50 senior citizens and students, children free; free the 3rd Sat. of the month.* ☉ *Wed.–Sun. 10–5.*

⑩ **Kidspace** is a children's museum housed in the gymnasium of an elementary school. Here kids can talk to a robot; direct a television or radio station; dress up in the real (and very heavy) uniforms of a firefighter, an astronaut, a football player; and more. "Critter Caverns" beckons with its large tree house and secret tunnels for exploring insect life up close (don't worry, the bugs are fake). A child-size rendition of a supermarket lets younger visitors try their hand at the cash register. *390 S. El Molino Ave.,* ☎ *818/449–9143.* ✒ *$5 adults, $3.50 senior citizens, $2.50 children 1–2.* ☉ *Sept.–May, Wed. 2–5, weekends 12:30–5, school vacations, weekdays 1–5 and weekends 12:30–5; June–Aug., Tues.–Fri. 1–5.*

⑪ The **Ritz-Carlton, Huntington Hotel** (1401 S. Oak Knoll Ave., ☎ 818/568–3900) is situated in Pasadena's most genteel neighborhood, Oak Knoll, close to San Marino. The hotel, built in 1906, reopened in March 1991, after five years of renovations necessary to bring it up to earthquake code standards. The original design was scrupulously preserved, including the Japanese and Horseshoe Gardens. Don't miss the historic Picture Bridge with its murals depicting scenes of California along its 20 gables.

San Marino

★ ⑫ If you only have time for one stop in the Pasadena area, it should be the **Huntington Library, Art Gallery, and Botanical Gardens,** the area's most important site. Railroad tycoon Henry E. Huntington built his hilltop home in the early 1900s; since then it has established a reputation as one of the most extraordinary cultural complexes in the world, annually receiving more than a half million visitors. The library contains 6 million items, including such treasures as a Gutenberg Bible, the earliest known edition of Chaucer's *Canterbury Tales,* George Washington's genealogy in his own handwriting, and first editions by Ben Franklin and Shakespeare. In the library's hallway are five tall hexagonal towers displaying important books and manuscripts. The art gallery, devoted to British art from the 18th and 19th centuries, contains the original *Blue Boy* by Gainsborough, *Pinkie,* a companion piece by Lawrence, and the monumental *Sarah Siddons as the Tragic Muse* by Reynolds.

The Huntington's awesome 130-acre garden, formerly the grounds of the estate, now includes a 12-acre Desert Garden featuring the largest group of mature cacti and other succulents in the world, all arranged by continent. The Japanese Garden offers traditional Japanese plants, stone ornaments, a moon bridge, a Japanese house, a bonsai court, and a Zen rock garden. Besides these gardens, there are collections of azaleas and 1,500 varieties of camellias, the world's largest public collection. The 1,000-variety rose garden is displayed chronologically, so the development leading to today's strains of roses can be observed. There are also herb, palm, and jungle gardens plus a Shakespeare garden, where plants mentioned in Shakespeare's works are grown.

The Huntington Pavilion, built in 1980, offers visitors unmatched views of the surrounding mountains and valleys and houses a bookstore, displays, and information kiosks as well. Both the east and west wings of the pavilion display paintings on public exhibition for the first time. The Ralph M. Parsons Botanical Center at the pavilion includes a botanical library, a herbarium, and a laboratory for research on plants.

Visitors to this vast property have several options, including a 12-minute slide show introducing the Huntington; a 1¼-hour guided tour of the gardens; a 45-minute audiotape about the art gallery (which can be rented for a nominal fee); a 15-minute introductory talk about the library; and inexpensive, self-guided tour leaflets. *1151 Oxford Rd.,* ☎ *818/405–2100.* ✒ *(suggested) $7.50 adults, $6 senior citizens, $4 children 12–18, under 12 free.* ☉ *Tues.–Fri. 1–4:30, weekends 11–4:30.*

THE SAN FERNANDO VALLEY

Although there are other valleys in the Los Angeles area, this is the one that people refer to simply as "the Valley." Sometimes there is a note of derision in their tone, since the Valley is struggling with its stepchild status. City people still see it as a mere collection of bedroom communities, not worth serious thought. But the Valley has come a long way since the early 20th century when it was mainly orange groves and small ranches. Now home to more than 1 million people, this large portion of Los Angeles (with its own monthly magazine) is an area of neat bungalows and ranch-style homes situated on tidy parcels of land, with shopping centers never too far away. Fine restaurants and several major movie and television studios are an integral part of this community.

We group the major attractions of the Valley into one Exploring section to give you a sense of the place, but because the Valley is such a vast area, focus on one or two attractions and make them the destination for a half- or full-day trip. Rush-hour traffic jams on the San Diego and Hollywood freeways can be brutal.

Universal City

If you drive into the area on the Hollywood Freeway, through the Cahuenga Pass, you'll come first to Universal City, a one-industry town and that industry is Universal Studios. Its history goes back decades as a major film and television studio, but in the past few years Universal has also become a major tourist attraction. Today this hilly area boasts the Universal Studios Tour, the Universal Amphitheater, City-Walk (fun shopping and dining along a narrow thoroughfare that resembles a movie back lot), a major movie complex, and two major hotels.

★ **Universal Studios Hollywood and CityWalk** is the best place in Los Angeles for seeing behind the scenes of the movie industry. The five-to seven-hour Universal tour is an enlightening and amusing (if a bit sensational) day at the world's largest television and movie studio. The complex stretches across more than 420 acres, many of which are traversed during the course of the tour by trams featuring usually witty running commentary by enthusiastic guides. You can experience the parting of the Red Sea, an avalanche, and a flood; meet a 30-foot-tall version of King Kong; live through an encounter with a runaway train; be attacked by the ravenous killer shark of *Jaws* fame; and endure a confrontation by aliens armed with death rays—all without ever leaving the safety of the tram. And now, thanks to the magic of Hollywood, you can also experience the perils of The Big One—an all-too-real simulation of an 8.3 earthquake, complete with collapsing earth, deafening train wrecks, floods, and other life-threatening amusements. There is a New England village, an aged European town, and a replica of an archetypal New York street. The newest exhibits are *Back to the Future,* a $60-million flight simulator disguised as a DeLorean car that shows off state-of-the-art special effects, and *Lucy: A Tribute to Lucille Ball,* a 2,200-square-foot heart-shape museum containing a re-creation of the set from the *I Love Lucy* television show, plus other artifacts from the hit 1950s program. At the Entertainment Center, the longest and last stop of the day, you can stroll around to enjoy various shows: In one theater animals beguile you with their tricks; in another you can pose for a photo session with the Incredible Hulk; at Castle Dracula you'll confront a variety of terrifying monsters; and at the Star Trek Theater, you can have yourself filmed and inserted as an extra in a scene from a galactic adventure already released. Bedrock is represented in the "Flintstone's Live Music Extravaganza," a stunning Stone Age revue. CityWalk opened in 1993, with a slew of quaint shops and restaurants, including Spago, a copy of the star-studded Sunset Strip restaurant. *100 Universal City Pl.,* ☎ *818/508–9600.* ☛ *$33 adults, $27 senior citizens 60 and over, $25 children 3–11. Box office open daily 9–7.*

Burbank

Warner Brothers Studios offers a two-hour tour, which involves a lot of walking, so you should dress comfortably and casually. This tour is somewhat technically oriented and centered more on the actual workings of filmmaking than the one at Universal. It also varies from day to day to take advantage of goings-on on the lot. Most tours see the back-lot sets, prop construction department, and sound complex. *4000 Warner Blvd.,* ☎ *818/954–1744.* ☛ *$27. Tours on the hr, weekdays 9–4. No children under 10 permitted. Reservations essential, 1 wk in advance. AE, MC, V.*

NBC Television Studios are also in Burbank, as any regular viewer of *The Tonight Show* can't help knowing. For those who wish to be part of a live studio audience, free tickets are made available for tapings of the various NBC shows, and studio tours are offered daily. *3000 W. Alameda Ave., Burbank,* ☎ *818/840–3537.* ☛ *$6 adults, $3.75 children, under 5 free. Tours daily 1–3.*

San Fernando

San Fernando, in the northeast corner of the valley that bears its name, is one of the few separate cities in the Valley. It has only one important attraction: **Mission San Fernando Rey de España,** one of a chain of 21 missions established by 1823, which extend from San Diego to Sonoma along the coastal route known as El Camino Real. Today U.S. 101 parallels the historic Mission Trail and is one of the state's most popular tour ways. San Fernando Mission was established in 1797 and named in honor of King Ferdinand III of Spain. Fifty-six Native Americans joined the mission to make it a self-supporting community. Soon wheat, corn, beans, and olives were grown and harvested there. In addition workshops produced metalwork, leather goods, cloth, soap, and candles. Herds of cattle, sheep, and hogs also began to prosper. By 1833, after Mexico extended its rule over California, a civil administrator was appointed for the mission and the priests were restricted to religious duties. The Native Americans began leaving, and what had been flourishing one year before became unproductive. Thirteen years later the mission, along with its properties (those being the entire San Fernando Valley), was sold for $14,000. During the next 40 years, the mission buildings were neglected; settlers stripped roof tiles, and the adobe walls were ravaged by the weather. Finally in 1923 a restoration program was initiated. Today, as you walk through the mission's arched corridors, you may experience déjà vu—and you probably have seen it before, in an episode of *Gunsmoke, Dragnet,* or dozens of movies. The church's interior is decorated with Native American designs and artifacts of Spanish craftsmanship depicting the mission's 18th-century culture. There is a small museum and gift shop. In 1991, the wacky Steve Martin comedy *L.A. Story* was filmed here. *15151 San Fernando Mission Blvd.,* ☎ *818/361–0186.* ☛ *$4 adults, $3 senior citizens and children 7–15.* ⊙ *Daily 9–5.*

Calabasas

Calabasas, in the southwest corner of the Valley, was once a stagecoach stop on the way from Ventura to Los Angeles. The name means "pumpkins" in Spanish. The little town has retained some of the flavor of its early days. The **Leonis Adobe** is one of the most charming adobes in the county, due in part to its fairly rural setting and barnyard animals, especially the Spanish red hens. With a little concentration, visitors can imagine life in the early years. The house was originally built as a one-story adobe, but in 1844 Miguel Leonis decided to remodel rather than move and added a second story with a balcony. Voilà! A Monterey-style home. *23537 Calabasas Rd., ☎ 818/222–6511. ☞ Free. ☉ Wed.–Sun. 1–4.*

TIME OUT The **Sagebrush Cantina** (23527 Calabasas Rd., ☎ 818/222–6062), just next door to the Leonis Adobe, is a casual, outdoorsy place, and perfect for families. The specialty here, as the name suggests, is Mexican fare.

OTHER PLACES OF INTEREST

Scattered across Los Angeles County are attractions that don't fit neatly into any organized drive or walk. Some, such as Dodger Stadium, are major sites. Others, such as Watts Towers, are quirky places. If Los Angeles is anything, it's a something-for-everybody city.

Dodger Stadium has been home of the Los Angeles Dodgers since 1961, when Chavez Ravine was chosen as the site of the newly arrived-from-Brooklyn team's home base. The stadium seats 56,000 and parking is fairly easy. *1000 Elysian Park Ave., ☎ 213/224–1400, accessible from Pasadena Fwy. just north of downtown L.A. ☉ Only during games.*

Exposition Park was the site of the 1932 Olympics and the impressive architecture still stands. Adjoining the University of Southern California (*see below*), Exposition Park is the location of two major museums: the **California Museum of Science and Industry** and the **Natural History Museum** (*see* Museums, *below*). Also included in the 114-acre park are the **Los Angeles Swimming Stadium** (home of Los Angeles aquatic competitions), which is open to the public in summer, and **Memorial Coliseum,** the major stadium for the 1932 and 1984 Olympics, which was severely damaged in the 1994 earthquake. At press time (summer 1995) the swimming stadium was still closed for repairs. There are plenty of picnic areas on the grounds as well as a sunken rose garden. *Figueroa St. at Exposition Blvd., Los Angeles.*

Forest Lawn Memorial Park is more than just a cemetery: It covers 300 formally landscaped acres and features a major collection of marble statuary and art treasures, including a replica of Leonardo da Vinci's *The Last Supper* done entirely in stained glass. In the Hall of the Crucifixion-Resurrection is one of the world's largest oil paintings incorporating a religious theme, *The Crucifixion* by artist Jan Styka. The picturesque grounds are perfect for a leisurely walk. Forest Lawn was the model for the setting of Evelyn Waugh's novel *The Loved One.* Many celebrities are buried here, some more flamboyantly than others. Markers for Walt Disney and Errol Flynn are near the Freedom Mausoleum. Inside the mausoleum are the wall crypts of Nat King Cole, Clara Bow, Gracie Allen, and Alan Ladd. Clark Gable, Carole Lombard, Theda Bara, and Jean Harlow are among the luminaries buried in the Great Mausoleum. *1712 S. Glendale Ave., Glendale, ☎ 213/254–3131. ☉ Daily 8–5.*

Forest Lawn Memorial Park–Hollywood Hills is the 340-acre sister park to Forest Lawn Glendale, situated just west of Griffith Park on the north slope of the Hollywood Hills. Dedicated to the theme of American liberty, it features bronze and marble statuary, including Thomas Ball's 60-foot Washington Memorial and a replica of the Liberty Bell. There are also reproductions of Boston's Old North Church and Longfellow's

Church of the Hills. The film *The Many Voices of Freedom* is shown daily and Revolutionary War documents are on permanent display. Among the famous people buried here are Buster Keaton, Stan Laurel, Liberace, Charles Laughton, and Freddie Prinze. *6300 Forest Lawn Dr., Hollywood,* ☎ *213/254–7251.* ⊙ *Daily 8–5.*

Gene Autry Western Heritage Museum celebrates the American West, both the movie and real-life versions, with memorabilia, artifacts, and art in a structure that draws on Spanish Mission and early Western architecture, located just north of the Los Angeles Zoo. The collection includes Teddy Roosevelt's Colt revolver, Buffalo Bill Cody's saddle, and Annie Oakley's gold-plated Smith and Wesson guns, alongside video screens showing clips from old Westerns. *4700 W. Heritage Way, Los Angeles,* ☎ *213/667–2000.* ☛ *$7 adults, $5 senior citizens, $3 children 2–12.* ⊙ *Tues.–Sun. 10–5.*

★ **Griffith Park Observatory and Planetarium,** on the south side of Mt. Hollywood in the heart of Griffith Park, offers exhibits, a laserium, and dazzling daily shows that duplicate the starry sky. A guide narrates the show and points out constellations. One of the largest telescopes in the world is open to the public for free viewing every clear night. *Griffith Park,* ☎ *213/664–1191. Enter at Los Feliz Blvd. and Vermont Ave. entrance. Hall of Science and telescope are free. Planetarium shows: $4 adults, $3 senior citizens, $2 children. Laserium show: $6.50 adults, $5.50 children. Call for schedule.* ⊙ *Tues.–Fri. 2–10, weekends 12:30–10.*

Hollyhock House was the first of several houses Frank Lloyd Wright designed in the Los Angeles area. Built in 1921 and commissioned by heiress Aline Barnsdall, it exemplifies the pre-Columbian style Wright was fond of at that time. As a unifying theme, he used a stylized hollyhock flower, which appears in a broad band around the exterior of the house and even on the dining room chairs. Hollyhock House has been restored and furnished with original furniture designed by Wright and reproductions. *4800 Hollywood Blvd., Hollywood,* ☎ *213/662–7272.* ☛ *$2 adults, $1 senior citizens, children under 12 free. Tours conducted Tues.–Sun., at noon, 1, 2, and 3.*

Mulholland Drive, one of the most famous thoroughfares in Los Angeles, makes its very winding way from the Hollywood Hills across the spine of the Santa Monica Mountains west almost to the Pacific Ocean. Driving its length is slow, but the reward is sensational views of the city, the San Fernando Valley, and the expensive homes along the way.

University of Southern California (USC, or simply "SC" to locals) is the oldest major private university on the West Coast. The pleasant campus, which is home to nearly 30,000 students, is often used as a backdrop for television shows and movies. Two of the more notable of its 191 buildings are the Romanesque **Doheny Memorial Library** and **Widney Hall,** the oldest building on campus, a two-story clapboard dated 1880. The **Mudd Memorial Hall of Philosophy** contains a collection of rare books from the 13th through 15th centuries. *Bounded by Figueroa, Jefferson, Exposition, and Vermont, and adjacent to Exposition Park,* ☎ *213/740–2300. Free 1-hr campus tours weekdays 10–2, on the hr.*

OFF THE BEATEN TRACK

El Mercado lies in East Los Angeles, the heart of the Mexican barrio. While Olvera Street draws both Mexican and gringo customers, this is the real thing: a huge, three-story marketplace that's a close cousin to places like Libertad in Guadalajara. There are trinkets (piñatas and soft-clay pottery) to buy here, but the real draw is the authentic foods and mariachi music. You'll either love it or hate it here. *3425 E. 1st St., Los Angeles,* ☎ *213/268–3451.* ⊙ *Weekdays 10–8, later on weekends.*

The **Flower Market** (just east of downtown, in the 700 block of Wall Street) is a block-long series of stores and stalls that open up in the middle of the night to sell wholesale flowers and houseplants to the city's florists, who rush them to their shops to sell that day. Many of the stalls stay open until late morning to sell leftovers to the general public at the same bargain prices. The public is officially welcome after 9 AM, although many come earlier since the stock is quickly depleted.

Laurel and Hardy's Piano Stairway (923–927 Vendome St., in the Silver Lake section of Los Angeles, a few mi northeast of downtown) was the setting for the famous scene in the 1932 film *The Music Box*, where Stan Laurel and Oliver Hardy try to get a piano up an outdoor stairway. The stairway remains today much as it was then.

Orcutt Ranch Horticultural Center (23600 Roscoe Blvd., Canoga Park, ☎ 818/883–6641, ☛ Free), once owned by William Orcutt, a well-known geologist who was one of the excavators of the La Brea Tar Pits, is a surprisingly lush and varied garden in the west San Fernando Valley. Orcutt is filled with interesting little areas to explore, such as the rose garden, herb garden, and streambank with shady trees and ferns (a wonderful picnic site). The first weekend after the 4th of July, the extensive orange and grapefruit groves are open for public picking. It's a chance to enjoy the Valley as it was in the years when groves like these covered the landscape for miles. You'll need an A-frame ladder or a special pole for dislodging the fruit up high. Bring along grocery sacks. ⊙ *Daily, 8–5.*

Pig murals (on the corner of Bandini and Soto Sts. in Vernon) were probably the first public murals in Los Angeles. They were originally painted on the outside walls of the Farmer John Company by Leslie Grimes, who was killed in a fall from the scaffolding while painting. They depict bucolic scenes of farms and contented pigs, rather an odd juxtaposition to what goes on inside the packing plant. Vernon is the heart of Los Angeles's meatpacking industry, and to be stuck in traffic on a hot summer afternoon in this part of town is an odoriferous experience not soon forgotten.

Watts Towers is the folk-art legacy of an Italian immigrant tile-setter, Simon Rodia, and one of the great folk-art structures in the world. From 1920 until 1945, without helpers, this eccentric and driven man erected three cement towers, using pipes, bed frames, and anything else he could find, and embellished them with bits of colored glass, broken pottery, seashells, and assorted discards. The tallest tower is 107 feet. *1765 E. 107th St., Los Angeles.*

SIGHTSEEING CHECKLISTS

Historical Buildings and Sites

When Los Angeles celebrated its bicentennial in 1981, it came as something of a shock to many Americans. Until then most people had assumed that Los Angeles came into being in the 1920s or thereabouts. The city's historical heritage has not always been carefully preserved—in fact, city officials and developers have been quite cavalier about saving many of the best examples of the city's architectural past. However, active restoration projects are taking place all the time, and there is a great deal to be seen that predates the arrival of moving pictures.

Adamson House. *See* Tour 5, *above.*
Banning Residence Museum. *See* Tour 6, *above.*

Bullocks Wilshire. *See* Tour 3, *above.*

Bradbury Building. *See* Tour 1, *above.*

California Heritage Museum. *See* Tour 5, *above.*

Carroll Avenue (1300 block Carroll Ave., Angelino Heights) has the highest concentration of Victorian homes in the city and has been designated a historical monument. It's in Angelino Heights, one of the oldest neighborhoods in Los Angeles, developed when the upper middle class of the 1880s sought out homes in this hilly section just northwest of downtown. The entire area has many fine examples of Victorian architecture, but this block is the best. Most of the homes have been renovated with a careful eye for historical accuracy. The Carroll Avenue Foundation sponsors several events during the year that include tours to the best restored homes. The **Sessions House,** at 1330 Carroll, is one of the finest. At 1345 Carroll, you'll run across the Haunted House seen in Michael Jackson's *Thriller* video.

El Alisal. *See* Tour 7, *above.*

El Pueblo de Los Angeles Historical Monument. *See* Tour 1, *above.*

Gamble House. *See* Tour 7, *above.*

Heritage Square. *See* Tour 7, *above.*

Hollyhock House. *See* Other Places of Interest, *above.*

May Company Department Store. *See* Tour 3, *above.*

Mission San Fernando Rey de España. *See* The San Fernando Valley, *above.*

Mission San Gabriel Archangel. More than 200 years ago Father Junipero Serra dedicated this mission to the great archangel and messenger from God, St. Gabriel. As the founders approached the mission site, they were confronted by "savage" Native Americans. In the heat of battle, one of the padres produced the canvas painting *Our Lady of Sorrows,* which so impressed the Indians that they laid down their bows and arrows. Within the next 50 years, the San Gabriel Archangel became the wealthiest of all California missions. In 1833 the Mexican government confiscated the mission and it began to decline; in 1855 the U.S. government returned the mission to the church, but by this time the Franciscans had departed. In 1908 the Claretian Fathers took charge, and much care and respect has since been poured into the mission. Today, Mission San Gabriel Archangel's adobe walls preserve an era of history, and the magnificent cemetery stands witness to the many people who lived here, although you can only gaze at the structure because the 1994 earthquake left it unsafe to enter. *537 W. Mission Dr., San Gabriel,* ☎ *818/457–3048.* ☛ *To grounds: $3 adults, $1 children 6–12.* ☉ *Daily 9:30–4:15.*

Rancho Los Alamitos. *See* Tour 6, *above.*

Rancho Los Cerritos. *See* Tour 6, *above.*

Virginia Robinson Gardens, the former estate of the heir to the Robinson Department Store chain, sits on 6.2 terraced acres in Beverly Hills. A guide will take you on an hour-long tour of the gardens and the exquisite exteriors of the main house, guest house, servants' quarters, swimming pool, and tennis court. A highlight of the tour is the collection of rare and exotic palms. Visitors must call for reservations and be told the address and directions. ☎ *310/276–5367.* ☛ *$5. Tours by appointment Tues.–Thurs., 10 AM and 1 PM, Fri. 10 AM.*

Watts Towers. *See* Off the Beaten Track, *above.*

William S. Hart Regional Park. *See* Parks and Gardens, *below.*

Will Rogers State Historic Park. *See* Tour 5, *above.*

Wiltern Theater. *See* Tour 3, *above.*

Museums

Banning Residence Museum. *See* Tour 6, *above.*

Cabrillo Marine Aquarium. *See* Tour 6, *above.*

California Heritage Museum. *See* Tour 5, *above.*

California Museum of Science and Industry is especially intriguing to children, with many exhibits they can operate by punching buttons, twisting knobs, or turning levers. The Aerospace Complex features a DC-3, DC-8, rockets, and satellites plus an IMAX motion picture theater. The Hall of Health reveals the inner workings of the body, with side displays on AIDS awareness, substance abuse, and Health for Life. The Urban Environment exhibit looks at recycling, reusing, and reducing waste. Exciting Beginnings shows how chicks, frogs, and humans develop from eggs. *700 State Dr., Exposition Park,* ☎ *213/744–7400.* ☛ *Free, parking $3.* ☉ *Daily 10–5.*

Carole & Barry Kaye Museum of Miniatures. *See* Tour 3, *above.*

Craft and Folk Art Museum. *See* Tour 3, *above.*

George C. Page Museum of La Brea Discoveries. *See* Tour 3, *above.*

Hollywood Guinness World of Records Museum. *See* Tour 2, *above.*

Hollywood Studio Museum (Lasky–DeMille Barn). *See* Tour 2, *above.*

Hollywood Wax Museum. *See* Tour 2, *above.*

Huntington Library, Art Gallery, and Botanical Gardens. *See* Tour 7, *above.*

J. Paul Getty Museum. *See* Tour 5, *above.*

Lomita Railroad Museum, hidden away in a typical suburban neighborhood, is a replica of a turn-of-the-century Massachusetts train station. Beyond the gate, discover one of the largest collections of railroad memorabilia in the West. Climb aboard a real steam engine and take a look at the immaculate interior of the car itself. You'll get to inspect a 1910 caboose. *2137 250th St., Lomita,* ☎ *310/326–6255.* ☛ *$1 adults, 50¢ children under 12.* ☉ *Wed.–Sun. 10–5.*

Long Beach Children's Museum, situated in a Long Beach mall, features the regulation-issue children's-museum exhibits such as the Art Cafe and Granny's Attic. All exhibits welcome curious minds and eager hands. A children's art gallery showcases young artist's works. Stick around after the viewing and you'll get to reel in a stunning array of Velcro fish. *445 Long Beach Blvd. at Long Beach Plaza, Long Beach,* ☎ *310/495–1163.* ☛ *$3.95, children under 1 free.* ☉ *Thurs.–Sat. 11–4, Sun. noon–4.*

Los Angeles Children's Museum. *See* Tour 1, *above.*

Los Angeles County Museum of Art. *See* Tour 3, *above.*

Max Factor Museum. *See* Tour 2, *above.*

Museum of Contemporary Art. *See* Tour 1, *above.*

Natural History Museum of Los Angeles County is the third-largest natural history museum in the United States, with more than 35 halls and galleries. The main building is an attraction in itself: Spanish Renaissance in structure, it has travertine columns, walls, and domes; an inlaid marble floor heightens the overall magnificence. Opened in 1913, the museum has a rich collection of prehistoric fossils, an extensive bird- and marine-life exhibit, and a vast display of insect life. A brilliant display of stones can be seen in the Hall of Gems and Minerals, and there's an elaborate taxidermy exhibit of North American and African mammals set in detailed replicas of their natural habitats. Exhibits typifying various cultural groups include pre-Columbian artifacts and a display of crafts from the South Pacific. The Times-Mirror Hall of Native American Cultures delves into the Indian history of Los Angeles. The Ralph M. Parsons Discovery Center is like a children's museum, with many hands-on, science-oriented exhibits. *900 Exposition Blvd.,*

Exposition Park, ☎ *213/744–3466 or 213/744–3414.* ☛ *$6 adults, $3.50 senior citizens and students, $2 children 5–12; free first Tues. of month.* ○ *Tues.–Sun. 10–5. 1-hr docent tours at 1.*

Norton Simon Museum. *See* Tour 7, *above.*
Pacific Asia Museum. *See* Tour 7, *above.*
Petersen Automotive Museum. *See* Tour 3, *above.*
Ripley's Believe It or Not. *See* Tour 2, *above.*
Southwest Museum. *See* Tour 7, *above.*

Parks and Gardens

The extensive Los Angeles park system provides a welcome oasis after the myriad concrete freeways and urban sprawl. The parks range from small, grassy knolls for picnicking and relaxing to huge wilderness areas offering a wide spectrum of recreational facilities, including tennis courts, golf courses, and lakes.

The **Los Angeles Department of Parks and Recreation** (☎ 213/485–5555) provides helpful information on locating and identifying park facilities. Parks and Rec also sponsors various activities such as marathon races, interpark sports contests, poetry readings, art shows, and chess tournaments. For visits to parks on the westside of town, call the **Santa Monica Department of Parks and Recreation** (☎ 310/458–8311).

Banning Residence Museum and Park. *See* Tour 6, *above.*
Burton Chase Park. *See* Tour 5, *above.*
Descanso Gardens, once part of the vast Spanish Rancho San Rafael that covered more than 30,000 acres, now encompasses 165 acres of native chaparral-covered slopes. A forest of California live oak trees furnishes a dramatic backdrop for thousands of camellias, azaleas, and a 4-acre rose garden. Descanso's Tea House features pools, waterfalls, a Zen garden, and a gift shop as well as a relaxing spot to stop for refreshments. Trams traverse the grounds. *1418 Descanso Dr., La Canada,* ☎ *818/952–4400.* ☛ *$5 adults, $3 senior citizens and students, $1 children; half price 3rd Tues. of month.* ○ *Daily 9–4:30.*
Douglas Park is a postage-stamp-size park (4 acres) that's jam-packed every weekend with Westside families. It offers pleasant spots for blanket picnics close to the playgrounds so parents can monitor their children and read the Sunday *Times* at the same time. The playground area seldom has an empty swing. A former wading pool is now a dry track for tiny children and their three-wheelers. Well-kept and frequented by friendly people, this park deserves its favorable word-of-mouth reputation among locals. *1155 Chelsea Ave., Wilshire Blvd. near 25th St., Santa Monica.*
Eaton Canyon Park celebrates native plants and animals in a big but low-key way. It may look a bit dry and scrubby, compared to parks planted with lush East Coast trees and bushes, but for those who take the time to study the variety of plants and how they adapt to the meager rainfall, it is well worth a trip. From September through June (the best times to visit), docents offer easy, guided walks. They leave from the parking lot Saturdays beginning at 9 AM. *1750 N. Altadena Dr., Pasadena,* ☎ *818/398–5420.*
Echo Park manages to rise above the seedy, urban patina it can't escape. If you're a half-full kind of person, you'll find plenty to rave about here. There's a feeling of romance, of a bygone era, of history, stories untold. Set in one of the older, tougher neighborhoods in the city, Echo Park is mostly lake with a little edging all around. Echo Park is at its best in the late afternoon, when the area takes on a warm glow as the

sun sets. Weekdays are quiet; weekends filled with families. *1632 Bellevue Ave., Echo Park.*

El Dorado Regional Park. *See* Tour 6, *above.*

Elysian Park covers 575 hilly acres overlooking downtown Los Angeles. Despite its size, Elysian Park should be classified as an "urban" park, because it offers refuge to downtowners who live in cramped apartments. It's full of families enjoying some fresh air on weekends, and these crowded family areas are the safest parts (despite the presence of the L.A. Police Academy in the park, solo wanderings should be taken with caution, and explorations after dark forgotten altogether). *929 Academy Rd., Los Angeles,* ☎ *213/485–1759.*

Franklin Canyon Ranch has been embraced with a vengeance by Westside nature-buff do-gooders, who keep it busy with special-interest hikes and other outdoor events. The big draws are the picnic areas and the nature walks for preschoolers and their parents. *1936 N. Lake Dr., north of Beverly Hills,* ☎ *310/858–3834.*

Griffith Park is the largest city park in the United States. Donated to the city in 1896 by mining tycoon Griffith J. Griffith, it contains 4,000 acres. There are seemingly endless picnic areas, as well as hiking and horseback riding trails. Travel Town, with its miniature railroad, is a favorite with children. Pony rides and stagecoach rides are also available. The park is home to two 18-hole golf courses (Harding and Wilson) and one nine-hole executive course (Roosevelt), a pro shop, a driving range, and tennis courts. A swimming pool and soccer fields are nearby. The world-famous **Los Angeles Zoo** (*see below*) is on the park's north side. The Griffith Park Observatory and Planetarium is on the park's south side, high atop the Hollywood Hills (*see* Other Places of Interest, *above*). Near the Western Avenue entrance is Fern Dell, a half mile of shade that includes paths winding their way amid waterfalls, pools, and thousands of ferns. *Entrances at north end of Vermont Ave., Los Feliz district,* ☎ *213/665–5188.*

Hannah Carter Japanese Garden, in Bel Air just north of the UCLA campus, is owned by UCLA and may be visited by making phone reservations two weeks in advance. ☎ *310/825–4574.* ☉ *Tues. 10–1, Wed. noon–3.*

Huntington Botanical Gardens. *See* Huntington Library, Art Gallery, and Botanical Gardens, in Tour 7, *above.*

Los Angeles Zoo, one of the major zoos in the United States, is noted for its breeding of endangered species—koalas and white tigers are the latest additions. The 113-acre compound holds more than 2,000 mammals, birds, amphibians, and reptiles, grouped according to the geographic areas where they are naturally found—Africa, Australia, Eurasia, North America, and South America. A tram is available for stops at all areas. *See* Chapter 10, Los Angeles for Children, for more details. *Junction of Ventura and Golden State fwys. Griffith Park,* ☎ *213/666–4090.* ☛ *$8.25 adults, $5.25 senior citizens, $3.25 children 2–12. Safari Shuttle Tours available; fare $3 adults, $1 senior citizens and children over 12.* ☉ *Daily 10–5.*

MacArthur Park was a popular hangout for the elite during the 1920s and 1930s—a favorite spot for a leisurely stroll, boating, or an afternoon concert. How times have changed! The surrounding neighborhood is now a rundown section of town, teeming with Mexican and Central American immigrants and more than its share of winos. The park has suffered, but it remains well-used by the local population. For people who enjoy street life and consider themselves urban explorers, MacArthur Park still has something to offer. It's best to visit on weekends when the crowds provide some safety as well as a wonderfully rich panoply of human life. The grassy areas surrounding the lake are the most picturesque. The rental pedal boats allow visitors to observe the human condition from a safe distance. You can even get here on the subway line from Union Station. *2230 W. 6th St., Los Angeles.*

Malibu Creek State Park, nestled deep in the Santa Monica Mountains, crystallizes what the mountains are all about: an incredibly varied chaparral landscape and a get-away-from-it-all feeling. Century Lake, a small, man-made lake a mile from the road, is an excellent picnic site. *¼ mi south of intersection of Las Virgenes Rd. and Mulholland Hwy., Malibu.*

Malibu Lagoon State Park. *See* Tour 5, *above.*

Peter Strauss Ranch is named for its former owner, actor Peter Strauss, who lived in the splendidly cozy stone house, now park headquarters. The hiking trails are easy enough for the whole family. Throughout the year there are weekend entertainments, from folk dance ensembles to puppet shows. *Mulholland Hwy. at Kanon, Agoura,* ☎ *818/889–3150.*

Placerita Canyon Nature Center is perfect for hiking, with 8 miles of trails through 350 acres of both flat and hilly terrain along a streambed and through oak trees. Because the park is a wildlife refuge, picnicking is limited to the designated area. The half-mile ecology trail focuses on the flora and fauna of the area. Gold was first discovered in California in 1842 in this park (not in the Mother Lode as most assume), at a site designated by the Oak of the Golden Dream. *19152 W. Placerita Canyon Rd., Newhall,* ☎ *805/259–7721.*

Roxbury Park is centrally located and attracts a good crowd every weekend. *471 S. Roxbury Dr., at Olympic Blvd., Beverly Hills, just east of Century City,* ☎ *310/550–4761.*

Shoreline Aquatic Park. *See* Tour 6, *above.*

Vasquez Rocks offers one of Los Angeles County's best photo opportunities. Sure, it's a two-hour drive from downtown, but that doesn't stop the dozens of film, television, and ad-agency crews who truck out here each year to use the 45-degree-angle rocks as the archetypal Western backdrop. *10700 E. Escondido Rd., Agua Dulce, off Antelope Valley Fwy.*

William S. Hart Regional County Park was once owned by cowboy star William S. Hart, who took his movie money and bought a large tract of land in the Santa Clarita Valley—in those days, far in the country. Hart is long dead, civilization (in the guise of housing tracts and shopping malls) has surrounded the area, but 253 acres remain a bucolic and very Western preserve. *24151 N. San Fernando Rd., Newhall,* ☎ *805/259–0855. House open Wed.–Fri. 10–12:30 and weekends 11–3:30, with tours every ½ hr. Park open 7 AM–sunset.*

Will Rogers State Historic Park. *See* Tour 5, *above.*

3 Shopping

By Jane E.
Lasky

WHEN ASKED WHERE THEY WANT TO SHOP, visitors to Los Angeles inevitably answer, "Rodeo Drive." But this famous thoroughfare is only one of many enticing shopping streets in Los Angeles. There's also mall shopping, which in this metropolis is an experience unto itself—the mall is the modern-day Angeleno's equivalent of a main street, town square, back fence, malt shop, and county fair, all rolled into one. Distances between shopping spots can be vast, however, so don't choose too many different stops in one day—if you do, you'll spend more time driving than spending!

Most Los Angeles shops are open from 10 to 6 although many remain open until 9 or later, particularly at the shopping centers, on Melrose Avenue, and in Westwood Village during the summer. Melrose shops, on the whole, don't get moving until 11 AM but are often open Sunday, too. At most stores around town, credit cards are almost universally accepted and traveler's checks are also often allowed with proper identification. If you're looking for sales, check the *Los Angeles Times*.

Shopping Districts

Downtown

Although downtown Los Angeles has many enclaves to explore, we suggest that the bargain hunter head straight for the **Cooper Building** (860 S. Los Angeles St., ☎ 213/622–1139). Eight floors of small clothing and shoe shops (mostly for women) offer some of the most fantastic discounts in the city. Grab a free map in the lobby, and seek out as many of the 50 shops as you can handle. Nearby are myriad discount outlets selling everything from shoes to suits to linens.

Near the Hilton Hotel, **Seventh Street Marketplace** (735 S. Figueroa, ☎ 213/955–7150) is an indoor/outdoor multilevel shopping center with an extensive courtyard that boasts many busy cafés and lively music. The stores surrounding this courtyard include **G. B. Harb** (☎ 213/624–4785), a fine shop for fashion, and **Bullocks** (☎ 213/ 624–9494), a small version of the big department store, geared to the businessperson.

Melrose Avenue

West Hollywood, especially Melrose Avenue, is where young shoppers should try their luck, as should those who appreciate vintage styles in clothing and furnishings. The 1½ miles of Melrose from La Brea to a few blocks west of Crescent Heights is definitely one of Los Angeles's trendiest shopping areas, with loads of intriguing one-of-a-kind shops and bistros; both east and west of this delineation, Melrose has some other very worthwhile stores, too. *See* Tour 4 *in* Chapter 2, Exploring Los Angeles, for other stores along Melrose. A sampling of Melrose stores:

Betsey Johnson (7311 Melrose Ave., ☎ 213/931–4490) offers the designer's vivid, hip women's fashions. Watch for twice-yearly sales.
Comme des Fous (7384 Melrose Ave., ☎ 213/653–5330) is an avant-garde (and pricey) clothing shop packed with innovative European designs many women would consider daring to wear.
Cottura (7215 Melrose Ave., ☎ 213/933–1928) offers brightly colored Italian ceramics.
Emphasis (7361 Melrose Ave., ☎ 213/653–7174) offers a pristine collection of fashion-forward clothes for women, as well as hats, belts, accessories, and a selection of unique lingerie.

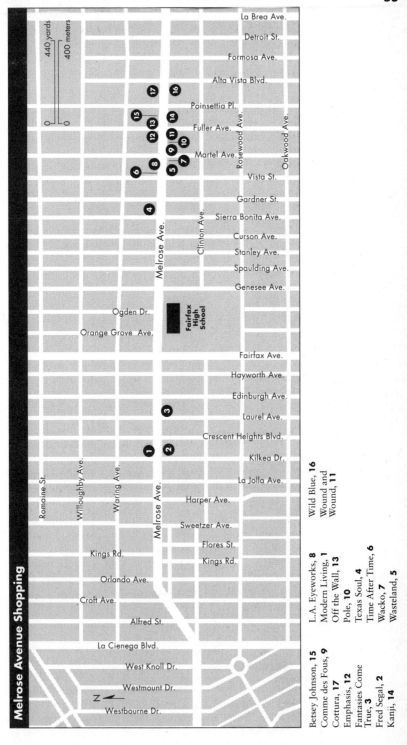

Fantasies Come True (8012 Melrose Ave., ☎ 213/655–2636) greets you with "When You Wish upon a Star" playing from a tape deck. The store, needless to say, is packed with Walt Disney memorabilia.

Fred Segal (8118 Melrose Ave., ☎ 213/651–1935) has a collection of shops that provide stylish clothing for men and women. Among the designers and manufacturers they carry: Nancy Heller, New Man, Ralph Lauren, Calvin Klein. Children's clothing, accessories, and shoes—an impressive array—are also stocked at the Melrose store.

Kanji (7320½ Melrose Ave., ☎ 213/933–6364) carries an alluring mixture of conservative fashions and clothing with flair. You'll find European-style dresses, pants, and suits.

L.A. Eyeworks (7407 Melrose Ave., ☎ 213/653–8255) is a hip boutique run by the world's most successful eye-fashion prognosticators; frame-wise, whatever's next in style around the globe will probably show up first in this leading-edge L.A. shop.

Modern Living (8125 Melrose Ave., ☎ 213/655–3898) is a gallery of 20th-century design, representing renowned international furniture designers, including Philippe Starck, Ettore Sottsass, and Massino Iosaghini.

Off the Wall (7325 Melrose Ave., ☎ 213/930–1185) specializes in "antiques and weird stuff": translation—20th-century nostalgia items, such as rare Bakelite radios, vintage vending machines, and period furnishings.

Pole (7378 Melrose Ave., ☎ 213/653–3784) offers very progressive women's clothing, with predominantly French labels like Morgan, Tehen, and Kookai. The clientele tends to be body-conscious and fashion-conscious.

Texas Soul (7515 Melrose Ave., ☎ 213/658–5571) is the place for Western footwear made in—you guessed it—the Lone Star State. Top-of-the-line boots, such as Tony Lama's, are big sellers, as are the tooled belts, leather jackets, and spurs that adorn this popular shop.

Time After Time (7425 Melrose Ave., ☎ 213/653–8463), decorated to resemble a Victorian garden, has time-honored garments ranging from turn-of-the-century to the 1960s, especially antique wedding dresses.

Wacko (7416 Melrose Ave., ☎ 213/651–3811) is a wild space crammed with all manner of blow-up toys, cards, and other semi-useless items that make good Los Angeles keepsakes.

Wasteland (7428 Melrose Ave., ☎ 213/653–3028) carries an extensive collection of retro clothing, both used and never-worn, all reasonably priced. It's a fun place to shop for '50s bowling shirts, '40s rayon dresses, funky ties, worn jeans, and leather jackets.

Wild Blue (7220 Melrose Ave., ☎ 213/939–8434) is a fine shop-gallery specializing in functional and wearable art created by exceptional contemporary artists, many of whom hail from the L.A. area.

Wound and Wound (7374 Melrose Ave., ☎ 213/653–6703) has an impressive collection of windup toys and music boxes.

Larchmont

One of L.A.'s most picturesque streets is Larchmont Boulevard, adjacent to the expensive residential neighborhood of Hancock Park. Stores that make Larchmont Village worth a detour include **Hollyhock** (214 N. Larchmont Blvd., ☎ 213/931–3400), for exceptional new and antique furnishings; **Lavender & Lace** (660 N. Larchmont Blvd., ☎ 213/856–4846), specializing in antique textiles, linens, and English pine furniture; **My Favorite Place** (202 N. Larchmont Blvd., ☎ 213/461–5713), for comfortable women's clothing—silks and ethnic pieces in particular; and **Robert Grounds** (119 N. Larchmont Blvd., ☎ 213/464–8304), for distinctive gifts and antiques.

Westwood

Westwood Village, near the UCLA campus, is a young and lively area
for shopping. The atmosphere is invigorating, especially on summer
evenings when there are movie lines around every corner, all kinds of
people strolling the streets (an unusual phenomenon in L.A., where few
folks walk anywhere), and cars cruising along to take in the scene. Among
the shops worth scouting out in this part of the city:

Aah's (1083 Broxton, ☎ 310/824–1688) is good for stationery and
fun gift items.
Copelands Sporting Goods (1001 Westwood Blvd., ☎ 310/208–6444)
offers a cornucopia of sportswear, beachwear, shoes, and shorts, along
with a variety of skiing, camping, and other outdoor equipment.
Morgan and Company (1131 Glendon, ☎ 310/208–3377) is recommended for California jewelry.
Shanes Jewelers (1065 Broxton, ☎ 310/208–8404) is a youth-oriented
jewelry store specializing in earrings, engagement rings, chains, and
watches, at prices that are comparable to wholesale. There is a good
repair department.
Sisterhood Book Store (1351 Westwood Blvd., ☎ 310/477–7300)
stocks an incredible collection of women's books in all areas—history,
health, and psychology among them.
Wilger Company (10924 Weyburn, ☎ 310/208–4321) offers fine
men's clothing with a conservative look, most of it carrying the store's
own private label, though other lines like Polo are also stocked.

The Beverly Center and Environs

The **Beverly Center** (☎ 310/854–0070), bound by Beverly Boulevard,
La Cienega Boulevard, San Vicente Boulevard, and 3rd Street, covers
more than 7 acres and contains some 200 stores. Call the center for
information about any of the shops. Examples are **By Design,** for contemporary home furnishings; **Shauna Stein** and **Ice,** for fashionable (and
very pricey) women's clothes; **Alexio,** for fashionable men's garments;
and two stores called **Traffic,** for contemporary clothing for both genders. One of the more innovative and popular stores here is **MAC,** which
offers a line of professional makeup at reasonable prices, sold by
knowledgeable staff who help with quick-to-apply beauty hints. *See*
Tour 4 *in* Chapter 2, Exploring Los Angeles, for other stores.

The shopping center is anchored by **The Broadway** department store
on one end and **Bullocks** on the other, and it has one of Los Angeles's
finest multitheater complexes, with 14 individual movie theaters. There
are also some interesting restaurants, like the **California Pizza Club,** a
fun place renowned for its unusual designer pies (like Tandoori Chicken
Pizza and Thai Pizza) and healthy salads, as well as its quick counter
service, and the **Hard Rock Cafe,** known for its bargain cuisine and fascinating decor, including a 1959 Caddy that dives into the roof of the
building above the restaurant.

Directly across the street from the Beverly Center, on the east side of
La Cienega between Beverly Boulevard and 3rd Street, is another mall,
the **Beverly Connection** (100 N. La Cienega, ☎ 213/651–3611), opened
in 1990. Following are some stores found here: **Book Star** (☎ 213/289–
1734) is a giant warehouselike store selling every conceivable sort of
reading material at low prices. **Old Navy** (☎ 213/658–5292) is a bot-
tom-of-the-line clothing store like the Gap, hawking all sorts of sweats,
shirts, and jeans. **Rexall Square Drug** (☎ 213/653–0880), a.k.a. "Drug-
store of the Stars," is where people like Dustin Hoffman and Goldie
Hawn have been seen lurking in the amply stocked aisles filled with
over-the-counter drugs, cleaning supplies, jewelry, cosmetics, and lots

of imaginative gifts. **Sports Chalet** (☎ 213/657–3210) is one of Southern California's premier places to buy all kinds of athletic equipment.

In the immediate neighborhood you'll find some other interesting shops:

Charlie's (8234 W. 3rd. St., ☎ 213/653–3657) sells a cornucopia of '40s, '50s, and '60s clothing, along with a few choice furnishings. This place has vintage evening gowns in impeccable condition as well as wild, wonderful hats designed by the namesake owner.
Cheap Frills (8325 W. 3rd St., ☎ 213/653–9997) is maintained by an athletic owner who knows how much dance wear costs and is determined to beat the high prices. Her excellent selection ranges from leotards to jazz shoes to cover-ups.
Freehand (8413 W. 3rd St., ☎ 213/655–2607) is a gallery shop featuring contemporary American crafts, clothing, and jewelry, mostly by California artists.
Trashy Lingerie (402 N. La Cienega, ☎ 310/652–4543) is just what the name suggests. This is a place for the daring; models try on the sexy garments to help customers decide what to buy.

Century City
Century City Shopping Center & Marketplace (☎ 310/277–3898), set among gleaming, tall office buildings on what used to be Twentieth Century Fox Film Studios' back lot, is an open-air mall with an excellent roster of shops. Besides The Broadway and Bullocks, both department stores, you'll find individual boutiques like the following:

Wild Pair (10250 Santa Monica Blvd., ☎ 310/203–8769) is *the* place to go for trendy shoes and bags. **Ann Taylor** (10250 Santa Monica Blvd., ☎ 310/277–3041) offers stylish but not outlandish clothing. The **Pottery Barn** (10250 Santa Monica Blvd., ☎ 310/552–0170) is a great source for contemporary furnishings and glassware at comfortable prices. Of particular note are decorative accessories such as candleholders and place mats. **Card Fever** (10250 Santa Monica Blvd., ☎ 310/553–7332) is a whimsical boutique with fun and funky messages to send. **Brentano's** (10250 Santa Monica Blvd., ☎ 310/785–0204) is one of the city's largest bookstores. **Gelson's** (10250 Santa Monica Blvd., ☎ 310/277–4288) is a gourmet food market.

Besides dozens of stores, there are many restaurants on the premises, among them **Houston's,** which gets down with its American fare of grilled fish and steak, and **Stage Deli,** the kind of New York–style deli that previously was hard to find in L.A. Also at Century City is the **AMC Century** 14-screen movie complex.

West Los Angeles
The **Westside Pavilion** (☎ 310/474–6255) is a pastel-color postmodern mall on Pico and Overland boulevards, a couple of minutes' drive from Century City. The three levels of shops and restaurants run the gamut from high-fashion boutiques for men and women to toy stores and housewares shops. Among them are the **Disney Store** (☎ 310/474–7022), filled with novelties to make all your fantasies come true; **Robinsons-May** (☎ 310/475–4911) and **Nordstrom** (☎ 310/470–6155), two full-scale department stores; **Mr. Gs for Toys** (☎ 310/475–9554), a good place for children's gifts; **Barami** (☎ 310/470–4742) for women's designer clothing; and **Victoria's Secret** (☎ 310/441-5007), a scented lingerie boutique. Worth visiting even if you're not here to shop—and a welcome stop, if you are—is **Sisley Italian Kitchen** (☎ 310/446–3030), which serves California-Italian dishes, pizzas, and terrific salads.

Santa Monica

Go west all the way to the ocean to find Santa Monica, an increasingly rewarding area for shopping. It almost feels like a self-contained small town, with a combination of both malls and street shopping.

Santa Monica Place Mall (315 Broadway, ☎ 310/394–5451) is a three-story enclosed mall that's nothing special. Some of the stores inside are **Pacific Sunwear** (☎ 310/451–8891), selling super bathing suits; **Card Fever** (☎ 310/451–8912), so you can write the folks back home; **Lechter's** (☎ 310/393–8684), for stocking up on your favorite gourmet utensils; and **Wherehouse Records** (☎ 310/394–1060), for the latest tunes. **Robinson's** (☎ 310/451–2411) and **The Broadway** (☎ 310/393–1441) are department stores in this complex.

Next door, **Third Street Promenade** (☎ 310/393–8355) is a pedestrians-only street lined with boutiques, movie theaters, clubs, pubs, and restaurants. It's as busy at night as it is in the day, with wacky street performers to entertain as you mosey along.

Along **Montana Avenue,** a stretch of a dozen or so blocks from 7th to 17th streets, showcases boutique after boutique of high-quality goods, many of them exclusive to this street. Among the more interesting:

ABS Clothing (1533 Montana Ave., ☎ 310/393–8770) sells contemporary sportswear designed in Los Angeles.
Brenda Cain (1211 Montana Ave., ☎ 310/395–1559) features nostalgic clothes and antique jewelry. The hot ticket here is the amazing array of Hawaiian shirts for men and women.
Brenda Himmel (1126 Montana Ave., ☎ 310/395–2437) is known for its fine stationery, but antiques, frames, photo albums, and books also enhance this homey boutique.
Lisa Norman Lingerie (1134 Montana Ave., ☎ 310/451–2026) sells high-quality lingerie from Europe and the United States—slips, camisoles, robes, silk stockings, and at-home clothes.
Weathervane II (1209 Montana, ☎ 310/393–5344) is one of the street's larger shops, with a friendly staff who make browsing among the classic and offbeat fashions more fun.

The stretch of **Main Street** leading from Santa Monica to Venice (Pico Blvd. to Rose Ave.) is another of those rare places in Los Angeles where you can indulge in a pleasant walk. While enjoying the ocean breeze, you'll pass some quite good restaurants and unusual shops and galleries. Some of the best:

Arts & Letters (2665A Main St., ☎ 310/392–9076) is a very special stationery boutique, selling lots of picture frames and personalized gift items as well.
Bootz (2736 Main St., ☎ 310/396–2466) stocks an incredible array of Western footwear.
Malina (2654C Main St., ☎ 310/392–2611) sells French fashions like Le Petit Bateau for children and Kenzo for women, as well as the store's own line, often described as conservative with a twist.

Farther down the street, where Santa Monica turns into Venice, is an area known as **Abbott Kinney,** a quiet artists' colony amid what is otherwise the wilder part of town. Among its galleries, cafés, boutiques, and antiques shops, look for the **Psychic Eye Bookstore** (218 Main St., ☎ 310/396–0110), a spiritual haven selling wind chimes, incense, and crystal jewelry, as well as books on sorcery and other occult subjects. It's worth a look even for skeptics.

San Fernando and San Gabriel Valleys

This is mall country; among the many outlets are **Sherman Oaks Galleria** (15301 Ventura Blvd., Sherman Oaks, ☎ 818/783–7100), **The Promenade** (6100 Topanga Canyon Blvd., ☎ 818/884–7090) in Woodland Hills, and **Glendale Galleria** (2148 Central Blvd., ☎ 818/240–9481) and **Encino Town Center** and **Plaza de Oro** (☎ 818/788–6100) in Encino.

Aside from shopping centers, some individual stores stand out along sections of Ventura Boulevard, which runs through Universal City, Sherman Oaks, Topanga, and Calabasas. One of the top shops: **Cranberry House** (12318 Ventura Blvd., Studio City, ☎ 818/506–8945) is a huge shopping arena covering half a city block, packed with 140 kiosks run by L.A.'s leading antiques dealers. Come here for vintage furniture, clothing, jewelry, and furnishings.

Beverly Hills

We've saved the most famous section of town for last. **Rodeo Drive** is often compared to such famous streets as 5th Avenue in New York and the Via Condotti in Rome. Along the couple of blocks between Wilshire and Santa Monica boulevards, you'll find an abundance of big-name retailers—but don't shop Beverly Hills without shopping the streets that surround illustrious Rodeo Drive. There are plenty of treasures to be purchased on those other thoroughfares as well.

Even Beverly Hills has a couple of shopping centers, although owners wouldn't dare call their collection of stores and cafés "malls." The **Rodeo Collection** (421 N. Rodeo Dr. ☎ 310/276–9600), between Brighton Way and Santa Monica Boulevard, is nothing less than the epitome of opulence and high fashion. Many famous upscale European designers opened their doors in this piazza-like area of marble and brass. Among them: **Fila** (☎ 310/276–1732), for the best in sports gear; **Mondi** (☎ 310/274–8380), for high-style German fashions; and **Gianni Versace** (☎ 310/276–6799), for trendsetting Italian designs.

A collection of glossy retail shops called **Two Rodeo Drive** (a.k.a. Via Rodeo, on the corner of Rodeo Dr. and Wilshire Blvd., ☎ 310/247–7040) is housed on a private cobblestone street that somewhat resembles a Hollywood back lot. Amid the Italianate piazza, outdoor cafés, and sculpted fountains of Two Rodeo are some two dozen boutiques, including **Christian Dior** (☎ 310/859-4700), for couture fashions known the world over; **Davidoff of Geneva** (☎ 310/278–8884), for the finest tobacco and accessories; **Gian Franco Ferre** (☎ 310/273–6311), for high-quality Italian designs; and **A. Sulka** (☎ 310/859–9940), a noted men's haberdasher.

The Beverly Hills branch of **Saks Fifth Avenue** (9600 Wilshire Blvd., ☎ 310/275–4211) isn't as impressive as the one you'll find across the street from St. Patrick's Cathedral in Manhattan. Still, the buyers have good taste.

Barneys New York (9570 Wilshire, ☎ 310/276–4400) was the most exciting new resident to take up shop in Beverly Hills in 1994. The West Coast branch of this uptown and very hip Manhattan store is especially popular with Generation Xers who come for the cutting-edge (and pricey) designer clothing (including threads by Comme des Garçons, Giorgio Armani, Donna Karan, and Azzedine Alaia), as well as a pristine collection of home furnishings in its Chelsea Passage department on the second floor.

Beverly Hills Shopping

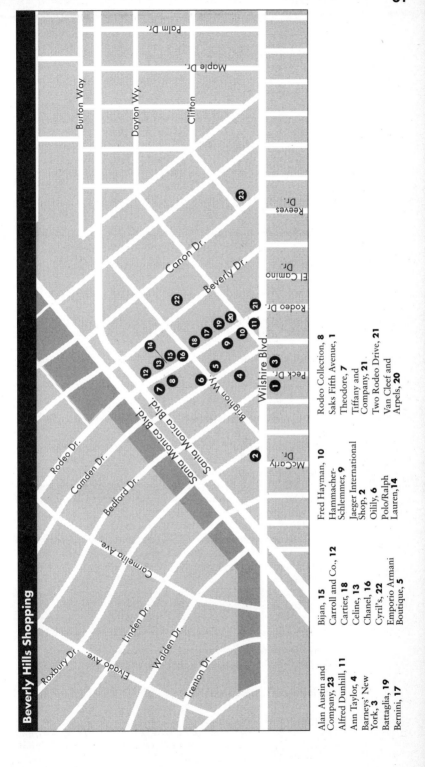

Alan Austin and
Company, **23**
Alfred Dunhill, **11**
Ann Taylor, **4**
Barneys' New
York, **3**
Battaglia, **19**
Bernini, **17**

Bijan, **15**
Carroll and Co., **12**
Cartier, **18**
Celine, **13**
Chanel, **16**
Cyril's, **22**
Emporio Armani
Boutique, **5**

Fred Hayman, **10**
Hammacher-
Schlemmer, **9**
Jaeger International
Shop, **2**
Oilily, **6**
Polo/Ralph
Lauren,**14**

Rodeo Collection, **8**
Saks Fifth Avenue, **1**
Theodore, **7**
Tiffany and
Company, **21**
Two Rodeo Drive, **21**
Van Cleef and
Arpels, **20**

Some of the many other shops, boutiques, and department stores in Beverly Hills:

FASHIONS AND HOME DECOR

Emporio Armani Boutique (9533 Brighton Way, ☎ 310/271–7790) hangs the lower-priced line of this famous Italian designer, as well as his accessories and perfumes.

Oilily (9520 Brighton Way, ☎ 310/859–9145) features fun, colorful clothing and gift items for women, children, and even infants.

Polo/Ralph Lauren (444 N. Rodeo Dr., ☎ 310/281–7200) serves up a complete presentation of Lauren's all-encompassing lifestyle philosophy. The men's area, reminiscent of a posh British men's club, offers rough wear and active wear. Some 200 antiques are used as a backdrop for the women's area. Upstairs resides the world's most extensive selection of Lauren's home-furnishing designs.

GIFTS

Hammacher-Schlemmer (309 N. Rodeo Dr., ☎ 310/859–7255) is a fabulous place to unearth those hard-to-find presents for adults who never grew up.

JEWELRY

Cartier (370 N. Rodeo Dr., ☎ 310/275–4272) offers all manner of luxury gifts and jewelry.

Tiffany and Company (210 N. Rodeo Dr., ☎ 310/273–8880), the famous name in fine jewelry, silver, and more, packages each purchase in a signature blue Tiffany box.

Van Cleef and Arpels (300 N. Rodeo Dr., ☎ 310/276–1161) sells expensive baubles and fine jewelry.

MEN'S FASHIONS

Alfred Dunhill of London (201 N. Rodeo Dr., ☎ 310/274–5351) is an elegant shop selling British-made suits, shirts, sweaters, and slacks. Pipes, tobacco, and cigars, however, are this store's claim to fame.

Battaglia (306 N. Rodeo Dr., ☎ 310/276–7184) features accessories, shoes, and men's apparel—the richest Italian fashions in luxurious silks, woolens, cottons, and cashmeres.

Bernini (362 N. Rodeo Dr., ☎ 310/278–6287) specializes in contemporary Italian designer fashions. Look for fine leather accessories from Giorgio Armani.

Bijan (420 N. Rodeo Dr., ☎ 310/273–6544) is a store where it helps to make an appointment. Bijan claims that many Arabian sheiks and other royalty shop here, along with some of the wealthiest men in the United States. Many designs are created especially by the owner.

Carroll and Co. (466 N. Rodeo Dr., ☎ 310/273–9060) is a conservative men's shop that's been in business for more than a decade. It's known for quality, service, and its exclusive clientele.

Cyril's (370 N. Beverly Dr., ☎ 310/278–1330) features fine clothing in the latest European styles and carries labels like Cerruti and Haupt.

WOMEN'S FASHIONS

Alan Austin and Company (184 N. Canon Dr., ☎ 310/275–1162) has traditional clothing in a wide selection of fabrics.

Ann Taylor (357 N. Camden Dr., ☎ 310/858–7840) is the flagship shop of this chain of women's clothing stores, offering the epitome of the young executive look.

Celine (460 N. Rodeo Dr., ☎ 310/273–1243) is for luggage, shoes, and accessories as well as traditionally tailored clothing made of fine fabrics. Expect Old World craftsmanship and classic designs.

Chanel (400 N. Rodeo Dr., ☎ 310/278–5500), known for its fashions and cosmetics, now also features fine jewelry, including copies of the original Coco designs popular in the 1920s and '30s.

Fred Hayman (273 N. Rodeo Dr., ☎ 310/271–3000) is an illustrious store where one does not merely shop for glitzy American and European clothing, accessories, and footwear; one also refreshes oneself at the stunning Oak Bar.

Jaeger International Shop (9699 Wilshire Blvd., ☎ 310/276–1062) is one of Britain's best-known clothiers, with a complete line of cashmere and woolen separates in traditionally designed fashions.

Theodore (453 N. Rodeo Dr., ☎ 310/276–9691) offers trendy items in fabulous fabrics for men and women from Kenzo, Sonia Rykiel, Issey Miyake, and Donna Karan. Everything is done with a real eye for color.

Department Stores

The Broadway (the Beverly Center, 8500 Beverly Blvd., ☎ 310/854–7200) offers merchandise in the moderate price range, from cosmetics to housewares to linens to clothing for men and women.

Bullocks (the Beverly Center, 8500 Beverly Blvd., ☎ 310/854–6655) is more upscale than The Broadway, but also carries an extensive collection of clothing for men and women, as well as housewares and cosmetics.

Nordstrom (Westside Pavilion, 10830 W. Pico Blvd., West Los Angeles, ☎ 310/470–6155) offers a wide selection of clothing for men and women and a reputation for fine customer service.

Robinsons-May (9900 Wilshire Blvd., ☎ 310/275–5464) is a high-end department store that has many women's selections, a few men's selections, and a good housewares department.

Specialty Shops

Antiques

La Cienega Boulevard, between Santa Monica Boulevard and Beverly Boulevard, is lined with antiques dealers selling everything from Chinese to French to Viennese collectibles.

Nearby lies L.A.'s poshest antiquarian niche: Melrose Place. **Rose Tarlow Antiques** (8454 Melrose Pl., ☎ 213/653–2122) and **Licorne** (8432 Melrose Pl., ☎ 213/852–4765), operated by French émigrés, sell fine 17th-century furnishings. **City Antiques** (8444 Melrose Ave., ☎ 213/658–6354) provides an eclectic assortment of French and English antiques. **J. F. Chen Antiques** (8414 Melrose Ave., ☎ 213/655–6310) specializes in ancient Oriental pieces, among them bronzes and tapestries. **French Kings Antiques** (8408 Melrose Pl., ☎ 213/383–4430) features furniture, bronzes, and clocks.

At the **Antique Guild** (3225 Helms Ave., ☎ 310/838–3131), you'll find treasures from all over the world and a gigantic inventory in a warehouse-size space.

Clothing

American Rag Company (124–150 S. La Brea Ave., ☎ 213/935–3154) is a series of six stylish boutiques set along a city block on the east side of this artsy boulevard. You can find everything from carefully handpicked European fashions and accessories for men and women, Provençal and Mediterranean home furnishings, and a hip shoe collection, to smaller-sized kids' versions of all of their lines and a range of retro (both new and used) clothes for both genders.

Maxfield (8825 Melrose Ave., ☎ 310/274–8800) is among the most elite clothing stores in L.A. Designers carried here include Azzedine Alaia, Comme des Garçons, Maud Frizon, Issey Miyake, Giorgio Armani, Byblos, Missoni. The store also houses Yohiji Yamamoto's only L.A. boutique. Maxfield is the supplier of choice for sundry celebrities as well as the wardrobe staff responsible for dressing the more fashionable shows on television.

Gifts and Crafts

Del Mano Gallery (11981 San Vicente Blvd., Brentwood, ☎ 310/476–8508), owned by Jan Peters and Ray Leier, handles the work of contemporary artists. Del Mano stocks everything from handcrafted handbags to glass and ceramic treasures.

Tesoro (319 S. Robertson Blvd., ☎ 310/273–9890) is a large boutique that stocks everything from trendy Swid-Powell dishware to Southwestern blankets, ceramics, and art furniture. The wide-ranging work by area artists is well worth a browse.

Leather

North Beach Leather (8500 Sunset Blvd., West Hollywood, ☎ 310/652–3224) offers a great selection of clothing made of leather and suede, for both men and women.

4 Sports and Fitness

SPECTATOR SPORTS

IF YOU ENJOY WATCHING PROFESSIONAL SPORTS, you'll never hunger for action in this town. Los Angeles is the home of some of the greatest franchises in pro basket-ball, football, and baseball. And while most cities would be content simply to have one team in each of those categories, L.A. fans often can root for two. If you want to participate, the best source for tickets to all sporting events is **Ticketmaster** (☎ 213/365–3500).

Some of the major sports venues in the area are **Anaheim Stadium** (2000 Gene Autry Way, ☎ 714/254–3100), **Great Western Forum** (3900 W. Manchester, Inglewood, ☎ 310/673–1773), and **L.A. Sports Arena** (downtown, next to Coliseum, at 3939 S. Figueroa, ☎ 213/748–6131). The **L.A. Coliseum** (3911 S. Figueroa, downtown, ☎ 213/748–6131), another major venue, was totally rebuilt after the 1994 earthquake.

Baseball

The **Dodgers** will take on all of their National League rivals in another eventful season at the ever-popular Dodger Stadium (1000 Elysian Park Ave., exit off I–110, the Pasadena Fwy.). For ticket information, call 213/224–1400. South down the freeway, in Anaheim, the **California Angels** continue their quest for the pennant in the American League West. For Angels ticket information, contact Anaheim Stadium (☎ 714/937–7200).

Basketball

Pro
The **Los Angeles Lakers'** home court is the Forum; for ticket information, call 310/419–3182. L.A.'s "other" team, the **Clippers,** make their home at the L.A. Sports Arena; for ticket information, call 213/748–8000.

College
The **University of Southern California** (for tickets, ☎ 213/740–2311) plays at the L.A. Sports Arena, and the Bruins of the **University of California at Los Angeles** (for tickets, ☎ 310/825–2101) play at Pauley Pavilion on the UCLA campus; these schools mix it up in Pac 10 competition each season. Another local team to watch is the Lions of **Loyola Marymount University** (for tickets, ☎ 310/338–4532).

Boxing and Wrestling

Championship competitions take place in both of these sports year-round at the Forum.

Football

Pro
The **L.A. Raiders** play at the Coliseum, downtown. For tickets, call 310/322–5901.

College
The **USC Trojans's** (for tickets, ☎ 213/740–2311) home turf is the Coliseum, pending the completion of repairs after the earthquake. The **UCLA Bruins** (for tickets, ☎ 310/825–2101) pack 'em in at the Rose Bowl in Pasadena. Each season, the two rivals face off in one of college football's oldest and most exciting rivalries.

Golf

The hot golf ticket in town each February is the **Los Angeles Open** (☎ 213/482–1311). The tournament attracts the best golfers in the world and is played in Pacific Palisades at the Riviera Country Club.

Hockey

The **L.A. Kings** (for tickets, ☎ 310/673–6003) put their show on ice at the Forum, October–April. Disney's **Mighty Ducks** (for tickets, ☎ 714/704–2500) push the puck at The Pond in Anaheim, October–April.

Horse Racing

Santa Anita Race Track (Huntington Dr. and Colorado Pl., Arcadia, ☎ 818/574–7223) is still the dominant site for exciting thoroughbred racing. You can always expect the best racing in the world at this beautiful facility.

Hollywood Park is another favorite racing venue. Since the completion of the Hollywood Park Casino in 1994, a sense of class and style has been restored to this nostalgic park. The track is next to the Forum in Inglewood, at Century Boulevard and Prairie, ☎ 310/419–1500. It's open late mid-November–December 24 and April–mid-July.

For harness racing, **Los Alamitos** (4961 Katella Ave., Anaheim) has both day and night racing. For track information, call 714/995–1234.

Several grand-prix jumping competitions and Western riding championships are held throughout the year at the **Los Angeles Equestrian Center** in Burbank (480 Riverside Dr., ☎ 818/840–9063). Show jumping and Western riding events are also featured at the **Orange County Fair Equestrian Center** (88 Fair Dr., Costa Mesa, ☎ 714/708–1652); ☛ is free.

Polo

Will Rogers State Park (1501 Will Rogers State Park Rd., Pacific Palisades) offers lovely picnic grounds where you can feast while enjoying an afternoon chukker of polo. For polo season information, call 310/454–8212. If it doesn't rain during the week, games are played Saturdays at 2 PM and Sundays at 10 AM. Parking fee is $5 per car.

Tennis

The **L.A. Open,** held in August at UCLA, usually attracts some of the top-seeded players on the pro tennis circuit. For information, call 310/208–3838.

PARTICIPANT SPORTS

If you're looking for a good workout, you've come to the right city. Whether your game is basketball, golf, billiards, or bowling, Los Angeles is a dream town for athletes of all kinds. Not only does the near-perfect climate allow sports enthusiasts to play outdoors almost year-round, but during some seasons it's not impossible to be surfing in the morning and snow skiing in the afternoon . . . all in the same county. For information, call the **City of Los Angeles Recreation and Parks Department** (200 N. Main St., Suite 1380, City Hall East, LA 90012, ☎ 213/485–5515) or **Los Angeles County Parks and Recreation Department** (433 S. Vermont Ave., LA 90020, ☎ 213/738–2961).

Bicycling

Perhaps the most famous bike path in the city, and definitely the most beautiful, can be found on the **Pacific Ocean beach,** from Temescal Canyon down to Redondo Beach. **San Vicente Boulevard** in Santa Monica has a nice wide cycling lane next to the sidewalk that runs for about 5 miles. **Balboa Park** in the San Fernando Valley is another haven for two-wheelers, as is the marked path for cyclers that traverses **Griffith Park** (entrance is at intersection of Riverside Drive and Los Feliz Boulevard).

Call the **L.A. County Parks and Recreation Department** (*see above*) for a map of bike trails.

Fishing

The best lakes for **freshwater fishing** in the area are **Big Bear** and **Arrowhead** in the San Bernardino National Forest, east of Los Angeles about two hours (*see* Chapter 8, Excursions from Los Angeles). Rainbow trout, bass, carp, blue gill, and catfish are the typical catch, and the scenery in these mountains will enhance your outing, whether you hook anything or not. Juniper Point on the north shore of Big Bear Lake is a favorite trout hangout. Call for fishing information in the area (☎ 909/866–5796).

If your fish stories are more abundant than the fish on your plate, a sure catch can be found at **Trout Dale** (in Agoura, 3 mi south of the Ventura Fwy. on Kanan Rd., ☎ 818/889–9993; open daily, 10–5), where they even go so far as to clean your catch. Three picturesque ponds are set up for picnicking or for fishing. A $3 entry fee includes your license and pole, but there's an extra charge for each trout you push up onto the banks.

Saltwater fishing in L.A. offers the gamesperson a number of different ways to get hold of a fresh catch from the Pacific. Shore fishing and surf casting are excellent on many of the beaches (*see* Beaches, *below*). Pier fishing is another popular method of hooking your dinner. The Malibu, Santa Monica, and Redondo Beach piers each offer nearby bait-and-tackle shops, and you can generally pull in a healthy catch.

If you want to break away from the piers, however, the **Malibu Pier Sport Fishing Company** (23000 Pacific Coast Hwy., ☎ 310/456–8030) offers boat excursions for $20 per half-day. The **Redondo Sport Fishing Company** (233 N. Harbor Dr., ☎ 310/372–2111) has various excursions available. Half-day charters start at $19 per person and a full day goes for $65. You can rent a pole for $7 and you'll need a license, which will cost $6.55. Sea bass, halibut, bonita, yellowtail, and barracuda are the usual catch. This company also runs whale-watching excursions in winter.

L.A. Harbor Sportfishing (☎ 310/547–9916) offers whale watching off Berth 79 from late December through March at the San Pedro Harbor, as well as just plain fishing. The cost of boating excursions ranges from $22 to $60; they take you as far as Catalina Island. **Skipper's Twenty Second Street Landing** (141 W. 22nd St., San Pedro, ☎ 310/832–8304) offers an overnight charter that affords you a look at the stars while waiting for a bite. These boats, complete with bunk beds and full galley, leave at 10 PM and 10:30 PM and dock between 5 PM and 9 PM the next night. Per-person price is $60. Day charters are available as well, at $28–$40, with half-day excursions on weekends for $22.

The most popular and unquestionably the most unusual form of fishing in the L.A. area involves no hooks, bait, or poles. The great **grunion runs**, which take place March–August, are a spectacular natural phenomenon in which hundreds of thousands of small silver fish, called grunion, wash up on Southern California beaches to spawn and lay their eggs in the sand. The **Cabrillo Marine Aquarium** in San Pedro (☎ 310/548–7562, *see* Tour 6 *in* Chapter 2, Exploring Los Angeles) has entertaining and educational programs about grunion throughout most of their spawning season. During certain months it is prohibited to touch the grunion, so please check with the Fish and Game Department (☎ 310/590–5132) before going to see them wash ashore.

Golf

The Parks and Recreation Department lists seven public 18-hole courses in Los Angeles. **Rancho Park Golf Course** (10460 W. Pico Blvd., ☎ 310/838–7373) is one of the most heavily played links in the entire country. It's a beautifully designed course but the towering pines will make those who slice or hook regret that they ever took up golf. There's a two-level driving range, a nine-hole pitch 'n' putt (☎ 310/839–4374), a snack bar, and a pro shop where you can rent clubs.

Several good public courses are in the San Fernando Valley. The **Balboa and Encino Golf Courses** (16821 Burbank Blvd., Encino, ☎ 818/995–1170) are right next to each other. The **Woodley Lakes Golf Course** (6331 Woodley Ave., Van Nuys, ☎ 818/780–6886) is flat as a board and has hardly any trees. In summer, however, the temperature in the Valley can get high enough to fry an egg on your putter, so be sure to bring lots of sunscreen and water. Down the road in Pacoima, you'll find little escape from the summer heat, but the **Hansen Dam Public Golf Course** (10400 Glen Oaks Blvd., ☎ 818/899–2200) has a buffet-style restaurant that serves plenty of cold drinks, as well as a driving range where you can warm up.

Perhaps the most concentrated area of golf courses in the city can be found in **Griffith Park.** Here you'll find two splendid 18-hole courses along with a challenging nine-hole course. **Harding Golf Course** and **Wilson Golf Course** (both at 4730 Crystal Springs Dr., ☎ 213/663–2555) are about 1½ miles inside the park entrance at Riverside Drive and Los Feliz Boulevard. Bridle paths surround the outer fairways, and the San Gabriel Mountains make a scenic background. The nine-hole **Roosevelt Course** (2650 N. Vermont Ave., ☎ 213/665–2011) can be reached through the park's Hillhurst Street entrance.

Yet another course in the Griffith Park vicinity, and one at which there's usually no waiting, is the nine-hole **Los Feliz Pitch 'n' Putt** (3207 Los Feliz Blvd., ☎ 213/663–7758). Other pitch 'n' putt courses in Los Angeles include **Holmby Hills** (601 Club View Dr., West Los Angeles, ☎ 310/276–1604) and **Penmar** (1233 Rose Ave., Venice, ☎ 310/396–6228).

Health Clubs

There are dozens of health-club chains in the city. **Bally's Nautilus Aerobics Plus** and **Bally's Holiday Spa Health Club and Sports Connection** are the most popular local chains. The Holiday Club, between Hollywood and Sunset boulevards (1628 El Centro, ☎ 213/461–0227), is the flagship operation, but to find the Bally's nearest you, call 800/695–8111. **Sports Club L.A.** (1835 S. Sepulveda Blvd., West Los Angeles, ☎ 310/473–1447) is a hot spot, attracting a diverse group of celebrities, such as James Woods and Monaco's Princess Stephanie.

Probably the most famous body-pumping facility of this nature in the city is **Gold's Gym** (358 Hampton Dr., Venice, ☎ 310/392–6004; another branch is in Hollywood at 1016 N. Cole Ave., ☎ 213/462–7012). This is where all the incredible hulks turn themselves into modern art. For $15 a day or $50 a week, several tons of weights and Nautilus machines can be yours. **World Gym** (812 Main St., Venice, ☎ 310/399–9888) is another famous iron-person's club. **Powerhouse Gym** (8053 Beverly Blvd., West Hollywood, ☎ 213/651–3636) is also a place to go if you're looking to pump yourself up while in town. The fee to use the facilities is $10 per day, or $40 per week.

Dance and Workout Studios

A popular place to reconfigure your figure is the trendy **Voight Fitness Center** (980 N. La Cienega Blvd., West Hollywood, ☎ 310/854–0741), providing the latest in hip-hop, step, and funk moves. For a less intimidating, neighborhoody kind of place that's convenient to downtown, visit **Studio A's** (2306 Hyperion Ave., Silverlake, ☎ 213/661–8311) user-friendly aerobics, jazz, and ballet classes.

Hiking

What makes Los Angeles a hiker's paradise is the multitude of different land- and seascapes to explore. **Arrowhead** and **Big Bear,** in the **San Bernardino National Forest** (*see* Chapter 8, Excursions from Los Angeles), many parts of the **Angeles National Forest,** and the **Angeles Crest** area have spectacular mountain hiking trails. Much of the terrain here is rugged, and if you're not familiar with these regions, it's advisable to contact the National Forest Service (☎ 818/790–1151) for information before you go.

Closer to the city, **Will Rogers Historic State Park** has a splendid nature trail. Other parks in the L.A. area that also have hiking trails include **Brookside Park, Elysian Park,** and **Griffith Park.** For more information on parks, *see* Chapter 2, Exploring Los Angeles.

In the Malibu area, **Leo Carillo State Beach** and the top of **Corral Canyon** offer incredible rock formations and caves to be explored on foot. In the hills east of **Paradise Cove,** a horse trail winds back into the canyons along a stream for several miles, eventually winding up at a beautiful waterfall. (*See also* Beaches, *below.*)

For further information on these or any other hiking locations in Los Angeles, contact the **Sierra Club** (3345 Wilshire Blvd., Suite 508, Los Angeles 90010, ☎ 213/387–4287).

Horseback Riding

Although horseback riding in Los Angeles is extremely popular, stables that rent horses are becoming an endangered species. Of the survivors, **Bar "S" Stables** (1850 Riverside Dr., Glendale, ☎ 818/242–8443) will rent you a horse for $13 an hour (plus a $10 deposit). Riders who come here can take advantage of over 50 miles of beautiful bridle trails in the Griffith Park area. **Sunset River Trails** (Rush St., at end of Peck Rd., El Monte, ☎ 818/444–2128) offers riders the nearby banks of the San Gabriel River to explore at $15 an hour. **Los Angeles Equestrian Center** (480 Riverside Dr., Burbank, ☎ 818/840–8401) rents pleasure horses—English and Western—for riding along bridle paths throughout the Griffith Park hills. Horses cost $13 per hour. **Sunset Ranch** (3400 Beachwood Dr., Hollywood, ☎ 213/469–5450) offers a $35 adventure (not including the cost of dinner). At sunset riders take a trail over the hill into Burbank, where they tie up their horses and dine at a Mexican restaurant.

Ice Skating

Rinks are all over the city. In the Valley, there's the **Pickwick Ice Center** (1001 Riverside Dr., Burbank, ☎ 818/846–0032). In Pasadena, try the **Ice Skating Center** (310 E. Green St., ☎ 818/578–0800) and, in Rolling Hills, try the **Culver City Ice Arena** (4545 Sepulveda Ave., ☎ 310/398–5718).

In-line and Roller Skating

All of the areas mentioned in Bicycling (*see above*) are also excellent for in-line and roller skating, though cyclists have the right of way. Venice Beach is the skating capital of the city—and maybe of the world.

If you're looking to get off the streets, there are a number of rinks in L.A. **Moonlight Rollerway** (5110 San Fernando Rd., Glendale, ☎ 818/241–3630) and **Skateland** (18140 Parthenia St., Northridge, ☎ 818/885–1491) are two of the more popular ones.

Jogging

A popular scenic course for students and downtown workers can be found at **Exposition Park.** Circling the Coliseum and Sports Arena is a jogging-workout trail with pull-up bars and other simple equipment placed every several hundred yards. **San Vicente Boulevard** in Santa Monica has a wide grassy median that splits the street for several picturesque miles. The **Hollywood Reservoir,** just east of Cahuenga Boulevard in the Hollywood Hills, is encircled by a 3.2-mile asphalt path and has a view of the Hollywood sign. Within hilly **Griffith Park** are thousands of acres' worth of hilly paths and challenging terrain, while Crystal Springs Drive from the main entrance at Los Feliz to the zoo is a relatively flat 5 miles. Circle Drive, around the perimeter of **UCLA** in Westwood, provides a 2½-mile run through academia, L.A.-style.

Racquetball and Handball

As with tennis, there are dozens of high schools and colleges all over town that have three-walled courts open to the public. The only catch is you have to wait until after school's out, or the weekend.

There are several indoor racquetball facilities throughout the city: the **Racquet Center** (10933 Ventura Blvd., Studio City, ☎ 818/760–2303), in the San Fernando Valley, offers court time for $10–$14, depending on when you play. There's another Racquet Center in South Pasadena (920 Lohman La., ☎ 213/258–4178). **YMCAs** throughout the city also have courts available based on hourly rates.

Skiing

Cross-Country
If you're into cross-country skiing, **Idyllwild,** above Palm Springs, offers excellent trails during most of the heavy-snow season. For information, call the Idyllwild Mountain Information Line (☎ 909/659–3259).

Downhill
A relatively short drive from downtown will bring you to some of the best snow skiing in the state. Just north of Pasadena, in the San Gabriel Mountains, are two ski areas: **Mt. Waterman** (☎ 818/440–1041) and

Kratka Ridge (☎ 818/449–1749), both of which have a couple of lifts and a range of slopes for beginning and advanced skiers. Farther east is **Mt. Baldy** (☎ 909/981–3344), off I–10 at the top of Mountain Avenue.

Ski resorts with accommodations can be found within 90 minutes of Los Angeles proper. **Big Bear** (*see* Chapter 8, Excursions from Los Angeles) is one of the most popular ski retreats on the West Coast, with a full range of accommodations, several ski lifts, night skiing, and one of the largest snowmaking operations in California. For information about Big Bear ski conditions, hotels, and special events, contact the Chamber of Commerce (☎ 909/878–3000).

Other ski areas in the vicinity of Big Bear include **Bear Mountain** (☎ 909/585–2519), **Snow Valley** (☎ 909/867–2751), **Mountain High** (☎ 714/972–9242), and **Snow Summit** (☎ 909/866–4621). All have snowmaking capabilities, and many have lights for night skiing. Call for directions and information about ski conditions.

Tennis

Many public parks have courts that require an hourly fee. **Lincoln Park** (Lincoln and Wilshire Blvd., Santa Monica), **Griffith Park** (Riverside Dr. and Los Feliz Blvd.), and **Barrington Park** (Barrington just south of Sunset Blvd. in L.A.) all have well-maintained courts with lights.

For a shorter wait, and no fee at all, there are a number of local high schools and colleges that leave their court gates unlocked on the weekends. Contact the school in question to obtain the required permit. There are several nice courts on the campus of **USC** (off Vermont St. entrance), a few on the campus of **Paul Revere Junior High School** (Sunset Blvd. and Mandeville Canyon Rd., Brentwood), and a few more at **Palisades High School** (Temescal Canyon Rd., Pacific Palisades)—and that's only the tip of this iceberg.

For a complete list of the public tennis courts in Los Angeles, contact the **L.A. Department of Recreation and Parks** (☎ 213/485–5515) or the **Southern California Tennis Association** (Los Angeles Tennis Center, UCLA Campus, 420 Circle Dr., Los Angeles 90024, ☎ 310/208–3838).

Water Sports

Boating and Kayaking

Sailing is one of the most popular activities in Southern California, and you don't have to own a boat to captain one. **Rent-A-Sail** (13719 Fiji Way, Marina del Rey, ☎ 310/822–1868) will rent you everything from canoes to powerboats or 14- to 25-foot sailboats for anywhere from $16 to $36 per hour plus a $20 deposit. No boating licenses are required, but if you've got your eye on one of the larger vessels, you must have prior sailing experience.

Big Bear and **Lake Arrowhead** (*see* Chapter 8, Excursions from Los Angeles) open up a whole different world of freshwater adventure. Canoes, motorboats, and waterskiing equipment can be rented from a number of outfits in both towns. Big Bear even offers parasailing for those who'd rather be above it all. For information about both of these lakes and nearby rental facilities, contact the Big Bear Chamber of Commerce (☎ 909/878–3000).

Action Water Sports (4144 Lincoln Blvd., Marina del Rey, ☎ 310/306–9539) rents kayaks for $35 per day during the summer.

Jetskiing

This is another booming sport on the lakes at Big Bear and Arrow-head, although Jet Skis can be expensive to rent. For information, con-tact the Big Bear Chamber of Commerce (☎ 909/878–3000).

Scuba Diving and Snorkeling

Diving and snorkeling off Leo Carillo State Beach, Catalina, and the Channel Islands is considered some of the best on the Pacific coast. Dive shops, such as **New England Divers** (4148 Viking Way, Long Beach, ☎ 310/421–8939) and **Dive & Surf** (504 N. Broadway, Redondo Beach, ☎ 310/372–8423), will provide you with everything you need for your voyage beneath the waves. Snorkeling equipment runs $9–$14 per day, while full scuba gear for certified divers runs $50–$62.50 per day, with prices cut for subsequent days. Diving charters to Catalina and the Channel Islands as well as certification training can be arranged through these dive shops.

Surfing

The signature water sport in L.A. is surfing . . . and rightfully so. Southern California beaches offer a wide variety of surfing venues, along with a number of places to rent boards. For a complete listing of the best surfing areas, *see* Beaches, *below.*

Windsurfing

Hanging 10 has traditionally involved a surfer, a board, a wave, and a few toes. Since a sail was added to this equipment, however, wind-surfing has become one of the most popular water sports ever. Good windsurfing can be found all along the coast, and there are a number of places from which certified windsurfers can rent equipment. **Natural Progression** (22935 Pacific Coast Hwy., Malibu, ☎ 310/456–6302) leases windsurfing equipment for about $40 per day.

BEACHES

The beach scene is an integral part of the Southern California lifestyle. There is no public attraction more popular in L.A. than the white, sandy playgrounds that line the deep blue Pacific.

From downtown, the easiest way to hit the coast is by taking the Santa Monica Freeway (I–10) due west. Once you reach the end of the free-way, I–10 turns into the famous Highway 1, better known as the Pa-cific Coast Highway, or PCH, and continues up to Oregon. Other basic routes from the downtown area include Pico, Olympic, Santa Mon-ica, Sunset, or Wilshire boulevards. The RTD bus line runs every 20 minutes to and from the beaches along each of these streets.

Los Angeles County beaches (and state beaches operated by the county) have lifeguards. Public parking (for a fee) is available at most. The fol-lowing beaches are listed in north–south order. Some are excellent for swimming, some for surfing (check with lifeguards for current condi-tions), and others are better for exploring.

Leo Carillo State Beach. This beach along a rough and mountainous stretch of coastline is the most fun at low tide, when a spectacular array of tide pools blossom for all to see. Rock formations on the beach have created some great secret coves for picnickers looking for solitude. There are hik-ing trails, sea caves, and tunnels, and whales, dolphins, and sea lions are often seen swimming in the offshore kelp beds. The waters here are rocky and best for experienced surfers and scuba divers; fishing is good. Pic-turesque campgrounds are set back from the beach. Camping fee is $16

Los Angeles Area Beaches

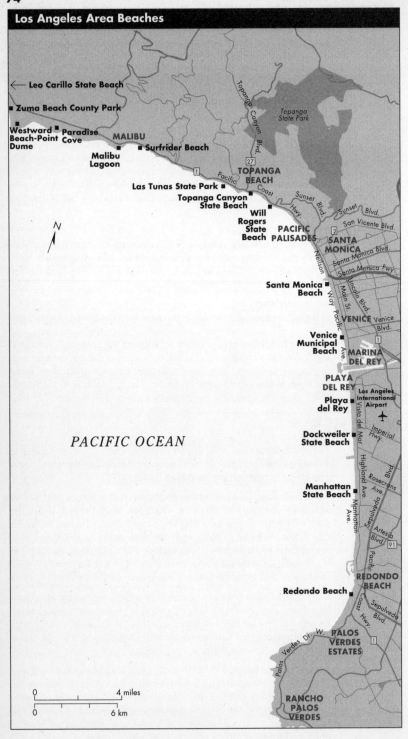

← Leo Carillo State Beach

■ Zuma Beach County Park

■ Westward Beach-Point Dume   ■ Paradise Cove   **MALIBU**

Malibu Lagoon   ■ Surfrider Beach

Topanga State Park

Topanga Canyon Blvd.

27   **TOPANGA BEACH**

1   Pacific   Coast

Las Tunas State Park ■

Topanga Canyon State Beach ■

Will Rogers State Beach ■   Sunset Blvd.

Sunset   Blvd.

PACIFIC PALISADES

San Vicente Blvd.

2   **SANTA MONICA**

Santa Monica Blvd.

Santa Monica Fwy.

Santa Monica Beach ■

Nielson

Pacific   Way

Main St.

Lincoln Blvd.

VENICE   Venice Blvd.

1

Venice Municipal Beach ■

Pacific   Ave.

MARINA DEL REY

PLAYA DEL REY

Los Angeles International Airport ✈

Playa del Rey ■

Vista del Mar

Imperial Hwy.

Dockweiler State Beach ■

Highland Ave.

Rosecrans   Blvd.

Manhattan State Beach ■

Manhattan Ave.

Sepulveda

Artesia Blvd.   91

PACIFIC OCEAN

REDONDO BEACH

Redondo Beach ■

Pacific   Coast   Hwy.

Sepulveda Blvd.

W. Palos Verdes Dr.   **PALOS VERDES ESTATES**   1

Palos Verdes Dr.

| 0 | | 4 miles |
| 0 | | 6 km |

RANCHO PALOS VERDES

per night. *35000 block of PCH, Malibu, ☎ 818/880–0350 or 800/444–7275. Facilities: parking, lifeguard, rest rooms, showers, fire pits.*

Zuma Beach County Park. This is Malibu's largest and sandiest beach, and a favorite spot of surfers. It's also a haven for high-school students who have discovered Nautilus Plus. *30050 PCH, Malibu, ☎ 310/457–9891. Facilities: parking, lifeguard, rest rooms, showers, food, playground, volleyball.*

Westward Beach/Point Dume State Beach. Another favorite spot for surfing, this ½-mile-long sandy beach has tide pools and sandstone cliffs. *South end of Westward Beach Rd., Malibu, ☎ 310/457–9891. Facilities: parking, lifeguard, rest rooms, food.*

Paradise Cove. With its pier and equipment rentals, this sandy beach is a mecca for sportfishing boats. Though swimming is allowed, there are lifeguards during the summer only. *28128 PCH, Malibu, ☎ 310/457–9891. Facilities: parking, rest rooms, showers, food (concessions open summer only).*

Malibu Lagoon State Beach/Surfrider Beach. The steady 3- to 5-foot waves make this beach, just north of Malibu Pier, a great long-board surfing beach. The International Surfing Contest is held here in September. Water runoff from Malibu Canyon forms a natural lagoon, which is a sanctuary for many birds. There are also nature trails perfect for romantic sunset strolls. *23200 block of PCH, Malibu, ☎ 818/880–0350. Facilities: parking, lifeguard, rest rooms, picnicking, visitor center.*

Las Tunas State Beach. Las Tunas is small (1,300 feet long, covering a total of only 2 acres), narrow, and sandy, with some rocky areas, and set beneath a bluff. Surf fishing is the biggest attraction here. There is no lifeguard, and swimming is not encouraged because of steel groins set offshore to prevent erosion. *19400 block of PCH, Malibu, ☎ 310/457–9891. Facilities: parking, rest rooms.*

Topanga Canyon State Beach. This rocky beach stretches from the mouth of the Topanga Canyon down to Coastline Drive. Catamarans dance in these waves and skid onto the sands of this popular beach, where dolphins sometimes come close enough to shore to startle sunbathers. The area near the canyon is a great surfing spot. *18700 block of PCH, Malibu, ☎ 310/394–3266. Facilities: parking, lifeguard, rest rooms, food.*

Will Rogers State Beach. This wide, sandy beach is several miles long and has even surf. Parking in the lot here is limited, but there is plenty of beach, volleyball, and bodysurfing, attracting a predominantly gay crowd. *15800 PCH, Pacific Palisades, ☎ 310/394–3266. Facilities: parking, lifeguard, rest rooms.*

Santa Monica Beach. This is one of L.A.'s most popular beaches. In addition to a pier and a promenade, a man-made breakwater just offshore has caused the sand to collect and form the widest stretch of beach on the entire Pacific coast. And wider beaches mean more bodies. If you're up for some sightseeing on land, this is one of the more popular gathering places for L.A.'s young, toned, and bronzed. All in all, the 2-mile-long beach is well equipped with bike paths, facilities for the disabled, playgrounds, and volleyball. In summer, free rock and jazz concerts are held at the pier on Thursday nights. *West of PCH, Santa Monica, ☎ 310/394–3266. Facilities: parking, lifeguard, rest rooms, showers.*

Venice Municipal Beach. While the surf and sands of Venice are fine, the main attraction here is the boardwalk scene. Venice combines the beefcake of some of L.A.'s most serious bodybuilders with the productions of lively crafts merchants and street musicians. There are roller skaters, comedians, and rappers to entertain you, and cafés to feed you. You can rent bikes at Venice Pier Bike Shop (21 Washington St.) and skates at Skatey's (102 Washington St.). *1531 Ocean Front Walk,*

Venice, ☎ *310/394–3266. Facilities: parking, rest rooms, showers, food, picnicking.*

Playa del Rey. South of Marina del Rey lies one of the more under-rated beaches in Southern California. Its sprawling white sands stretch from the southern tip of Marina del Rey almost 2 miles down to Dock-weiler Beach. The majority of the crowds that frequent these sands are young. One of the more attractive features of this beach is an area called Del Rey Lagoon, a grassy oasis in the heart of Playa del Rey. A lovely pond is inhabited by dozens of ducks, and barbecue pits and tables are available to picnickers. *6660 Esplanade, Playa del Rey. Facilities: parking, lifeguard, rest rooms, food.*

Dockweiler State Beach. There are consistent waves for surfing here, and it is not crowded, due to an unsightly powerplant with towering smokestacks parked right on the beach. While the plant presents no danger to swimmers in the area, its mere presence, combined with the jumbo jets taking off overhead from L.A.'s International Airport, makes this beach a better place for surfing or working out than for lying out. There is firewood for sale for barbecues on the beach; beach fires are legal in this area as long as they are contained within the special pits that are already set up along the beach. *Harbor Channel to Vista del Mar and Grand Ave., Playa del Rey,* ☎ *310/322–5008. Facilities: parking, lifeguard, rest rooms, showers.*

Manhattan State Beach. Here are 44 acres of sandy beach for swimming, diving, surfing, and fishing. Polliwog Park is a charming, grassy landscape a few yards back from the beach that parents with young children may appreciate. Ducks waddle around a small pond, and picnickers enjoy some convenient facilities like showers and rest rooms. *West of Strand, Manhattan Beach,* ☎ *310/372–2166. Facilities: volleyball, parking, lifeguard, rest rooms, showers, food.*

Redondo State Beach. The beach is wide, sandy, and usually packed in summer, and parking is limited. The Redondo Pier marks the starting point of the beach area, which continues south for more than 2 miles along a heavily developed shoreline community. Storms have damaged some of the restaurants and shops along the pier, but plenty of others are still functioning. Excursion boats, boat launching ramps, and fishing are other attractions. There is a series of rock and jazz concerts held at the pier during the summer. *Foot of Torrance Blvd., Redondo Beach,* ☎ *310/372–2166. Facilities: volleyball, parking, lifeguard, rest rooms, showers, food.*

5 Dining

By Bruce David
Colen

Updated by
Jane E. Lasky

IN THE HIGH-LIVING '80S, Los Angeles emerged as a top gastronomic capital of the world, and as the 90s progress, there are no signs of slowing down. Where once the city was known only for its chopped Cobb salad, Green Goddess dressing, drive-in hamburger stands, and outdoor barbecues, today it is home to many of the best French and Northern Italian restaurants in the United States and so many places featuring international cuisines that listing them would be like a roll call at the United Nations. Despite the recession, many new—and good—dining establishments open every week, and sometimes it seems that there are more chairs, booths, and banquettes than there are bodies to fill them. The result is a fierce competition among upscale restaurateurs that has made L.A. one of the least expensive big cities—here or abroad—in which to eat well.

Locals tend to dine early, between 7:30 and 9 PM, in part a holdover from when this was a "studio" town, and the filmmaking day started at 6 AM (these days it's more to allow for early-morning jogging and gym time). Reservations are essential at the best restaurants, and at almost all restaurants on weekend evenings.

One caveat: The city recently enforced a no-smoking ordinance that applies to all restaurants. If you do want to smoke, there are ways around this—choose a restaurant with an outdoor area (smoking is allowed outdoors) or one that incorporates a full-scale bar (lounge areas are exempt from the no-smoking rule). Also, some of the incorporated cities like West Hollywood and Beverly Hills make their own rules, so call ahead to see if the place where you want to dine permits smoking.

CATEGORY	COST*
$$$$	over $50
$$$	$30–$50
$$	$20–$30
$	under $20

per person, excluding 8.25% tax, service, and drinks

American

Beverly Hills

$$$ **Grill on the Alley.** This is the closest Los Angeles gets in terms of look and atmosphere to a traditional San Francisco bar and grill, with its dark-wood paneling and brass trim. The food is basic American, cleanly and simply prepared—the Grill is known for great steaks, fresh seafood, chicken pot pies, and crab cakes. Repeat customers like the restaurant's creamy Cobb salad and homemade rice pudding. This is a great place for a power lunch. ✕ *9560 Dayton Way,* ☎ *310/276–0615. Reservations required. AE, DC, MC, V. Closed Sun. Valet parking in evening.*

$ **Ed Debevic's.** This is a good place to take the kids or to go yourself if you're feeling nostalgic. Old Coca-Cola signs, a blaring jukebox, gum-chewing waitresses in bobby socks, and meat loaf and mashed potatoes take you back to the diners of the '50s. Soda jerks are on hand to serve fountain delights like a black cow or the world's smallest hot-fudge sundae. ✕ *134 N. La Cienega,* ☎ *310/659–1952. Reservations for large parties only. AE, D, DC, MC, V. Valet parking.*

$ **RJ'S the Rib Joint.** The large barrel of free peanuts at the door and the sawdust on the floor set a folksy atmosphere. An outstanding salad bar has dozens of fresh choices and return privileges, and there are gi-

Los Angeles Dining (Boxes Refer to Detail Maps)

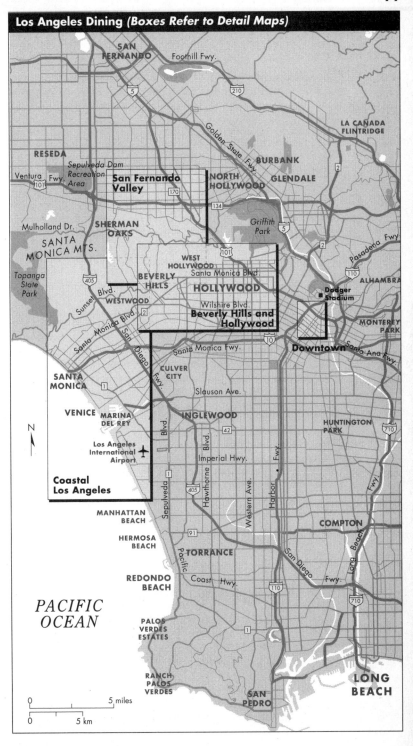

SAN FERNANDO

Foothill Fwy.

LA CAÑADA FLINTRIDGE

RESEDA

Golden State Fwy.

BURBANK

GLENDALE

Ventura Fwy.

Sepulveda Dam Recreation Area

San Fernando Valley

NORTH HOLLYWOOD

Pasadena Fwy.

Mulholland Dr.

SHERMAN OAKS

Griffith Park

SANTA MONICA MTS.

Topanga State Park

WEST HOLLYWOOD

BEVERLY HILLS

Santa Monica Blvd

HOLLYWOOD

ALHAMBRA

WESTWOOD

Sunset Blvd.

Santa Monica Blvd.

Wilshire Blvd.

Beverly Hills and Hollywood

Dodger Stadium

MONTEREY PARK

San Diego Fwy.

Santa Monica Fwy.

Downtown

Santa Ana Fwy.

SANTA MONICA

CULVER CITY

Slauson Ave.

VENICE

MARINA DEL REY

INGLEWOOD

HUNTINGTON PARK

N

Los Angeles International Airport

Hawthorne Blvd.

Imperial Hwy.

Western Ave.

Harbor Fwy.

Coastal Los Angeles

Sepulveda Blvd.

MANHATTAN BEACH

COMPTON

HERMOSA BEACH

TORRANCE

Long Beach Fwy.

REDONDO BEACH

Pacific Coast Hwy.

San Diego Fwy.

PACIFIC OCEAN

PALOS VERDES ESTATES

RANCH PALOS VERDES

SAN PEDRO

LONG BEACH

0   5 miles

0   5 km

gantic portions of everything—from ribs, chili, and barbecued chicken, to mile-high layer cakes—all at very reasonable prices. ✕ *252 N. Beverly Dr.,* ☎ *310/274–7427. Reservations advised. AE, D, DC, MC, V. Valet parking in evening.*

Century City

$ **Dive!** When you walk into this Century City eatery, you'll feel as though you've just climbed down the hatch of a submarine. The sandwiches are nautical miles ahead of what you might find at a traditional deli, with such specialties as fajita sub cucina, a Chinese chicken salad sub, and a brick oven–baked Tuscan steak sub. Be sure not to miss out on the sublime desserts: Try the Dive, s'mores, or lemon-bar concoction with white chocolate and raspberry sauce. ✕ *10250 Santa Monica Blvd.,* ☎ *310/788–DIVE. No reservations. AE, D, DC, MC, V.*

Downtown

$$$ **Pacific Dining Car.** This 70-year-old restaurant, one of L.A.'s oldest, is open around the clock. Best known for well-aged steaks, rack of lamb, and an extensive California wine list at fair prices, it's a favorite haunt of politicians and lawyers around City Hall and of sports fans after Dodgers games. High tea is served every day from 3 to 5:30 PM. ✕ *1310 W. 6th St.,* ☎ *213/483–6000. Reservations advised. AE, DC, MC, V. Valet parking.*

$ **Philippe's The Original.** This downtown landmark near Union Station and Chinatown has been serving its famous French dip sandwich (four kinds of meat on a freshly baked roll) since 1908. Still a family-run establishment, the Phillipe keeps with tradition, from sawdust on the floor to long, wooden tables for customers to sit around and schmooze like one big, happy family. The home cooking includes potato salad, cole slaw, hearty breakfasts, and an enormous pie selection brought in fresh daily from a nearby bakery. The best bargain: a cup of java for only 10¢. ✕ *1001 N. Alameda St.,* ☎ *213/628–3781. No reservations. No credit cards.*

$$–$$$ **Nicola.** Renowned local architect Michael Rotondi created the contemporary backdrop for this restaurant—celebrity chef Larry Nicola's latest venture—in the Sanwa Bank Building. The two-room restaurant provides a contrast in moods, one an intimate dining arena, the other more open and airy; both see a lot of business deals sealed over lunch and dinner. Although the seasonal menu is largely American, ethnic touches abound with entrées, such as broiled Chilean sea bass with caramelized orange and ginger potatoes, roasted prime rib of pork with tomatillo sauce and corn succotash, and Mediterranean range chicken with tabbouleh and Lebanese fried potatoes. The wine list is very impressive, with plenty of California favorites. A kiosk in the courtyard operated by Nicola is popular with area workers looking for a quick (but tasty) bite. ✕ *601 S. Figueroa St.,* ☎ *213/485–0927. Reservations advised. AE, D, DC, MC, V. No Sat. lunch, closed Sun. Valet parking.*

San Fernando Valley

$ **Paty's.** Located near NBC, Warner Brothers, and the Disney Studio, Paty's is a good place for stargazing without having to mortgage your home to pay for the meal. This is an all-American–style upgraded coffee shop with comfortable, eclectic decor. Breakfasts are charming; the omelets are plump, and the biscuits are homemade and served with high-quality jam. Lunches and dinners include Swiss steak and a hearty beef stew that is served in a hollowed-out loaf of home-baked bread. Roast turkey is served with dressing and a moist, sweet loaf of home-baked nut or raisin bread. All desserts are worth saving room for: New Orleans bread pudding with a hot brandy sauce is popular, and the Dan-

Downtown Los Angeles Dining

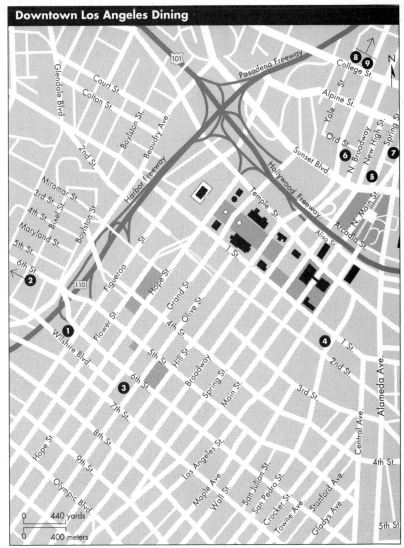

Clearwater Cafe, **8**
Mon Kee Seafood
Restaurant, **5**
Nicola, **1**
Ocean Seafood
Restaurant, **6**
Pacific Dining Car, **2**
Philippe The
Original, **7**

Restaurant
Horikawa, **4**
Rex Il Ristorante, **3**
Yujean Kang's
Gourmet Chinese
Cuisine, **9**

Beverly Hills and Hollywood Dining

Antonio's
Restaurant, **35**
Arnie Morton's of
Chicago, **28**
Bistro Garden, **13**
Ca' Brea, **36**
California Pizza
Kitchen, **15**
Canter's, **25**
Cava, **30**
Cha Cha Cha, **42**
Chan Dara, **39**
Chopstix, **34**

Citrus, **37**
Dining Room, **14**
Dive, **3**
Ed Debevic's, **29**
El Cholo, **43**
Greenblatt's, **20**
Grill on the Alley, **11**
Hard Rock Cafe, **26**
Harry's Bar &
American Grill, **2**
Il Fornaio Cucina
Italiana, **10**
Jimmy's, **4**

Joss, **17**
La Veranda, **16**
La Chardonnay, **24**
Le Dome, **21**
Locanda Veneta, **27**
L'Orangerie, **22**
Louise's Trattoria, **40**
The Mandarin, **6**
Morton's, **23**
Nate 'n' Al's, **8**
The Palm, **18**
Prego, **9**

Primi, **1**
RJ's the Rib Joint, **12**
Restaurant Katsu, **41**
Roscoe's House of
Chicken 'n'
Waffles, **38**
Rustica, **7**
Sofi, **31**
Spago, **19**
Tavola Calda, **32**
Tommy Tang's, **33**
Trader Vic's, **5**

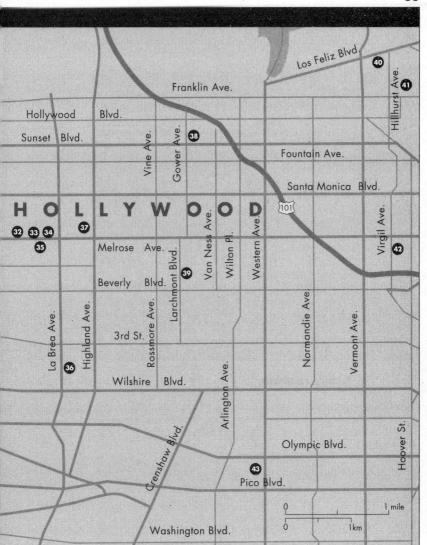

ishes are gigantic. If you're in a hurry, call ahead with your order and the restaurant will deliver directly to your car. ✕ *10001 Riverside Dr., Toluca Lake,* ☎ *818/760–9164. No reservations. No credit cards.*

West Hollywood

$$$–$$$$ **Arnie Morton's of Chicago.** The West Coast addition to this ever-ex-
★   panding national chain brought joy and cholesterol to the hearts of Los Angeles meat lovers, many of whom claim that Morton's serves the best steaks in town. In addition to a 24-ounce porterhouse, a New York strip, and a double-cut filet mignon, there are giant veal and lamb chops, thick cuts of prime rib, and imported lobsters at market prices. ✕ *435 S. La Cienega Blvd.,* ☎ *310/246–1501. Reservations advised. Jacket required. AE, D, DC, MC, V. No lunch.*

$$$ **Morton's.** When the brother-and-sister owners of this trendy restaurant decided to open an upscale clubhouse for the music and entertainment industry, it was only natural that choice steaks should be the cornerstone of the menu—their father is *the* Arnie Morton of Chicago (*see above*). Good broiled fish and chicken, as well as pasta, veal, and pizza have since been added. ✕ *8764 Melrose Ave.,* ☎ *310/276– 5205. Reservations required. Jacket required. AE, D, MC, V. Closed Sun. Valet parking.*

$$$ **The Palm.** A West-Coast replay of the famous Manhattan steak house— down to the New York–style waiters rushing you through your Bronx cheesecake—this is where you'll find the biggest and best lobster, good steaks and chops, great french-fried onion rings, and paper-thin potato slices. The big deal for dinner, though, is the prime rib. ✕ *9001 Santa Monica Blvd.,* ☎ *310/550–8811. Reservations advised. AE, DC, MC, V. No weekend lunch. Valet parking.*

$$ **Hard Rock Cafe.** Big burgers, rich milk shakes, banana splits, BLTs, and other prenouvelle food delights, along with loud music and rock-and-roll memorabilia, have made this '50s-era barn of a café the favorite of local teenagers. The large, busy bar is where people hang out, even if they're not waiting for a table. You'll know the place by the fishtail Cadillac jutting out of the roof, a trademark of the chain. ✕ *8600 Beverly Blvd.,* ☎ *310/276–7605. No reservations. AE, DC, MC, V. Valet parking in Beverly Center.*

$ **Roscoe's House of Chicken 'n' Waffles.** The name of this very casual eatery doesn't sound all that appetizing, but don't be fooled: This is *the* place for real down-home southern cooking. Just ask the people who drive from all over the L.A. basin for Roscoe's fried chicken, waffles, grits, and potatoes at bargain prices. ✕ *1514 N. Gower St.,* ☎ *213/466–9329. AE, D, DC, MC, V.*

Westside

(COASTAL LOS ANGELES DINING MAP)

$$–$$$ **West Beach Cafe.** It seems that Bruce Marder can do no wrong. More
★   than 15 years ago he opened this upscale restaurant within a Frisbee toss of the action on the Venice Beach strand. Next came Rebecca's, just across the street, where Mexican food is treated as semi-haute cuisine and idolized by the upscale. Then came his most recent hit, the Broadway Deli in Santa Monica (*see below*). Best bets at the West Beach are Caesar salad, rack of lamb, ravioli with port and radicchio, fisherman's soup, and what many consider the best hamburger and fries in all of Los Angeles. There's also a fabulous selection of French wines and liqueurs. ✕ *60 N. Venice Blvd.,* ☎ *310/823–5396. Reservations advised. AE, D, DC, MC, V. Closed Mon. Valet parking.*

$$ **Gilliland's.** Gerri Gilliland was teaching cooking in her native Ireland, took a vacation in Southern California, and never went back. Instead, she stayed and created this charming, warm restaurant, which offers

Beaurivage, **2**
Border Grill, **9**
Broadway Deli, **7**
Chinois on Main, **11**
Dynasty Room, **16**
Gilliland's, **10**
Gladstone's 4 Fish, **4**
Granita, **1**
Hotel Bel-Air, **17**
Ocean Avenue, **8**
Orleans, **13**
Remi, **6**
Schatsi on Main, **12**
Tra di Noi, **3**
Valentino, **15**
Warszawa, **5**
West Beach Cafe, **14**

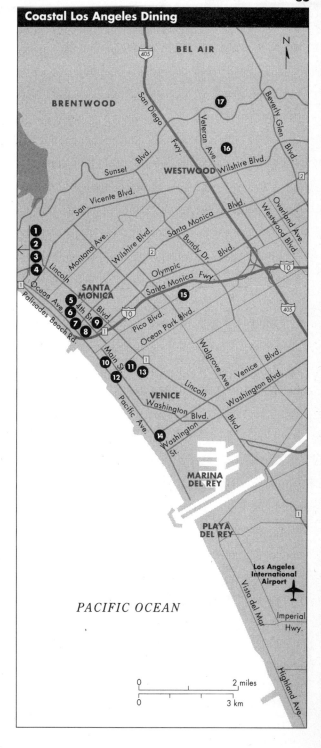

Coastal Los Angeles Dining

the best of both culinary worlds and showcases her fascination with Mediterranean dishes. The soda bread, Irish stew, and corned beef and cabbage are wonderful. A real treat are the Louisiana crab cakes served with fresh corn, herbs, onions, tomatillo sauce, and sour cream. ✕ *2424 Main St., Santa Monica,* ☎ *310/392–3901. Reservations advised. AE, D, DC, MC, V.*

$$ Ocean Avenue. This cavernous restaurant, operating since 1946, isn't right on the water, but the Pacific is just across the street, so ask for a table by the window. Low ceilings and mood lighting set an intimate atmosphere, with well-spaced tables and attentive service. Daily specials are always a good choice, but if in doubt, order the cioppino, a fish stew made with Dungeness crab, clams, mussels, and prawns, or the Maine lobster, either boiled or steamed. To start, try the crab cakes with ginger horseradish. Try the apple phyllo with caramel sauce, a light confection that melts in the mouth. ✕ *1401 Ocean Ave., Santa Monica,* ☎ *310/394–5669. Reservations advised. AE, DC, MC, V. Valet parking.*

$–$$ Broadway Deli. The name is misleading, so don't come here expecting hot corned beef and pastrami sandwiches. This joint venture of Michel Richard and Bruce Marder is a cross between a European brasserie and an upscale diner. Whatever you feel like eating, you will probably find it on the menu, from a platter of assorted smoked fish or Caesar salad to shepherd's pie, carpaccio, steak, and broiled salmon with creamed spinach. There are also excellent side dishes (such as corn muffins, mashed potatoes with mushroom gravy, and potato pancakes), desserts, and freshly baked breads. ✕ *1457 3rd St. Promenade, Santa Monica,* ☎ *310/451–0616. No reservations. AE, MC, V. Valet parking weekends and evenings.*

$ Gladstone's 4 Fish. This is undoubtedly the most popular restaurant along the Southern California coast, serving well over a million beach-goers a year; it has spawned a sister restaurant in Universal Studios' CityWalk, also worth a visit. Perhaps the food is not the greatest in the world, but familiar seashore fare is prepared adequately and in large portions, and the prices are certainly right. Best bets: crab chowder, steamed clams, three-egg omelets, hamburgers, barbecued ribs, and chili. And then there's the wonderful view, especially from the beachside terrace—ideal for whale-, porpoise-, and people-watching. ✕ *17300 Pacific Coast Hwy. (at Sunset Blvd.), Pacific Palisades,* ☎ *310/454–3474. Reservations advised. AE, D, DC, MC, V. Valet parking.*

Cajun

Westside

(COASTAL LOS ANGELES DINING MAP)

$$–$$$ Orleans. The jambalaya and gumbo dishes are hot—in more ways than one—at this spacious eatery, where the cuisine was created with the help of New Orleans celebrity-chef Paul Prudhomme. The blackened salmon is probably the best catch on the menu. Most menu items are available in low-sodium, low-fat versions; just ask. ✕ *11705 National Blvd., W. Los Angeles,* ☎ *310/479–4187. Reservations advised. AE, DC, MC, V. Valet parking.*

California Cuisine

Beverly Hills

$$$ Bistro Garden. The flower-banked outdoor dining terrace makes this the quintessential Southern California "ladies who lunch" experience. It's chic and lively without being overly pretentious or too "Hollywood." There's excellent smoked salmon, fresh cracked crab, steak tartare, calves'

Adriano's Ristorante, **1**

Art's Delicatessen, **5**

Barzac Brasserie, **6**

Europa, **3**

Paty's, **7**

Pinot Bistro, **4**

Posto, **2**

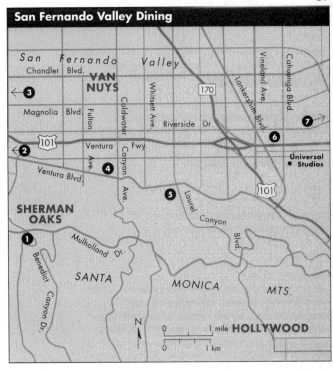

San Fernando Valley Dining

liver with bacon, and a unique apple pancake. ✗ *176 N. Canon Dr.,* ☎ *310/550–3900. Reservations required. Jacket and tie at dinner. AE, DC, MC, V. Closed Sun. Valet parking.*

$$$ Dining Room. ★ Located in the Regent Beverly Wilshire, this elegant, European-looking salon is the best thing to happen to L.A. hotel dining in decades. It offers wonderful California cuisine (try the loin of Colorado lamb accompanied by eggplant and sweet pepper lasagna), plus splendid service, at prices that are relatively reasonable. A three-course fixed-price menu costs $38; a four-course sampler dinner is priced at $75. Adjoining the Dining Room is an equally attractive, sophisticated cocktail lounge, with romantic lighting and a pianist playing show tunes. ✗ *9500 Wilshire Blvd.,* ☎ *310/275–5200. Reservations advised. Jacket and tie. AE, D, DC, MC, V. Valet parking.*

$$ La Veranda. David Slay had a very popular restaurant of the same name in St. Louis, then came West. He has succeeded in making his fortune in hypercritical Beverly Hills, serving, of all things, regional American cooking with Italian overtones. His warm, intimate place is loaded with celebrities and just plain folk back for more of Slay's pan-seared calves' liver with caramelized onions and sweet marsala sauce, or the herb-crusted rack of lamb with chili mint au jus and pancetta-and-pine-nut wild rice. A grazing menu on Sunday nights allows you to sample the cuisine in smaller portions: Good bets are sautéed spinach tossed with lemon and Parmesan cheese and roasted garlic with grilled bread. ✗ *225 S. Beverly Dr.,* ☎ *310/274–7246. Reservations advised. Jacket required. AE, DC, MC, V. No weekend lunch.*

$ California Pizza Kitchen. This member of the popular West Coast chain is *the* place to go for a good wood-fired pizza at a fair price, without the usual pizza-parlor surroundings. There's an immaculate, pleasingly modern dining room, plus counter service by the open kitchen, and a wide, rather esoteric choice of pizza toppings. Try the tandoori pie, which is made without cheese. The pastas are equally interesting and carefully prepared. The few sidewalk tables are in great demand. ✕ *207 S. Beverly Dr.,* ☎ *310/275–1101. No reservations. AE, D, DC, MC, V.*

West Hollywood

$$–$$$ **Citrus.** One of L.A.'s most prominent chefs, Michel Richard, creates
★ superb dishes by blending French and American cuisines. You can't miss with the delectable tuna burger, the impossibly thin angel-hair pasta, or the deep-fried potatoes, sautéed foie gras, rare duck, or carpaccio salad. For an unusual taste treat, try the chicken in mushroom skin. Get your doctor's permission before even looking at Richard's irresistible desserts. ✕ *6703 Melrose Ave.,* ☎ *213/857–0034. Reservations advised. Jacket required. AE, DC, MC, V. Closed Sun. Valet parking.*

$$–$$$ **Spago.** This is the restaurant that propelled owner/chef Wolfgang Puck
★ into the international culinary spotlight. He deserves every accolade for raising California cuisine to a totally tantalizing gastronomic experience, using only the finest West Coast produce. The proof is in the tasting: roasted cumin lamb on lentil salad with fresh coriander and yogurt chutney, fresh oysters with green chili and black pepper mignonette, grilled free-range chickens, and grilled Alaskan baby salmon. The biggest seller is not on the menu, so ask: It's known as the Jewish pizza, with cream cheese and smoked salmon as toppings. As for Puck's incredible desserts, they're on Weight Watchers' Most Wanted List. This is the place to see *People* magazine live, but you'll have to put up with the noise in exchange. Be safe: Make reservations at least two weeks in advance. ✕ *1114 Horn Ave.,* ☎ *310/652–4025. Reservations required. Jacket required. D, DC, MC, V. No lunch. Valet parking.*

Westside

(COASTAL LOS ANGELES DINING MAP)

$$$ **Hotel Bel-Air.** You couldn't ask for a lovelier setting, in a romantic country garden, and the menu matches—the California-Continental cooking is very good indeed, be it for breakfast, lunch, or dinner. Seasonal dishes use fresh fare in a fanciful way, like tuna and monkfish medallions with chive mashed potatoes; peppered swordfish medallions on a bed of artichokes, mushrooms, asparagus, and corn in a tarragon lobster sauce; and grilled fillet of Great Lakes whitefish with saffron couscous. ✕ *701 Stone Canyon Rd., Bel Air,* ☎ *310/472–1211. Reservations advised. Jacket and tie at dinner. AE, D, DC, MC, V. Valet parking.*

$$–$$$ **Granita.** Wolfgang Puck's Granita has such stunning interior details as handmade tiles embedded with seashells, blown-glass lighting fixtures, and etched-glass panels with wavy glass. It's as close as you'll come to the beach without getting sand in your shoes. Even the blasé Malibu film colony is impressed. While Puck's menu here favors seafood items, such as grilled John Dory with stir-fried vegetables and curry lime sauce and grilled Atlantic salmon in lemongrass broth with seared carrots and wild mushrooms, the menu also features some of his standard favorites. Among the greats are spicy shrimp pizza with sun-dried tomatoes and herb pesto, roasted Chinese duck with dried fruit chutney, seared foie gras with caramelized walnuts and blood-orange port-wine glaze, and Caesar salad with oven-baked bruschetta. ✕ *23725 W. Malibu Rd., Malibu,* ☎ *310/456–0488. Reservations required far ahead, especially for weekends. D, DC, MC, V. No lunch Mon. and Tues.*

Caribbean

Hollywood

$–$$ **Cha Cha Cha.** Off the beaten path, this small shack of a Caribbean restaurant attracts a discerning, eclectic crowd—the place is hip, yet not pretentious or overly trendy. Sit indoors in a cozy room, or in the enclosed patio, very tropical in its decor, à la Carmen Miranda. There's Jamaican jerk chicken, swordfish brochette, fried plantain chips, and assorted flans. If you're in the mood for pizza, try Cha Cha Cha's Caribbean versions. A "Valley" branch (17499 Ventura Blvd., Encino, ☎ 818/789–3600) exists in much more stylish quarters. ✕ *656 N. Virgil Ave.,* ☎ *213/664–7723. Reservations advised. AE, D, DC, MC, V. Valet parking available (and advised).*

Chinese

Beverly Hills

$$–$$$ **Joss.** This very elegant, attractively modern restaurant, popular with Beverly Hills and Hollywood Hills locals, offers beautifully presented, aristocratic multiregional Chinese cuisine. Try the varied dim sum and the Peking duck served as two courses. Many claim Joss has the best cooking west of Downtown Chinatown. Service can be haughty. The sidewalk tables are a popular rendezvous for lunch. ✕ *9255 Sunset Blvd.,* ☎ *310/276–1886. Reservations advised. AE, D, DC, MC, V. No weekend lunch.*

$–$$ **The Mandarin.** Who said you find great Chinese food only in hole-in-
★ the-wall places with oilcloth tabletops? Here is a good-looking restaurant with the best crystal and linens, serving an equally bright mixture of Szechuan and Chinese country-cooking dishes. Minced chicken in lettuce-leaf tacos, Peking duck (order ahead of time), a superb beggar's chicken, scallion pancakes, and any of the noodle dishes are recommended. ✕ *430 N. Camden Dr.,* ☎ *310/859–0926. Reservations required. AE, DC, MC, V. No weekend lunch. Valet parking evening only.*

Downtown

$–$$ **Mon Kee Seafood Restaurant.** The name pretty much tells you what
★ to expect—except it doesn't convey how good the cooking is and how morning-fresh the fish are. The garlic crab is addictive; the steamed catfish is a masterpiece of gentle flavors. In fact, almost everything on the menu is excellent. Despite its wonderful cuisine, this is a crowded, messy place; be prepared to wait for a table. ✕ *679 N. Spring St.,* ☎ *213/628–6717. No reservations. AE, DC, MC, V. Pay parking lot.*

Pasadena

(DOWNTOWN LOS ANGELES DINING MAP)

$$–$$$ **Yujean Kang's Gourmet Chinese Cuisine.** Despite its length, this name
★ doesn't say it all. Mr. Kang, formerly of San Francisco, is one of the finest nouvelle-Chinese chefs in the nation. Forget any and all preconceived notions of what Chinese food should look and taste like. Start with the tender slices of veal on a bed of enoki and black mushrooms, topped with a tangle of quick-fried shoestring yams, or the sea bass with kumquats and a passion-fruit sauce, and finish with poached plums, or watermelon ice under a mantle of white chocolate, and you will appreciate that this is no chop-suey joint. No MSG is used in any dish. ✕ *67 N. Raymond Ave.,* ☎ *818/585–0855. Reservations advised. AE, D, DC, MC, V.*

West Hollywood

$ **Chopstix.** Never underestimate the ability of Californians to adopt—and adapt—an ethnic-food vogue: in this case, dim sum, subtly doctored for non-Asian tastes. The result is MSG-free, nouvelle Asian fast food served in a mod setting, at high tables with stools, or at a diner-like counter. The dishes are interesting (spicy black bean beef, Thai tacos, Bangkok noodles), but don't expect a native Chinese to agree. There's another branch of Chopstix in Pasadena. ✕ *7229 Melrose Ave., ☎ 213/937–1111. No reservations. AE, D, MC, V.*

Continental

Beverly Hills

$$–$$$ **Rustica.** Popular on a sunny day (out back there's a retractable roof that allows you to dine alfresco when weather warrants), this contemporary bistro serves a mixture of California and Italian cuisine. It's one of Beverly Hills' most romantic spots, especially the cozy, dimly lit front room, and the service is ace. All entrées are under $25, which is very good for this part of town. Try the grilled swordfish; tricolor mushroom ravioli with sun-dried tomatoes, pesto, and Parmesan; and the blackened goat-cheese salad with roasted walnut vinaigrette. More than 200 wines make up the top-notch wine list. ✕ *435 N. Beverly Dr., Beverly Hills, ☎ 310/247–9331. Reservations advised. AE, D, DC, MC, V. Valet parking. No weekend lunch.*

Century City
[BEVERLY HILLS AND HOLLYWOOD DINING MAP]

$$$–$$$$ **Jimmy's.** When Beverly Hills CEOs are not dining at home, they often head here. Owner Jimmy Murphy provides the warmth in this expensive, decorator-elegant restaurant. The best dishes on the broad menu include peppered salmon, veal medallions with orange coffee-bean sauce, roast duckling, and chateaubriand. There's a fine steak or salmon tartare at lunch and, if you're feeling flush, start your meal with beluga caviar. ✕ *201 Moreno Dr., ☎ 310/552–2394. Reservations required. Jacket and tie. AE, DC, MC, V. Valet parking.*

Santa Monica
[COASTAL LOS ANGELES DINING MAP]

$$ **Schatsi on Main.** Owner Arnold Schwarzenegger has seen to it that the chef's dishes include his Austrian homeland favorites such as Wiener schnitzel, bratwurst, and smoked pork chops. The bulk of the dishes, however, range from Peking roast duck and pasta with shrimp to seared swordfish medallions and New York–style pizza. The indoor area, with brick walls, is warmly decorated with low lighting. The patio, designated for smoking, has retractable canvas panels, allowing outdoor seating in all kinds of weather. This cultural experience goes so far as to have German lessons piped into the rest rooms. *3110 Main St., ☎ 310/399–4800. Reservations recommended. AE, D, DC, MC, V. Valet parking.*

Westwood
[COASTAL LOS ANGELES DINING MAP]

$$$ **Dynasty Room.** This peaceful, elegant dining room in the Westwood Marquis Hotel has a European flair and tables set far enough apart for privacy. The well-handled Continental fare includes grilled *opaka-paka* (whitefish on a bed of couscous) with fennel and *ahi* (tuna) in Thai-curried seaweed. For dessert, the mixed-fruit tart is highly recommended. ✕ *930 Hilgard Ave., ☎ 310/208–8765. Reservations required. AE, D, DC, MC, V. No lunch. Valet parking.*

Deli

Beverly Hills

$ **Nate 'n' Al's.** A famous gathering place for Hollywood comedians, gag writers, and their agents, Nate 'n' Al's serves first-rate matzo-ball soup, lox and scrambled eggs, cheese blintzes, potato pancakes, and the best deli sandwiches west of Manhattan. ✕ *414 N. Beverly Dr.,* ☎ *310/274–0101. No reservations. AE, MC, V. Free parking.*

San Fernando Valley

$ ★ **Art's Delicatessen.** One of the best Jewish-style delicatessens in the city, this Kosher mecca serves mammoth sandwiches named after celebrities and made from some of the best corned beef, pastrami, and other cold cuts around. Matzo-ball soup and sweet-and-sour cabbage soup are specialties, and there is good chopped chicken liver. ✕ *12224 Ventura Blvd., Studio City,* ☎ *818/762–1221. No reservations. AE, D, DC, MC, V.*

West Hollywood

$ **Canter's.** Ex–New Yorkers claim that this granddaddy of delicatessens (it opened in 1928) is the closest in atmosphere, smell, and menu to a Big Apple corned-beef and pastrami hangout. The elderly waitresses even speak with New York accents. It's open 24 hours a day (attracting an eclectic late-night crowd) and has a yummy in-house bakery. ✕ *419 N. Fairfax Ave.,* ☎ *213/651–2030. Reservations accepted. MC, V. Valet parking.*

French

San Fernando Valley

$$–$$$ ★ **Pinot Bistro.** Joachim Spliechel, owner-chef of top-rated Patina, opened this perfectly designed synthesis of Parisian bistros. One can smell the fumes of perfectly seasoned escargots and the aroma of perfectly brewed espressos. Dishes are authentic: an array of fresh oysters, country pâtés, bouillabaisse, braised tongue and spinach, pot-au-feu, and steak with french fries. The pastry chef specializes in chocolate desserts. There's a long wine list. ✕ *12969 Ventura Blvd.,* ☎ *818/990–0500. Reservations advised. AE, D, DC, MC, V. No weekend lunch. Valet parking.*

$$ **Barzac Brasserie.** Just north of Universal Studios, show business types and other locals seeking French comfort food satiate themselves on chef Didier Poirier's Gallic menu. It's also an interesting place to eat, as the contemporary dining room surrounds an open kitchen, so you can watch your meal being prepared. Start with roasted potato shells with golden and black caviar or sautéed baby escargots with shiitake mushrooms in a puffed pastry. Popular entrées are grilled baby coho salmon over couscous and curry sauce and rack of lamb roasted with Dijon mustard served with red Swiss chard. ✕ *4212 Lankershim Blvd., Universal City,* ☎ *818/760–7081. Reservations advised. AE, DC, MC, V. No weekend lunch. Valet parking.*

West Hollywood

$$$–$$$$ ★ **L'Orangerie.** For sheer elegance and classic good taste, it would be hard to find a lovelier restaurant in this country. And the cuisine, albeit nouvelle-light, is as French as the l'Orangerie at Versailles. Specialties include coddled eggs served in the shell and topped with caviar, duck with foie gras, John Dory with bay leaves, rack of lamb for two, and an unbeatable apple tart served with a jug of double cream. ✕ *903 N. La Cienega Blvd.,* ☎ *310/652–9770. Reservations required. Jacket and tie. AE, D, DC, MC, V. No lunch, closed Mon. Valet parking.*

$$$ Le Dome. For some reason, local food critics have never given this brasserie as much attention as it deserves. Perhaps they are intimidated by the hordes of show- and music-biz celebrities who keep the place humming. By and large the food is honest, down-to-earth French: cockles in white wine and shallots; veal ragout; veal tortellini with prosciutto, sundried tomatoes, peas, and Parmesan sauce; and a genuine, stick-to-the-ribs cassoulet. ✕ *8720 Sunset Blvd.,* ☎ *310/659–6919. Reservations required. AE, DC, MC, V. No lunch Sat., closed Sun. Valet parking.*

$$–$$$ Le Chardonnay. The interiors are Art Deco in this look-alike of a famous Left Bank bistro, circa 1920. Despite the high noise level, it's a most romantic rendezvous, with comfortable, cozy booths. Specialties include warm sweetbread salad, goat-cheese ravioli, roast venison, grilled fish, Peking duck with a ginger and honey sauce, and lots of lush desserts. ✕ *8284 Melrose Ave.,* ☎ *213/655–8880. Reservations required. AE, D, DC, MC, V. Closed Sat. and Sun. Valet parking.*

Westside
(COASTAL LOS ANGELES DINING MAP)

$$–$$$ Beaurivage. A charming, romantic restaurant designed in the fashion of an auberge on the Cote d'Azur, this is one of the few Malibu dining places with a view of the beach and ocean. The menu complements the Provençal atmosphere: roast duckling Mirabelle, pasta with shellfish, mussel soup, filet mignon with a mushroom marsala sauce, and, in season, wild game specials. It's a satisfying getaway. ✕ *26025 Pacific Coast Hwy.,* ☎ *310/456–5733. Reservations required. AE, DC, MC, V. No lunch, except Sun. brunch. Parking lot.*

$$–$$$ Chinois on Main. The third of the Wolfgang Puck pack of restaurants,
★ this one was designed in tongue-in-cheek kitsch by his wife, Barbara Lazaroff. Both the look of the place and Puck's merging of Asian and French cuisines are great fun. A few of the least resistible dishes on the irresistible seasonal menu include grilled Mongolian lamb chops with cilantro vinaigrette and wok-fried vegetables, Shanghai lobster with spicy ginger curry sauce, and rare duck with a wondrous plum sauce. The best desserts are three differently flavored crèmes brûlées. This is one of L.A.'s most crowded spots—and one of the noisiest. ✕ *2709 Main St., Santa Monica,* ☎ *310/392–9025. Dinner reservations required. AE, D, DC, MC, V. No lunch Sat.–Tues. Valet parking.*

Greek

Mid-Wilshire
(BEVERLY HILLS AND HOLLYWOOD DINING MAP)

$ Sofi. Hidden down a narrow passageway is this friendly little taverna that makes you feel like you've been transported straight to Mykonos. Enjoy your meal in the stone-wall dining room or under a vine-shaded patio. The food is authentic Greek cuisine: *dolmades* (stuffed grape leaves), lamb gyros, a sampling of traditional salads, phyllo pies, spanakopita, and souvlakia. ✕ *8030¼ W. 3rd St.,* ☎ *213/651–0346. Reservations advised. AE, D, DC, MC, V. No Sun. lunch.*

Health Food

Pasadena
(DOWNTOWN LOS ANGELES DINING MAP)

$–$$ Clearwater Cafe. Not only for the health conscious but also for the environmentally correct diner, this spiffy restaurant in Pasadena's Old Town district prints its menus with vegetable-based inks and serves food in reusable containers. Dishes cater to low-fat, low-sodium palates, but that doesn't mean a loss in taste—the spicy catfish has a certain bite and the mixed vegetable grill with creamy polenta satisfies even the most discerning vegetarian. Sit in the courtyard patio of this two-level restaurant if the sun is shining. ✕ *168 W. Colorado Blvd.,* ☎ *818/356–0959. Reservations accepted. AE, D, MC, V. Valet parking.*

Italian

Beverly Hills

$–$$ **Il Fornaio Cucina Italiana.** What was once a bakery-café has been ★ transformed into one of the best-looking contemporary trattorias in California, and the food is more than worthy of the setting. From the huge brass-and-stainless-steel rotisserie come crispy roasted duck, herb-basted chickens, and juicy rabbit. Nearby, cooks paddle a tasty variety of pizzas and calzones in and out of the oakwood-burning oven. Also emerging from the latter is a *bomba,* a plate-size, dome-shape focaccia shell draped with strips of smoked prosciutto. The thick porterhouse steak alla Florentina at $17.95 is clearly the best beef buy around; another top choice is pasta stuffed with lobster, ricotta, and leeks, served with a lemon cream sauce. The wines come from vineyards Il Fornaio owns in Italy. Stop by for Sunday brunch; it's terrific. ✕ *301 N. Beverly Dr.,* ☎ *310/550–8330. Reservations accepted. AE, DC, MC, V. Valet parking.*

$–$$ **Prego.** The baby lamb chops, large broiled veal chop (the specialty), fresh Dover sole, and T-bone steak here are more than satisfying, considering the low prices and attentive service. Grilled vegetable dishes are worth asking about, too. The baked-in-house bread sticks and freshly made pasta are great. ✕ *362 N. Camden Dr.,* ☎ *310/277–7346. Reservations advised. AE, DC, MC, V. No Sun. lunch. Valet parking in evening.*

Century City
(BEVERLY HILLS AND HOLLYWOOD DINING MAP)

$$–$$$ **Harry's Bar & American Grill.** A more posh, private, and uptown version of Prego (*see above*), it's run by the same management. The decor and selection of dishes are acknowledged copies of Harry's Bar in Florence. But for first-rate food—paper-thin carpaccio, grilled fish and steaks, and excellent pastas like ravioli filled with artichokes or tortellini with Maine lobster and shiitake sauce—the check will be far lower than it would be in Italy. ✕ *2020 Ave. of the Stars,* ☎ *310/277–2333. Reservations required. AE, DC, MC, V. No weekend lunch. Valet parking.*

Downtown

$$$$ **Rex Il Ristorante.** Owner Mauro Vincenti may know more about Ital-★ ian cuisine than any other restaurateur in this country. The Rex is the ideal showcase for his talents: Two ground floors of a historic Art Deco building were remodeled to resemble the main dining salon of the circa-1930 Italian luxury liner *Rex.* The cuisine, the lightest of *nuova cucina,* is equally special. Be prepared for small and costly portions of such delights as herb-breaded lamb chops with spinach or calamari with black squid-ink pasta. ✕ *617 S. Olive St.,* ☎ *213/627–2300. Reservations required. Jacket and tie. AE, DC, MC, V. Closed Sun. No lunch Sat.–Wed. Valet parking.*

Los Feliz
(BEVERLY HILLS AND HOLLYWOOD DINING MAP)

$–$$ **Louise's Trattoria.** Definitely for people who want to party and aren't necessarily concerned with culinary excellence, this fun restaurant (one of a chain) serves mostly Southern Italian fare. Portions tend to be bigger than even Arnold Schwarzenegger could handle. Recommendations include black pepper linguine with roasted turkey breast, sweet red peppers, and cilantro; grilled chicken Caesar salad; and the goat cheese, tomato, and basil pizza. Next door is the Derby Room, a resurrection of one of the three famed Brown Derbys, where for a fee you can dance to a live jazz band. ✕ *4500 Los Feliz Blvd.,* ☎ *213/667–0777. Reservations advised. AE, DC, MC, V. Valet parking.*

San Fernando Valley

$$–$$$ **Adriano's Ristorante.** A five-minute drive north of Sunset Boulevard is this countrified retreat, near the top of the Santa Monica Mountains. There's nothing backwoods about the food, though—homemade lobster ravioli, breaded veal with capers and anchovies, risotto with seafood, soft-shell crab sautéed in garlic and a delicious *tiramisù.* ✕ *2930 Beverly Glen Circle,* ☎ *310/475–9807. Reservations required. AE, DC, MC, V. No weekend lunch. Closed Mon. Free parking.*

$$ **Posto.** Thanks to Piero Selvaggio, Valley residents no longer have to drive to the Westside for good modern Italian cuisine. His chef makes a tissue-thin pizza topped with flavorful ingredients, and the chicken, duck, and veal sausages are made each morning, as are the different herb breads, fried polenta, and wonderful risotto with porcini mushrooms. And, if you are not too stuffed after that, the desserts are delicious. ✕ *14928 Ventura Blvd., Sherman Oaks,* ☎ *818/784–4400. AE, MC, V. No weekend lunch.*

West Hollywood

$$ **Ca'Brea.** Signoris de Mori and Tomassi were so successful with Locanda
★   Veneta (*see below*) that they took a gamble and opened a much larger and lower-price place only 20 blocks away. Ca'Brea has turned into the Italian-restaurant smash hit of the penny-pinching '90s, and there isn't a pizza on the menu. You won't care, either, what with the osso buco, the linguine and baby clams, gnocchi with fresh herbs in a beef and veal sauce, grilled lamb chops covered in a black truffle and mustard sauce, roasted chicken and pork sausage with braised Napa Valley cabbage, and homemade mozzarella salads. Daily specials include soup, salad, pasta, and fish. ✕ *348 S. La Brea Ave.,* ☎ *213/938–2863. Reservations advised. AE, D, DC, MC, V. Closed Sun. No weekend lunch.*

$$ **Locanda Veneta.** The food may be more finely wrought at one or two
★   other spots, but the combination of a splendid Venetian chef, Antonio Tomassi, and a simpatico co-owner, Jean Louis de Mori, have re-created the atmospheric equivalent of a genuine Italian trattoria, at reasonable prices. Specialties include risotto with lobster, veal chop, potato dumplings with tomatoes and shrimp, linguine with clams, lobster ravioli with saffron sauce, and a delectable apple tart. ✕ *8638 W. 3rd St.,* ☎ *310/274–1893. Reservations required. AE, D, DC, MC, V. Closed Sun. No Sat. lunch. Valet parking.*

$ **Tavola Calda.** This low-tech Italian nirvana draws the budget-watching crowd, who are attracted to the inexpensive entrées that are all under $10. Cabaret tables are scattered about the roomy place, with a piano player, high ceilings, and intimate lighting all working together to set the upbeat tone (don't be surprised if one of the customers gets up to do a rendition from a popular opera). Best bets on the limited menu are unusual gourmet pizzas (like the vegetarian pie that doesn't include cheese) and risotto that reminds you of being in Milan. ✕ *7371 Melrose Ave.,* ☎ *213/658–6340. No reservations. AE, DC, MC, V. Valet parking.*

Westside

[COASTAL LOS ANGELES DINING MAP]

$$$–$$$$ **Valentino.** Rated among the best Italian restaurants in the nation,
★   Valentino is generally considered to have the best wine list outside Italy, although the 1994 earthquake wreaked havoc with the wine cellar.

LOOK AT VACATIONS DIFFERENTLY. BETTER YET, LOOK AT EVERYTHING DIFFERENTLY.

From the train it's a whole new world out there. A world you can see clearly when you plan your next trip with Amtrak's® Great American Vacations. Because we'll help you plan everything. Train reservations. Hotel reservations. Car rentals. Sightseeing tours. Admission to local attractions. And whatever else you want to do. Wherever you want to go.

On Amtrak your vacation starts the moment you board the train. Because you start your trip off in a comfortable seat, not a confining one. Where you have the choice of watching not only movies, but sunsets and wide open spaces roll by. Where even before you get there, you can get away from it all in a private bedroom.

And with Amtrak's Air-Rail Travel Plan, you can combine the magic of the train with the speed of the plane, all at one special price that includes one-way coach on Amtrak and one-way coach on United Airlines.

To find out more call your travel agent or 1-800-321-8684. Send in this coupon for an Amtrak travel planner.

Things are looking better already.

NAME_____
ADDRESS _____
CITY _____ STATE _____ ZIP_____
TELEPHONE _____

AMTRAK'S
Great American
VACATIONS

Mail to: Amtrak,
Dept. TP3, P.O. Box 7717,
Itasca, IL 60143

No matter where you go, travel is easier when you know the code.^{SM}

dial 1 8 0 0
C A L L
A T T®

Dial 1 800 CALL ATT
and you'll always get
through from any phone
with any card* and you'll
always get AT&T's best
deal.** It's the one number
to remember when calling
away from home.

*Other long distance company calling cards excluded.
**Additional discounts available.

AT&T
Your True Choice

©1995 AT&T

Owner Piero Selvaggio is the man who introduced Los Angeles to the best and lightest of modern-day Italian cuisine. There's superb prosciutto, fried calamari, lobster cannelloni, fresh broiled porcini mushrooms, and osso buco. ✕ *3115 Pico Blvd., Santa Monica,* ☎ *310/829–4313. Reservations required. AE, DC, MC, V. Closed Sun. No lunch Sat.–Thurs. Valet parking.*

$$ **Remi.** It's not easy to find authentic Venetian cuisine in Southern California, but this is a top-rated source tucked away in Santa Monica's Third Street Promenade, an outdoor shopping mall. Order the linguine with scallops, mussels, shrimp, and fresh chopped tomatoes; the whole wheat crepes with ricotta and spinach, topped with a tomato, carrot, and celery sauce; or the roasted pork chop stuffed with smoked mozzarella and prosciutto, served with mashed potatoes and fennel. ✕ *1451 Third St. Promenade, Santa Monica,* ☎ *310/393–6545. Reservations required. AE, DC, MC, V. Parking in nearby multistory mall parking lots.*

$–$$ **Tra di Noi.** The name means "between us," and Malibu natives are trying to keep this charming, simple *ristorante* just that—a local secret. It's run by a mama (who does the cooking), son, and daughter-in-law. Regular customers, film celebrities and non–show-biz folk alike love the unpretentious atmosphere and bring their kids. Nothing fancy or *nuovo* on the menu, just great lasagna, freshly made pasta, mushroom and veal dishes, and crisp fresh salads. ✕ *3835 Cross Creek Rd.,* ☎ *310/456–0169. Reservations advised. AE. Closed Sun. lunch.*

Japanese

Downtown

$$–$$$ **Restaurant Horikawa.** A department store of Japanese cuisines includes sushi, teppan steak tables, tempura, sashimi, shabu-shabu, teriyaki, and a $75-per-person seven-course dinner. All are good or excellent, but the sushi bar is the best. The decor is traditional Japanese, with private dining rooms, where guests sit on tatami floor mats, for two to 24. ✕ *111 S. San Pedro St.,* ☎ *213/ 680–9355. Reservations advised. AE, MC, V. No Sat. lunch. Valet parking.*

Los Feliz
(BEVERLY HILLS AND HOLLYWOOD DINING MAP)

$$$ **Restaurant Katsu.** A stark, simple, perfectly designed sushi bar with a
★ small table area serves some of the most exquisite and delicious delicacies east of Japan. You can't go wrong when ordering—whether it is the seafood shabu-shabu or the *yadokari nabe* (an assortment of seafood in an abalone shell). This is probably the most authentic Japanese restaurant in the city and definitely a treat for both the eye and the palate. ✕ *1972 N. Hillhurst Ave.,* ☎ *213/665–1891. Reservations advised. AE, DC, MC, V. No weekend lunch. Valet parking.*

Mexican

Hollywood

$ **El Cholo.** The progenitor of the upscale chain, this place has been packing them in since the '20s. It serves good-size margaritas, a zesty assortment of tacos, make-your-own tacos and, from July through October, green-corn tamales. It's friendly and fun, with large portions for only a few pesos. ✕ *1121 S. Western Ave.,* ☎ *213/ 734–2773. Reservations advised. AE, DC, MC, V. Valet parking and parking meters.*

Santa Monica
(COASTAL LOS ANGELES DINING MAP)

$–$$ **Border Grill.** This very trendy, very loud eating hall is owned by two talented female chefs with the most eclectic tastes in town. The menu ranges from Yucatán seafood tacos to vinegar-and-pepper-grilled turkey to spicy baby-back ribs. It's worth dropping by for the fun of it, if you don't mind the noise. ✕ *1445 4th St., ☎ 310/451–1655. Reservations advised. AE, D, DC, MC, V. No lunch.*

Polynesian

Beverly Hills

$$–$$$ **Trader Vic's.** Sure, it's corny, but this Trader Vic's, inside the Beverly Hilton, is the most restrained and elegant of the late Victor Bergeron's South Sea extravaganzas. Besides, who says corn can't be fun—and tasty, too. The crab Rangoon, grilled cheese wafers, skewered shrimp, grilled pork ribs, and the steaks, chops, and peanut butter–coated lamb cooked in the huge clay ovens, are just fine. As for the array of exotic rum drinks, watch your sips. ✕ *9876 Wilshire Blvd., ☎ 310/276–6345. Reservations required. Jacket and tie. AE, D, DC, MC, V. No lunch. Valet parking.*

Spanish

Mid-Wilshire
[BEVERLY HILLS AND HOLLYWOOD DINING MAP]

$$–$$$ **Cava.** In Spanish, *cava* loosely means "celebration," and that's just what a meal here should prove to be. Not far from the Farmer's Market is this trendy two-level tapas bar and restaurant inside the Beverly Plaza Hotel that opened in 1993. The decor is artsy (larger-than-life roses are painted on the walls), the atmosphere a bit noisy but lots of fun, and the cuisine alluring. You can graze on tapas—tiny snacks such as baked artichoke topped with bread crumbs and tomato or a fluffy potato omelet served with crème fraîche—or feast on bigger entrées: The paella is a must, but you may also want to try *zarzuela* (lightly baked shrimp, scallops, clams, mussels, and fresh fish in a hearty tomato wine sauce) or *bistec flamenco* (aged New York steak with caramelized onions and a traditional Argentine steak sauce). Wash it all down with a glass or three of Sangria, and you'll be assured a very Spanish experience. ✕ *8384 W. 3rd St., ☎ 213/658–8898. Reservations advised. AE, D, DC, MC, V. Valet parking.*

Thai

Hollywood

$–$$ **Chan Dara.** Here you'll find excellent Thai food in a bright and shiny Swiss chalet! Try any of the noodle dishes, especially those with crab and shrimp. Also tops on the extensive menu are *satay* (appetizers on skewers) and barbecued chicken and catfish. ✕ *310 N. Larchmont Blvd., ☎ 213/467–1052. Reservations advised for parties of more than 4. AE, DC, MC, V. No lunch on weekends.*

West Hollywood

$$ **Tommy Tang's.** At this grazing ground for yuppies and celebs, a lot of people-watching goes on. Although portions are on the small side, they are decidedly innovative. The kitchen features crisp duck marinated in ginger and plum sauce, blackened sea scallops, and a spinach salad tossed with grilled chicken. There is also a happening sushi bar overlooking the parade of eccentric people who frequent Melrose Avenue. ✕ *7313 Melrose Ave., ☎ 213/651–1810. Reservations advised. AE, DC, MC, V. Valet parking.*

6 Lodging

BECAUSE LOS ANGELES IS SO SPREAD OUT—it's actually a series of suburbs connected by freeways—it's good to select a hotel room not only for its ambience, amenities, and price but also for a location that is convenient to where you plan to spend most of your time.

By Jane E.
Lasky

After you decide which area of the city is best suited to your needs, reserve a room. Many hotels offer tickets to amusement parks or plays as well as special prices for weekend visits. A travel agent can help in making your arrangements.

Hotels listed below are organized according to their location, then by price category, following this scale:

CATEGORY	COST*
$$$$	over $160
$$$	$100–$160
$$	$65–$100
$	under $65

*All prices are for a double room excluding tax.

To reserve a room in any property in this chapter, you can contact **Fodor's new Toll-Free Lodging Reservations Hotline** (☎ 1–800/FODORS–1 or 1–800/363–6771; 0800/89–1030 in Great Britain; 0014/800–12–8271 in Australia; 1800/55–9101 in Ireland).

Downtown

$$$$ **Biltmore Hotel.** Since its 1923 opening, the Biltmore has hosted such notables as Mary Pickford, J. Paul Getty, Eleanor Roosevelt, Princess Margaret, and several U.S. presidents. The guest rooms in this historic landmark have been updated, with pastel color schemes and traditional French furniture and armoires. The lobby ceiling was painted by Italian artist Giovanni Smeraldi; imported Italian marble and plum-color velvet grace the Grand Avenue Sports Bar. There's also Bernard's, an acclaimed Continental restaurant. The swank health club has a Roman-bath motif. On the 9th and 11th floors, designated as the Executive floors, desks are specially equipped for business travelers. The 10th floor, the Club floor, comes complete with a concierge and a lounge that offers afternoon tea, Continental breakfast, board games, a fax machine, and big-screen TV. ☎ 506 S. Grand Ave., 90071, ☎ 213/624–1011 or 800/245–8673, FAX 213/612–1545. 683 rooms. 3 restaurants, lounge, no-smoking floors, room service, health club. AE, DC, MC, V.

$$$$ **Hotel Inter-Continental Los Angeles.** This imposing 17-story structure was introduced to the downtown skyline at the end of 1992, the first hotel to be built in this section of town in the past decade. Part of California Plaza (where the Museum of Contemporary Art is) and within walking distance of the Music Center, the sleek Inter-Continental boasts floor-to-ceiling views. Guest rooms are decorated in contemporary style, with glass-topped tables and desks, in color schemes of either ivory and peach or celadon and brown. The sculpture Yellow Fin, by Richard Serra, dominates the large lobby, and other artwork is on view throughout, on loan from the Museum of Contemporary Art. The Grand Cafe serves California cuisine in an arty atmosphere. ☎ 251 S. Olive St., 90012, ☎ 213/617–3300 or 800/442–5251, FAX 213/617–3399. 429 rooms. Restaurant, no-smoking floors, room service, outdoor pool, indoor pool, health club, business services. AE, D, DC, MC, V.

Los Angeles Lodging *(Boxes Refer to Detail Maps)*

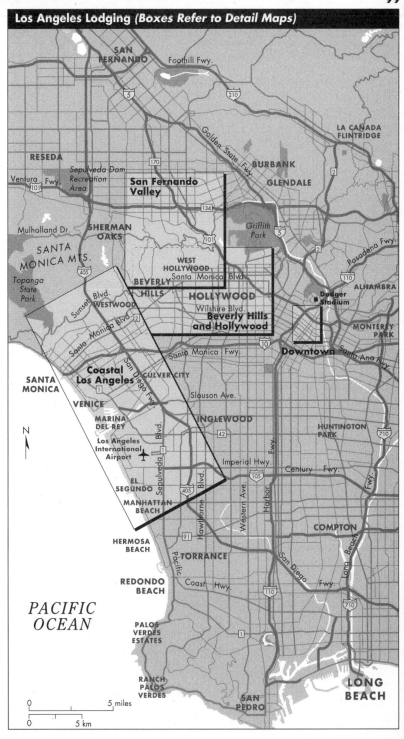

SAN FERNANDO

Foothill Fwy.

LA CAÑADA
FLINTRIDGE

RESEDA

Ventura Fwy.

Sepulveda Dam
Recreation
Area

BURBANK

GLENDALE

Golden State Fwy.

**San Fernando
Valley**

Mulholland Dr.

SHERMAN
OAKS

Griffith
Park

SANTA
MONICA MTS.

WEST
HOLLYWOOD

Santa Monica Blvd.

Pasadena Fwy.

ALHAMBRA

Topanga
State
Park

Sunset Blvd.

BEVERLY
HILLS

WESTWOOD

HOLLYWOOD

Dodger
Stadium

MONTEREY
PARK

Wilshire Blvd.

**Beverly Hills
and Hollywood**

Santa Monica Blvd.

Santa Ana Fwy.

SANTA
MONICA

N

Santa Monica Fwy.

Santa Monica Fwy.

Downtown

**Coastal
Los Angeles**

CULVER CITY

San Diego Fwy.

VENICE

Slauson Ave.

MARINA
DEL REY

INGLEWOOD

HUNTINGTON
PARK

Los Angeles
International
Airport

Sepulveda Blvd.

Century Fwy.

Imperial Hwy.

Harbor Fwy.

Western Ave.

EL
SEGUNDO

Hawthorne Blvd.

MANHATTAN
BEACH

COMPTON

HERMOSA
BEACH

San Diego Fwy.

Long Beach Fwy.

Pacific

TORRANCE

REDONDO
BEACH

Coast Hwy.

PACIFIC
OCEAN

PALOS
VERDES
ESTATES

RANCH
PALOS
VERDES

SAN
PEDRO

**LONG
BEACH**

0   5 miles

0   5 km

Downtown Los Angeles Lodging

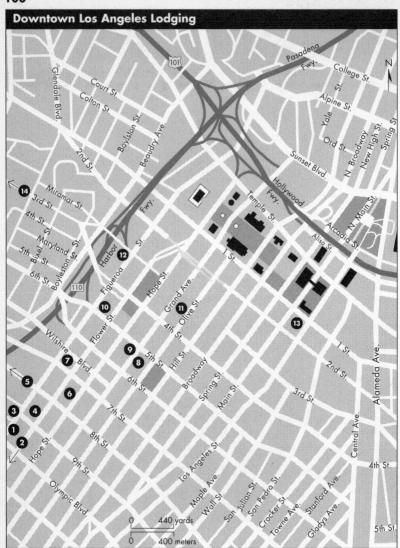

Biltmore Hotel, **8**

EconoLodge, **14**

Figueroa Hotel, **3**

Holiday Inn L.A.
Downtown, **5**

Hotel
Inter-Continental
Los Angeles, **11**

Hyatt Regency
Los Angeles, **6**

Inn at 657, **2**

The Inntowne, **1**

Los Angeles Hilton
Hotel and Towers, **7**

New Otani Hotel
and Garden, **13**

Orchid Hotel, **4**

Sheraton Grande
Hotel, **12**

Westin
Bonaventure
Hotel & Suites, **10**

Wyndham Checkers
Hotel, **9**

$$$$ **Hyatt Regency Los Angeles.** The Hyatt is in the heart of the downtown financial district, minutes away from the Convention Center, Dodger Stadium, and the Music Center. Each room, traditionally furnished with rich mahogany and cherry woods and marble baths, has a wall of windows with city views. Security is high at this downtown hotel, with well-lit hallways and no blind corners. The hotel is part of the Broadway Plaza, comprising 35 shops. ☎ *711 S. Hope St., 90017,* ☎ *213/683–1234 or 800/233–1234,* FAX *213/629–3230. 485 rooms, 41 suites. Restaurant, coffee shop, 2 lounges, no-smoking floors, health club, parking. AE, D, DC, MC, V.*

$$$$ **Los Angeles Hilton Hotel and Towers.** Located on Wilshire Boulevard, the Hilton is convenient to Dodger Stadium, museums, Chinatown, and the Music Center. The sparse-looking contemporary decor of the guest rooms is in beige, blue, and green. ☎ *930 Wilshire Blvd., 90017,* ☎ *213/629–4321 or 800/445–8667,* FAX *213/612–3977. 900 rooms. 4 restaurants, coffee shop, lounge, exercise room, parking (fee). AE, D, DC, MC, V.*

$$$$ **Sheraton Grande Hotel.** This 14-story hotel, with its reflecting glass
★ facade, is near Dodger Stadium, the Music Center, and downtown's Bunker Hill District. Guest rooms are oversize, with wall-to-wall windows and awesome city views. The decor features dark wood furniture, sofas, and minibars; colors are mauve, peach, and gray; baths are marble. There's butler service with every room. There are complimentary privileges at a local, state-of-the-art YMCA and a lovely landscaped pool on the premises. ☎ *333 S. Figueroa St., 90071,* ☎ *213/617–1133 or 800/524–7263,* FAX *213/613–0291. 469 rooms. 3 restaurants, bar, room service, no-smoking floors, pool, 4 cinemas. AE, D, DC, MC, V.*

$$$$ **Westin Bonaventure Hotel & Suites.** This is architect John Portman's striking 1976 contribution to downtown Los Angeles: a 35-story, five-tower, mirrored-glass high-rise in the center of downtown. Rooms—a number of which are on the small side—have a wall of glass, streamlined pale furnishings, and comfortable appointments. One tower is endowed with oversize suites, 94 in all. The outside elevators provide stunning city views; there are also 5 acres of ponds, and waterfalls in the lobby, which was renovated in 1994. ☎ *404 S. Figueroa St., 90071,* ☎ *213/624–1000 or 800/228–3000,* FAX *213/612-4894. 1,368 rooms. 3 restaurants, lounge, no-smoking floors, pool, shops, parking (fee). AE, D, DC, MC, V.*

$$$$ **Wyndham Checkers Hotel.** Set in one of this neighborhood's few remaining historical buildings—it opened as the Mayflower Hotel in 1927—this hotel offers much the same sophistication and luxury as the Biltmore across the street, but on a smaller scale. Guest rooms are furnished with oversize beds, upholstered easy chairs, and writing tables and have marble baths. A library is available for small meetings or tea. ☎ *535 S. Grand Ave., 90071,* ☎ *213/624–0000 or 800/996–3426,* FAX *213/626–9906. 188 rooms. Restaurant, no-smoking floors, lap pool, spa, exercise room, valet parking (fee). AE, D, DC, MC, V.*

$$$–$$$$ **New Otani Hotel and Garden.** For a quintessential Japanese hotel ex-
★ perience, visit this 21-story, ultramodern hotel, with its ½-acre rooftop Japanese-style garden. The decor is a serene blend of Westernized luxury and Eastern simplicity. Each room has a phone in the bathroom, a refrigerator, an alarm clock, and a color TV; most rooms have a *yukata* (robe). If you're so inclined, book a Japanese suite, where you'll sleep on a futon on the floor. The hotel's concrete exterior walls reduce noise from the street. ☎ *120 S. Los Angeles St., 90012,* ☎ *213/629–1200, 800/421–8795, or 800/273–2294 in CA;* FAX *213/622-0989. 435*

rooms. *3 restaurants, 3 lounges, room service, massage (fee), sauna, parking (fee). AE, D, DC, MC, V.*

$$ **Figueroa Hotel.** This 12-story hotel, built in 1926, has managed to keep its charming Spanish style intact. Terra-cotta-color rooms carry out the Spanish look, with hand-painted furniture and, in many rooms, ceiling fans. ☎ *939 S. Figueroa St., 90015,* ☎ *213/627–8971 or 800/421–9092,* FAX *213/689–0305. 285 rooms. 3 restaurants, lounge, coffee shop, pool, free parking. AE, DC, MC, V.*

$$ **Holiday Inn L.A. Downtown.** This six-floor hotel offers Holiday Inn's usual professional staff and services and standard no-frills room decor. The rooms—large, by downtown standards—are decorated with light-green carpets and pink-and-green curtains, walls, and bedspreads. The hotel is convenient, close to the Museum of Contemporary Art, convention center, and Los Angeles Sports Arena. Guests are invited to work out for free at the nearby Family Fitness Center at ARCO Plaza. ☎ *750 Garland Ave., 90017,* ☎ *213/628–5242 or 800/628–5240,* FAX *213/628–1201. 205 rooms. Restaurant, lounge, no-smoking floors, pool, free parking. AE, D, DC, MC, V.*

$$ **The Inntowne.** This three-story hotel with large beige-and-white rooms is 1½ blocks from the convention center. The swimming pool is surrounded by palm trees and a small garden. ☎ *925 S. Figueroa St., 90015,* ☎ *213/628–2222 or 800/457–8520,* FAX *213/687–0566. 170 rooms. Lounge, coffee shop, pool, free parking. AE, D, DC, MC, V.*

$ **Inn at 657.** This unassuming inn is a surprise entrant to the downtown
★ hotel scene. The homey accommodation, run by retired attorney Patsy Carter, is reminiscent of a tiny European-style hotel. It operates like a small apartment building (which it originally was, when it was built in the 1930s), with stocked kitchens containing coffee, tea, and soft drinks, all included in the price. The rate also includes a hearty breakfast, local telephone calls, gratuities, taxes, and parking. All-suite accommodations are roomy and tastefully decorated, with down comforters on the beds and Oriental silks on the walls. The inn's location is convenient, close to the convention center and the University of Southern California campus. ☎ *657 W. 23rd St., 90027,* ☎ *213/741–2200 or 800/347–7512. 6 suites. No-smoking rooms, outdoor hot tub. No credit cards.*

$ **Orchid Hotel.** One of the smaller downtown hotels, this 1920s vintage property is very reasonably priced. There are no frills, but the standard rooms are clean, with modern decor in pastel tones. Note that there is no parking at the hotel, but public lots are close by. If you're staying at least a week, ask about lower weekly rates. ☎ *819 S. Flower St., 90017,* ☎ *213/624–5855,* FAX *213/624–8740. 63 rooms and 2 suites. Coin laundry. AE, D, DC, MC, V.*

Mid-Wilshire

$$$–$$$$ **Radisson Wilshire Plaza Hotel.** One of Wilshire Boulevard's largest hotels, this 12-story building with green-and-ivory-stripe awnings was completely renovated inside in 1992. The rooms have views of either Hollywood or downtown and have contemporary decor in light beige or gray. Corporate clients often use the large banquet and meeting rooms. ☎ *3515 Wilshire Blvd., 90010,* ☎ *213/381–7411 or 800/333–3333,* FAX *213/386–7379. 391 rooms. 2 restaurants, lounge, no-smoking floor, pool, health club, parking (fee). AE, D, DC, MC, V.*

Hollywood and West Hollywood

$$$$ **The Argyle.** Located on the Sunset Strip, this early Art Deco building has been around since the 1930s. All its current furnishings are fine

replicas of Art Deco masterpieces, the originals of which are in New York's Metropolitan Museum of Art. Staying here is like checking into an exclusive private club; you feel as if you're a celebrity (and many a star called this address home, among them Marilyn Monroe, John Wayne, Clark Gable, and Errol Flynn). Ask for a city (more expensive) or mountain view. ☎ *8358 Sunset Blvd., West Hollywood 90069, ☎ 213/654–7100 or 800/225–2637, ℻ 213/654-9287. 64 rooms. Restaurant, pool, sauna, health club, business services, meeting rooms. AE, DC, MC, V.*

$$$$ **Mondrian Hotel.** This giant structure is a monument to the Dutch artist from whom the hotel takes its name. The exterior of the 12-story hotel is actually a giant surrealistic mural; inside there's fine artwork. Accommodations are spacious, with pale-wood furniture and curved sofas in the seating area. Ask for south-corner suites; they tend to be quieter than the rest. The hotel is convenient to major recording, film, and TV studios and is popular with the rock-and-roll crowd. ☎ *8440 Sunset Blvd., West Hollywood 90069, ☎ 213/650–8999 or 800/525–8029, ℻ 213/650–5215. 224 suites. Restaurant, room service, pool, health club, parking (fee). AE, D, DC, MC, V.*

$$$$ **Summerfield Suites Hotel.** This four-story luxury hotel features all suites, decorated in a modern style in shades of blue and pink. All have private balconies, fireplaces, and kitchens. Great for business travelers— it's near "Restaurant Row on La Cienega"—it's not as expensive as other hotels in this price category, and rates even include breakfast. ☎ *1000 Westmont Dr., West Hollywood 90069, ☎ 310/657–7400, 800/833–4353, ℻ 310/854–6744. 109 suites. Bar, pool, health club, parking (fee). AE, D, DC, MC, V.*

$$$$ **Sunset Marquis Hotel and Villas.** Lovely landscaping highlights this three-story property near La Cienega and Sunset boulevards. The hotel is decorated in Mediterranean style; most guests stay in either suites or individual villas. Fashion-magazine photographs are often shot in the lush gardens. ☎ *1200 N. Alta Loma Rd., West Hollywood 90069, ☎ 310/657–1333 or 800/858–9758, ℻ 310/652–5300. 118 rooms. Dining room, room service, refrigerators, 2 pools, sauna, exercise room, free parking. AE, DC, MC, V.*

$$$$ **Wyndham Bel Age Hotel.** This elegant, European-style, all-suite hotel
★ just off the Sunset Strip has a soothing, residential feel. The understated country-French decor is in dark woods and rose and mauve color schemes; the suites are spacious, with large living rooms. South-facing rooms have private terraces that look out over the Los Angeles skyline as far as the Pacific. Some touches are downright extravagant, such as multiline telephones with voice mail, original art, private terraces, and a daily newspaper. The hotel has a distinctive restaurant that serves fine Russian meals with a French flair. ☎ *1020 N. San Vicente Blvd., West Hollywood 90069, ☎ 310/854–1111 or 800/424–4443, ℻ 310/854-0926. 200 suites. 3 restaurants, lounge, room service, pool, health club, concierge, parking (fee). AE, D, DC, MC, V.*

$$$ **Chateau Marmont Hotel.** Although planted on the Sunset Strip amid giant billboards and much sun-bleached Hollywood glitz, this castle of Old World charm and French Normandy design still promises its guests a secluded hideaway close to Hollywood's hot spots. A haunt for many reclusive show-biz personalities and discriminating world travelers since it opened in 1929, this is the ultimate in privacy. All kinds of accommodations are available, including fully equipped cottages, bungalows, and a penthouse. Small pets are allowed. ☎ *8221 Sunset Blvd., Hollywood 90046, ☎ 213/656–1010 or 800/242–8328, ℻ 213/655–5311. 63 rooms. Dining room, room service, pool, exercise room, concierge, free parking. AE, MC, V.*

Beverly Hills and Hollywood Lodging

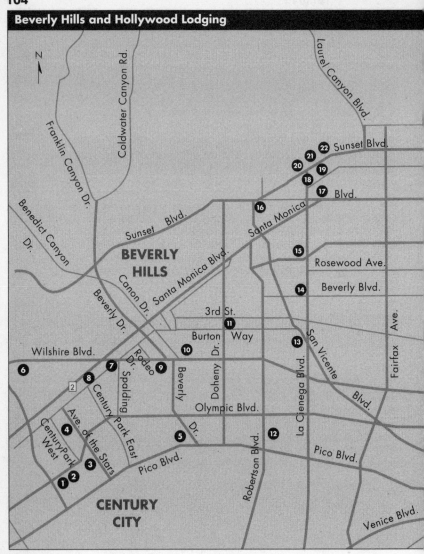

The Argyle, **19**

Banana Bungalow
Hotel and
International
Hostel, **24**

Beverly Hills Ritz
Hotel, **6**

Beverly Hilton, **8**

Beverly Prescott
Hotel, **5**

Carlyle Inn, **12**

Century City
Courtyard by
Marriott, **2**

Century City Inn, **1**

Century Plaza Hotel
and Tower, **4**

Chateau Marmont
Hotel, **22**

Four Seasons Los
Angeles, **11**

Hollywood Holiday
Inn, **25**

Hotel Nikko, **13**

Hotel Sofitel Ma
Maison, **14**

Hyatt on Sunset, **21**

J.W. Marriott Hotel at
Century City, **3**

Le Parc Hotel, **15**

Mondrian Hotel, **18**

Peninsula
Beverly Hills, **7**

Radisson Beverly
Pavilion Hotel, **10**

Radisson Hollywood
Roosevelt, **23**

Radisson Wilshire
Plaza Hotel , **26**

Regent Beverly
Wilshire, **9**

Summerfield Suites
Hotel, **17**

Sunset Marquis Hotel
and Villas, **20**

Wyndham Bel Age
Hotel, **16**

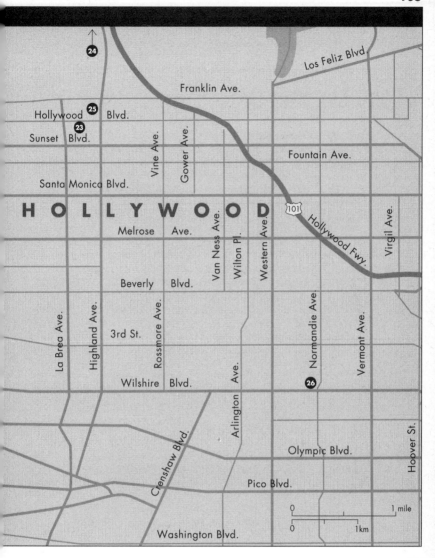

$$$ Hyatt on Sunset. In the heart of the Sunset Strip, this Hyatt is a favorite of music-biz execs and rock stars who appreciate the two-line phones and voice mail available here. There are penthouse suites, and all rooms facing the boulevard have private patios. The rooms are decorated in peach colors and modern furniture; some have aquariums. The Silver Screen sports bar is a fun spot. ☎ *8401 Sunset Blvd., West Hollywood 90069,* ☎ *213/656–1234 or 800/233–1234,* FAX *213/650–7024. 262 rooms. Restaurant, lounge, no-smoking floors, pool, parking (fee). AE, D, DC, MC, V.*

$$$ Radisson Hollywood Roosevelt. This hotel, across from Mann's Chinese Theater, was considered state-of-the-art Hollywood glamour and luxury before it gradually fell into disrepair. But in true Hollywood fashion, this site of the first Academy Awards ceremony made a comeback in 1985, thoroughly restored right down to the ornate Art Deco lobby and elegant courtyard. Highlights are the Olympic-size pool decorated by artist David Hockney and the Tropicana Bar in the courtyard. Most rooms have pastel decor with pine furniture, but for a treat, try one of the 40 Hollywood-theme suites, such as the Gable/Lombard Suite or the Shirley Temple Suite. The 65 poolside cabana rooms are also fun accommodations. At night, a hot spot is the Cinegrill, for dining and dancing to a mellifluous jazz band. ☎ *7000 Hollywood Blvd., Hollywood 90028,* ☎ *213/466–7000 or 800/950–7667,* FAX *213/462–8056. 311 rooms. 3 restaurants, lounge, no-smoking floor, car rental, parking (fee). AE, D, DC, MC, V.*

$$ Hollywood Holiday Inn. You can't miss this hotel, one of the tallest buildings in Hollywood. It's 23 stories high, topped by Windows, a revolving restaurant-lounge (the Sunday brunch served here is a local favorite). The rooms are decorated in floral prints and pastels in standard-issue Holiday Inn fashion. There is a safekeeping box in each room. The hotel is only minutes from the Hollywood Bowl, Universal Studios, and Mann's Chinese Theater, and it's a tour stop. ☎ *1755 N. Highland Ave., Hollywood 90028,* ☎ *213/462–7181 or 800/465–4329,* FAX *213/466–9072. 470 rooms. Restaurant, coffee shop, pool, coin laundry, parking (fee). AE, D, DC, MC, V.*

$ Banana Bungalow Hotel and International Hostel. You'll get the most for your money at this friendly miniresort in the Hollywood Hills, about ½ mile from the Hollywood Bowl. It's popular with backpackers and college students—don't expect a palace. Mostly hostel-style rooms are offered here, with three to six beds in each; you'll be sharing a room with people you don't know, unless you book one of the 12 double-occupancy rooms—be sure to specify what you want when booking. The decor is white and gray, with light wood furniture and plants. Checkout is early, by 10:30 AM. ☎ *2775 Cahuenga Blvd. W, Hollywood 90068,* ☎ *213/851–1129 or 800/446–7835,* FAX *213/851–1569. 56 rooms. Pool, exercise room, billiards, recreation room, theater, airport shuttle, free parking. MC, V.*

Beverly Hills

$$$$ Beverly Hilton. Opened in 1955, this large, contemporary-design hotel complex, with its wide selection of restaurants and shops, may seem nondescript, but in fact it's a popular place for big spenders and Hollywood bigwigs. The large lobby is a favorite meeting place; sitting areas are upholstered with tropical-style fabrics, while other areas look more upscale, with leather furniture surrounded by plenty of marble. Most rooms, decorated in warm tones, have balconies overlooking Beverly Hills or downtown. The on-premises Trader Vic's is one of the city's better restaurants, but you're also within walking distance of Century

City and downtown Beverly Hills eateries. ☎ *9876 Wilshire Blvd., 90210,* ☎ *310/274–7777 or 800/445–8667,* FAX *310/285–1313. 581 rooms. 3 restaurants, refrigerators, pool, wading pool, exercise room, parking (fee). AE, D, DC, MC, V.*

$$$$ **Four Seasons Los Angeles.** Some say this property resembles a French
★ château with the refinement of a European manor house; formal European decorative details are complemented by outpourings of flora from the porte cochere to the pool deck on the second-story rooftop. Rooms are eclectic, some done in pastels, others in a black-and-beige scheme. All suites have French doors and a balcony. There is an outstanding restaurant on the premises serving California cuisine, and there's great shopping only five minutes away on Rodeo Drive and Melrose Avenue. ☎ *300 S. Doheny Dr., Los Angeles 90048,* ☎ *310/273–2222 or 800/332–3442,* FAX *310/859–3824. 285 rooms. Restaurant, lounge, room service, pool, exercise room, free parking and parking (fee). AE, DC, MC, V.*

$$$$ **Hotel Nikko.** Distinctive Japanese accents distinguish this contemporary hotel located near Restaurant Row. Large guest rooms done in traditional pastels cater to business travelers. Traditional Japanese soaking tubs dominate luxurious bathrooms, and a bedside remote-control conveniently operates in-room lighting, temperature, TV, VCRs, and CD players. Pangaea, the hotel restaurant, serves Pacific Rim cuisine. ☎ *465 S. La Cienega Blvd., Los Angeles 90048,* ☎ *310/247– 0400, 800/645–5687, or 800/645–5624,* FAX *310/247–0315. 300 rooms. Restaurant, lounge, room service, pool, fitness center, business services, parking. AE, D, DC, MC, V.*

$$$$ **Hotel Sofitel Ma Maison.** This hotel offers first-class service and the sort of intimacy you usually expect in small European-style hotels. The country-French guest rooms are done in terra-cotta and blues, with small prints. The back of the property faces a large brick wall, so insist on a southern view. ☎ *8555 Beverly Blvd., Los Angeles 90048,* ☎ *310/278–5444 or 800/521–7772,* FAX *310/657–2816. 311 rooms. Restaurant, pool, sauna, fitness center, parking (fee). AE, DC, MC, V.*

$$$$ **Le Parc Hotel.** A boutique hotel housed in a modern low-rise building, the four-story Le Parc is in a lovely residential area. Suites are decorated in earth tones and shades of wine and rust with sunken living rooms, balconies, fireplaces, VCRs, and kitchenettes. The hotel is near Farmer's Market, CBS Television City, and the Los Angeles County Museum of Art. Cafe Le Parc is a private dining room for hotel guests only. ☎ *733 N. West Knoll, West Hollywood 90069,* ☎ *310/855–8888 or 800/578–4837,* FAX *310/659–5230. 154 suites. Restaurant, pool, tennis courts, health club, parking (fee). AE, DC, MC, V.*

$$$$ **Peninsula Beverly Hills.** This luxury hotel was the first new property to open in Beverly Hills in more than two decades when it made its debut in 1991. Surrounded by flowered hedges, poplar trees, and philodendrons, a circular motor court greets guests in rare style. The hotel's appearance is classic, done in French Renaissance architecture with contemporary overtones. Rooms are decorated like luxury homes, with antiques, rich fabrics, and marble floors. ☎ *9882 Little Santa Monica Blvd., 90212,* ☎ *310/551–2888 or 800/462–7899,* FAX *310/ 788– 2319. 195 rooms. 2 restaurants, bar, lap pool, health club, concierge, business services, parking. AE, D, DC, MC, V.*

$$$$ **Regent Beverly Wilshire.** Reigning over the heart of Beverly Hills at
★ the foot of Rodeo Drive, this famous hotel was the setting for much of the film *Pretty Woman.* Warren Beatty once lived here; so did heiress Barbara Hutton. This landmark 12-story property has Italian Renaissance–style architecture with a French neoclassic influence; the guest

rooms have appropriate period furnishings in subtle hues of soft beige and cream, wheat, peach, rose, and celery and glorious marble bathrooms. The multilingual staff offers personal service (like private butlers) and many other extras, such as the fresh strawberries and cream and designer water that are delivered to your room upon arrival. ☎ *9500 Wilshire Blvd., 90212,* ☎ *310/275–5200, 800/421–4354, or 800/427–4354 in CA,* FAX *310/274–2851. 300 rooms and 48 suites. 3 restaurants, no-smoking floors, pool, spa, concierge, business services, parking (fee). AE, D, DC, MC, V.*

$$$ **Beverly Hills Ritz Hotel.** There's a very family-style European feel at this
★ low-rise hotel; the friendly staff will get to know you by name, given half the chance. The cozy black-and-white lobby has overstuffed sofas and lots of plants. All the suites are off the pool. Furnishings are smart and contemporary; all accommodations feature kitchen/living room, one bedroom, and bath. ☎ *10300 Wilshire Blvd., 90024,* ☎ *310/275– 5575 or 800/800–1234. 116 rooms. Restaurant, pool, exercise room, parking (fee). AE, D, DC, MC, V.*

$$$ **Beverly Prescott Hotel.** This small, 12-story luxury hotel, perched on a hill overlooking Beverly Hills, Century City, and the mighty Pacific, opened in May 1993. The open-air architecture is enhanced by soothing rooms decorated in warm salmon and caramel tones. Furnishings are stylish, and the rooms are spacious, with private balconies. Six suites are equipped with their own personal Jacuzzis. ☎ *1224 S. Beverwil Dr., 90035,* ☎ *310/277–2800 or 800/421–3212,* FAX *310/203–9537. 140 rooms. Restaurant, room service, pool, health club, business services, parking (fee). AE, D, DC, MC, V.*

$$$ **Carlyle Inn.** Service is the byword of this intimate, small hostelry in the city's design district. The four-story, contemporary property offers guests several extras: a buffet breakfast in the morning, a glass of wine in the late afternoon. Rooms are decorated in peach with light pine furniture and black accents. ☎ *1119 S. Robertson Blvd., 90035,* ☎ *310/275–4445 or 800/3–227–5953,* FAX *310/859–0496. 32 rooms. Restaurant, exercise room, parking (fee). AE, D, DC, MC, V.*

$$$ **Radisson Beverly Pavilion Hotel.** This eight-floor boutique hotel has a small but cozy lobby with plenty of plants. Located near movie theaters and fashionable shopping, it's popular with commercial travelers, and features the well-known restaurant Colette, with California cuisine and a cocktail lounge. The average-size rooms and executive suites have balconies and are decorated in contemporary styles, mostly in beige, blue, and mauve. ☎ *9360 Wilshire Blvd., 90212,* ☎ *310/273– 1400 or 800/441–5050,* FAX *310/859–8551. 110 rooms. Restaurant, lounge, pool. AE, D, DC, MC, V.*

Century City

$$$$ **Century Plaza Hotel and Tower.** Beside the 20-story hotel (on 10 acres
★ of tropical plants and reflecting pools) is a 30-story tower, which is lavishly decorated with signature art and antiques. Rooms in both are furnished like a mansion, with a mix of classic and contemporary appointments. Each room has a refrigerator and balcony with an ocean or a city view. There are three excellent restaurants here: the award-winning La Chaumiere for California/French cuisine, the Terrace for Mediterranean/Italian, and the Cafe Plaza, a French-style café that serves American fare. ☎ *2025 Ave. of the Stars, 90067,* ☎ *310/277–2000 or 800/228–3000,* FAX *310/551–3355. 1,072 rooms. 3 restaurants, 2 pools, health club, parking. AE, D, DC, MC, V.*

$$$$ **J. W. Marriott Hotel at Century City.** The West Coast flagship for the
★ multifaceted Marriott chain, this hotel has elegant, modern rooms

decorated in soft pastels and equipped with minibars, lavish marble baths, and facilities for travelers with disabilities. ☎ *2151 Ave. of the Stars, 90067, ☎ 310/277–2777 or 800/228–9290, FAX 310/785–9240. 367 rooms. Restaurant, indoor and outdoor pools, health club. AE, D, DC, MC, V.*

$$$ **Century City Courtyard by Marriott.** Located near the Century City business complex, this more-than-comfortable hotel mixes California architecture with traditional fabrics and furnishings in soft hues. ☎ *10320 W. Olympic Blvd., Los Angeles 90067, ☎ 310/556–2777 or 800/947–8521. 133 rooms. Restaurant, exercise room, free parking. AE, D, DC, MC, V.*

$$ **Century City Inn.** This hotel is small but designed for comfort. Baths have whirlpool tubs and a phone. Complimentary Continental breakfast is served. ☎ *10330 W. Olympic Blvd., Los Angeles 90064, ☎ 310/553–1000 or 800/553–1005, FAX 310/277–1633. 48 rooms. Parking (fee). AE, D, DC, MC, V.*

Bel-Air, Westwood, and West Los Angeles

$$$$ **Hotel Bel-Air.** This charming, secluded hotel—a celebrity mecca—is one
★ of Los Angeles's best. Extensive exotic gardens and a creek complete with swans give it the ambience of a top-rated resort. The lovely rooms and suites are impeccably decorated in peach and earth tones. All are villa/bungalow style with Mediterranean decor offering the feel of fine homes. For their quietest accommodation, ask for a room near the former stable area. ☎ *701 Stone Canyon Rd., Bel-Air 90077, ☎ 310/472–1211 or 800/648–4097, FAX 310/476–5890. 92 rooms. Restaurant, lounge, pool, fitness center, parking (fee). AE, DC, MC, V.*

$$$$ **Westwood Marquis Hotel and Gardens.** This hotel near UCLA is a favorite of corporate and entertainment types. Each individualized suite in its 15 stories has a view of Bel-Air, the Pacific Ocean, or Century City. South-facing suites overlooking the pool also offer expansive views of the city and sea. ☎ *930 Hilgard Ave., Los Angeles 90024, ☎ 310/208–8765 or 800/421–2317, FAX 310/824–0355. 257 suites. 2 restaurants, lounge, room service, no-smoking floor, 2 pools, health club, parking (fee). AE, D, DC, MC, V.*

$$$ **Radisson Bel-Air.** In its lovely garden setting, this two-story hotel feels very southern Californian, with patios and terraces overlooking the lush tropical greenery. Despite lots of marble, the lobby is comfortable and fairly intimate and is dominated by a huge tropical flower arrangement. Guest rooms are decorated in muted tones of cream and gray, with furniture in sleek, modern shapes and art deco–style fixtures. Echo, the hotel restaurant featuring California cuisine, is worth checking out. ☎ *11461 Sunset Blvd., Los Angeles 90049, ☎ 310/476–6571 or 800/333–3333. 162 rooms. Restaurant, lounge. no-smoking rooms, pool, tennis courts, health club, concierge, business services, parking (fee). AE, D, DC, MC, V.*

$$–$$$ **Century Wilshire.** Most units in this three-story European-style hotel are suites with kitchenettes and tiled baths, all set in a homey English-style pastel decor. Within walking distance of UCLA and Westwood Village, this simple hotel has views of Wilshire and the courtyard. The clientele here is mostly European. ☎ *10776 Wilshire Blvd., West Los Angeles 90024, ☎ 310/474–4506 or 800/421–7223 (outside CA), FAX 310/474–2535. 99 rooms. Pool, free parking. AE, DC, MC, V.*

$ **Best Western Royal Palace Inn and Suites.** This small hotel, located just off I–405 (San Diego Freeway), is decorated with modern touches, lots of wood, and mirrors. Guest rooms are done in rich greens and teals, with contrasting soft peach and rose tones. All the rooms are suites with cooking facilities, such as microwaves and refrigerators, and a queen sleeper sofa, in addition to the two queen-size beds in each unit. ☏ *2528 S. Sepulveda Blvd., West Los Angeles 90064, ☏ 310/477–9066 or 800/251–3888, FAX 310/478–4133. 55 suites. Pool, exercise room, billiards, laundry service, free parking. AE, D, DC, MC, V.*

Santa Monica

$$$$ **Loews Santa Monica Beach Hotel.** Set on the most precious of Los Angeles's real estate—beachfront—this hotel is two blocks south of the landmark Santa Monica Pier. The property's centerpiece is a five-story glass atrium with views of the Pacific; though it's basically contemporary in design, several details hark back to the Victorian era, when Santa Monica first flourished as a resort community. The restaurant, Riva, serves northern Italian cuisine with an emphasis on seafood. Rooms are California casual with bleached rattan and wicker furniture and quilted bedspreads, in mauve, peach, coral, and sky-blue color schemes. Most have ocean views and private balconies, and all guests have direct access to the beach. ☏ *1700 Ocean Ave., 90401, ☏ 310/458–6700 or 800/325–6397, FAX 310/458–6761. 350 rooms, 35 suites. Restaurant, café, no-smoking floors, indoor-outdoor pool, fitness center, concierge, business services, parking (fee). AE, D, DC, MC, V.*

$$$$ **Miramar Sheraton.** This hotel, "where Wilshire meets the sea," is close to all area beaches, across the street from Pacific Palisades Park, and near deluxe shopping areas and many quaint eateries. The landscape is dominated by a gigantic rubber tree. Divided into three buildings, the hotel includes The Palisades, done in traditional furnishings; The Tower, which sports contemporary decor; and The Bungalows, incorporating separate little cottages in a garden setting. Many rooms have balconies overlooking the ocean. ☏ *101 Wilshire Blvd., 90401, ☏ 310/576–7777 or 800/325–3535. 302 rooms. 2 restaurants, lounge, pool, health club, parking (fee). AE, D, DC, MC, V.*

$$$$ **Shutters on the Beach.** At first glance, this hotel looks like an overgrown beach house. Three separate buildings—just yards from the Pacific—are linked by trellises, balconies, and awnings, like resorts and cottages of the 1920s. Two fireplaces dominate a cozy lobby, which has a vast balcony overlooking the ocean. Contemporary rooms are on the small side but tidily decorated in pastels, with white walls, round-back tufted chairs, and desks and nightstands of dark walnut. Each room has sliding shutter doors (hence the hotel's name), and in the marble bathroom you'll find an oversize Jacuzzi tub with a glass window that opens to look across the room to the outdoors. ☏ *1 Pico Blvd., Santa Monica 90405, ☏ 310/458–0030 or 800/334–9000, FAX 310/458–4589. 198 rooms. 2 restaurants, no-smoking floors, in-room safes, pool, health club, concierge, parking (fee). AE, D, DC, MC, V.*

$$ **Pacific Shore.** This modern, eight-story hotel is one block from the beach and near many highly recommended restaurants. The well-appointed rooms are decorated with contemporary fabrics and modern furniture; some have ocean views. ☏ *1819 Ocean Ave., 90401, ☏ 310/451–8711 or 800/622–8711, FAX 310/394–6657. 168 rooms. Restaurant, lounge, pool, sauna, laundry service, car rental, free parking. AE, D, DC, MC, V.*

$ **Carmel Hotel.** This charming four-story hotel, built in the 1920s, is one block from the beach and Santa Monica Place, as well as from movie theaters and many fine restaurants. The art–deco-style lobby is appealing, and electric ceiling fans add to the simple room decor done in wine, hunter green, and beige tones. ☏ *201 Broadway, 90401, ☏ 310/451–*

Airport Marina
Hotel, **20**

Airport Park View
Hotel, **25**

Barnaby's Hotel, **27**

Best Western Royal
Palace Inn
and Suites, **18**

Carmel Hotel, **1**

Century Wilshire, **14**

Crowne Plaza Redondo
Beach and Marina
Hotel, **28**

Doubletree Hotel LAX, **24**

Doubletree Marina del
Rey L.A., **10**

Holiday Inn LAX, **23**

Holiday Inn Santa
Monica Beach , **6**

Hotel Bel-Air, **16**

Hyatt Hotel LAX, **21**

Loews Santa Monica
Beach Hotel, **3**

Los Angeles Airport
Marriott, **26**

Marina del Rey
Hotel, **11**

Marina del Rey
Marriott Inn, **13**

Marina International
Hotel, **9**

Marina Pacific
Hotel & Suites, **8**

Miramar Sheraton, **2**

Pacific Shore, **4**

Palm Motel, **7**

Radisson Bel-Air, **15**

Red Lion Inn, **19**

Ritz-Carlton, Marina
del Rey, **12**

Sheraton Gateway
Hotel at LAX, **22**

Shutters on the
Beach, **5**

Westwood Marquis
Hotel and Gardens, **17**

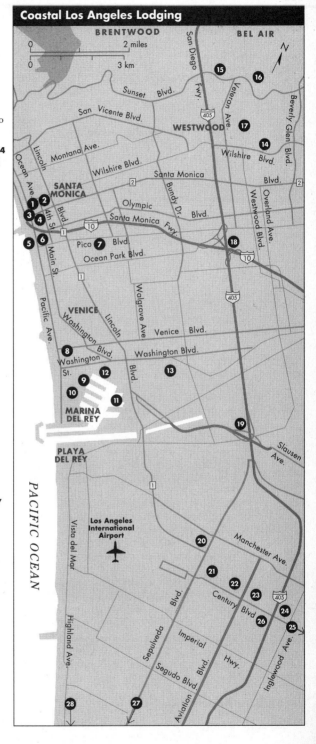

Coastal Los Angeles Lodging

2469 or 800/445–8695, FAX 310/393–4180. 102 rooms, 8 suites. Restaurant, parking (fee). AE, D, DC, MC, V.

Marina del Rey

$$$$ **Doubletree Marina del Rey L.A.** This luxurious, nine-story, high-rise prop-
★ erty has a high-tech design softened by a pastel-toned decor accented in brass and marble. Ask for upper-floor rooms that face the marina. There are lovely touches in this Mediterranean-style hotel, such as a gazebo in the patio and rooms with water views. The restaurant Stones is known for its fresh seafood. 🔁 4100 Admiralty Way, 90292, ☎ 310/301–3000, 800/222–8733, or 800/528–0444, FAX 310/301–6890. 375 rooms. Restaurant, lounges, pool, fitness center, business services, airport shuttle, parking (fee). AE, D, DC, MC, V.

$$$$ **Marina del Rey Hotel.** Completely surrounded by water, this deluxe waterfront hotel is on the marina's main channel, making cruises and char-
ters easily accessible. Guest rooms (contemporary with a nautical touch) have balconies and patios, and many have harbor views. The hotel is within walking distance of shopping and only a bike ride away from Fish-
erman's Village. There are meeting rooms, a beautiful gazebo area for parties, and complimentary access to the nearby fitness club. 🔁 13534 Bali Way, 90292, ☎ 310/301–1000, 800/882–4000, or 800/862–7462 in CA, FAX 310/ 301–8167. 158 rooms. Restaurant, lounge, pool, putting green, airport shuttle, free parking. AE, DC, MC, V.

$$$–$$$$ **Marina International Hotel.** Across from a sandy beach within the ma-
rina, this hotel's village-style decor is done in earth tones with Califor-
nia-style furniture. Each of the very private rooms offers a balcony or patio that faces the garden or the courtyard. Ask for one of the bunga-
lows—they're huge. The Crystal Fountain restaurant has Continental cui-
sine. Boat charters are available for up to 200 people. 🔁 4200 Admiralty Way, 90292, ☎ 310/301–2000, 800/862–7462, or 800/529–2525, FAX 310/301–6687. 110 rooms, 25 bungalows. Restaurant, lounge, pool, health club, airport shuttle, free parking. AE, DC, MC, V.

$$$–$$$$ **Ritz-Carlton, Marina del Rey.** This sumptuous property sits on some prime real estate at the northern end of a basin, offering a panoramic view of the Pacific. The well-appointed contemporary rooms have French doors, marble baths, honor bars, and plenty of amenities—from plush terry robes to maid service twice a day. 🔁 4375 Admiralty Way, 90292, ☎ 310/823–1700, FAX 310/823–7318. 306 rooms. 2 restau-
rants, pool, fitness center, tennis courts, business services, parking (fee). AE, D, DC, MC, V.

$$ **Marina Pacific Hotel & Suites.** This hotel faces the Pacific and one of the world's most vibrant boardwalks; it's nestled among Venice's art galleries, shops, and elegant, offbeat restaurants. The marina is just a stroll away. Comfortable accommodations include suites, conference facilities, full-service amenities, and a delightful sidewalk café. For active travelers, there are ocean swimming, roller skating along the strand, racquetball, and tennis nearby. 🔁 1697 Pacific Ave., Venice 90291, ☎ 310/399–7770 or 800/421–8151, FAX 310/452–5479. 57 rooms, 35 suites; 1-bedroom apartments available. Restaurant, laundry service, free parking. AE, D, DC, MC, V.

South Bay Beach Cities

$$$–$$$$ **Crowne Plaza Redondo Beach and Marina Hotel.** Across the street from the Redondo Beach Pier, this swank five-story hotel overlooks the Pa-
cific. The magnificent lobby has a 2,200-gallon saltwater aquarium as the focal point, and there are plenty of amenities and special touches

throughout the property, including indoor and outdoor dining, a night-club, and the famous Gold's Gym. Rooms are decorated in a seaside theme with light woods and soft colors. The hotel is within walking distance of 15 restaurants. ☎ *300 N. Harbor Dr., Redondo Beach 90277,* ☎ *310/318–8888 or 800/368–9760,* FAX *310/376–1930. 339 rooms. Restaurant, lounge, pool, sauna, tennis, exercise room, business services, parking (fee). AE, D, DC, MC, V.*

$$ **Barnabey's Hotel.** Modeled after a 19th-century English inn, with four-
★ poster beds, lace curtains, and antique decorations, Barnaby's also has an enclosed greenhouse pool. The London Pub resembles a cozy English hangout, with entertainment nightly; Barnabey's Restaurant serves Continental cuisine and has private, curtained booths. A complimentary English buffet breakfast is served. A 1-mile walking path begins at the hotel and ends at the water's edge. ☎ *3501 Sepulveda Blvd. (at Rosecrans), Manhattan Beach 90266,* ☎ *310/545–8466 or 800/552–5285,* FAX *310/545–8621. 126 rooms. 2 restaurants, lounge, no-smoking floor, pool, airport shuttle, free parking. AE, D, DC, MC, V.*

Airport

$$$–$$$$ **Sheraton Gateway Hotel at LAX.** This luxurious 14-story hotel is in the perfect setting for business and leisure travelers alike. The contemporary rooms are decorated in muted shades and are not exceptional but adequate. Forty-eight of the rooms were designed especially for people with disabilities. ☎ *6101 W. Century Blvd., Los Angeles 90045,* ☎ *310/642–1111 or 800/325–3535,* FAX *310/645–1414. 807 rooms. 2 restaurants, lounges, pool, exercise room, concierge. AE, D, DC, MC, V.*

$$$ **Doubletree Hotel LAX.** This three-wing hotel is a good place to stay if
★ you want to be pampered but also need to be close to the airport. Rooms and suites are decorated in muted earth tones to complement the contemporary decor; many suites have private outdoor spas. The expansive, luxurious lobby is decorated in marble and brass. The Trattoria Grande restaurant features pasta and seafood specialties. ☎ *5400 W. Century Blvd., Los Angeles 90045,* ☎ *310/216–5858,* FAX *310/670–1948. 729 rooms. 2 restaurants, lounge, pool, sauna, fitness center, business services, parking (fee). AE, D, DC, MC, V.*

$$$ **Hyatt Hotel–LAX.** Rich brown marble in the lobby entrance and dark wood columns delineate the neoclassical decor of this contemporary 12-story building close to LAX, Hollywood Park, the Forum, and Marina del Rey. The Hyatt keeps business travelers in mind, offering in-room fax machines, computer hookups, and voice mail, plus large meeting rooms with ample banquet space. ☎ *6225 W. Century Blvd., Los Angeles 90045,* ☎ *310/337–1234 or 800/233–1234,* FAX *310/641–6924. 594 rooms. 2 restaurants, lounge, no-smoking floors, pool, health club, parking (fee). AE, D, DC, MC, V.*

$$$ **Los Angeles Airport Marriott.** This 18-story Marriott is a fully equipped convention center, convenient to the beach, Marina del Rey, Fisherman's Village, the Forum, and the Coliseum. Complimentary airport bus service gets you to LAX in just about four minutes. All guest rooms are designed to provide maximum space and comfort in relaxing earth tones; some have sitting areas and balconies. ☎ *5855 W. Century Blvd., Los Angeles 90045,* ☎ *310/641–5700 or 800/228–9290,* FAX *310/337–5358. 1,010 rooms. 4 restaurants, lounge, pool, health club, laundry facilities, business services, parking (fee). AE, D, DC, MC, V.*

$$ **Airport Marina Hotel.** Located in a quiet, residential area, perfect for jogging, tennis, and golf, is this contemporary hotel, with four separate wings and several buildings, the main one a 12-story high-rise. The

large marble lobby boasts writing tables, plants, and comfortable sofas. The rooms are warm, with plenty of wood; all have either a pool, ocean, or airport view. In the restaurant, Marina Cafe, you can get New York–style deli favorites. A shuttle service goes to LAX, Marina del Rey, and Fox Hills Mall. ☎ *8601 Lincoln Blvd., Los Angeles 90045,* ✆ *310/670–8111 or 800/800–6333,* ﬀ﹩ *310/337–1883. 770 rooms. Restaurant, pool, airport shuttle. AE, D, DC, MC, V.*

$ **Holiday Inn–LAX.** This international-style hotel appeals to families as well as business types, with standard Holiday Inn rooms decorated in earth tones—beige, burgundy, orange, and green. Amenities include a California-cuisine restaurant and cocktail lounge, multilingual telephone operators, and tour information. ☎ *9901 La Cienega Blvd., Los Angeles 90045,* ✆ *310/649–5151 or 800/624–0025,* ﬀ﹩ *310/670–3619. 403 rooms. Restaurant, pool, exercise room, airport shuttle, parking (fee). AE, D, DC, MC, V.*

$ **Red Lion Inn.** Just 3 miles north of LAX and a few minutes from Marina del Rey, this deluxe hotel is convenient for business types. There is both elegant and casual dining. The Culver's Club Lounge has lively entertainment and dancing. The oversize guest rooms on 12 floors have a '90s version of art deco–style decor. Extra special is the California Suite, with beautiful decorations and its own Jacuzzi. ☎ *6161 Centinela Ave., Culver City 90231,* ✆ *310/649–1776 or 800/547–8010,* ﬀ﹩ *310/649–4411. 368 rooms. 2 restaurants, lounge, no-smoking floors, pool, sauna, health club, free parking. AE, D, DC, MC, V.*

Pasadena

$$$–$$$$ **Ritz-Carlton Huntington Hotel.** This landmark hotel, built in 1906, was closed in 1986 for five years and virtually rebuilt to conform to earthquake-code standards. Reopened in 1991, it justifies the enormous effort. The main building, a Mediterranean-style structure in warm-color stucco, fits perfectly with the lavish houses of the surrounding Oak Knoll neighborhood, Pasadena's best. Walk through the intimate lobby into the central courtyard, dotted with tiny ponds and lush plantings, to the wood-paneled grand lounge, where you can have afternoon tea while enjoying a sweeping view of Los Angeles in the distance. Guest rooms are traditionally furnished and handsome, although a bit small for the price; the large marble-fitted bathrooms also look old-fashioned. The landscaped grounds are lovely, with their Japanese and horseshoe gardens and the historic Picture Bridge, which has murals depicting scenes of California along its 20 gables. The food is excellent and the service attentive. ☎ *1401 S. Oak Knoll Ave., Pasadena 91106,* ✆ *818/568–3900 or 800/241–3333,* ﬀ﹩ *818/568–3700. 383 rooms. 2 restaurants, no-smoking floors, pool, tennis courts, health club, parking (fee). AE, D, DC, MC, V.*

San Fernando Valley

$$$$ **Sheraton Universal.** You're apt to see movie and TV stars in this large, 21-story hotel (with a three-story poolside wing). It's on the way up the hill to Universal Studios, overlooking Hollywood and within walking distance of the Universal Amphitheater, Universal Studios Tour, and CityWalk (*see* Chapter 2, Exploring Los Angeles, for details). The rooms are decorated in natural tones, with floor-to-ceiling windows that actually open, should you care to get some fresh air. ☎ *333 Universal Terrace Pkwy., Universal City 91608,* ✆ *818/980–1212 or 800/325–3535,* ﬀ﹩ *818/985–4980. 442 rooms. Restaurant, lounge, no-smoking floors, pool, health club, business services, parking (fee). AE, D, DC, MC, V.*

Beverly
Garland's
Holiday Inn, **3**

Burbank
Airport
Hilton, **6**

Radisson Valley
Center Hotel
Los Angeles, **2**

Ritz-Carlton
Huntington
Hotel, **8**

Safari Inn, **7**

Sheraton
Universal, **5**

Sportsman's
Lodge Hotel, **1**

Universal City
Hilton and
Towers, **4**

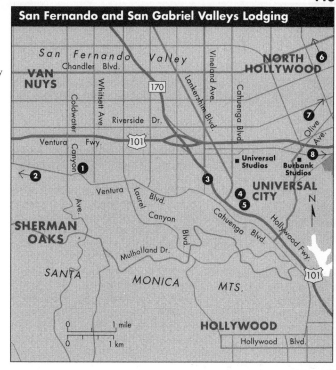

San Fernando and San Gabriel Valleys Lodging

$$$$ **Universal City Hilton and Towers.** This 24-story glass tower blends contemporary luxury with the charm of an Old World European hotel. The pleasant rooms are decorated in warm tones of burgundy and hunter green, and the bathrooms have wall-to-wall marble. Breathtaking views of the San Fernando Valley and hills can be enjoyed through floor-to-ceiling windows. Inside the 40-foot-high pavilions next to the guest tower is a restaurant and two lounges. There is a nearby tennis center and an equestrian center, and golf courses are a short drive away. A popular place for TV location filming, the hotel is also close to the Universal Amphitheater, Universal Studios Tour, CityWalk, and the Hollywood Bowl. ⌨ *555 Universal Terrace Pkwy., Universal City 91608,* ☎ *818/506–2500,* ℻ *818/ 509–2058. 446 rooms. Restaurant, 2 lounges, no-smoking floors, pool, health club, parking (fee). AE, D, DC, MC, V.*

$$$ **Burbank Airport Hilton.** Across the street from the Hollywood–Burbank Airport and close to Universal Studios is this contemporary Hilton with two towers, one with eight floors and the other with nine. It's geared to business meetings—there's a state-of-the-art convention center on the premises. The mauve-and-pink lobby is large; rooms have standard-issue hotel decor with no particularly nice views. In other words, don't expect anything snazzy. ⌨ *2500 Hollywood Way, Burbank 91505,* ☎ *818/843–6000, 800/643–7400 in CA, 800/468–3576 outside CA,* ℻ *818/842–9720. 500 rooms. Restaurant, in-room VCRs, pool, spa, parking (fee). AE, D, DC, MC, V.*

$$ **Beverly Garland's Holiday Inn.** There's a country-club atmosphere to this lodgelike hotel in two separate buildings. It's popular with business and entertainment folk and offers private balconies and patios. Rooms carry out the early California look with distressed furniture and muted color schemes, and there are Sierra Madre and Santa Monica mountain views from their balconies. The property is convenient to Universal Studios, but it's also right next to the Hollywood Freeway, so ask for a room facing the front of the main entrance. ☎ *4222 Vineland Ave., North Hollywood 91602,* ☎ *818/980–8000 or 800/238–3759,* FAX *818/766–5230. 258 rooms. Restaurant, lounge, pool, wading pool, tennis courts, meeting rooms, free parking. AE, D, DC, MC, V.*

$$ **Radisson Valley Center Hotel Los Angeles.** In addition to excellent service and comfort, this contemporary hotel boasts a convenient location (at the intersection of I–405 and Hwy. 101), fairly near to Universal Studios and other Southland attractions. The pastel-toned decor incorporates whitewashed-wood furniture. This hotel is well equipped for conventioneers, and there are plush executive suites. A fitness center in the penthouse provides private trainers. ☎ *15433 Ventura Blvd., Sherman Oaks 91403,* ☎ *818/981–5400 or 800/333–3333,* FAX *818/981–3175. 216 rooms. Restaurant, lounge, no-smoking floors, pool, health club, parking (fee). AE, DC, MC, V.*

$$ **Sportsman's Lodge Hotel.** An English country–style building with a resort atmosphere, this hotel features beautiful grounds with waterfalls, a swan-filled lagoon, and a bright white gazebo. Guest rooms are large, and are decorated in soft colors like mauve and blue. Studio suites with private patios are available, and there's an Olympic-size swimming pool and a restaurant that serves American and Continental cuisine. The hotel is close to the Universal Studios Tour and Universal Amphitheater. ☎ *12825 Ventura Blvd., North Hollywood 91604,* ☎ *818/769–4700 or 800/821–8511,* FAX *213/877–3898. 193 rooms. 3 restaurants, pool, health club, free parking. AE, D, DC, MC, V.*

$ **Safari Inn.** Often used for location filming, this motel-like property near Warner Brothers Studios, encompassing two buildings, has a homey, neighborhood feel. The decor, in antique white and gold, has a modern flair, as for example in the rooms with sleek rattan-and-bamboo furniture. There's a fine Italian restaurant called Jane's Cucina on the premises. ☎ *1911 W. Olive, Burbank 91506,* ☎ *818/845–8586 or 800/782–4373,* FAX *818/845–0054. 110 rooms. Restaurant, lounge, refrigerators, pool, free parking. AE, DC, MC, V.*

7 The Arts and Nightlife

FOR THE MOST COMPLETE LISTING OF WEEKLY EVENTS, get the current issue of *Los Angeles* magazine. The Calendar section of the *Los Angeles Times* also offers a wide survey of Los Angeles arts events, as do the more irreverent free publications, the *L.A. Weekly* and the *L.A. Reader*. For a telephone report on current music, theater, dance, film, and special events, plus a discount ticket source, call 213/688–2787.

Most tickets can be purchased by phone (with a credit card) from **Ticketmaster** (☎ 213/365–3500), **TeleCharge** (☎ 800/762–7666), **Good Time Tickets** (☎ 213/464–7383), **Tickets L.A.** (☎ 213/660–8587), or **Murray's Tickets** (☎ 213/234–0123).

THE ARTS

Theater

Los Angeles isn't quite the "Broadway of the West" as some have claimed—the scope of theater here really doesn't compare to that in New York. Still, there are plenty of offerings worth any visitor's time in this entertainment-oriented city.

The theater scene's growth has been astounding. In 1978 only about 370 professional productions were brought to stages in Los Angeles; now well over 1,000 are scheduled each year. Small theaters are blossoming all over town, and the larger houses, despite price hikes to $35 for a single ticket, are usually full.

Even small productions might boast big names from "the Business" (the Los Angeles entertainment empire). Many film and television actors love to work on the stage between "big" projects or while on hiatus from a TV series as a way to refresh their talents or regenerate their creativity in this demanding medium. Doing theater is also an excellent way to be seen by those who matter in the glitzier end of show biz. Hence there is a need for both large houses—which usually mount productions that are road-company imports of Broadway hits or, on occasion, where Broadway-bound material gets a tryout—and a host of small, intimate theaters to showcase the talent that abounds in this city.

Major Theaters
The **Music Center** (135 N. Grand Ave., ☎ 213/972–7211). This big downtown complex includes three theaters: the **Ahmanson Theater,** presenting both classics and new plays; the 3,200-seat **Dorothy Chandler Pavilion,** which offers a smattering of plays in between performances of the L.A. Philharmonic, L.A. Master Chorale, and L.A. Opera; and the 760-seat **Mark Taper Forum,** under the direction of Gordon Davidson, which presents new works that often go on to Broadway, such as *Angels in America* and *Jelly's Last Jam.*
James A. Doolittle Theater (1615 N. Vine St., Hollywood, ☎ 213/972–0700, or call Ticketmaster, ☎ 213/365–3500). Located in the heart of Hollywood, this house offers an intimate feeling despite its 1,038-seat capacity. New plays, dramas, comedies, and musicals are presented here year-round.
John Anson Ford Theater (2580 Cahuenga Blvd., Hollywood, ☎ 213/744–3466). This 1,300-seat outdoor house in the Hollywood Hills is best known for its Shakespeare and free summer jazz, dance, and cabaret concerts.

Pantages (6233 Hollywood Blvd., Hollywood, ☎ 213/468–1770, or call Ticketmaster, ☎ 213/365–3500). Once the home of the Academy Awards telecast and Hollywood premieres, this house is massive (2,600 seats) and a splendid example of high-style Hollywood Art Deco, although the acoustics could use some updating. Large-scale musicals from Broadway are usually presented here.

Westwood Playhouse (10886 Le Conte Ave., Westwood, ☎ 310/208–6500 or 310/208–5454). An acoustically superior theater with great sight lines, the 498-seat playhouse showcases new plays in the summer, primarily musicals and comedies. Many of the productions here are on their way to or from Broadway. This is also where Jason Robards and Nick Nolte got their starts.

Wilshire Theater (8440 Wilshire Blvd., Beverly Hills, ☎ 213/468–1716 and 213/468–1799, or call Ticketmaster, ☎ 213/365–3500). The interior of this 1,900-seat house is Art Deco–style; musicals from Broadway are the usual fare.

Smaller Theaters

Cast Theater (804 N. El Centro, Hollywood, ☎ 213/462–0265). Musicals, revivals, and avant-garde improv pieces are done here.

The **Coast Playhouse** (8325 Santa Monica Blvd., West Hollywood, ☎ 213/650–8507). The specialty of this 99-seat house is excellent original musicals and new dramas.

Fountain Theater (5060 Fountain Ave., Hollywood, ☎ 213/663–1525). This theater, which seats 80, presents original American dramas and stages flamenco dance concerts. Marian Mercer and Rob Reiner got their starts here.

Japan America Theater (244 S. San Pedro St., downtown, ☎ 213/680–3700). This community-oriented 880-seat theater at the Japan Cultural Arts Center is home to local theater, dance troupes, and the L.A. Chamber Orchestra, plus numerous children's theater groups.

Santa Monica Playhouse (1211 4th St., Santa Monica, ☎ 310/394–9779). With 99 seats, this house is worth visiting for its cozy, library-like atmosphere; the good comedies, dramas, and children's programs presented here are a further incentive.

Skylight Theater (1816½ N. Vermont Ave., Los Feliz, ☎ 213/666–2202). Many highly inventive productions have been hosted in this 99-seat theater.

Theatre/Theater (1713 Cahuenga Blvd., Hollywood, ☎ 213/871–0210). Angelenos crowd into this 70-seat house to view original works by local authors as well as international playwrights.

Concerts

Los Angeles is not only the focus of America's pop/rock music recording scene, but now, after years of being denigrated as a cultural invalid, is also a center for classical music and opera.

Major Concert Halls

Dorothy Chandler Pavilion (135 N. Grand Ave., ☎ 213/972–7211). Part of the Los Angeles Music Center and—with the Hollywood Bowl—the center of L.A.'s classical music scene, the 3,200-seat Pavilion is the home of the Los Angeles Philharmonic. The L.A. Opera presents classics from September through June.

The **Greek Theater** (2700 N. Vermont Ave., ☎ 213/665–1927). This open-air auditorium near Griffith Park offers some classical performances in its mainly pop/rock/jazz schedule from June through October. Its Doric columns evoke the amphitheaters of ancient Greece.

The **Hollywood Bowl** (2301 Highland Ave., ☎ 213/850–2000). Open since 1920, the Bowl has been one of the world's largest outdoor amphitheaters, located in a park surrounded by mountains, trees, and gardens. The Bowl's season runs early July–mid-September; the L.A. Philharmonic spends its summer season here. There are performances daily except Mondays (and some Sundays); the program ranges from jazz to pop to classical. Concert goers usually arrive early, bringing or buying picnic suppers. There are plenty of picnic tables, and box-seat subscribers can reserve a table right in their own box. Restaurant dining is available on the grounds (reservations recommended, ☎ 213/851–3588). The seats are wood, so you might bring or rent a cushion—and bring a sweater; it gets chilly here in the evening. A convenient way to enjoy the Hollywood Bowl experience without the hassle of parking is to take one of the Park-and-Ride buses, which leave from various locations around town; call the Bowl for information.

The **Shrine Auditorium** (665 W. Jefferson Blvd., ☎ 213/749–5123). Built in 1926 by the Al Malaikah Temple, the auditorium's decor could be called Baghdad and Beyond. Touring companies from all over the world, along with assorted gospel and choral groups, appear in this one-of-a-kind, 6,200-seat theater.

The **Wilshire Ebell Theater** (4401 W. 8th St., ☎ 213/939–1128). The Los Angeles Opera Theatre comes to this Spanish-style building, erected in 1924, as do a broad spectrum of other musical performers.

Wiltern Theater (Wilshire Blvd. and Western Ave., ☎ 213/380–5005 or 213/388–1400). Reopened in 1985 as a venue for the Los Angeles Opera Theater, the building was constructed in 1930 and is listed in the National Register of Historic Places. It is a magnificent example of Art Deco in its green terra-cotta glory.

Dance

Due to lack of Music Center funding, Los Angeles lost the Joffrey Ballet in 1991, and Angelenos have since turned to local dance companies. You can find talented companies dancing at various performance spaces around town. Check the *L.A. Weekly* free newspaper under "dance" to see who is dancing where, or call the **Dance Resource Center** (☎ 213/622–0815) or the **Art's Line** (☎ 213/688–2787).

L.A. has one major resident company, the **Bella Lewistsky Dance Co.** (☎ 213/580–6338), which performs around town.

Visiting companies, such as Martha Graham, Paul Taylor, and Hubbard Street Dance Company, perform in UCLA Dance Company's home space at **UCLA Center for the Arts** (405 N. Hilgard Ave., ☎ 310/825–2101).

Larger companies, such as the Kirov, the Bolshoi, and the American Ballet Theater (ABT), perform at various times during the year at the **Shrine Auditorium** (665 W. Jefferson Blvd., ☎ 213/749–5123).

Also, two prominent dance events occur annually: the Dance Fair in March and Dance Kaleidoscope in July. Both events take place at **Cal State L.A.'s Dance Department** (5151 State University Dr., ☎ 213/343–5124).

Film

Spending two hours at a movie while visiting Los Angeles needn't be taking time out from sightseeing. Some of the country's most historic and beautiful theaters are found here, hosting both first-run and revival films. Movie listings are advertised daily in the *Los Angeles Times* Calendar section. The price of admission to first-run movies is, as of this writing, $6.50–$7.50. Bargain prices as low as $4 are common for the first showing of the day.

Movie Palaces

Mann's Chinese Theater (6925 Hollywood Blvd., Hollywood, ☎ 213/464–8111). Perhaps the world's best-known theater houses three movie screens, and it still hosts many gala premieres.

Pacific Cinerama Dome (6360 Sunset Blvd., Hollywood, ☎ 213/466–3401). This futuristic, geodesic structure was the first theater designed specifically for Cinerama in the United States. The gigantic screen and multitrack sound system create an unparalleled cinematic experience.

Pacific's El Capitan (6838 Hollywood Blvd., Hollywood, ☎ 213/467–7674). Restored to its original Art Deco splendor, this classic movie palace reopened across the street from Mann's Chinese in 1991. First-run movies are on the bill.

Vista Theater (4473 Sunset Dr., Los Feliz, ☎ 213/660–6639). At the intersection of Hollywood and Sunset boulevards, this 70-year-old cinema was once Bard's Hollywood Theater, where both moving pictures and vaudeville played. A Spanish-style facade leads to an ornate Egyptian interior.

Art Houses

The **Laemmle Theater** chain hosts the best of the latest foreign releases. See its *Los Angeles Times* Calendar ad for listings.

Cineplex (8522 Beverly Blvd., 8th Floor of Beverly Center, ☎ 310/652–7760). This 14-screen cinema offers foreign films as well as first-run features.

Los Feliz Theater (1822 N. Vermont Ave., Los Feliz, ☎ 213/664–2169). This multiscreen cinema has a comfortable feel, more like a neighborhood theater than a chain multiplex.

Melnitz Hall (405 Hilgard Ave., ☎ 310/825–2345). UCLA's main film theater runs a mixture of the old, the avant-garde, and the neglected.

New Beverly Cinema (7165 Beverly Blvd., ☎ 213/938–4038). Film festivals, Hollywood classics, documentaries, and notable foreign films are the fare at this theater. There is always a double bill.

Nuart (11272 Santa Monica Blvd., West Los Angeles, ☎ 310/478–6379). The best-kept of L.A.'s revival houses, this place has an excellent screen, good double bills, and special midnight shows.

Royal Theatre (11523 Santa Monica Blvd., Santa Monica, ☎ 310/478–1041). New films by independent filmmakers and foreign films are the usual fare at this art house.

Silent Movie (611 N. Fairfax Ave., ☎ 213/653–2389). This theater revives classics like Charlie Chaplin's *The Gold Rush* and the portfolio of Buster Keaton films. Open Wednesday, Friday, and Saturday evenings, it's known as the only silent movie house in the world, complete with a vintage organ.

Television

Audiences Unlimited (100 Universal City Plaza, Bldg. 153, Universal City 91608, ☎ 818/506–0043) is a nifty organization that helps fill seats for television programs (and sometimes theater events, as well). There's no charge, but the tickets are on a first- come, first-served basis. Shows to see include *Roseanne, Family Matters, Home Improvement, Mad About You, Coach, Murphy Brown,* and *Married . . .with Children.* Tickets can be picked up at Fox Television Center (5746 Sunset Blvd., Van Ness Ave. entrance, weekdays 8:30–6, weekends 11–6) or at the Glendale Galleria Information Desk between 10 and 9 daily. Note: You must be 16 or older to attend a television taping. For a schedule, send a self-addressed envelope to the address above a couple of weeks prior to your visit.

NIGHTLIFE

Despite the high energy level of the nightlife crowd, Los Angeles nightclubs aren't known for keeping their doors open until the wee hours. This is still an early-to-bed city, and it's safe to say that by 2 AM, most jazz, rock, and disco clubs have closed for the night.

The accent in this city is on trendy rock clubs, smooth country-and-western establishments, intimate jazz spots, and comedy clubs. Consult *Los Angeles* magazine for current listings. The Sunday *Los Angeles Times* Calendar section and the free *L.A. Weekly* and *L.A. Reader* also provide listings.

The Sunset Strip offers a wide assortment of nighttime diversions. Comedy stores, restaurants with piano bars, cocktail lounges, and hard-rock clubs proliferate. Westwood, home of UCLA, is a college town, and this section of Los Angeles comes alive at night with rock and new-wave clubs playing canned and live music. It's one of the few areas in the city with a true neighborhood spirit. In past years, downtown Los Angeles hasn't offered much in the way of nighttime entertainment (with the exception of the Music Center for concerts and theater), but that is gradually changing, with the openings of more theaters and trendy clubs. Some of Los Angeles's best jazz clubs, discos, and comedy clubs are scattered throughout the San Fernando and San Gabriel valleys.

Dress codes vary, depending on the place you visit. Jackets are expected at cabarets and hotels. Discos are generally casual, although some will turn away the denim-clad. The rule of thumb is to phone ahead and check the dress code, but on the whole, Los Angeles is oriented toward casual wear.

Jazz

Atlas Bar & Grill (3760 Wilshire Blvd., ☎ 213/380–8400). The eclectic entertainment at this snazzy supper club includes torch singers as well as a jazz band.

Baked Potato (3787 Cahuenga Blvd. W, North Hollywood, ☎ 818/980–1615). In this tiny club they pack you in like sardines to hear a powerhouse of jazz. The featured item on the menu is, of course, baked potatoes; they're jumbo and stuffed with everything from steak to vegetables.

Bird of Paradise (1800 E. Broadway, Long Beach, ☎ 310/590–8773). This is a casual place to come for contemporary jazz, Art Deco decor, and popular happy hours.

Catalina Bar and Grill (1640 N. Cahuenga Blvd., Hollywood, ☎ 213/466–2210). Big-name acts and innovators like Latin-influenced saxophonist Paquito D. Rivera have played at this top Hollywood jazz spot. Continental cuisine is served.

House of Blues (8430 Sunset Blvd., Hollywood, ☎ 213/650–1451). The most happening nightclub on the Sunset Strip, this house has an impressive following, with three bars surrounding the large dance floor. Past performers have included Etta James, Lou Rawls, Joe Cocker, and the Commodores. Some shows are presented in cabaret style, where dinner is served. Every Sunday there's a gospel brunch.

Jax (339 N. Brand Blvd., Glendale, ☎ 818/500–1604). This intimate
club serves a wide variety of food, from ribs to pasta; live music is an
added draw.

Jazz Bakery (3221 Hutchison, Culver City, ☎ 310/271–9039). On weekends Jim Britt opens his photography studio, adjacent to the Helms
Bakery Building, to serve coffee, desserts, and a nice selection of world-
class jazz, enhanced by great acoustics and a smoke-free environment.
The $15 admission (no credit cards) includes refreshments.

Le Cafe (14633 Ventura Blvd., Sherman Oaks, ☎ 818/986–2662). The
Room Upstairs has high-tech decor and features mellow jazz. Downstairs is a dynamic restaurant-café offering everything from onion
soup to some of the best stuffed mushrooms in town.

The Lighthouse (30 Pier Ave., Hermosa Beach, ☎ 310/372–6911 or
310/376–9833). Once one of Los Angeles's finest jazz venues, this club
now offers a broad spectrum of music, from blues to Motown to reggae—though not much jazz anymore, except at Sunday brunch.

Marla's Jazz Supper Club (2323 W. Martin Luther King Jr. Blvd., Los
Angeles, ☎ 213/294–8430). Owned by comedy star Marla Gibbs of
The Jeffersons and *227,* the room pops with blues, jazz, and easy lis-
tening. James Ingram plays here from time to time.

Studio City Bar and Grill (11002 Ventura Blvd., Studio City, ☎ 8l8/763–
7912). This neighborhood club in the heart of the Studio district draws
casual customers who want to play pool or shoot darts while they imbibe. Jazz and blues musicians play Wednesday through Sunday.

Folk, Pop, and Rock

Alligator Lounge (3321 Pico Blvd., Santa Monica, ☎ 310/449–1843).
A wide range of musical acts appear at this bar/restaurant that serves
Cajun cuisine. ⊙ Friday through Monday.

Anti-Club (4658 Melrose Ave., Hollywood, ☎ 213/661–3913). If
you're looking for the underground (in rock bands, that is), seek out
this dimly lit, smoke-filled hangout.

Blue Saloon (4657 Lankershim Blvd., North Hollywood, ☎ 818/766–
4644). For rock and roll, this is the place to go. (You'll also catch a
smattering of country and blues at times.) If your seat gets tired while
listening to the music, rustle up a game of billiards or darts. This is the
friendliest club around.

Club Lingerie (6507 Sunset Blvd., Hollywood, ☎ 213/466–8557). One
local describes this place as "clean enough for the timid, yet seasoned
quite nicely for the tenured scenester." Best of all is its mix of really
hot bands.

Ghengis Cohen Cantina (740 N. Fairfax Ave., West Hollywood, ☎
213/653–0640). At this longtime music industry hangout, you can hear
up-and-coming talent, usually in a refreshingly mellow format like MTV's
"Unplugged" performances. A plus is the restaurant's Chinese cuisine.

Kingston 12 (814 Broadway, Santa Monica, ☎ 310/451–4423). This
Santa Monica club is known for its rap music, although reggae is also
on tap, as is a menu of fine Jamaican food.

McCabe's Guitar Shop (3101 Pico Blvd., Santa Monica, ☎ 310/828–
4497; concert information, 310/828–4403). Folk, acoustic rock, blue-
grass, and soul concerts are featured in this guitar store on weekend
nights. Coffee, herbal tea, apple juice, and homemade sweets are served
during intermission. Make reservations well in advance.

The Palace (1735 N. Vine St., Hollywood, ☎ 213/462–3000). The "in"
spot for the upwardly mobile, this plush Art Deco palace boasts lively
entertainment, a fabulous sound system, a full bar, and dining upstairs.
The patrons here dress to kill.

The Palladium (6215 W. Sunset Blvd., Hollywood, ☎ 213/962–7600). The Palladium is often the place to "be." Occasionally, rock bands appear here, drawing a funky crowd.

Pier 52 (52 Pier Ave., Hermosa Beach, ☎ 310/376–1629). From Wednesday through Saturday dance bands play pure rock and roll. Sunday, however, is designated the day of blues.

The Roxy (9009 Sunset Blvd., West Hollywood, ☎ 310/276–2222). The premier Los Angeles rock club, classy and comfortable, offers performance art as well as theatrical productions.

The Strand (1700 S. Pacific Coast Hwy., Redondo Beach, ☎ 310/316–1700). This major concert venue covers a lot of ground, hosting hot new acts or such old favorites as Asleep at the Wheel, blues man Albert King, rock vet Robin Trower, and Billy Vera, all in the same week.

The Troubadour (9081 Santa Monica Blvd., West Hollywood, ☎ 310/276–6168). In the early '70s this was one of the hottest clubs in town for major talent and it's rolling again.

Viper Room (8852 Sunset Blvd., West Hollywood, ☎ 310/358–1880). This musicians' hangout, part-owned by actor Johnny Depp, devotes itself to music and dance in the pop, rock, blues, and jazz/fusion genres.

Whiskey A Go Go (8901 Sunset Blvd., West Hollywood, ☎ 310/652–4202). This, the most famous rock-and-roll club on the Sunset Strip, presents up-and-coming alternative, very hard rock, and punk bands.

Cabaret

Gardena Club (7066 Santa Monica Blvd., Hollywood, ☎ 213/467–7444). This East Coast–style cabaret offers an elegant setting for its singers, comedy, and variety performances. The menu offers mediocre Italian fare.

L.A. Cabaret (17271 Ventura Blvd., Encino, ☎ 818/501–3737). This two-room club features a variety of comedy acts as well as karaoke. Famous entertainers often make surprise appearances. Light fare such as chicken and fish dishes are served.

Luna Park (665 Robertson Blvd., West Hollywood, ☎ 310/652–0611). A self-described "club in progress," this New York–style cabaret features an eclectic mix of music, with three stages and two bars. Locally famous drag queens strut their stuff here.

Queen Mary (12449 Ventura Blvd., Sherman Oaks, ☎ 818/506–5619). Female impersonators vamp it up as Diana Ross, Barbra Streisand, and Bette Midler in this small club where every seat is a good one.

Discos and Dancing

Bar One (9229 Sunset Blvd., Beverly Hills, ☎ 310/271–8355).This hot, hip place for dancing, is considered L.A.'s club of the moment.

Circus Disco and Arena (6655 Santa Monica Blvd., Hollywood, ☎ 213/462–1291 or 213/462–1742). A gay and mixed crowd flocks to these two huge side-by-side discos, which feature techno and rock music.

Coconut Teaszer (8117 Sunset Blvd., Los Angeles, ☎ 213/654–4773). Dancing to live music, a great barbecue menu, and killer drinks make for lively fun. Pool tables are always crowded.

Crush Bar Continental Club (1743 Cahuenga Ave., Hollywood, ☎ 213/463–7685). If the 1960s is a decade that appeals to you, stop by this happening dance club, open Friday and Saturday evenings.

Florentine Gardens (5951 Hollywood Blvd., Hollywood, ☎ 213/464–0706). Here's one of Los Angeles's largest dance areas, with spectacular lighting to match. It's open Friday, Saturday, and Sunday.

Glam Slam (333 S. Boylston, Los Angeles, ☎ 213/482–6626). A New York–style club, this hot spot has a restricted entrance policy—there's a large celebrity clientele, and everybody's dressed to kill. It's open Friday and Saturday until 4 AM. This club is in a terrible neighborhood, so be prepared to shell out for valet parking.

Moonlight Tango Cafe (13730 Ventura Blvd., Sherman Oaks, ☎ 818/788–2000). This high-energy club-restaurant, big on the swing era, really gets moving in the wee hours, when a conga line inevitably takes shape on the dance floor.

Oar House (2941 Main St., Santa Monica, ☎ 310/396–4725). Perhaps because there's no cover charge, or maybe just because this is a relaxing place to hang out, this club is frequented by Westsiders who like pop music. Monday is oldies night.

Roxbury (8225 Sunset Blvd., West Hollywood, ☎ 213/656–1750). Live music, from hip-hop to oldies from the '70s, fills the air at this lively night spot that's also known for its gourmet pizza.

7969 (7969 Santa Monica Blvd., West Hollywood, ☎ 213/654–0280). This fun bar caters to a gay clientele, with live music and drag shows. There's a large dance floor and a super sound system.

Tatou (233 N. Beverly Dr., Beverly Hills, ☎ 310/274–9955).This contemporary downstairs club/restaurant attracts a world-weary older crowd who often wander upstairs to mingle with the younger set on the spacious dance floor.

Country Music

In Cahoots (223 N. Glendale Ave., Glendale, ☎ 818/500–1665). At this raucous dance hall, à la Nashville, you can learn how to two-step if you don't already know how. All week long there's live music. Open seven nights.

The Palomino (6907 Lankershim Blvd., North Hollywood, ☎ 818/764–4010). There's occasionally a wild crowd at this premier country showcase, where good old boys and urban cowboys meet and everybody has a good time.

Hotel Lounges and Piano Bars

Alberto's Ristorante (8826 Melrose Ave., Los Angeles, ☎ 310/278–2770). This piano bar draws a neighborhood crowd, mostly over 40 and well-to-do. Alberto's also serves excellent Italian food.

Century Plaza Hotel and Tower (2025 Ave. of the Stars, Century City, ☎ 310/277–2000). The Lobby Court features piano music nightly.

Hollywood Roosevelt (700 Hollywood Blvd., Hollywood, ☎ 213/466–7000). The grand lobby, done in shades of rose and taupe, is an elegant setting for cocktails.

Hotel Bel-Air (701 Stone Canyon Rd., Bel Air, ☎ 310/472–1211). There's entertainment every night, alternating between a pianist and a vocalist, in one of Los Angeles's most famous hotels.

Hyatt Regency (711 S. Hope St., Los Angeles, ☎ 213/683–1234). There's a good piano lounge in this spectacularly designed hotel.

New Otani Hotel and Garden (120 S. Los Angeles St., Los Angeles, ☎ 213/629–1200). The Rendezvous Lounge of this Japanese-style hotel offers a sentimental pianist.

Radisson Bel-Air (11461 Sunset Blvd., Bel Air, ☎ 310/476–6571). The Oasis Bar here features a singer-pianist who performs music from the '40s as well as more contemporary tunes.

Regent Beverly Wilshire (9500 Wilshire Blvd., Beverly Hills, ☎ 310/275–5200). Plush sofas and high tables set the atmosphere for this elegant piano bar, in one of L.A.'s premier and most historic hotels.

Ritz-Carlton Huntington Hotel (1401 S. Oak Knoll Ave., Pasadena, ☎ 818/568–3900). Entertainment is offered at The Bar, a lounge that resembles a genteel private library, with brass fixtures, an oversize fireplace, and a marble-topped bar.

Smoke House (4420 Lakeside Dr., Burbank, ☎ 818/845–3731). There's a lounge room with assorted entertainment separate from the restaurant.

Sportsmen's Lodge Restaurant (12833 Ventura Blvd., Studio City, ☎ 818/984–0202). The lounge connected to the main hotel features a tranquil setting, with brooks and swan-filled ponds.

Westin Bonaventure Hotel (5th and Figueroa Sts., Los Angeles, ☎ 213/624–1000). In the Lobby Court there is music nightly, consisting of popular favorites at the piano bar or more jazz-oriented musical entertainers.

Westwood Marquis (930 Hilgard Ave., Westwood, ☎ 310/208–8765). The Westwood Lounge of this chic hotel offers cozy settees, soft lights, and a piano or harp player. Vocalists are featured occasionally.

Comedy and Magic

Comedy Act Theater (3339 W. 43rd St., near Crenshaw, ☎ 310/677–4101). This club features comedy by and for the black community, Thursday through Saturday nights.

Comedy and Magic Club (1018 Hermosa Ave., Hermosa Beach, ☎ 310/372–1193). This beachfront club features many magicians and comedians seen on TV and in Las Vegas. The Unknown Comic, Elayne Boosler, Pat Paulsen, Jay Leno, and Harry Anderson have all played here.

Comedy Store (8433 Sunset Blvd., Hollywood, ☎ 213/656–6225). Los Angeles's premier comedy showcase has been going strong for over a decade. Many famous comedians, including Robin Williams and Steve Martin, occasionally make unannounced appearances here.

Groundlings Theater (7307 Melrose Ave., Hollywood, ☎ 213/934–9700). The entertainment here consists of original skits, music, and improv, with each player contributing his/her own flavor to the usually hilarious performance.

Ice House Comedy Showroom (24 N. Mentor Ave., Pasadena, ☎ 818/577–1894). Three-act shows here feature comedians, celebrity impressionists, and magicians from Las Vegas, as well as from television shows.

Igby's Comedy Cabaret (11637 Pico Blvd., Los Angeles, ☎ 310/477–3553). You'll see familiar television faces, as well as up-and-coming comedians Wednesday through Sunday in this friendly club. Reservations are necessary.

The Improvisation (8162 Melrose Ave., West Hollywood, ☎ 213/651–2583). The Improv is a transplanted New York establishment showcasing comedians and some vocalists. This place was the proving ground for Liza Minnelli and Richard Pryor, among others. Reservations are recommended. Hell's Kitchen, inside the Improv, is the place to dine.

Laugh Factory (8001 Sunset Blvd., Hollywood, ☎ 213/656–8860). A variety of comedy acts and improvisation are performed here seven days a week.

Casinos

Just 15 miles south of the Los Angeles Civic Center is the community of **Gardena,** home of six combination card rooms, restaurants, and cocktail lounges. These are not full gaming casinos, and there are no attached hotels. Although California law prohibits gambling, Gardena enacted an ordinance years ago allowing operators to run draw-poker, low-ball, and pan. The six card rooms are fairly standardized, even though the decor varies, and limits on maximum bets differ. A card room, for example, can have no more than 35 tables. Typically a poker table has eight seats and a designated limit on bets. The minimum bet is $1 before the draw and $2 after the draw, with no limits on the number of raises. Some tables have a "house" dealer; the card room collects a fee, ranging from $1 up to $24 an hour in the $100–$200 games, from the players every half hour.

Gardena card rooms are open 24 hours a day, and you can play as long as your cash and stamina hold out. Card rooms also have surprisingly good food in their restaurants at reasonable prices. The law requires that the bar be separate and outside the building.

Eldorado Club (15411 S. Vermont Ave., Gardena, ☎ 310/323–2800). This popular casino holds court over games like Keno, Pai Gow (like poker), and pan. American and Chinese food, at bargain prices, is not outstanding but more than palatable. Credit cards accepted.
Normandie Casino (1045 W. Rosecrans, Gardena, ☎ 310/515–1466). Seven-card stud, blackjack, Texas holdem, and Pai Gow poker are offered, and there's Las Vegas–style entertainment with headliners like Juice Newton. Free instruction is offered by staffers. Coffee shop on premises.

Bars

Despite its well-publicized penchant for hedonism, Los Angeles, unlike New York, Chicago, and San Francisco, is not a saloon town. The practiced art of pub-crawling has never flourished here, mainly because the city has few real neighborhoods and plenty of freeways. Traditionally, unlike New Yorkers, Angelenos rarely pledge loyalty to any libational hangout; they're too nomadic. But there are hundreds of great cozy bars, lively pubs, and festive watering holes to quench your thirst for conversation and fine spirits.

South Bay bars and any place near the water have younger, hipper, and livelier crowds. Rugby shirts and cutoffs are commonplace, and the talk is largely about volleyball, beach parties, real estate syndications, and sports cars. **Westside** is typically more trendy; casual chic is the watchword. In **West Hollywood** and **Hollywood** environs, the attire is even more relaxed: young directors in jogging suits, out-of-work actors in jeans. Here bars buzz with the intoxicating talk of "deals," as in "three-picture deals," "development deals," "album deals." Autograph hounding of celebrities is discouraged by owner-managers, who are thrilled whenever stars frequent their places. **Pasadena** pubs, once fiercely conservative, have loosened and livened up. But the attire is still traditional: button-down shirts, rep ties, blue blazers—decidedly preppy. **Downtown** bars are generally a bastion for bankers, brokers, and other business folk; two- and three-piece suits are de rigueur.

Monitor your intake of spirits if you're driving. California has enacted some very tough laws to rid its roads of intoxicated motorists. A first-time offender who has more than a .08% blood-alcohol reading gets 20 hours in jail and a stiff fine. So beware—or, better yet, find yourself a designated driver if you want to imbibe while you're out on the town.

Otherwise, welcome to Los Angeles—and bottoms up!

Airport and South Bay

El Torito (3290 Sepulveda Blvd., Manhattan Beach, ☎ 310/545–4569). This lively spot features backgammon. The club is attached to a budget-priced Mexican restaurant.

Orville and Wilbur's (401 W. Rosecrans, ☎ 310/545–6639). The clientele is an eclectic mix of surfers, business folks, and rugby-shirted beach rats. With its spectacular view of the Pacific, this is a real sundown place.

Beverly Hills

La Scala (410 N. Canon, ☎ 310/275–0579). A quaint bar with an immense wine cellar, La Scala is honeycombed with celebrities nightly.

R.J.'s (252 N. Beverly Dr., ☎ 310/274–3474 or 310/274–7427). Behind the oak bar and brass rail are 800 bottles stacked to the ceiling. Bend your elbow at the bar with a brace of new buddies during happy hour.

Century City

Harper's Bar and Grill (2040 Ave. of the Stars, ☎ 310/553–1855). A central place to meet friends for cocktails before or after a show at the Shubert Theater, it offers warm decor and generous drinks.

Harry's Bar and American Grill (ABC Entertainment Center, 2020 Ave. of the Stars, ☎ 310/277–2333). A reasonably authentic version of the famed Florentine bar and grill that Hemingway and other Lost Generation scribblers frequented, Harry's is unrivaled in L.A. for its potent cappuccino.

Downtown

When bar-hopping downtown, go with someone who knows the territory; the area isn't the safest place for a novice to go exploring.

Engine Co. #28 (644 S. Figueroa St., ☎ 213/624–6996). This cozy bar (and restaurant), with dark mahogany accents and high-back booths, attracts a lot of stockbrokers and lawyers.

Grand Avenue Sports Bar (506 S. Grand St., ☎ 213/612–1595). This sleek bar in the Biltmore Hotel serves until 2 AM. Bring a lot of money.

Little Joe's (900 N. Broadway, ☎ 213/489–4900). A must for sports buffs. The prices are low and the big-screen TV is always tuned to the hottest game. W.C. Fields frequented the bar in the '30s.

Pacific Dining Car (1310 W. 6th St., ☎ 213/483–6000). A Los Angeles landmark, this large bar is open 24 hours and serves gourmet hors d'oeuvres nightly at no charge.

Redwood Second Street Saloon (316 W. 2nd St., ☎ 213/617–2867). Reporters from the *Los Angeles Times* and United Press International pack this gaudy, gabby place after 5 PM to trade postmortems of the day's stories or to drink their lunch if they're working nightside.

Rex (617 S. Olive St., ☎ 213/627–2300). This piano bar on the ground floor of the historic Oviatt Building radiates the Art Deco ambience of a 1930s cruise liner.

Stepps (Wells Fargo Court, 350 S. Hope St., ☎ 213/626–0900). In warmer months, TGIF celebrants gather at the portable outdoor bars of this major business-crowd hangout.

The Tower (1150 S. Olive St., ☎ 213/746–1554). This bar and restaurant atop the 32-story Transamerica Building provides a terrific view and an elegant cocktail environment.

Hollywood

Cobalt Cantina (4326 Sunset Blvd., ☎ 213/953–9991). The bar, next door to a Tex-Mex restaurant, is decorated Santa Fe style. The clientele is a mix of business and "biz" folk who take advantage of its proximity to PBS and to ABC's Prospect Studios. The signature drink here is a cobalt blue margarita made with blue Curaçao.

Dresden Room (1760 N. Vermont Ave., ☎ 213/665–4294). Everything old is new again in L.A., as evidenced in this unassuming '40s-style bar that has been rediscovered by a happening '90s crowd.

El Coyote (7312 Beverly Blvd., ☎ 213/939–7766). For a pick-me-up margarita, stop by this kitschy restaurant/bar and get a glass of the best—and cheapest—in town.

Hollywood Athletic Club (6525 Sunset Blvd., ☎ 213/962–6600). A hip place to hang out is this old billiard parlor. To escape from the rowdy pool crowd, head upstairs for some blues and a chance to mellow out.

Martoni's (1523 Cahuenga Blvd., ☎ 213/466–3441). A venerable Italian restaurant launched decades ago by Frank Sinatra's former valet, this cozy bar is packed nightly with agents, studio musicians, and stars on the ascent.

Musso and Franks (6667 Hollywood Blvd., ☎ 213/467–5123). Film-studio moguls and $2-a-day extras alike flock to this long-running hit, where the Rob Roys are just as smooth and the clientele just as eclectic as ever.

Smalls (5574 Melrose Ave., ☎ 213/469–8258). The clientele here is mostly social moguls—upscale business types who kick back and dress down in designer jeans.

Tiki Ti (4427 W. Sunset Blvd., ☎ 213/669–9381). This small cocktail lounge is big with the singles crowd. The building, housing some of the city's best tropical rum drinks, emulates a Tahitian hut.

Windows on Hollywood (1755 N. Highland Ave., ☎ 213/462–7181). Located on the top floor of the giant Holiday Inn, this dizzying drinker's spot spins even if you don't drink too much. The view is, as expected, spectacular, so try to get here as the sun sinks in the West.

Yamashiro's (1999 N. Sycamore Ave., ☎ 213/466–5125). A lovely tradition is to meet at this Japanese restaurant/bar at sunset for cocktails on the terrace.

Marina del Rey/Venice

Black Whale (3016 Washington Blvd., ☎ 310/823–9898). For swash-buckling saloon goers, there are plenty of mates ready to swig rum with you.

Brennan's (4089 Lincoln Blvd., ☎ 310/821–6622). This Irish pub's big open bar is a pleasant backdrop for easy conversation. Turtle racing, a parking-lot grand prix on Thursday nights, is a fixture here.

Casablanca (220 Lincoln Blvd., ☎ 310/392–5751). At this Mexican bar and grill you can watch the cook make tortillas.

Crystal Fountain Lounge (Marina International Hotel, 4200 Admiralty Way, ☎ 310/301–2000). Even locals often overlook this dark and cozy spot. Jukebox music alternates with a guitarist's tunes.

Typhoon (3221 Donald Douglas Loop S, ☎ 310/390–6565). This fun-filled bar right off the Santa Monica Airport's runway is known for a Typhoon Punch (triple sec, rums, and fruit juices) so potent that the umbrella sticking out of the glass is blown inside-out.

The Warehouse (4499 Admiralty Way, ☎ 310/823–5451). Ex-cine-matographer Burt Hixon collected tropical drink recipes on his South Seas forays and whips up one of the most sinfully rich piña coladas this side of Samoa. The bar is popular, so get here early.

West Beach Cafe (60 N. Venice Blvd., ☎ 310/823–5396). A popular night spot, the bar is often crowded with Westside yuppies, and it has a changing contemporary art show.

Mid-Wilshire

HMS Bounty (3357 Wilshire Blvd., ☎ 213/385–7275). This is a businessperson's après-work watering hole; very clubby, very gabby.

Lowenbrau Keller (3211 Beverly Blvd., ☎ 213/382–5723). A little bit of Bavaria gone Hollywood, this is where locals go to gobble up a plate of bratwurst and knock back a few steins. A grand piano accompanies swaying punters belting out the requisite German drinking songs.

Molly Malone's (575 S. Fairfax Ave., ☎ 213/935–1577). A small, cozy Irish pub, it features Gaelic music (both contemporary and traditional), Harp beer all the time, and a hamburger that is a feast in itself.

Tom Bergin's (840 S. Fairfax Ave., ☎ 213/936–7151). One of L.A.'s best Irish pubs, it's plastered with Day-Glo shamrocks perpetuating the names of the thousands of patrons who have passed through its door.

Pasadena

Beckham Place (77 W. Walnut, ☎ 818/796–3399). A rather fancy "Olde English" pub, it's known for its huge drinks, free roast beef sandwiches, and wing chairs placed near a roaring fire.

Chronicle (897 Granite Dr., ☎ 818/792–1179). This restaurant/bar with the feel of a turn-of-the-century mansion features friendly bartenders and generous drinks.

Crown City Brewery (300 S. Raymond Ave., ☎ 818/577–5548). Beer brewed on the premises is the main attraction, and for good reason.

Islands (3533 Foothill Blvd., ☎ 818/351–6543). At this Polynesian-style bar, surf videos blare in the background. Order up some tacos, burgers, or chicken sandwiches, and turn drink time into feast time.

John Bull (958 S. Fair Oaks Ave., ☎ 818/441–4353). This British pub looks as if it came straight here from London.

Sports Edition (150 S. Los Robles Ave., ☎ 818/577–1000). You won't find any little old ladies from Pasadena in this bar (on the lower level of the Pasadena Hilton), devoted to contact sports: This is action central. Marble tables and wooden floors are featured decor.

Market City Cafe (33 S. Fair Oaks Ave., ☎ 818/568–0203). This light and airy bar in Pasadena's Old Town is popular at lunch or in the early evening.

San Fernando Valley

Commuters traverse the Ventura Freeway east to west and often stop to dine and drink at a potpourri of French, Italian, Asian, and trendy American bistros.

Sagebrush Cantina (23527 Calabassas Rd., ☎ 818/222–6062). An indoor-outdoor saloon next to a Mexican restaurant, this spot is the Valley's version of the Via Veneto café scene. Motorcycle hippies mix comfortably with computer moguls and showbiz folk, including a platoon of stunt people. There's classic rock entertainment.

Santa Monica and the Beaches

Chez Jay (1657 Ocean Ave., ☎ 310/395–1741). This shack of a saloon near Santa Monica Pier has endured for 30 years and seen the likes of Warren Beatty, Julie Christie, and former California governor Jerry Brown come through its door.

Galley Steak House (2442 Main St., ☎ 310/452–1934). This tiny restaurant-bar, thick with nautical mementos, is recommended for nostalgics who want to recapture Santa Monica circa 1940.

Oar House (2941 Main St., ☎ 310/396–4725). Something old has been glued or nailed to every square inch of this place, from motorcycles to carriages. Drinks are downright cheap.

Ye Olde King's Head (116 Santa Monica Blvd., ☎ 310/451–1402). Reeking of ale, this is a gathering place for Brits eager to hear or dispense news from home.

West Hollywood

Barefoot (8722 W. 3rd St., ☎ 310/276–6223). A mahogany bar and art-nouveau mirrors make this place as inviting as the expertly mixed martinis served here.

Checca (7323 Santa Monica Blvd., ☎ 213/850–7471). Facing the old Goldwyn Studios, this combination lively bar-restaurant offers everything in music from acid jazz to standard blues. Check out the waiters dressed in drag on Thursdays.

Dan Tana's (9071 Santa Monica Blvd., ☎ 310/275–9444). Although it's mainly a restaurant, the busy bar is a favorite late-night haunt.

Le Dome (8720 W. Sunset Blvd., ☎ 310/659–6919). The circular bar here draws the likes of Rod Stewart and Richard Gere. The best time to visit is after 11 PM, when it really starts to jump.

Morton's (8764 Melrose Ave., ☎ 310/276–1253). Although it's a small bar, Morton's has a big-name, mostly show-business, clientele.

Spago (1114 Horn Ave. at Sunset Blvd., ☎ 310/652–4025). Celebrity watching is a polished art here. The tiny bar tucked away inside this ultrachic bistro is immensely popular; consider yourself fortunate if you can stake out a bar stool.

Westwood/Westside

Westwood is the front door to UCLA and a popular hangout for kids of all ages. Both it and the area around it have some outstanding bars.

Acapulco (1109 Glendon, ☎ 310/208–3884). Once an Irish pub, this Mexican restaurant/bar still has an air of conviviality. It also stocks a good assortment of Mexican beers.

Hamburger Hamlet (11648 San Vicente Blvd., ☎ 310/826–3558). This is one of the Westside's hottest singles bars, so don't walk in here looking for solitude.

Q's (11835 Wilshire Blvd., West Los Angeles, ☎ 310/477–7550). This upscale pool hall and bar serves a yuppified clientele.

San Francisco Saloon (11501 W. Pico Blvd., ☎ 310/478–0152). The ambience is San Francisco–style, with old prints adorning the walls and friendly bartenders to tell your troubles to.

Shakespeare's (1043 Westwood Blvd., Westwood, ☎ 310/208–3171). In the heart of Westwood Village, this restaurant-bar has plenty of tables as well as a long, marble bar. Two television monitors are bound to be tuned to the latest sporting event.

8 Excursions from Los Angeles

E VEN IF LOS ANGELES IS THE CENTER OF YOUR VACA-
TION plans, you are probably planning trips out of the
city. Disneyland (*see* Chapter 9, Orange County) is less
than an hour's drive away; you can reach Santa Barbara and Palm Springs
in a couple hours. This chapter explores some excursions a little farther off the beaten track.

By Aaron
Sugarman

Updated by
William P.
Brown and
Jane E. Lasky

In the following restaurant reviews, these price categories have been
used: $$$$ (over $35), $$$ ($25–35), $$ ($15–25), and $ (under $15).
Unless otherwise noted, dress is casual and reservations are not required.

In hotel reviews, these price categories have been used: $$$$ (over $100),
$$$ ($75–100), $$ ($50–75), and $ (under $50).

BIG BEAR/LAKE ARROWHEAD

Local legend has it that in 1845, Don Benito Wilson—General George
Patton's grandfather—and his men charged up along the San Bernardino
River in pursuit of a troublesome band of Native Americans. As Wilson entered a clearing, he discovered a meadow teeming with bears.
The rest, of course, is history: Wilson later became mayor of Los Angeles, and the area he'd stumbled into was developed into a delightful
mountain playground, centered around the man-made lakes of Arrowhead and Big Bear.

Today Angelenos seeking escape from urban life and from other va-
cationers are far more plentiful in these mountain resort areas than bears
ever were. Visitors come in winter for downhill and cross-country skiing, and in summer to breathe cool mountain air, hike in the woods,
sniff the daffodils, and play in the water. Spring and fall bring clear,
sweeping views of the San Bernardino Valley, one of the most awesome
panoramas in southern California.

Along the edge of the San Bernardino Mountains, which connect Lake
Arrowhead and Big Bear Lake, is a truly great scenic drive: the Rim
of the World Scenic Byway. The alpine equivalent of the Pacific Coast
Highway, it reaches elevations of 8,000 feet, offering views of sprawling San Bernardino and east toward Palm Springs.

Exploring

*Numbers in the margin correspond to points of interest on the Big Bear
Lake map.*

This tour begins near the western end of the byway, near its intersection with Highway 138. As you wind your way along the Rim of the
World, there are several places to park, sip cool water from spring-fed
fountains, and enjoy the view. At the village of Crestline, a brief de-
❶ tour off Highway 18 leads you to **Lake Gregory.** The newest of the high
mountain lakes, Lake Gregory was formed by a dam constructed in
1938. Because the water temperature in summer is seldom extremely
cold—as it can be in the other lakes at this altitude—this is the best
swimming lake in the mountains, but it's open in summer only, and
there's a minimum charge to swim. You can rent rowboats at Lake Gregory Village.

❷ Continuing east on Highway 18, you will pass the **Baylis Park Picnic
Ground,** where you can have a barbecue in a wooded setting. A little
❸ farther along, just past the town of Rim Forest, is the **Strawberry Peak**

134

Beverly
Garland's
Holiday Inn, **3**

Burbank
Airport
Hilton, **6**

Radisson Valley
Center Hotel
Los Angeles, **2**

Ritz-Carlton
Huntington
Hotel, **8**

Safari Inn, **7**

Sheraton
Universal, **5**

Sportsman's
Lodge Hotel, **1**

Universal City
Hilton and
Towers, **4**

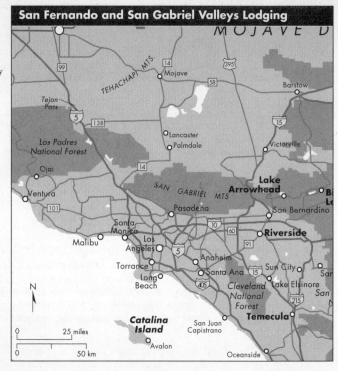

San Fernando and San Gabriel Valleys Lodging

fire lookout tower. Visitors who brave the steep stairway to the tower are treated to a magnificent view and a lesson on fire spotting by the lookout staff.

4 Heading north on Highway 173 will lead you to **Lake Arrowhead Village** and the lake itself. Arrowhead Village draws mixed reviews: For some, it is a quaint alpine community with shops and eateries; for others, it has all the ambience of a rustic-theme shopping mall. The lake, on the other hand, is decidedly a gem, although it can become crowded with speedboats and water-skiers in summer. The **Arrowhead Queen,** operated daily by LeRoy Sports (☎ 909/336–6992, reservations needed in summer, price varies, the maximum is $9.50) provides 50-minute cruises around the lake, leaving from the waterfront marina. The **Lake Arrowhead Children's Museum** (lower level of the village, ☎ 909/336–3093; ☛ $3.50 adults and children, senior citizens $2.50) has plenty to entertain pint-sized explorers: hands-on exhibits, a climbing maze, and a puppet stage. Call the Arrowhead Chamber of Commerce (☎ 909/337–3715) for information on events, camping, and lodging.

If you are traveling with children, you may also want to stop at nearby **5** **Santa's Village.** The petting zoo, rides, riding stables, and a bakery filled with goodies make this place a favorite of kids. *Located on Hwy. 18, Box 638, Skyforest 92385, ☎ 909/337–2484. ☛ (includes 12 rides): $10 adults and children. Hrs vary depending on the season, so call ahead.*

6 Farther along the Rim drive, 5 miles east of Running Springs, is **Snow Valley** (☎ 909/867–5151), one of the major ski areas in the San Bernardinos, with snowmaking capabilities and a dozen lifts. Summer visitors will find hiking trails, horseback riding, and fishing here, too.

Big Bear Lake

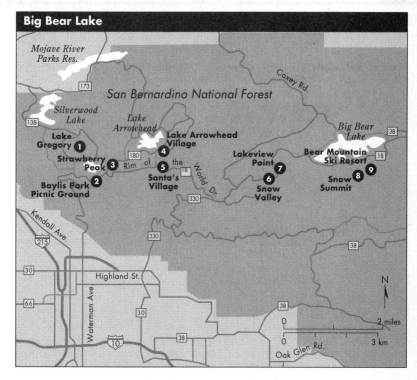

❼ Beyond Snow Valley, the road climbs to **Lakeview Point,** where a spectacular view of the deep Bear Creek Canyon unfolds; Big Bear Lake is usually visible in the distance. A 15½-mile drive will take you completely around the lake, and **Big Bear Lake Village** is on the lake's south shore. The town is a pleasant combination of alpine and Western-mountain style, with the occasional chaletlike building. The paddle wheeler *Big Bear Queen* (☎ 909/866–3218) departs daily, mid-March through October, from Big Bear Marina for 90-minute scenic tours of the lake. Fishing-boat and equipment rentals are available from several lakeside marinas, including Pine Knot Landing (☎ 909/866–2628), adjacent to Big Bear Village. For general information and lodging reservations, contact the Big Bear Resort Association (☎ 909/866–7000).

❽ ❾ **Snow Summit** (☎ 909/866–5766) and **Bear Mountain Ski Resort** (☎ 909/585–2517) are both just to the southeast of the village. Snow Summit, which has a 8,200-foot peak, is equipped with a high-speed quad chair, 12 chairlifts, and 20 miles of runs at all levels. Bear Mountain has 11 chairlifts and 35 trails, from beginner to expert. On busy winter weekends and holidays, your best bet is to reserve your tickets before you head for the mountain.

Dining

Big Bear

$$ Blue Ox Bar and Grill. This rustic, casual restaurant, complete with peanut shells on the floor, serves oversize steaks, ribs, burgers, and chicken—all cooked simply but well. ✕ *441 W. Big Bear Blvd., Big Bear City,* ☎ *909/585–7886. AE, MC, V.*

$$ George and Sigi's Knusperhauschen. Don't let the campy gingerbread-house look fool you: This restaurant offers wonderful Eastern European fare in a warm, charming atmosphere. The schnitzel and sauer-braten are a delight. ✕ *829 W. Big Bear Blvd., Big Bear City,* ☎ *909/585–8640. Reservations advised. MC, V. Closed Mon. and Tues. and lunches.* ⊙ *Holidays.*

$$ **Iron Squirrel.** Hearty French cooking with American influences is presented in a country-French setting. The veal Normandie comes highly recommended, and other traditional dishes, such as rack of lamb with garlic, are nicely prepared. ✕ *646 Pineknot Blvd., Big Bear Lake,* ☎ *909/866–9121. AE, MC, V.*

Lake Arrowhead (Arrowhead Village)

$$ **Woody's Boathouse.** If you want to sit and relax, lakefront, choose this casual eatery for its juicy steaks, fresh seafood, and generous salad bar. ✕ *28200 Hwy. 189, Suite 13–100,* ☎ *909/337–2628. AE, MC, V.*

Lodging

Rates for Big Bear lodgings fluctuate widely, depending upon the season. When winter snow brings droves of Angelenos to the mountain for skiing, expect to pay sky-high prices for any kind of room. **Big Bear Central Reservations** (☎ 909/866–7000) can answer any questions you have and make arrangements for you.

Big Bear

$$$$ **Apples Bed and Breakfast Inn.** Surrounded by an acre of pine trees, this inn offers individually decorated rooms (four are equipped with their own Jacuzzis), plus a large gathering room with a wood-burning stove, baby grand piano, game table, and library loft. Breakfast and after-dinner dessert are included in the rates. ☎ *Box 7172, Big Bear Lake 92315,* ☎ *909/866–0903. 12 rooms. AE, D, MC, V.*

$$$$ **Big Bear Inn.** This is more or less a mountain chateau in the European tradition. The rooms are furnished with brass beds and antiques. Developer Paul Rizo's family has three luxury hotels on the Greek island of Corfu, and the inn shows its lineage—right down to the giant Greek statues in front of the property. ☎ *Box 1814, Big Bear Lake 92315,* ☎ *909/866–3471 or 800/232–7466. 75 rooms, 3 suites. Restaurant (open weekends only), lounge, pool. AE, MC, V.*

$$$–$$$$ **Gold Mountain Manor.** A restored mansion made of logs and dating back to the 1930s, the manor now serves as a historic bed-and-breakfast inn. It earned its fame when Clark Gable and Carole Lombard honeymooned in what is now the Clark Gable Room. The rooms are furnished with quilts and antiques. Rates include breakfast. ☎ *Box 2027, Big Bear City 92314,* ☎ *909/585–6997. 7 rooms. No smoking. MC, V.*

$$$–$$$$ **Robinhood Inn and Lodge.** Near Snow Summit, this well-located property has reasonably priced rooms (with or without kitchens) and condos. Each room (some with fireplaces and/or Jacuzzis) is individually decorated with simple modern furniture and bright colors. All accommodations face a courtyard with an outdoor whirlpool spa. ☎ *Box 1881, Big Bear Lake 92315,* ☎ *909/866–4643. 21 rooms. Restaurant, spa. AE, MC, V.*

Lake Arrowhead

$$$$ **Lake Arrowhead Resort.** The design and Old World graciousness of the lodge are reminiscent of the Alps. In addition to the lakeside luxury, guests receive membership privileges at the Village Bay Club and Spa (fee is $5). ☎ *Box 1699, 92352,* ☎ *909/336–1511 or 800/800–6791. 261 rooms. Restaurant, coffee shop, lounge, pool, tennis, health club, beach. AE, MC, V.*

$$$–$$$$ **Carriage House Bed and Breakfast.** Within walking distance of the lake and village, this New England–style country home offers lake views from all guest rooms. Breakfast and afternoon refreshments are included in the rates. ✉ *Box 982, 92352,* ☎ *909/336–1400. 3 rooms. MC, V.*

Big Bear/Lake Arrowhead Essentials

Arriving and Departing

BY CAR

Take I–10 east from Los Angeles to Highway 330, which connects with Highway 18—the Rim of the World Scenic Byway—at Running Springs. This is approximately the midpoint of the scenic drive, which hugs the mountainside from Big Bear Lake to Cajon Pass. The trip should take about 90 minutes to Lake Arrowhead, and two hours to Big Bear. Highway 38, the back way into Big Bear, is actually longer, but it can be faster when the traffic on the more direct route is heavy.

CATALINA ISLAND

When you approach Catalina Island through the typical early morning ocean fog, it's easy to wonder if perhaps there has been some mistake. What is a Mediterranean island doing 22 miles off the coast of California? Don't worry, you haven't left the Pacific—you've arrived at one of the Los Angeles area's most popular resorts.

Though lacking the sophistication of some European pleasure islands, Catalina does offer virtually unspoiled mountains, canyons, coves, and beaches. In fine weather, it draws thousands of southern California boaters, who tie up their vessels at moorings spotted in coves along the coast. The exceptionally clear water surrounding the island lures divers and snorkelers. Although there's not much sandy beach, sunbathing and water sports are also popular. The main town, Avalon, is a charming, old-fashioned beach community, where palm trees rim the main street and yachts bob in the crescent-shape bay.

Cruise ships sail into Avalon twice a week. The Catalina Island Company, which has a near-monopoly on sightseeing tours on the island beyond Avalon, has excellent service.

Discovered by Juan Rodriguez Cabrillo in 1542, the island has sheltered many dubious characters, from Russian fur trappers (seeking sea-otter skins), slave traders, pirates, and gold miners to bootleggers, filmmakers, and movie stars. In 1919, William Wrigley, Jr., the chewing-gum magnate, purchased a controlling interest in the company developing the island. Wrigley had the island's most famous landmark, the Casino, built in 1929, and he made Catalina the site of spring training for his Chicago Cubs baseball team.

In 1975 the Santa Catalina Island Conservancy, a nonprofit foundation, acquired about 86% of the island to help preserve the natural resources here. Although boat tours hug the island's coast, to explore Catalina you should take one of several bus or van tours into the rugged interior country, which the conservancy is restoring with plantings of native grasses and trees. Depending on which route you take, you can expect to see buffalo (brought to the island for the 1924 filming of *The Vanishing American*), goats, and boar or unusual species of sea life, including such oddities as electric perch, saltwater goldfish, and flying fish.

Although Catalina can certainly be seen in a day, there are several inviting hotels that make it worth extending your stay for one or more nights.

Between Memorial Day and Labor Day, be sure to make reservations *before* heading here. After Labor Day, rooms are much easier to find on shorter notice, rates drop dramatically, and a number of hotels offer packages that include transportation from the mainland and/or sight-seeing tours.

Exploring

Everybody walks in Avalon, where private autos are restricted and there are no rental cars. But taxis, trams, and shuttles can take you to hotels, attractions, and restaurants. If you are determined to have a set of wheels, you can rent a bicycle (about $6 an hr) or a golf cart ($35 an hr, cash only) along Crescent Avenue as you walk in from the dock. To hike into the interior of the island you will need a permit, available free from Doug Bombard Enterprises (Island Plaza, Avalon, ☎ 310/510–7265).

The **Chamber of Commerce Visitors Bureau,** on Green Pier, is a good place to get your bearings, check into special events, and plan your itinerary. The **Catalina Island Company Visitors Center** (☎ 310/510–1520) is on the corner of Crescent and Catalina avenues, across from Green Pier.

On the northwest point of Crescent Bay is the **Casino,** Avalon's most prominent landmark. The circular structure, considered one of the finest examples of Art Deco architecture anywhere, has lots of Span-ish-influence details. Its floors and murals show off brilliant blue and green Catalina tiles. "Casino" is the Italian word for "gathering place," and has nothing to do with gambling here. Instead, you can visit the **Catalina Island Museum** (lower level of Casino, ☛ $1), which displays the history of the island; in the evening, you can see a first-run movie at the **Avalon Theater** (☎ 310/510–0179), which has a classic 1929 the-ater pipe organ; or on holiday weekends you can go to big-band dances similar to those that made the Casino famous in the 1930s and '40s.

If modern architecture interests you, be sure to stop by the **Wolfe House** (124 Chimes Tower Rd.). Built in Avalon in 1928 by noted ar-chitect Rudolph Schindler, its terraced frame is carefully set into a steep site, affording extraordinary views. The house is a private residence, rarely open for public tours, but you can get a good view of it from the path below it and from the street.

The **Wrigley Memorial and Botanical Garden** is 2 miles south of Avalon via Avalon Canyon Road. The garden displays only plants native to southern California, including several that grow only on Catalina Is-land: Catalina ironwood, wild tomato, and rare Catalina mahogany. The Wrigley family commissioned the garden as well as the monument, which has a grand staircase and a Spanish mausoleum that's decorated with colorful Catalina tile. Although the mausoleum was never used by the Wrigleys, who are instead buried in Los Angeles, the structure—and the view from it—are worth a look. Tram service between the memo-rial and Avalon is available daily between 8 AM and 5 PM. There is a nominal entry fee of $1.

El Rancho Escondido is a ranch in Catalina's interior, home to some of the country's finest Arabian horses. Horse shows are presented for pas-sengers on the inland motor tour (*see* Guided Tours, *below*).

Snorkelers and divers can explore the crystal-clear waters of **Under-water Marine Park at Casino Point,** where moray eels, bat rays, spiny lobsters, halibut, and other sea animals cruise around kelp forests and along the sandy bottom.

Catalina Island

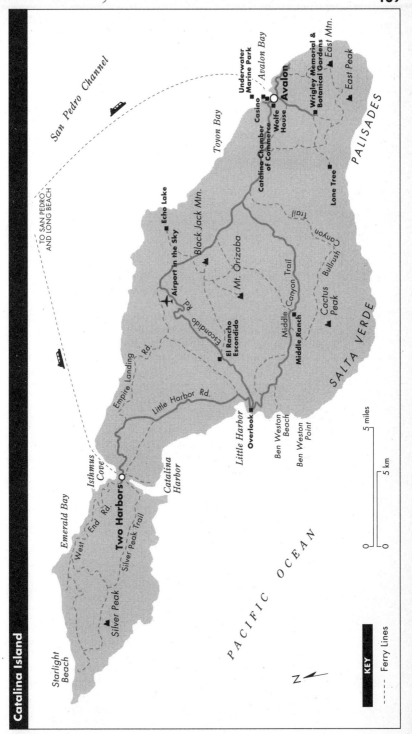

San Pedro Channel

TO SAN PEDRO
AND LONG BEACH

Underwater
Marine Park

Avalon Bay

Casino

Wrigley Memorial &
Botanical Gardens

East Mtn.

Avalon

Catalina Chamber
of Commerce

Wolfe
House

East Peak

PALISADES

Toyon Bay

Lone Tree

Echo Lake

Black Jack Mtn.

Canyon Trail

Airport in the Sky

Mt. Orizaba

Bullrush Canyon

Escondido Rd.

Middle Canyon Trail

Cactus Peak

El Rancho
Escondido

Middle Ranch

SALTA VERDE

Empire Landing Rd.

Little Harbor Rd.

Little Harbor
Overlook

Ben Weston Beach

Ben Weston Point

Isthmus Cove

Catalina
Harbor

Two Harbors

PACIFIC OCEAN

West End Rd.

Silver Peak Trail

Emerald Bay

Silver Peak

Starlight Beach

5 miles

5 km

N

KEY

----- Ferry Lines

Two Harbors is a fairly primitive resort at the west end of the island and a longtime summer destination popular with southern California boaters. The area is named for its two harbors, separated by a ½-mile-wide strip of land that is the isthmus of the island. Once inhabited by pirates and smugglers and later frequently used as a movie location, it recalls the days before tourism was the island's major industry. Popular activities here include swimming, diving, boating, hiking, and beachcombing. Limited accommodations are available at the **Banning House Lodge,** in camping cabins and at campgrounds (☎ 310/510–2800). **Catalina Safari Shuttle Bus** (☎ 310/510–2800) has regular bus service between Avalon and Two Harbors; **Catalina Express Coastal Shuttle** (☎ 310/519–1212) takes visitors on a 45-minute cruise from Avalon to Two Harbors; **Catalina Express** also has service from the mainland (*see* Arriving and Departing, *below*).

Dining

$$–$$$ **Cafe Prego.** This waterfront restaurant specializes in pasta, seafood, and steak. ✗ *603 Crescent Ave.,* ☎ *310/510–1218. AE, D, DC, MC, V.*

$$–$$$ **Pirrone's.** Located on the second floor of the Vista del Mar hotel, Pirrone's has a bird's-eye view of the bay. The menu includes local seafood, prime rib, steaks, and pasta. ✗ *417 Crescent Ave.,* ☎ *310/510–0333. AE, D, DC, MC, V.*

$ **Sand Trap.** Basically an expanded taco stand on the way to the Wrigley Memorial, the Sand Trap specializes in omelets, burritos, *tortas* (layered tortilla casseroles), and quesadillas. There's a shaded patio dining area and a tranquil golf-course view. ✗ *Falls Canyon,* ☎ *310/510–1349. No credit cards. Closed for dinner.*

Lodging

$$$$ **Hotel Metropole and Marketplace.** This romantic hotel has a French Quarter ambience: It overlooks a flower-decked courtyard of restaurants and shops. Some guest rooms have balconies, ocean views, fireplaces, and Jacuzzis. Continental breakfast is served in the lounge. ⊞ *225 Crescent Ave., Avalon 90704,* ☎ *310/510–1884, 48 rooms. AE, MC, V.*

$$$$ **Inn on Mt. Ada.** Occupying the former Wrigley Mansion, the island's most exclusive hotel offers the comforts of a millionaire's mansion—and at millionaire's prices, beginning at $320 a night during the summer season. The six bedrooms are elegantly decorated, some with canopy beds, traditional furniture, and overstuffed chairs. The views across the water to the mainland are spectacular, and the service is discreet. All meals, beverages, snacks, and the use of a golf cart are complimentary. ⊞ *Box 2560, Avalon 90704,* ☎ *310/510–2030. 6 rooms. MC, V.*

$$$$ **Pavilion Lodge.** Across the street from the beach, this motel, operated by the Santa Catalina Island Company, has simply furnished but spacious rooms. There's a large, attractively furnished garden courtyard in the center of the complex. Rates include Continental breakfast. ⊞ *Box 737, Avalon 90704,* ☎ *800/851-0217. 72 rooms. AE, D, DC, MC, V.*

$$$–$$$$ **Hotel Vista del Mar.** This friendly, freshly decorated hotel offers surprisingly bright rooms, most of which open onto a skylighted atrium. There are fireplaces, Jacuzzis, wet bars, contemporary rattan decor, and abundant greenery. Two suites have ocean views. Rates include Continental breakfast. ⊞ *417 Crescent Ave., Avalon 90704,* ☎ *310/510–1452. 15 rooms. AE, D, MC, V.*

Catalina Island Essentials

Arriving and Departing

BY BOAT

Catalina Express (☎ 310/519–1212 or 800/995–4386) makes the hour-long run from Long Beach or San Pedro to Avalon and Two Harbors; round-trip fare from Long Beach and San Pedro is $35 for adults, $32 for seniors, $26 for children 2–11, $2 for children under 2. Service is also available from Newport Beach through **Catalina Passenger Service** (☎ 714/673–5245), which leaves from Balboa Pavilion at 9 AM, takes 75 minutes to reach the island, and costs $33 round-trip for adults, $30.50 for senior citizens, $16.50 for children 12 and under. The return boat leaves Catalina at 4:30 PM. You can make arrangements to boat in one direction and fly in the other, but you must make reservations separately. Reservations are advised.

BY PLANE

Island Express (☎ 310/436–2012) flies hourly from San Pedro and Long Beach. The trip takes about 15 minutes and costs $66 one-way, $121 round-trip.

Guided Tours

Santa Catalina Island Company (☎ 310/510–2000 or 800/428–2566) tours include coastal cruise to Seal Rocks (summer only), the *Flying Fish* boat trip (evenings, summer only) inland motor tour, the Skyline Drive, the Casino tour, the Avalon scenic tour, a traditional glass-bottom-boat tour, and a submerged glass-bottom-boat tour, where the vessel sinks 5 feet under. Reservations are highly recommended for the inland tours; the others are offered several times daily. Tours range in cost from $7.50 to $34.50 for adults; discounts are available for senior citizens over 55, for children under 12, and for two or more tours booked in combination.

The **Catalina Conservancy** (☎ 310/510–1421) offers walks led by area docents.

RIVERSIDE

Whereas Los Angeles tends to focus on the newest and latest—it's a city where '50s furniture is considered antique—Riverside wears its history on its sleeve. A delightful array of historic buildings rise upon almost every street corner in downtown Riverside. For most of the 20th century, the reason people visited Riverside was to see the Mission Inn, a romantic landmark sprouting turrets, towers, and balconies above an arched courtyard area with fountains and sculptures. The inn fell on hard times and was closed for a number of years, but now that it has been renovated and reopened, it is, once again, the *real* reason to visit Riverside. Once you're here, though, take time for a leisurely stroll around town: You'll enjoy its eclectic architecture, its charming shops, its museums, and its abundance of citrus trees—evidence of the billion-dollar citrus industry that was founded here a century ago.

Exploring

Start your exploration with a stop at the **Mission Inn,** the resplendent Mission Revival landmark. A grand pile on the order of Hearst Castle, it occupies an entire block of Seventh Street at Orange Street. If you are staying at the hotel, you can explore its bell towers, relax in flower-decked courtyards, stroll along tiled balconies and arcades, and walk in the footsteps of movie stars and politicians (including Ronald and Nancy Reagan, who honeymooned here). Other members of the public can linger for a meal in the blue-tiled Spanish dining room or patio or nurse a drink in the Presidential lounge, where Teddy Roosevelt stayed in 1903 and Richard Nixon was married in 1940. Or you can take a one-hour guided tour of the property, starting from the hotel museum (☎ 909/781–8241, daily, starting at 10, ☛ $6). A small museum on the premises (open daily, 10–4; $1 suggested donation) displays inn memorabilia. *3649 7th St., Riverside 92501, ☎ 800/843–7755. 230 rooms. AE, MC, V.*

Across the street from the inn is the **Municipal Museum.** Built in 1912, this Renaissance Revival building contains exhibits on early days of the citrus industry, local history, Native American culture, and natural history. *3720 Orange St., ☎ 909/782–5273. Donations accepted.*

Continuing down Seventh Street, you'll pass the **First Congregational Church,** a good example of the Mission Revival style, built in 1914, and clearly inspired by the California missions' spare, earthy look. Note the differences between it and the **Municipal Auditorium** across the street. Built in 1929 in Hispanic Revival style, the auditorium has distinctive blue, yellow, and white tile domes and is topped by an all-American eagle.

At Seventh and Lime streets is the **Riverside Art Museum,** designed in 1929 by Julia Morgan, the chief architect of Hearst Castle. Several galleries display the work of southern California artists. *3425 7th St., ☎ 909/684–7111. ☛ $1.*

Riverside's other main strip is **Main Street,** a pedestrian mall running from 5th Street to 11th Street, where there are several shops and cafés to look into.

The **California Museum of Photography,** in the historic Kress Variety Store building, is one of the largest photography museums on the West Coast. *3824 Main St., ☎ 909/787–4787. ☛ $2, free on Wed. ☉ Wed.–Sat. 11–5, Sun. noon–5.*

When you reach the **Riverside County Courthouse,** built in 1903, be prepared for a bit of a shock. Not even remotely like any typical California architectural style, this Beaux Arts beauty was modeled after the Grand Palace of Fine Arts in Paris.

A short drive south of downtown Riverside is the **Heritage House,** a Victorian building dating from 1891. The house, built for the family of a successful citrus grower, features period furniture, gas lamps, and tile fireplaces in every room. *8193 Magnolia Ave., between Adams and Jefferson, ☎ 909/689–1333. ☛ Suggested donation $1 adults, 50¢ senior citizens and children under 13. ☉ Tues. and Thurs. noon–2:30, Sun. noon–3:30.*

The **Parent Tree** (intersection of Magnolia St. and Arlington Ave.), a navel-orange tree planted in 1875 that still bears fruit, is the sole survivor of two trees brought to Riverside from Brazil. Cuttings from this tree have grown into today's acres of citrus groves. To get a historical perspective on the citrus industry, visit the **California Citrus State Historic Park** in Arlington Heights (9400 Dufferin Ave., open daily 8–3). Its entrance is marked by a replica of a giant orange-juice stand. The park illustrates the history of the citrus industry in the 1920s and preserves 150 acres of navel-orange groves.

Castle Park is a family-oriented amusement park spread over 27 pleasantly landscaped acres. A state-of-the-art video arcade, a miniature golf course, and a collection of rides—including a restored carousel dating from 1909—are sure to keep the kids entertained. *3500 Polk St.,* ☎ *909/785–4140.* ☛ *$5 adults, $3.75 children under 11 for golf. Golf and arcade open daily 10–midnight; ride park open Fri. 6–11, Sat. noon–11, Sun. noon–8.*

The **Riverside Botanic Gardens,** on the campus of the University of California, covers 37 acres of hilly terrain. Spring, when many of the 2,000 plant species bloom, is the best time to visit. *University of California–Riverside,* ☎ *909/787–4650.* ☛ *Free.* ⊙ *Daily 8–5.*

Riverside Essentials

Arriving and Departing

BY BUS
Greyhound (☎ 800/231–2222) offers more than a dozen daily departures to Riverside. The ride costs $5 one-way, $10 round-trip, and it takes about 1½ hours. The station is within walking distance of all downtown attractions.

BY CAR
Take Highway 60 east out of Los Angeles to Highway 91 heading south. The trip should take about 90 minutes.

BY TRAIN
Metrolink (☎ 800/371–5465) commuter service operates six trains daily between Los Angeles's Union Station and Marketplace Station in Riverside, with morning and afternoon runs. The fare is $7.50 one-way, $14 round-trip.

TEMECULA

Southern California's only developed wine region, Temecula (pronounced teh-MEH-cyoo-la) is a popular day or overnight excursion from Los Angeles, Orange County, or San Diego. More than 10 premium wineries can be found along Rancho California Road as it snakes through the hills.

Exploring

The wineries are strung out along Rancho California Road east of the town. Most allow wine tasting for a fee. **Thornton** (32575 Rancho California Rd., ☎ 909/699–0099) produces several varieties of wine, including Culbertson champagne; it offers tours on weekends and tastings daily. **Callaway Vineyard & Winery** (32720 Rancho California Rd., ☎ 909/676–4001) has a visitor center for tastings and tours, operates a gift shop, and offers special theme dinners and luncheons. **Maurice Car'rie Vineyard & Winery** (34225 Rancho California Rd., ☎ 909/676–1711) has a tasting room, a gift shop, and a picnic area, and it's often the site of barn dances and art shows.

Old Town Temecula was once a hangout for cowboys, and still looks the part. It now has a number of antiques shops that specialize in local and Old West memorabilia. **Temecula Historic Museum** (28690 Front St., ☎ 909/676–0021; ☛ Free; open Wed.–Sun. 11–4) displays Native American and local farming memorabilia. Guided walking tours of Old Temecula are conducted from here by appointment (donations appreciated).

Santa Rosa Plateau Ecological Reserve (22115 Tenaja Rd., Murietta, ☎ 909/677–6951) offers a rich look at what this countryside was like before the developers took over. Trails wind through oak forests, past vernal pools and rolling grassland.

Dining

$$–$$$ **Cafe Champagne.** Part of the Thornton Winery, this café serves pasta and seafood. The appetizers, made with Culbertson champagne, are the stars. ✕ *32575 Rancho California Rd., Temecula 92591,* ☎ *909/699–0099. AE, DC, MC, V.*

$–$$ **Baily Wine Country Cafe.** Tucked in the back of a shopping center, this pleasant café with patio dining area features tasty California cuisine with light sauces. Picnics can be ordered 24 hours in advance. ✕ *27644 Ynez Rd., Temecula 92591,* ☎ *909/676–9567. AE, DC, MC, V.*

Lodging

$$$$ **Temecula Creek Inn.** Minutes away from wine country proper, this up-scale resort offers wine-country packages. ▦ *44501 Rainbow Canyon Rd., Temecula,* ☎ *909/676–5631. 80 rooms. Restaurant, pool, 27-hole golf course, tennis courts. AE, D, DC, MC, V.*

$$$–$$$$ **Loma Vista Bed and Breakfast.** This Mission-style bed-and-breakfast is currently the only overnight accommodation right in the Temecula wine country. It has tranquil vineyard views and its own gardens. ▦ *3350 La Serena Way, Temecula,* ☎ *909/676–7047. 6 rooms. D, MC, V.*

Temecula Essentials

Arriving and Departing
BY CAR
Temecula is about 85 fast freeway miles from Los Angeles; count on 1½ hours' travel time. From Los Angeles or Orange County take Highway 60 east to the intersection with I–215, or take Highway 91 east to the intersection with I–15; then go south to Rancho California Road. From San Diego take I–15 north to Rancho California Road. The wineries are east of I–15.

9 Orange County

Updated by
Jane E. Lasky
and William P.
Brown

ORANGE COUNTY is one of the top tourist destinations in California, and once you've arrived here it doesn't take long to see why. The county has made tourism its number-one industry, attracting nearly 40 million visitors annually. Two theme parks, Disneyland and Knott's Berry Farm, attract millions on their own. Orange County also offers year-round pro sports action, with the California Angels baseball team and the Mighty Ducks of Anaheim hockey team. The Anaheim Convention Center is an enormous facility that's constantly booked with conferences and trade shows. There are plenty of places to stay, and they're generally of high quality.

People actually live in Orange County, too—many of them in high-priced Mediterranean-style suburbs strung along the 24-mile-long coastline. Orange County residents shop in the classy malls that lure visitors as well. Like visitors, locals can be found at the beach sunning themselves or waiting for the big wave. Locals even dine and stay at the luxurious oceanfront resorts that perch on the edge of the Pacific.

Served by convenient airports and only an hour's drive from Los Angeles, Orange County is both a destination on its own and a very popular excursion from Los Angeles.

EXPLORING

Before visiting Orange County, select a primary attraction and then plan excursions to other sights. If Disneyland is the highlight, you'll probably want to organize your activities around the tourist attractions that fill the central county and take excursions to selected coastal spots. The reverse is true, of course, if you're planning to hang out on the beach. In that case, select a coastal headquarters and make forays to the Magic Kingdom.

If you're traveling with children, you could easily devote several days to the theme parks: a day or two for Disneyland, a day for Knott's Berry Farm, and perhaps a day driving to some of the area's lesser-known attractions.

Inland Orange County

Numbers in the margin correspond to points of interest on the Orange County map.

With Disneyland as its centerpiece, Anaheim is indisputably the West's capital of family entertainment. Now at the center of a vast tourism complex that also includes the Anaheim Convention Center, Anaheim Stadium, and the Pond in Anaheim, Disneyland still dominates the city. The Anaheim Convention Center lures almost as many conventioneers as Disneyland attracts children, and for many visitors, a trip to the Magic Kingdom may be the bonus of an Anaheim meeting.

★ ❶ Perhaps more than any other place in the world, **Disneyland,** the first Disney theme park and the enduring physical evidence of Walt Disney's dream, is a symbol of the eternal child in all of us. It's a place of delight and enchantment, an exceptionally clean and imaginatively developed wonder.

When Disney carved the park out of the orange groves in 1955, it consisted of four lands and fewer than 20 major attractions radiating from his idealized American Main Street. Much has changed in the intervening years, including the massive expansion of the park to include four more lands and some 40 more attractions. But Main Street retains its turn-of-the-century charm, and in ever-sharper contrast with the world just outside the gates of the park. Disney's vision of the Magic Kingdom was one of a never-ending fantasy. Thus designers and engineers continue to devise new ways to tantalize and treat guests, the latest being the Indiana Jones Adventure, a chance to explore the ruins of an ancient excavation site to look for the lost Temple of the Forbidden Eye.

Disneyland is big and, during the busy summer season, crowded. Planning a strategy for your visit, as the locals do, will help you get the most out of it. If you can, pick a rainy midweek day; surprisingly, most Disney attractions are indoors. Arrive early; the box office opens a half hour before the park's scheduled opening time. Go immediately to the most popular attractions: Space Mountain, Star Tours, Pirates of the Caribbean, Haunted Mansion, It's a Small World, and Splash Mountain. Mickey's Toontown tends to be most crowded in the mornings. Lines for rides will also be shorter during the evening Fantasmic! show, parades, and fireworks display (usually around 9:30), as well as near opening or closing times. Just the same, even on a slow day expect to wait in line for 15 minutes or so. As with the rides, strategize your eating as well. Restaurants are less crowded toward the beginning and end of meal periods. Also, fast-food spots abound, and you can now get healthy fare, such as fruit, pasta, and frozen yogurt, at various locations throughout the park. Whatever you wind up eating, food prices are higher than on the outside. When shopping, remember that there are lockers just off Main Street in which you can store purchases and thereby avoid lugging bundles around all day or shopping just before the park's closing time when stores are crowded. If your feet get tired, you can move from one area of the park to another on the train or monorail or even in a horse-drawn carriage.

Each of Disney's lands has its own theme rides. Stepping through the doors of Sleeping Beauty's castle into **Fantasyland** can be a dream come true for children. Mickey Mouse may even be there to greet them. Once inside, they can join **Peter Pan's Flight;** go down the rabbit hole with **Alice in Wonderland;** take an aerial spin with **Dumbo the Flying Elephant;** take **Mr. Toad's Wild Ride;** spin around in giant cups at the **Mad Tea Party;** swoosh through the **Matterhorn;** or visit **It's a Small World,** where figures of children from 100 countries worldwide sing of unity and peace.

In **Frontierland** you can take a cruise on the **steamboat** *Mark Twain* or the **sailing ship** *Columbia* and experience the sights and sounds of the spectacular **Rivers of America.** Kids of every age enjoy rafting to **Tom Sawyer's Island** for an hour or so of climbing and exploring.

Some visitors to **Adventureland** have taken the **Jungle Cruise** so many times that they know the patter offered up by the operators by heart. Other attractions here include shops with African and South Seas wares.

The twisting streets of **New Orleans Square** offer interesting browsing and shopping, strolling Dixieland musicians, and the ever-popular **Pirates of the Caribbean** ride. The **Haunted Mansion,** populated by 999 holographic ghosts, is nearby. Theme shops purvey hats, perfume, Mardi Gras merchandise, and gourmet items. The **Disney Gallery** here has trendy (and expensive) original Disney art.

148

Anaheim Museum, **4**
Balboa Peninsula, **15**
Bolsa Chica Ecological Reserve, **12**
Bowers Museum of Cultural Art, **7**
Crystal Cathedral, **6**
Dana Point, **21**
Disneyland, **1**
Fashion Island, **16**
Fiesta Marketplace, **8**
Huntington Beach, **13**
Irvine Museum, **9**
Knott's Berry Farm, **2**
Laguna Art Museum, **19**
Mission San Juan Capistrano, **23**
Movieland Wax Museum, **3**
Newport Harbor, **14**
Newport Harbor Art Museum, **17**
Orange County Marine Institute, **22**
Richard Nixon Library and Birthplace, **5**
Ritz-Carlton Laguna Niguel, **20**
San Juan Capistrano Library, **24**
Sherman Library and Gardens, **18**
South Coast Plaza, **11**
University of California at Irvine, **10**

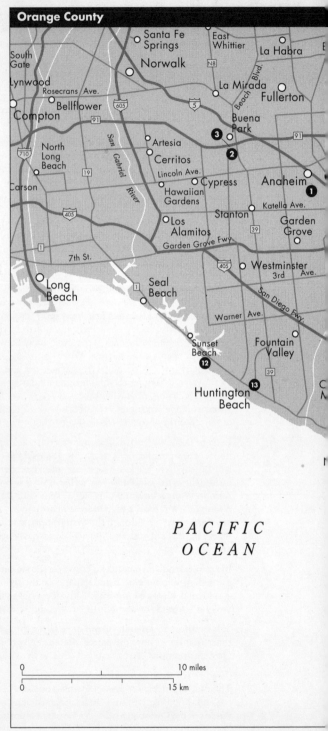

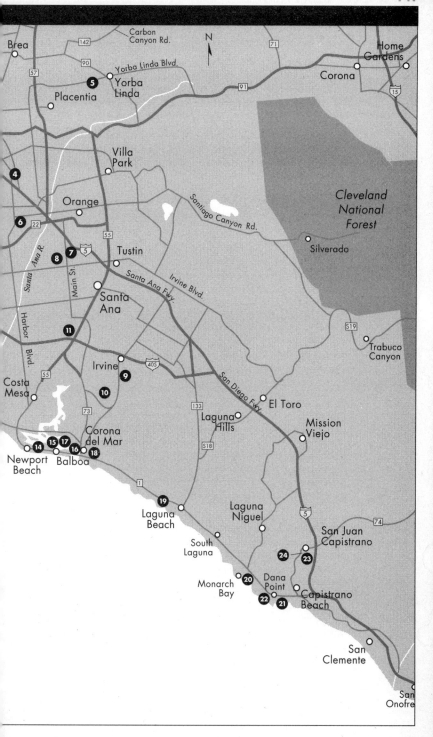

The animated bears in **Critter Country** may charm kids of all ages, but it's **Splash Mountain,** the steepest, wettest Disney adventure, that keeps them coming back for more.

Disney's vision of the future in **Tomorrowland** has undergone the most changes over the years, reflecting advances in technology. You can still take a **Submarine Voyage** or ride the monorail, but you can also be hurled into outer space on **Space Mountain,** take **Star Tours,** or watch Michael Jackson perform in the 3-D movie *Captain E-0.*

Designed to delight small children, **Mickey's Toontown** is actually a pint-size playground. Kids can climb up a rope ladder on the **"Miss Daisy," Donald's Boat,** talk to a mailbox, and walk through **Mickey's House** and **meet Mickey,** all the while feeling that they're inside a cartoon. Bring your camera; there are photo opportunities everywhere. The **Roger Rabbit Car Toon Spin,** the largest and most unusual black-light ride in Disneyland history, has been packing them in since it opened here in 1994.

A stroll along **Main Street** evokes a small-town America, circa 1900, that never existed except in the popular imagination and fiction and films. Interconnected shops and restaurants line both sides of the street. The **Emporium,** the largest and most comprehensive of the shops, offers a full line of Disney products. But you'll also find magic tricks, crystal, hobby and sports memorabilia, clothing, and photo supplies here. *1313 Harbor Blvd., Anaheim,* ☎ *714/999–4565.* ☛ *$33 adults, $25 children 3–11.* ⊙ *June–mid-Sept., Sun.–Fri. 9 AM–midnight, Sat. 9 AM–1 AM; mid-Sept.–May, weekdays 10–6, Sat. 9–midnight, Sun. 9–10. Hrs and prices subject to change.*

★ ❷   If Disneyland specializes in a high-tech brand of fantasy, **Knott's Berry Farm,** in nearby Buena Park, offers a dose of reality. The farm has been rooted in the community since 1934, when Cordelia Knott began serving chicken dinners on her wedding china to supplement the family's meager income. The dinners and the boysenberry pies proved more profitable than husband Walter's berry farm, so the family moved first into the restaurant business and then into the entertainment business. The park, with its Old West theme, is now a 150-acre complex with 100-plus rides and attractions, 60 eating places, and 60 shops.

Like Disneyland, the park has theme areas. **Ghost Town** offers a delightful human-scale visit to the Old West. Many of the buildings were relocated here from their original mining-town sites. You can stroll down the street, stop and chat with the blacksmith, pan for gold, crack open a geode, ride in an authentic 1880s passenger train, or take the **Gold Mine** ride and descend into a replica of a working gold mine. A real treasure here is the antique **Dentzel carousel** with a menagerie of animals. **Camp Snoopy** is a kid-size High Sierra wonderland where Snoopy and his Peanuts-gang friends hang out. Tall trees frame **Wild Water Wilderness,** where you can ride white water in an inner tube in **Big Foot Rapids** and commune with the native peoples of the Northwest coast in the spooky **Mystery Lodge.** Themes aside, thrill rides are placed throughout the park. Teenagers, especially, love the **Boomerang** roller coaster; **X-K-1,** a living version of a video game; **Kingdom of the Dinosaurs;** and **Montezooma's Revenge,** a roller coaster that goes from 0 to 55 mph in less than five seconds. Costumed interpreters offer insight into the natural and human history of the attractions.

Knott's also offers entertainment throughout the day with shows scheduled in Ghost Town, the Bird Cage Theater, and the Good Time Theater; occasionally stars appear here. *8039 Beach Blvd., Buena*

Park, ☎ *714/220–5200.* ☛ *$28.50 adults, $18.50 senior citizens and children 3–11.* ☉ *June–early Sept., daily 9* AM*–midnight; mid-Sept.–May, weekdays 10–6, Sat. 10–10, Sun. 10–7. Park closes during inclement weather. Hrs and prices subject to change.*

TIME OUT   Don't forget what made Knott's famous: Mrs. Knott's fried chicken dinners and boysenberry pies at **Mrs. Knott's Chicken Dinner Restaurant.** It's
just outside the park gates in Knott's California MarketPlace, a collection
of 32 shops and restaurants.

Visitors will find more than 70 years of movie magic immortalized at
③ **Movieland Wax Museum** in 400 wax sculptures of Hollywood's greatest stars including Michael Jackson, Cindy Crawford, John Wayne, Marilyn Monroe, and George Burns. Figures are displayed in a maze of
realistic sets from movies such as *Gone with the Wind, Star Trek, The
Wizard of Oz,* and *Home Alone.* The Chamber of Horrors is designed
to scare the daylights out of you. You can buy a combination ticket
($16.50 adults, $9.75 children) that also allows you ☛ to Ripley's Believe It or Not, the somewhat schlocky chain attraction across the street.
7711 Beach Blvd., 1 block north of Knott's, ☎ *714/522–1155.* ☛ *$12.95
adults, $6.95 children.* ☉ *Sun.–Thurs. 9–7, Fri.–Sat. 9–8.*

④ The **Anaheim Museum,** housed in a 1908 Carnegie Library building,
illustrates the history of Anaheim including the original wine-produc-
ing colony. Changing exhibits include art collections, women's history,
and hobbies. *241 S. Anaheim Blvd.,* ☎ *714/778–3301. Suggested* ☛
$1.50; children free. ☉ *Wed.–Fri. 10–4, Sat. noon–4.*

About 7 miles north of Anaheim, off Highway 57 (Yorba Linda Blvd.
★ **⑤** exit), the **Richard Nixon Library and Birthplace** is the final resting
place of the 37th president and his wife Pat. Displays illustrate the check-
ered career of Nixon, the only president forced to resign from office.
Interactive exhibits give visitors a chance to interview Nixon, press-
conference style, and receive prerecorded replies on 300 topics. Displays include impressive life-size sculptures of world leaders, gifts
Nixon received from international heads of state, and a large graffiti-
covered section of the Berlin Wall. Visitors can listen to Nixon's Checkers speech or to the so-called smoking-gun tape from the Watergate
days, among other recorded material. In contrast to the high-tech exhibits are Pat Nixon's tranquil rose garden and the small farmhouse
where Nixon was born in 1913. The farmhouse contains original furnishings such as a cast-iron stove, a piano, a Bible, and family photos.
Within the main building is a small but interesting gift shop that contains presidential souvenir items. *18001 Yorba Linda Blvd., Yorba Linda,*
☎ *714/993–3393.* ☛ *$5.95 adults, $3.95 senior citizens, $2 children
8–11.* ☉ *Mon.–Sat. 10–5, Sun. 11–5.*

Garden Grove, a community just south of Anaheim and Buena Park,
is the home of one of the most impressive churches in the country, the
⑥ **Crystal Cathedral.** The domain of television evangelist Robert Schuller,
this sparkling glass structure resembles a four-pointed star with more
than 10,000 panes of glass covering a weblike steel truss to form
translucent walls. The feeling as you enter is nothing less than mysti-
cal. In addition to tours of the cathedral, two pageants are offered
yearly—"The Glory of Christmas" and "The Glory of Easter"—featuring live animals, flying angels, and other special effects. *12141
Lewis St., Garden Grove,* ☎ *714/971–4013. Donation requested.
Guided tours Mon.–Sat. 9–3:30. Call for schedule.* ☎ *714/544–5679
for reservations for Easter and Christmas productions.*

❼ The **Bowers Museum of Cultural Art,** once a quaint cultural-arts gallery, is now the largest museum in Orange County, having tripled in size after a $12 million expansion and restoration of its original 1936 Spanish-style buildings. The museum houses a first-rate, 85,000-piece collection of artwork by indigenous peoples from around the world. Permanent galleries display sculpture, costumes, and artifacts from Oceania; sculpture from west and central Africa; Pacific Northwest wood carvings; dazzling beadwork of the Plains cultures; and California basketry. The museum's trendy Topaz Cafe offers an ethnically eclectic menu. *2002 N. Main St., Santa Ana,* ☎ *714/567–3600.* ☛ *$4.50 adults, $3 senior citizens and students, $1.50 children, under 5 free.* ☉ *Tues.–Wed. and Fri.–Sun. 10–4, Thurs. 10–9.*

Santa Ana, the county seat, is undergoing a dramatic restoration in its downtown area. Gleaming new government buildings meld with turn-of-the-century structures to give a sense of where the county came from **❽** and where it is going. The **Fiesta Marketplace,** along Fourth Street downtown, offers a glimpse into contemporary Hispanic culture. The best time to visit is on the weekend, when the place takes on a lively fiesta atmosphere. You'll find bargain Western wear, imports from Mexico and Guatemala, and authentic tacos and quesadillas. Just a block away is the **Old Orange County Courthouse,** which has been a backdrop for more than 30 movies and TV shows since 1915; it is now a county museum and historical center (*400 W. Santa Ana Blvd.;* ☛ Free; open weekdays 9–5).

To glimpse the pristine California landscape as it was before development brought houses and freeways to hillsides, visit the **Irvine Museum.** **❾** Located on the 12th floor of a circular marble-and-glass office building, the museum displays a collection of California impressionist landscape paintings dated 1890 to 1930. The collection was assembled by Joan Irvine Smith, granddaughter of James Irvine, who once owned one-quarter of what is now Orange County. *18881 Von Karman Ave., Irvine,* ☎ *714/476–2565.* ☛ *Free.* ☉ *Tues.–Sat. 11–5.*

Known for its forward-looking concept of community planning, Irvine **❿** is also a center for higher education. The **University of California** at Irvine was established on 1,000 acres of rolling ranch land donated by the Irvine family in the mid-1950s. The **Bren Events Center Fine Art Gallery** (☎ 714/824–6610; ☛ Free; open Tues.–Sat. noon–5) on campus sponsors exhibitions of 20th-century art. Tree lovers will be enthralled by the campus; it's an arboretum with more than 11,000 trees from all over the world. *San Diego Fwy. (I–405) to Jamboree Rd., west to Campus Dr. S.*

It is no small irony that the Costa Mesa/South Coast metro area is known first for its posh shopping mall and second for its performing-arts cen-★ **⓫** ter. A mega-shopping complex, **South Coast Plaza** (3333 S. Bristol St., Costa Mesa, ☎ 714/435–2000), along with its annexes, the Crystal Court and South Coast Village, attracts more than 20 million visitors per year, making it the busiest mall in southern California. It's so big and posh that a shuttle bus transports shoppers among the three complexes. The adjacent theater-arts complex contains the acclaimed avant-garde **South Coast Repertory Theater**(655 Town Center Dr., ☎ 714/957–4033) and **Orange County Performing Arts Center** (600 Town Center Dr., ☎ 714/556–2787). This dramatic 3,000-seat facility for opera, ballet, and symphony hosts such notables as the Los Angeles Philharmonic, the Pacific Symphony, and the New York City Opera. The **California Scenario,** a 1.6-acre sculpture garden designed by Isamu

Noguchi, surrounds the theater complex, which also houses restaurants and the Westin South Coast Plaza Hotel.

TIME OUT Take a spin around Arnold Schwarzenegger's **Planet Hollywood** (1641 W. Sunflower St., across from South Coast Plaza, ☎ 714/434–7827), a restaurant that recalls the 1930s and '40s with changing displays of movie memorabilia, giant TV screens showing clips of old movies, and loud rock music. The fare here has a '50s diner flair, with hamburgers topping the menu.

The Coast

Coastal Orange County, dotted with charming beach towns and punctuated with world-class resorts, offers the quintessential laid-back southern California experience. You can catch a monster wave with the bronzed local kids, get a glimpse of some rich and famous lifestyles, and take a walk through the shoreline's natural treasures. Sites and stops on this tour are strung out along some 42 miles of the Pacific Coast Highway, and we'll take this route north to south. Although there is bus service along the coast road, it's best to explore it by car.

★ ⑫ If you're interested in wildlife, a walk through **Bolsa Chica Ecological Reserve** (☎ 714/897–7003) will reward you with a chance to see an amazingly restored 300-acre salt marsh, which is home to 315 species of birds, plus other animals and plants. You can see many of them along the 1½-mile loop trail that meanders through the reserve. The walk is especially delightful in winter, when you're likely to see great blue heron, snowy and great egrets, common loons, and other migrating birds.

⑬ **Huntington Beach,** with its 9 miles of white sand and sometimes towering waves, offers one of the hippest surf scenes in southern California. Each year it hosts the Pro Surfing Championships competition. This beach is a favorite of Orange County residents and has ample parking, food concessions, fire pits, and lifeguards. For years, the town itself was little more than a string of small, tacky buildings across Pacific Coast Highway from the beach, containing surf shops, T-shirt emporiums, and hot-dog stands. In the early '90s, however, work began on a face-lift aimed at transforming the funky surf town into a shining resort area, with the newly reconstructed 1,800-foot-long **Huntington Pier** as its centerpiece. The **Pierside Pavilion,** across Pacific Coast Highway from the pier, contains shops, a restaurant, a nightclub, and a theater complex. The **International Surfing Museum in Huntington Beach** (411 Olive Ave., ☎ 714/960–3483; ☛ $2 adults, $1 students; open Wed.–Sun. noon–5) has an extensive collection of surfing memorabilia.

Newport Beach has a dual personality: It's best known as the quintessential (upscale) beach town, with its island-dotted yacht harbor and a history of such illustrious residents as John Wayne, author Joseph Wambaugh, and Watergate scandal figure Bob Haldeman. And then there's inland Newport Beach, just southwest of John Wayne Airport, a business and commercial hub with a major shopping center and a clutch of high-rise office buildings and hotels.

Even if you don't own a yacht and don't qualify as seaside high society, you can explore the charming avenues and alleys surrounding the famed
★ ⑭ **Newport Harbor,** which shelters nearly 10,000 small boats. To see it from the water, take a one-hour gondola cruise around the harbor (Gondola Company of Newport, 3404 Via Oporto, ☎ 714/675–1212).

⑮ The waterside portion of Newport Beach consists of a U-shaped harbor with the mainland along one leg and the **Balboa Peninsula** along the other leg, separating the marina from the ocean. Set within the harbor are eight small islands, including Balboa and Lido, both well-known for their famous residents. The homes lining the shore may seem modest, but remember that this is some of the most expensive real estate in the world.

You can reach the peninsula from Pacific Coast Highway at Newport Boulevard, which will take you to Balboa Boulevard. Begin your exploration of the peninsula at the **Newport Pier,** which juts out into the ocean near 20th Street. Street parking is difficult here, so grab the first space you find and be prepared to walk. A stroll along Ocean Front reveals much of the character of this place. On weekday mornings head for the beach near the pier, where you're likely to encounter the dory fishermen hawking their predawn catches, as they've done for generations. On weekends the walk is alive with kids (of all ages) on skates, skateboards, and bikes weaving among the strolling pedestrians and whizzing past fast-food joints, swimsuit shops, and seedy bars.

Continue your drive along Balboa Boulevard nearly to the end of the peninsula, where the charm is of quite a different character. On the bay side is the historic Victorian ★**Balboa Pavilion,** perched on the water's edge. Built in 1905 as a bath- and boathouse, it hosted big-band dances in the 1940s. Today it houses a restaurant and shops and is a departure point for harbor and whale-watching cruises. Adjacent to the pavilion is the three-car ferry, which connects the peninsula to Balboa Island. Several blocks surrounding the pavilion support restaurants, shops (all a little nicer than those at Newport Pier) and a small Fun Zone—a local hangout with a Ferris wheel, video games, rides, and arcades.

⑯ The attractions of inland Newport Beach are in striking contrast to the beach scene. **Fashion Island** (☎ 714/721–2022) is an upscale shopping mall anchored by department stores such as Robinsons–May and The Broadway. Atrium Court, an enclosed Mediterranean-style section, is popular with upscale shoppers and has boutiques. *Newport Center Dr. between Jamboree and MacArthur Blvds., off Pacific Coast Hwy.*

TIME OUT   **Farmer's Market at Atrium Court** (☎ 714/760–0403) is a grocery store and more, selling a vast array of exotic foods, prime meats, and glorious fresh produce arranged in color-coordinated patterns. Also on the ground floor of the Atrium Court is a gourmet food fair with a salsa bar, sushi bar, exotic coffees stand, fresh tropical fruit juice bar, and sandwich stalls with the usual deli selections.

⑰ The **Newport Harbor Art Museum** is internationally known for its impressive collection of abstract expressionist works and cutting-edge contemporary works by California artists. *850 San Clemente Dr.,* ☎ *714/759–1122.* ☞ *$4 adults, $2 students and senior citizens.* ☉ *Tues.–Sat. 10–5, Sun. noon–5.*

Just south of Newport Beach, **Corona del Mar** is a small jewel of a town with an exceptional beach. You can walk clear out onto the bay on a rough-and-tumble rock jetty. Much of the beach around here is backed by short cliffs that resemble scaled-down versions of the northern California coastline. The town itself stretches only a few blocks along Pacific Coast Highway, but some of the fanciest stores in the county are ⑱ here. **Sherman Library and Gardens,** a lush botanical garden and library specializing in Southwest flora and fauna, offers a diversion from sun and sand. You can wander among cactus gardens, rose gardens, a wheelchair-height touch-and-smell garden, and a tropical conservatory. *2647 E. Coast Hwy., Corona del Mar, ☎ 714/673–2261.* ☛ *$2; free Mon. Gardens open daily 10:30–4.*

The drive south to Laguna Beach passes some of southern California's most beautiful oceanfront; **Crystal Cove State Beach** stretches from Corona del Mar to Laguna, and its undersea park lures swimmers and divers. Each curve in the highway along here turns up a sparkling vista of crashing surf to one side and, to the other, gently rolling golden brown hills sweeping inland.

★ **Laguna Beach** has been called SoHo by the Sea, which is at least partly right. It is an artists' colony that, during the 1950s and '60s, attracted the beat, hip, and far-out, but it is also a colony of conservative wealth. The two camps coexist in relative harmony, with Art prevailing in the congested village, and Wealth entrenched in the canyons and on the hillsides surrounding the town. The November 1993 fire, which destroyed more than 300 homes in the hillsides surrounding Laguna Beach, miraculously left the village untouched.

Walk along Pacific Coast Highway in town or along side streets, such as Forest or Ocean, and you'll pass gallery after gallery filled with art ranging from billowy seascapes to neon sculpture and kinetic structures. In addition, you'll find a wide selection of crafts, high fashion, beachwear, and jewelry shops.

⑲ The **Laguna Art Museum,** near Heisler Park, has historical and contemporary California art. Special exhibits change quarterly. *307 Cliff Dr., ☎ 714/494–6531.* ☛ *$5 adults, $4 students and senior citizens, children under 12 free. ☉ Tues.–Sun. 11–5.*

In front of the Pottery Shack on Pacific Coast Highway is a bit of local nostalgia—a life-size **statue of Eiler Larsen,** the town greeter, who for years stood at the edge of town saying hello and goodbye to visitors. In recent years a man who calls himself Number One Archer has assumed the role of greeter, waving to tourists from a spot at the corner of Pacific Coast Highway and Forest Avenue.

Laguna's many arts festivals bring visitors here from all over the world. During July and August, the Sawdust Festival and Art-a-Fair, the Laguna Festival of the Arts, and the Pageant of the Masters take place. The **Pageant of the Masters** (☎ 714/494–1147) is Laguna's most impressive event, a blending of life and art. Live models and carefully orchestrated backgrounds are arranged in striking mimicry of famous paintings.

Going to Laguna without exploring its beaches would be a shame. To get away from the hubbub of Main Beach, go north to **Woods Cove,** off the Pacific Coast Highway at Diamond Street; it's especially quiet during the week. Big rock formations hide lurking crabs. As you climb the steps to leave, you'll see a stunning English-style mansion that was once the home of Bette Davis.

⑳ The **Ritz-Carlton Laguna Niguel** is the classiest hotel along the coast; it draws guests from around the world with its sweeping oceanside views, gleaming marble, and stunning antiques. Even if you're not a registered guest, you can enjoy the view and the elegant service by taking English tea, which is served each afternoon in the library. *1 Ritz-Carlton Dr., Dana Point, ☎ 714/240–2000.*

㉑ **Dana Point** is Orange County's newest aquatic playground, a small-boat marina tucked into a dramatic natural harbor surrounded by high bluffs. The harbor was first described more than 100 years ago by its namesake Richard Henry Dana in his book *Two Years Before the Mast*. The marina has docks for small boats and marine-oriented shops and restaurants. Recent development includes a hillside park with bike and walking trails, hotels, small shopping centers, and a collection of eateries. **Dana Wharf Sportfishing** (☎ 714/496–5794) has charters year-round and runs whale-watching excursions in winter, and the community sponsors an annual whale festival in late February.

A real treasure in Dana Point is the **Nautical Heritage Museum,** a collection of ship models, paintings, 18th- and 19th-century seafaring documents, and navigation instruments. *24532 Del Prado Ave., Dana Point,* ☎ *714/661–1001.* ☞ *Free.* ☉ *Weekdays 10–4.*

㉒ The **Orange County Marine Institute** offers a number of programs and excursions designed to entertain and educate about the ocean. Three tanks containing touchable sea creatures are available on weekends. Anchored near the institute is *The Pilgrim,* a full-size replica of the square-rigged vessel on which Richard Henry Dana sailed. Tours of *The Pilgrim* are offered Sunday from 11 to 2:30. A gallery and gift shop are open daily. *24200 Dana Point Harbor Dr.,* ☎ *714/496–2274.* ☉ *Daily 10–4:30.*

San Juan Capistrano is best known for its mission and, of course, for the swallows that migrate here each year from their winter haven in Argentina. The arrival of the birds on St. Joseph's Day, March 19, launches a week of festivities. After summering in the arches of the old stone church, the swallows head home on St. John's Day, October 23.

★ ㉓ Founded in 1776 by Father Junipero Serra, **Mission San Juan Capistrano** was the major Roman Catholic outpost between Los Angeles and San Diego. A main draw is a chance to see the original Great Stone Church, which is permanently supported by scaffolding. Many of the mission's adobe buildings have been restored to illustrate mission life, with exhibits of an olive millstone, tallow ovens, tanning vats, metalworking furnaces, and padres' living quarters. The bougainvillea-covered Serra Chapel is believed to be the oldest building still in use in California. *Camino Capistrano and Ortega Hwy.,* ☎ *714/248–2048.* ☞ *$4 adults, $3 children under 13.* ☉ *Daily 8:30–5; free tours Sun. at 1.*

㉔ Near the mission is the postmodern **San Juan Capistrano Library,** built in 1983. Architect Michael Graves mixed classical design with the style of the mission to striking effect. Its courtyard has secluded places for reading, as well as a running water fountain. *31495 El Camino Real,* ☎ *714/493–3984.* ☉ *Mon.–Tues. 11–9, Wed. 1–9, Thurs. noon–6, Sat. 10–5.*

Galleria Capistrano, occupying the historic Egan House, is one of southern California's leading galleries devoted to the art of Native Americans. Exhibits include first-rate paintings, prints, jewelry, and sculpture from Southwest and Northwest artists. *31892 Camino Capistrano,* ☎ *714/661–1781.* ☉ *Tues.–Sun. 11–6.*

TIME OUT The 1894 Spanish Revival **Capistrano Depot** (26701 Verdugo St., ☎ 714/496–8181) is not only the local Amtrak train station but also a restaurant. The eclectic menu runs from rack of lamb to Southwestern fare to pasta. It's a perfect way to see San Juan if you are based in Los Angeles—a train ride, a meal, and then a little sightseeing.

San Onofre State Beach, just south of San Clemente, boasts some of California's best surfing. Below the bluffs here are 3½ miles of sandy beach, where you can also swim, fish, and watch wildlife.

For avid bicyclists, the next 20 miles south of **San Clemente** (site of Richard Nixon's Western White House) are prime terrain. **Camp Pendleton,** the country's largest Marine Corps base, welcomes cyclists to use some of its roads—just don't be surprised to see a troop helicopter taking off right beside you.

Off the Beaten Track

Lido Isle, an island in Newport Harbor, the location of many elegant homes, provides some insight into the upper-crust Orange County mind-set. A number of grassy areas offer great harbor views; each is marked "Private Community Park." *Hwy. 55 to PCH in Newport Beach. Turn left at signal on Via Lido and follow onto island.*

Old Towne Orange contains at least 1,200 buildings documented as historically relevant. A walking tour explores some of the most interesting of these, including the Ainsworth House, a museum dedicated to the city's early lifestyle; the 1901 Finley Home, location of the 1945 film *Fallen Angels;* and O'Hara's Irish Pub, a hangout for local reporters. A brochure describing all the stops is available. *City of Orange, 300 E. Chapman Ave., Room 12, Orange,* ☎ *714/744–7220.*

Little Saigon, an area of the city of Westminster between Ward Street on the east and Magnolia on the west, is home to 115,000 or so Vietnamese residents, the largest Vietnamese community outside Vietnam. Check out the jewelry and gift shops, Asian herbalists, and restaurants in colorful Little Saigon Plaza (Bolsa and Buishard streets), where Song Phung Restaurant offers an extensive menu of authentic dishes. The Dynasty Seafood Restaurant, in the Asian Garden Mall (Bolsa between Magnolia and Bushard streets), is considered the best place in Orange County for Chinese dim sum.

SHOPPING

Upscale shopping is Orange County's favorite indoor sport, and the county has the shopping malls to prove it. The following is just a small selection of the shopping possibilities in the county.

South Coast Plaza (Bristol and Sunflower Sts., Costa Mesa), the most amazing of all the malls and the largest in Orange County, is actually two enclosed shopping centers, complete with greenery and tumbling waterfalls bisecting the wide aisles, plus a collection of boutiques and restaurants across the street. A free tram makes frequent runs among the three sections. The older section is anchored by Nordstrom, Sears, and Bullock's; the newer Crystal Court across the street has The Broadway department store as its centerpiece. It's the variety of stores, however, that makes this mall special. You'll find Rizzoli Bookstore, Gucci, Burberry's, Armani, F.A.O. Schwarz, Saks Fifth Avenue, and Mark Cross just up the aisle from Sears. Kids will want to browse through the Disney and Sesame Street stores.

Fashion Island on Newport Center Drive in Newport Beach sits on a hilltop, where shoppers can enjoy the ocean breeze. It is an open-air, single-level mall of more than 200 stores. Major department stores here include Neiman Marcus, Bullock's, and The Broadway. The enclosed **Atrium Court** is a Mediterranean-style plaza with three floors of boutiques and stores, such as Sharper Image, Benetton, and Caswell–Massey.

Main Place, just off I–5 in Santa Ana, has Robinsons–May, Bullock's, and Nordstrom as its anchors. Although many of the 190 shops are upscale, the mall resembles a warehouse. It's busy and noisy, and local teenagers tend to hang out here.

If you can look past the inflatable palm trees, unimaginative T-shirts, and other tourist novelties, there is some good browsing to be done in **Laguna Beach.** There are dozens of art galleries, antiques shops, one-of-a-kind craft boutiques, and custom jewelry stores. Some of the best can be found along arty Forest Avenue and nearby thoroughfares, just a few steps off Pacific Coast Highway. Tree Foxes Trot, at 264 Forest Avenue, features a delightful selection of handcrafted items from around the world; Georgeo's Art Glass and Jewelry, at 269 Forest Avenue, contains a large selection of etched and blown-glass bowls, vases, glassware, and jewelry; Rosovsky Gallery, at 303 Broadway, showcases the work of three Russian artists; Art Center Gallery, at 1492 South Coast Highway, features works for locally renowned artists; and Christie of Santa Fe, at 202 Forest Avenue, specializes in southwestern art.

SPORTS

For professional sports, *see* Spectator Sports in Chapter 4, Sports and Fitness.

Bicycling
Bicycles and roller and in-line skates are some of the most popular means of transportation along the beaches. A bike path spans the distance from Marina del Rey all the way to San Diego, with only some minor breaks. Most beaches have rental stands. In Laguna, try **Rainbow Bicycles** (☎ 714/494–5806) or, in Huntington Beach, **Team Bicycle Rentals** (☎ 714/969–5480).

Golf
Aliso Creek Golf Course (South Laguna, ☎ 714/499–1919); **Anaheim Hills Public Country Club** (☎ 714/748–8900); **Costa Mesa Public Golf and Country Club** (☎ 714/540–7500); **H.G. Dad Miller** (Anaheim, ☎ 714/774–8055); **Imperial Golf Course** (Brea, ☎ 714/529–3923); **Mile Square Golf Course** (Fountain Valley, ☎714/968–4556); **Newport Beach Golf Course** (☎ 714/852–8681); **San Clemente Municipal Golf Course** (☎ 714/492–3943); **San Juan Hills Country Club** (San Juan Capistrano, ☎ 714/837–0361).

Running
The **Santa Ana Riverbed Trail** hugs the Santa Ana River for 20.6 miles between the Pacific Coast Highway at Huntington State Beach and Imperial Highway in Yorba Linda; there are entrances, as well as rest rooms and drinking fountains, at all crossings. The **Beach Trail** runs along the beach from Huntington Beach to Newport. Paths throughout **Newport Back Bay** wrap around a marshy area inhabited by lizards, squirrels, rabbits, and waterfowl.

Snorkeling
The fact that **Corona del Mar** is off-limits to boats—along with its two colorful reefs—makes it a great place for snorkeling. **Laguna Beach** is also a good spot for snorkeling and diving; the whole beach area of the city is a marine preserve.

Surfing
There are 50 surf breaks along the Orange County coastline, with wave action ranging from beginner to expert. If you are not an expert, you can get a sense of the action on a boogie board at one of the begin-

ners' beaches. Surfing is permitted at most beaches year-round, except at **Huntington State Beach, Salt Creek Beach Park, Aliso County Beach, Capistrano Beach, Sunset Beach,** and **Newport Beach,** where it is permitted only in summer. "The Wedge" at **Newport Beach,** one of the most famous surfing spots in the world, is known for its steep, punishing shore break. Don't miss the spectacle of surfers, who appear tiny in the midst of the waves, flying through this treacherous place. San Clemente surfers usually take a great spot right across from the San Onofre Nuclear Reactor. Rental stands are found at all beaches.

Tennis

Most of the larger hotels have tennis courts. Here are some other choices; try the local Yellow Pages for additional listings.

ANAHEIM

Anaheim has 50 public tennis courts; phone the Parks and Recreation Department for information (☎ 714/254–5191).

HUNTINGTON BEACH

Edison Community Center (21377 Magnolia St., ☎ 714/960–8870) has four courts available on a first-come, first-served basis in the daytime. The **Murdy Community Center** (7000 Norma Dr., ☎ 714/960–8895) has four courts, also first-come, first-served during the day. Both facilities accept reservations for play after 5 PM; both charge $2 an hour.

LAGUNA BEACH

Six metered courts can be found at **Laguna Beach High School,** on Park Avenue. Two courts are available at the **Irvine Bowl,** on Laguna Canyon Road, and six new courts are available at **Alta Laguna Park,** at the end of Alta Laguna Boulevard, off Park Avenue, on a first-come, first-served basis. For more information, call the City of Laguna Beach Recreation Department (☎ 714/497–0716).

NEWPORT BEACH

Call the recreation department (☎ 714/644–3151) for information about court use at **Corona del Mar High School** (2101 E. Bluff Dr.). There are eight public courts.

Newport Beach Marriott Hotel and Tennis Club (900 Newport Center Dr., ☎ 714/640–4000) has eight courts.

SAN CLEMENTE

There are four courts at **San Luis Rey Park,** on Avenue San Luis Rey. They are offered on a first-come, first-served basis. Call the recreation department (☎ 714/361–8200) for further information.

Water Sports

Rental stands for surfboards, Windsurfers, small powerboats, and sailboats can be found near most of the piers. **Hobie Sports** has three locations for surfboard and boogie-board rentals—two in Dana Point (☎ 714/496–2366) and one in Laguna (☎ 714/497–3304).

In the biggest boating town of all, Newport Beach, you can rent sailboats and small motorboats at **Balboa Boat Rentals** (☎ 714/673–7200; open daily 11–5), in the harbor. Sailboats cost $25 an hour, and motorboats cost $29 an hour, half price for each subsequent hour. You must have a driver's license, and some knowledge of boating is helpful; rented boats are not allowed out of the bay.

Sportfishing is popular at **Davey's Locker** (☎ 714/673–1434; open summer, daily 9–5:30) in the Balboa Pavilion. The cost is $35 per person, for a day's worth; the half-day's cost is $22. Or, for $35 a half day you can rent a small motorboat to fish in the harbor for sea bass and other marine life.

In Dana Point, powerboats and sailboats can be rented at **Embarcadero Marina** (☎ 714/496–6177, open weekdays 8–5, weekends 7–5:30; open earlier June–Aug.), near the launching ramp at Dana Point Harbor. Boat sizes vary—sailboats range from $15 to $30 an hour; motorboats are $20 an hour. Only cash is accepted.

BEACHES

All the state, county, and city beaches in Orange County allow swimming. Make sure there is a staffed lifeguard stand nearby, and you should be pretty safe. Also keep on the lookout for posted signs about undertow: It can be mighty nasty around here. Recently, beaches have begun closing at night. Moving from north to south along the coast, here are some of the best beaches:

Huntington Beach State Beach (☎ 714/536–1454) runs for 9 miles along Pacific Coast Highway (Beach Blvd. [Hwy. 39] from inland). There are changing rooms, concessions, fire pits, and vigilant lifeguards on the premises, and there is parking. **Bolsa Chica State Beach** (☎ 714/846–3460), just north of Huntington and across from the Bolsa Chica Ecological Reserve, has barbecue pits and is usually less crowded than its neighbor.

Lower Newport Bay provides an enclave sheltered from the ocean. This area, off Pacific Coast Highway on Jamboree Boulevard, is a 740-acre preserve for ducks and geese. Nearby **Newport Dunes Resort** (☎ 714/729–3863) offers RV spaces, picnic facilities, changing rooms, watersports equipment rentals, and a place to launch boats.

Just south of Newport Beach, **Corona del Mar Beach** (☎ 714/644–3044) has a tidal pool and caves to explore. It also sports one of the best walks in the county—a beautiful rock pier that juts into the ocean. Facilities include fire pits, volleyball courts, food, rest rooms, and parking.

Crystal Cove State Park (☎ 714/494–3539, ☞ $6 per car), midway between Corona del Mar and Laguna, is a hidden treasure: 3½ miles of unspoiled beach with some of the best tide pooling in southern California. Here you can see starfish, crabs, and lobster on the rocks, and rangers conduct nature walks on Saturday morning.

Located at the end of Broadway at Pacific Coast Highway, Laguna Beach's **Main Beach Park** has sand volleyball, two half-basketball courts, children's play equipment, picnic areas, rest rooms, showers, and road parking.

The county's best spot for scuba diving is in the **Marine Life Refuge** (☎ 714/494–6571), which runs from Seal Rock to Diver's Cove in Laguna. Farther south, in South Laguna, **Aliso County Park** (☎ 714/661–7013) is a recreation area with a pier for fishing, barbecue pits, parking, food, and rest rooms. Swim Beach, inside **Dana Point Harbor,** also has a fishing pier, barbecues, food, parking, and rest rooms, as well as a shower.

Doheny State Park (☎ 714/496–6171), at the south end of Dana Point, one of the best surfing spots in southern California, has an interpretive center devoted to the wildlife of the Doheny Marine Refuge, and there are food stands and shops nearby. Camping is permitted here, and there are picnic facilities and a pier for fishing. **San Clemente State Beach** (☎ 714/492–3156) is a favorite of surfers and other locals. It has ample camping facilities, RV hookups, and food stands.

DINING AND LODGING

Dining

Central Orange County, in particular, boasts a number of ethnic restaurants, the result of an influx of people from all over the world. Some of these include **Sitar Indian Restaurant** (2632 W. La Palma Ave., Anaheim, ☎ 714/821–8333); **Lotus Court** (181 E. Commonwealth Ave., Fullerton, ☎ 714/738–3838), for Hong Kong–style Chinese cuisine; **Phoenix Club** (1340 Sanderson Ave., Anaheim, ☎ 714/563–4164), a German restaurant; **Sushi Seiha** (214 S. State College Blvd., Anaheim, ☎ 714/991–8980), a Japanese restaurant; **Anita's** (600 S. Harbor Blvd., Fullerton, ☎ 714/525–0977), for Southwestern fare; and **Song Long** (9361 Bolsa Ave., Westminster, ☎ 714/775–3724), a Vietnamese/French restaurant.

CATEGORY	COST*
$$$$	over $35
$$$	$25–$35
$$	$15–$25
$	under $15

per person, excluding 7.75% tax, service, and drinks

Lodging

A general upgrading of the area surrounding Disneyland has increased the number of reliable inexpensive and moderately priced chain motels. There are four **Travelodge** properties here, two along West Street across the street from the park, one on Katella Avenue on the south side of the park, and one on Harbor Boulevard next to the parking lot entrance. Reservations for all of them can be made by calling 800/826–1616. Two **Days Inn** properties can be found on Harbor Boulevard, the eastern boundary of the park: Days Inn Suites (1111 S. Harbor Blvd., ☎ 714/533–8830, FAX 714/758–0573) and Days Inn Maingate (1604 S. Harbor Blvd., ☎ 714/635–3630, FAX 714/520–3290). A **Motel 6** (100W. Freedman Way, ☎ 714/520–9696, FAX 714/533–7539) is about three blocks from the park.

Prices listed here are based on summer rates. Winter rates, especially near Disneyland, tend to be somewhat less. It pays to shop around for promotional and weekend rates.

CATEGORY	COST*
$$$$	over $100
$$$	$75–$100
$$	$50–$75
$	under $50

All prices are for a double room; local hotel taxes vary.

Anaheim

DINING

$$$$ **JW's.** This is an elegant French surprise in the heart of convention-busy
★ Anaheim. A quiet place where you can talk serious business or romance, the restaurant is a series of interconnected rooms. The decor is country French with fireplaces, books, subdued lighting, and original art on the walls. While French is the theme, the menu changes frequently to spotlight fresh seafood, game, and produce. The extensive wine list is fairly priced. ✗ *Marriott Hotel, 700 W. Convention Way,* ☎ *714/750–8000. Reservations suggested. AE, D, DC, MC, V. No lunch. Closed Sun. Valet parking.*

$$$–$$$$ **White House.** This mansion, built in 1909, which bears a striking resemblance to its namesake, is popular with conventioneers. There are

162

Dining

Angelo's & Vinci's Cafe Ristorante, **1**
Antoine, **33**
Bangkok IV, **28**
Beach House, **55**
The Cannery, **46**
The Catch, **22**
The Cellar, **2**
Chanteclair, **40**
City Club, **24**
Crab Cooker, **45**
Delaney's Restaurant, **62**
Dining Room, **61**
El Adobe, **67**
El Torito Grill, **43**
Emporio Armani Express, **29**
Etienne's, **69**
Five Feets, **58**
Hard Rock Cafe Newport Beach, **52**
JW's, **12**
Kachina, **57**
La Brasserie, **25**
La Vie En Rose, **4**
Le Biarritz, **47**
L'Hirondelle, **68**
Luciana's, **64**
Mandarin Gourmet, **42**
Marrakesh, **44**
McCormick & Schmick, **39**
Mulberry Street Ristorante, **3**
Pascal, **48**
Pavilion, **35**
Prego, **38**
Randall's, **27**
The Ritz, **49**
Tortilla Flats, **60**
Watercolors, **66**
White House, **20**
Wolfgang Puck Cafe, **30**

Lodging

Anaheim Hilton and Towers, **11**
Anaheim Marriott, **12**
Atrium Marquis Hotel, **32**
Best Western Marina Inn, **65**
Blue Lantern Inn, **63**
Buena Park Hotel, **5**
Candy Cane Inn, **16**
Castle Inn and Suites, **17**
Country Side Inn and Suites, **41**
Dana Point Resort, **66**

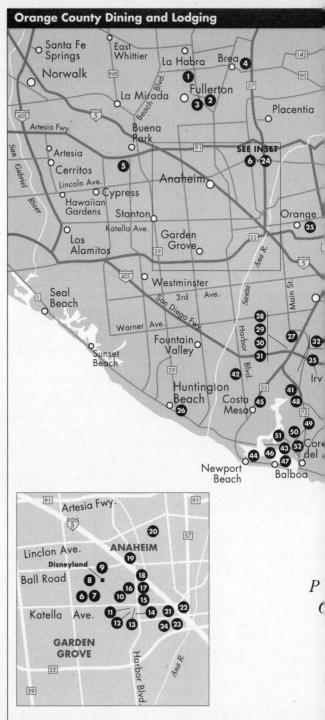

Orange County Dining and Lodging

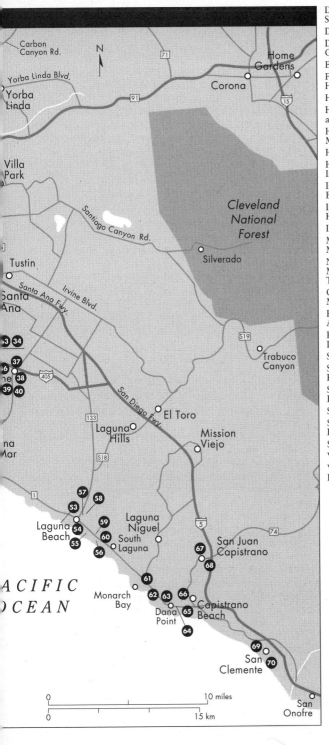

Desert Palm Inn and Suites, **10**

Disneyland Hotel, **8**

Doubletree Hotel Orange County, **23**

Eiler's Inn, **59**

Four Seasons Hotel, **50**

Hampton Inn, **21**

Holiday Inn at the Park, **19**

Holiday Inn Maingate, **15**

Hotel Laguna, **54**

Hyatt Regency Irvine, **37**

Inn at Laguna Beach, **53**

Inn at the Park Hotel, **13**

Irvine Marriott, **36**

Magic Carpet Motel, **7**

Newport Beach Marriott Hotel and Tennis Club, **51**

Quality Hotel Maingate, **14**

Ramada Maingate/ Anaheim, **18**

Ritz-Carlton Laguna Niguel, **61**

San Clemente Inn, **70**

Sheraton Anaheim Hotel, **9**

Sheraton Newport Beach, **34**

Stovall's Inn, **6**

Surf and Sand Hotel, **56**

Sutton Place Hotel, **33**

Waterfront Hilton, **26**

Westin South Coast Plaza, **31**

several small dining rooms with crisp linens, candles, flowers, and some fireplaces. The Northern Italian menu with French influence features a good selection from pasta to scaloppine, with a heavy emphasis on seafood. Vegetarian entrées are available. A four-course prix-fixe menu is available until 6:30 for $27.50 per person. ✗ *887 S. Anaheim Blvd.,* ☏ *714/772–1381. Reservations suggested. AE, DC, MC, V. No lunch weekends.*

$$–$$$ **The Catch.** This very reliable restaurant across the street from Anaheim Stadium is popular with sports fans, who enjoy its sports-bar atmosphere and friendly service. Dining rooms have a comfortable denlike ambience. The menu features hearty portions of steak, seafood, and salads. ✗ *1929 S. State College Blvd., Anaheim,* ☏ *714/634–1829. Reservations advised. AE, DC, MC, V. No weekend lunch.*

LODGING

$$$$ **Anaheim Hilton and Towers.** This hotel, the largest in southern California, is one of several choices convenient to the Anaheim Convention Center, which in fact is just a few steps from the front door. It is virtually a self-contained city—complete with its own post office. The lobby is dominated by a bright, airy atrium, and guest rooms are decorated in pinks and greens with light wood furniture. Because it caters to conventioneers, it can be busy and noisy, with long lines at restaurants. ☏ *777 Convention Way, 92802,* ☏ *714/750–4321 or 800/222–9923,* ☏ *714/740–4252. 1,576 rooms. 4 restaurants, 3 lounges, outdoor pool, shops, fitness center ($10 charge), concierge. AE, D, DC, MC, V.*

$$$$ **Anaheim Marriott.** This contemporary hotel, which consists of two towers with 16 and 18 floors, is another headquarters for Convention Center attendees. The busy lobby's huge windows allow sunlight to stream in, highlighting the gleaming marble and brass. The rooms are compact, but they have balconies and are well equipped for business travelers, with desks, two phones, and modem hookups. A concierge floor was added in 1994. Rooms on the north side have good views of Disneyland's summer fireworks shows. Discounted weekend and Disneyland packages are available. ☏ *700 W. Convention Way, 92802,* ☏ *714/750–8000 or 800/228–9290,* ☏ *714/750–9100. 979 rooms, 54 suites. 3 restaurants, 2 lounges, 2 pools, fitness center, video games, concierge. AE, D, DC, MC, V.*

$$$$ **Disneyland Hotel.** This hotel, which is connected to the Magic King-
★   dom by monorail, carries the Disney theme in the lobby, restaurants, entertainment, shops, and spacious guest rooms. Consisting of three towers surrounding lakes, streams, tumbling waterfalls, and lush landscaping, the once-tired hotel was recently renovated and now gleams with brass and marble. In Goofy's Kitchen, kids can breakfast with their favorite Disney characters. There are marina and park views, and rooms in the Bonita tower overlook the Fantasy Waters, a nighttime Disney-theme lighted fountain and music display. ☏ *1150 W. Cerritos Ave., 92802,* ☏ *714/778–6600,* ☏ *714/778–5946. 1,136 rooms. 6 restaurants, 5 lounges, 3 pools, spa, beach, concierge floor, fitness center, business center. AE, DC, MC, V.*

$$$$ **Sheraton Anaheim Hotel.** This Tudor-style hotel has a bright look, though it keeps its castle theme in large tapestries, faux stone walls, and frescoes in the public areas. The large guest rooms open onto interior gardens. A Disneyland shuttle and multilanguage services are available. ☏ *1015 W. Ball Rd., 92802,* ☏ *714/778–1700 or 800/325–3535,* ☏ *714/535–3889. 500 rooms. Dining room, bar, deli, pool, health club. AE, D, DC, MC, V.*

$$$ **Holiday Inn at the Park.** A big salmon-colored, Mediterranean-style building, set at the edge of Disneyland at the Santa Ana Freeway, this Holiday Inn was designed for families visiting the Magic Kingdom. It has pleasant, if functional, rooms sporting southwestern decor, some including separate sitting areas. Shuttle service is available to nearby attractions, including Knott's Berry Farm, Movieland Wax Museum, and Medieval Times. Children stay free with parents. ☎ *1221 S. Harbor Blvd., 92805,* ☎ *714/758–0900 or 800/545–7275,* FAX *714/533– 1804. 252 rooms, 2 suites. Restaurant, lounge, pool, spa, sauna, video games. AE, D, DC, MC, V.*

$$$ **Holiday Inn Maingate.** A trio of large glass chandeliers in the lobby set the tone at this establishment one block south of Disneyland. ☎ *1850 S. Harbor Blvd., 92802,* ☎ *714/750–2801 or 800/624-6855,* FAX *714/971–4754. 312 rooms, including 3 suites. Dining room, lounge, pool, video games. AE, D, DC, MC, V.*

$$$ **Inn at the Park Hotel.** This venerable hotel, a longtime favorite of conventioneers, has the spacious rooms of an earlier era. All rooms have balconies, and those in the tower offer good views of Disneyland's summer fireworks shows. The hotel also has one of the most spacious and attractive pool areas around. The refreshingly bright lobby is inviting, with a tropical feel. ☎ *1855 S. Harbor Blvd., 92802,* ☎ *714/750–1811 or 800/421–6662,* FAX *714/971–3626. 500 rooms. Restaurant, coffee shop, lounge, pool, spa, exercise room, video games. AE, D, DC, MC, V.*

$$ **Candy Cane Inn.** This very attractive motel has lush landscaping and spacious, clean rooms, just steps from the entrance to Disneyland's parking lot. Minirefrigerators and microwaves are available; Continental breakfast is included. ☎ *1747 S. Harbor Blvd. 92803,* ☎ *714/774– 5284 or 800/345–7057,* FAX *714/772–5462. 172 rooms. Pool. AE, D, MC, V.*

$$ **Castle Inn and Suites.** This colorful, cutesy motel across the street from Disneyland has been done up to resemble a castle with faux stone trim, turrets, and towers. Children under 18 are free. ☎ *1734 S. Harbor Blvd. 92802,* ☎ *714/774–8111 or 800/521–5653,* FAX *714/956–4736. 197 rooms. Refrigerators, pool, wading pool. AE, D, DC, MC, V.*

$$ **Quality Hotel Maingate.** A large, open, red-tile lobby is filled with mirrors, plants, and flowers; guest rooms are decorated in mauve and burgundy; and the furniture is made of blond wood. The hotel is close to Disneyland and the Convention Center. ☎ *616 Convention Way, 92802,* ☎ *714/750–3131 or 800/231–6215,* FAX *714/750–9027. 284 rooms. 2 restaurants, lounge, pool. AE, D, DC, MC, V.*

$$ **Ramada Maingate/Anaheim.** Clean and reliable, this chain hotel has pleasant guest rooms done in tones of mauve, indigenous landscaping, and room service from McDonald's. The property is across the street from Disneyland and offers free shuttle service to the park. ☎ *1460 S. Harbor Blvd., 92802,* ☎ *714/772–6777 or 800/447–4048,* FAX *714/999–1727. 465 rooms. Restaurant, pool. AE, D, DC, MC, V.*

$–$$ **Desert Palm Inn and Suites.** This budget hotel has many things going for it: It's midway between Disneyland and the Convention Center, it has large suites (some with balconies) that can accommodate as many as eight people, and every room has a microwave and a refrigerator. The brightly colored decor is attractive, though functional, and the staff is friendly. Book well in advance, especially when large conventions are in town. ☎ *631 W. Katella Ave., 92802,* ☎ *714/535–1133, 800/ 635–5423,* FAX *714/491–7409. 103 rooms and suites. Pool, sauna, exercise room, laundry service. D, MC, V.*

$–$$ **Stovall's Inn.** Very well-kept, this motel stacks up well against area hotels in a similar price range. Nice touches include the topiary gardens, room decor in soft desert colors, and a friendly staff. Ask about discounts if you're staying several nights. ⌕ *1110 W. Katella Ave. 92802,* ☎ *714/778–1880, 800/854–8175,* ℻ *714/778–3805. 290 rooms. Restaurant, lounge, 2 pools. D, MC, V.*

Brea
DINING

$$$$ **La Vie en Rose.** A reproduction of a Norman farmhouse with a large
★   turret, this restaurant, across from the Brea Mall, attracts visitors and locals for its artfully prepared French food. The fare includes seafood, lamb, veal, and melt-in-your-mouth pastries. With several cozy dining rooms, it has a warm atmosphere. ✕ *240 S. State College Blvd., 91621,* ☎ *714/529–8333. Reservations suggested. AE, DC, MC, V. Closed Sun.*

Buena Park
LODGING

$$–$$$ **Buena Park Hotel.** At the center of a lobby of marble, brass, and glass, a spiral staircase winds up to the mezzanine. Rooms are done in green and peach tones. The hotel, which is adjacent to Knott's Berry Farm, offers complimentary shuttle service to Disneyland. ⌕ *7675 Crescent Ave., 90620,* ☎ *714/995–1111 or 800/854–8792,* ℻ *714/828–8590. 350 rooms. Restaurant, coffee shop, lounge, pool, nightclub. AE, DC, MC, V.*

Costa Mesa
DINING

$$–$$$ **Bangkok IV.** Despite its shopping-mall location—it occupies an indoor
★   patio on the third floor of the Crystal Court—this restaurant serves artistically prepared and presented Thai cuisine. The decor is dramatic, with stylish flower arrangements and black-and-white appointments. Menu items designated as hot can be prepared with milder spices upon request. ✕ *3333 Bear St.,* ☎ *714/540–7661. Reservations required. AE, DC, MC, V.*

$$ **Mandarin Gourmet.** Dollar for bite, owner Michael Chang provides what the critics and locals consider the best Chinese cuisine in the area. His specialties include a crisp-yet-juicy Peking duck, cashew chicken, and, seemingly everyone's favorite, mu-shu pork. There is also a very good wine list. ✕ *1500 Adams Ave.,* ☎ *714/540–1937. Reservations accepted. AE, DC, MC, V.*

$ **Wolfgang Puck Cafe.** The famous chef has tried here to create an institutional-style café (read school cafeteria), complete with high noise level. Just the same, it's always jammed. The menu lists Wolf's famous pizzas, chicken salad, and pastas; the most popular item may be the half chicken with huge portions of garlic mashed potatoes. ✕ *South Coast Plaza, 3333 Bristol Ave.,* ☎ *714/546–9653. Reservations for parties of 5 or more only. MC, V.*

LODGING

$$$$ **Westin South Coast Plaza.** Located in the heart of Orange County's shopping-entertainment complex, this modern high-rise hotel has had a major face-lift. Rooms now sport soft colors, mostly cream and beige, and the pleasant public areas have been brightened. Fitness fans will enjoy the health club in the vicinity. The hotel is a short walk from 60 restaurants, theaters, and (across the new Unity Bridge) the South Coast Plaza shopping mall. Discounts are sometimes available on weekends. ⌕ *686 Anton Blvd., 92626,* ☎ *714/540–2500 or 800/228–3000,* ℻ *714/662–6695. 390 rooms, including 17 suites. Restaurant,*

lounge, pool, 2 tennis courts, shuffleboard, volleyball, concierge floor. AE, D, DC, MC, V.

$$–$$$ **Country Side Inn and Suites.** A taste of Europe can be found in these hotel rooms surrounding a flower-filled cobblestone courtyard. The accommodations here provide a good lodging value in this high-priced area. Rooms and lobbies are nicely decorated in Queen Anne–style furnishings with floral wall coverings. Breakfast is included in rates. Ask about discounts on room rates, which can reduce the price to well below this category. ☎ *325 Bristol St., 91626,* ☎ *714/549–0300 or 800/322–9992,* FAX *714/662–0828. 300 rooms and suites. Restaurant, lounge, 2 pools, exercise room. DC, MC, V.*

Dana Point

DINING

$$$ **Dining Room.** Long considered one of the best restaurants in Orange County, the Dining Room now boasts an innovative and very flexible prix-fixe menu featuring contemporary Mediterranean specialties: lobster risotto, grilled tuna chop, veal shank osso bucco, almond soufflé. You can choose two to seven courses; the price depends on the number of courses. Like the hotel, this is an elegant room with subdued lighting, crystal chandeliers, original paintings on the walls, and antiques tucked into corners. ✕ *1 Ritz-Carlton Dr., Dana Point,* ☎ *714/240–2000. Reservations required. Jacket required. AE, D, DC, MC, V. No lunch Sun., Mon.*

$$–$$$ **Watercolors.** This light, cheerful dining room provides a cliff-top view of the harbor and an equally enjoyable Continental/California menu, along with low-calorie choices. Try the baked breast of pheasant, roast rabbit, grilled swordfish, and either the Caesar or poached spinach salad. ✕ *Dana Point Resort,* ☎ *714/661–5000. Reservations advised. AE, D, DC, MC, V. Valet parking.*

$$ **Delaney's Restaurant.** Fresh seafood from nearby San Diego's fishing fleet is what this place is all about. Your choice is prepared as simply as possible. If you have to wait for a table, pass the time at the popular oyster bar, which is staffed only on the weekends. ✕ *25001 Dana Dr.,* ☎ *714/496–6195. Reservations advised. AE, D, DC, MC, V.*

$$ **Luciana's.** This small, intimate Italian restaurant is a real find, especially for couples seeking a romantic evening. Dining rooms are small, dressed with crisp white linens and warmed by fireplaces. The well-prepared food is served with care. ✕ *24312 Del Prado Ave.,* ☎ *714/661–6500. Reservations advised. AE, DC, MC, V. No lunch.*

LODGING

$$$$ **Blue Lantern Inn.** Perched atop the bluffs, this Contemporary Cape Cod–style bed-and-breakfast has stunning harbor and ocean views. Rooms are individually decorated with period furnishings, fireplaces, stocked refrigerators, and jetted baths. Breakfast and afternoon refreshments are included in the price. ☎ *34343 St. of the Blue Lantern, 92629,* ☎ *714/661–1304,* FAX *714/496–1483. 29 rooms. Concierge, fitness facilities, library. AE, MC, V.*

$$$$ **Dana Point Resort.** This Cape Cod–style hillside resort is decorated in
★ shades of sea-foam green and peach. The lobby is filled with large palm trees and original artwork, and most rooms have ocean views; all are done in rattan, with indoor plants. The ambience is casual yet elegant. In summer, the Capistrano Valley Symphony performs on the resort's attractively landscaped grounds. ☎ *25135 Park Lantern, 92629,* ☎ *714/661–5000 or 800/533–9748,* FAX *714/661–5358. 350 rooms. Restaurant, 2 lounges, 3 pools, 3 spas, basketball, croquet, health club, volleyball, concierge floor. AE, D, DC, MC, V.*

$$$$ **Ritz-Carlton Laguna Niguel.** This acclaimed hotel has earned world-class
★   status for its gorgeous setting right on the edge of the Pacific, its sump-
       tuous Mediterranean architecture and decor, and its reputation for flaw-
       less service. With colorful landscaping outside and an imposing
       marble-column entry, it feels like an Italian country villa. Every pos-
       sible amenity, and then some, is available to guests. Redecorated rooms
       still feature traditional furnishings, sumptuous fabrics, marble bath-
       rooms, and private balconies with ocean or garden views. Reduced-
       rate packages are sometimes available. Rental cars available on the
       premises. ⊡ *1 Ritz-Carlton Dr., 92677,* ☎ *714/240–2000 or 800/241–*
       3333, Ⓕⷞ *714/240–0829. 393 rooms. 2 restaurants, lounge, 2 pools,*
       beauty salon, golf privileges, 4 tennis courts, health club, concierge,
       nightclub. AE, D, DC, MC, V.

$$ **Best Western Marina Inn.** Set right in the marina, this fairly basic motel
       is convenient to docks, restaurants, and shops. Rooms vary in size from
       basic to family units with kitchens and fireplaces. Many rooms in this
       three-level motel have balconies and harbor views. ⊡ *24800 Dana Point*
       Harbor Dr., 92629, ☎ *714/496–1203 or 800/255–6843,* Ⓕⷞ *714/248–*
       0360. 136 rooms. Pool, fitness facilities. AE, D, DC, MC, V.

Fullerton
DINING

$$$$ **The Cellar.** The name tells the story here: an intimate subterranean din-
       ing room with a beamed ceiling and stone walls, wine racks, and casks.
       Appropriately, the list of wines from Europe and California is among
       the best in the West. The bill of fare is classic French cuisine that has
       been lightened for the California palate. ✕ *305 N. Harbor Blvd.,* ☎
       714/525–5682. Reservations required. AE, DC, MC, V. No lunch.
       Closed Sun., Mon.

$$ **Mulberry Street Ristorante.** The movers and shakers in north Orange
★   County gather regularly at this friendly, noisy, watering hole, designed
       to resemble a turn-of-the-century New York eatery. The kitchen serves
       up Northern Italian fare, prodigious, highly seasoned portions of pasta,
       seafood, chicken, and veal. Desserts are made on the premises. ✕ *114*
       W. Wilshire Ave., ☎ *714/525–1056. Reservations advised. AE, DC,*
       MC, V. No lunch Sun.

$ **Angelo's & Vinci's Cafe Ristorante.** The show's the thing at this funky
       Italian eatery created by actor-choreographer Steven Peck. Entertain-
       ing surroundings include giant knights in shining armor, tableaux of
       Italian street scenes, an altar with old family photos and cherubs from
       Sicily, and a pair of aerialist puppets and a tightrope walker overhead.
       Locally popular for huge portions of Sicilian-style pasta and pizza, this
       is a busy, noisy place. ✕ *550 N. Harbor Blvd.,* ☎ *714/879-4022. Reser-*
       vations accepted. AE, MC, V. $

Huntington Beach
LODGING

$$$$ **Waterfront Hilton.** This oceanfront hotel rises 12 stories above the surf.
       The Mediterranean-style resort is decorated in soft mauves, beiges, and
       greens and offers a panoramic ocean view from many guest rooms. Ocean-
       view suites have balconies and wet bars. ⊡ *21100 Pacific Coast Hwy.,*
       92648, ☎ *714/960–7873 or 800/822–7873,* Ⓕⷞ *714/960–3791. 290*
       rooms. 2 restaurants, lounge, pool, 2 tennis courts, fitness center, bike
       and beach-equipment rentals, concierge floor. AE, DC, MC, V.

Irvine
DINING

$$$ **Chanteclair.** This Franco-Italian country house is a lovely, tasteful re-
       treat amid an island of modern high-rise office buildings. French Riv-

iera–type cuisine is served, and the chateaubriand for two and rack of lamb are recommended. ✕ *18912 MacArthur Blvd.,* ☎ *714/752–8001. Reservations advised. Jacket required. AE, D, DC, MC, V. No Sat. lunch.*

$$ **Pavilion.** Excellent Chinese food is offered in what resembles a formal eating hall in Taiwan. Specialties include steamed whole fish, ginger duck, and Hunan lamb. ✕ *14110 Culver Dr., 714/551–1688. Reservations advised. AE, DC, MC, V.*

$$ **Prego.** A much larger version of the Beverly Hills Prego, this one is in
★ an attractive approximation of a Tuscan villa and has an outdoor patio. It's a favorite of Orange County yuppies, who rave about the watch-the-cooks-at-work open kitchen and the oak-burning pizza oven. Try the spit-roasted meats and chicken or the charcoal-grilled fresh fish. Also try one of the reasonably priced California or Italian wines. ✕ *18420 Von Karman Ave.,* ☎ *714/553–1333. Reservations advised. AE, DC, MC, V. No weekend lunch. Valet parking.*

LODGING

$$$$ **Hyatt Regency Irvine.** Offering all the amenities of a first-class resort, this hotel is elegantly decorated in contemporary colors, such as oatmeal, turquoise, jade, and salmon, and the marble lobby is flanked by glass-enclosed elevators. Soft cottons make guest furnishings comfortable and appealing. Special golf packages at nearby Tustin Ranch are available. The lower weekend rates are a great deal. ▥ *17900 Jamboree Rd., 92714,* ☎ *714/975–1234,* ℻ *714/852–1574. 526 rooms, 10 suites. 2 restaurants, 2 lounges, pool, 4 tennis courts, fitness facilities, bicycles, concierge. AE, D, DC, MC, V.*

$$$ **Atrium Marquis Hotel.** This hotel, reminiscent of one you'd discover along the Mediterranean, is across the street from John Wayne Airport and convenient to most area offices. The staff caters to business travelers, with rooms that have large work areas, coffeemakers, and two phones. All rooms have private balcony, some overlooking the pool and others looking out at the gardens. Special rates are available for weekend guests. ▥ *18700 MacArthur Blvd., 92715,* ☎ *714/833–2770,* ℻ *714/757–1228. 209 rooms. 2 restaurants, 2 lounges, pool, fitness center. AE, D, DC, MC, V.*

$$$ **Irvine Marriott.** This contemporary hotel towers over Koll Business Center, making it convenient for business travelers. Despite its size, the hotel has an intimate feel about it, due in part to the cozy lobby, the friendly staff, and the repeat guests. Oriental-style rooms, all with small balconies, are slated for renovation in 1996. Weekend discounts and packages are usually available. ▥ *1800 Von Karman Ave., 92715,* ☎ *714/553–0100,* ℻ *714/261–7059. 489 rooms, 24 suites. 2 restaurants, sports bar, indoor-outdoor pool, massage, spa, 4 tennis courts, health club, concierge floors, business services. AE, D, DC, MC, V.*

Laguna Beach

DINING

$$$–$$$$ **Five Feet.** The first of a number of Chinese-European restaurants in Orange County, Five Feet continues to delight diners with its innovative culinary approaches. You'll find delicate pot stickers, wontons stuffed with goat cheese, and a salad featuring sashimi, plus steak and fresh fish. The decor showcases the work of local artists. ✕ *328 Gleneyre St.,* ☎ *714/497–4955. Reservations advised. AE, MC, V. Lunch Fri. only.*

$$ **Beach House.** A Laguna tradition, the Beach House has a water view from every table. Fresh fish, lobster, and steamed clams are the drawing cards. It's open for breakfast, lunch, and dinner. ✕ *619 Sleepy Hollow La.,* ☎ *714/494–9707. Reservations advised. AE, MC, V.*

$$ **Kachina.** The creation of Orange County star chef David Wilhelm, this tiny restaurant housed beneath an art gallery draws locals and visitors with contemporary southwestern-style cuisine and a boisterous atmosphere. Even hearty eaters can make a meal by selecting several items from the appetizer portion of the menu. Kachina is a good place for Sunday brunch. ✕ *222 Forest Ave.,* ☎ *714/497–5546. Reservations advised. AE, MC, V.*

$ **Tortilla Flats.** This hacienda-style restaurant specializes in first-rate chile rellenos, carne Tampiquena, soft-shell tacos, and beef or chicken fajitas. There's also a wide selection of Mexican tequilas and beers. Sunday brunch is served. ✕ *1740 S. Coast Hwy.,* ☎ *714/494– 6588. Dinner reservations advised. AE, MC, V.*

LODGING

$$$$ **Surf and Sand Hotel.** Laguna's largest hotel is situated right on the beach. The rooms are decorated in soft sand colors and bleached wood and have wooden shutters and private balconies. The popular lounge on the top floor is a great place to end your evening, with piano bar and a welcoming fireplace. Weekend packages are available. ⌸ *1555 S. Coast Hwy., 92651,* ☎ *714/497–4477 or 800/524–8621,* 𝖥𝖠𝖷 *714/494– 7653. 157 rooms, including 5 suites. 2 restaurants, 2 lounges, pool, beach, concierge. AE, DC, MC, V.*

$$$–$$$$ **Inn at Laguna Beach.** This oceanfront Mediterranean-style inn, done
★ in warm mauves and sea greens, has one of the best locations in town. It's close to Main Beach and Las Brisas restaurant and bar, one of Laguna's most popular watering holes, yet far enough away to be secluded. Set on a bluff overlooking the ocean, the inn has luxurious amenities and many rooms with views. ⌸ *211 N. Coast Hwy., 92651,* ☎ *714/497–9722 or 800/544–4479,* 𝖥𝖠𝖷 *714/497–9972. 70 rooms. Pool, free parking. AE, D, DC, MC, V.*

$$$ **Eiler's Inn.** A light-filled courtyard is the focal point of this European-style B&B. Rooms are on the small side, but each is unique and decorated with antiques. Breakfast is served outdoors, and in the afternoon there's wine and cheese, often to the accompaniment of live music. A sun deck in back has an ocean view. ⌸ *741 S. Coast Hwy., 92651,* ☎ *714/494–3004,* 𝖥𝖠𝖷 *714/497–2215. 12 rooms. AE, MC, V.*

$$$ **Hotel Laguna.** This downtown landmark, the oldest hotel in Laguna, has been redone, with four rooms now featuring canopy beds and reproduction Victorian furnishings. Lobby windows look out onto manicured gardens, and a patio restaurant overlooks the ocean and the hotel's own private beach. ⌸ *425 S. Coast Hwy., 92651,* ☎ *714/494–1151 or 800/524–2927,* 𝖥𝖠𝖷 *714/497–2163. 65 rooms. 2 restaurants, lounge. AE, D, DC, MC, V.*

Newport Beach

DINING

$$$$ **Antoine.** This lovely, candlelighted hotel dining room is made for ro-
★ mance and quiet conversation. It serves the best French cuisine of any hotel in southern California; the fare is nouvelle, but is neither skimpy nor gimmicky. ✕ *Sutton Place Hotel, 4500 MacArthur Blvd.,* ☎ *714/476–2001. Reservations advised. Jacket and tie. AE, DC, MC, V. No lunch. Closed Sun., Mon.*

$$$$ **Pascal.** Although it's in a shopping center, you'll think that you're in
★ St-Tropez once you step inside this bright and cheerful bistro. And, after one taste of Pascal Olhat's light Provençale cuisine, the best in Orange County, you'll swear you're in the south of France. Try the sea bass with thyme, the rack of lamb, and the lemon tart. ✕ *1000 Bristol St.,* ☎ *714/752–0107. Reservations advised. AE, DC, MC, V. Closed Sun.*

$$$$ The Ritz. This is one of the most comfortable southern California restaurants—the bar area has red leather booths, etched-glass mirrors, and polished brass trim. Don't pass up the smorgasbord appetizer, the roast Bavarian duck, or the rack of lamb from the spit. This is one of those rare places that seems to please everyone. ✕ *880 Newport Center Dr., ☎ 714/720–1800. Reservations advised. AE, DC, MC, V. No lunch weekends.*

$$ The Cannery. The building once was a cannery, and it has wonderful wharf-side views. The seafood entrées are good, and the sandwiches at lunch are satisfying, but the location and lazy atmosphere are the real draw. If, however you're not into karaoke, you may want to consider booking elsewhere. ✕ *3010 Lafayette Ave., ☎ 714/675–5777. Reservations advised. AE, D, DC, MC, V.*

$$ Le Biarritz. Newport Beach natives have a deep affection for this restaurant, with its country-French decor, hanging greenery, and skylighted garden room. There's food to match the mood: a veal-and-pheasant pâté, seafood crepes, boned duckling and wild rice, sautéed pheasant with raspberries, and warm apple tart for dessert. ✕ *414 N. Old Newport Blvd., ☎ 714/645–6700. Reservations advised. AE, D, DC, MC, V. No Sat. lunch. Closed Sun.*

$$ Marrakesh. In a casbah setting straight out of a Hope-and-Crosby road movie, diners become part of the scene—you eat with your fingers while sitting on the floor or lolling on a hassock. Chicken *b'stilla* (traditional chicken dish served over rice), rabbit couscous, and skewered pieces of marinated lamb are the best of the Moroccan dishes. It's fun. ✕ *1100 Pacific Coast Hwy., ☎ 714/645–8384. Reservations advised. AE, DC, MC, V. No lunch.*

$ Crab Cooker. If you don't mind waiting in line, this shanty of a place serves fresh fish grilled over mesquite at low-low prices. The clam chowder and coleslaw are quite good, too. ✕ *2200 Newport Blvd., ☎ 714/673–0100. No reservations. No credit cards.*

$ Hard Rock Cafe Newport Beach. You can pick up your official Hard Rock Cafe T-shirt here while munching a hamburger or a sandwich. Like the other Hard Rocks, this one features an array of rock-star memorabilia and platinum records. ✕ *451 Newport Center Dr., ☎ 714/640–8844. No reservations. AE, DC, MC, V.*

$ ★ El Torito Grill. Southwestern cooking incorporating south-of-the-border specialties is the attraction here. The just-baked tortillas with a green-pepper salsa, the turkey molé enchilada, and the miniature blue-corn duck tamales are good choices. The bar serves hand-shaken margaritas and 20 brands of tequila. ✕ *Fashion Island, 951 Newport Center Dr., ☎ 714/640–2875. Reservations advised. AE, D, DC, MC, V.*

LODGING

$$$$ ★ Four Seasons Hotel. This 20-story hotel lives up to its chain's reputation. Marble and antiques fill the airy lobby; all rooms—decorated with beiges, peaches, and Southwestern touches—have spectacular views, private bars, and original art on the walls. Weekend golf packages are available in conjunction with the nearby Pelican Hill golf course, as well as fitness weekend packages. ☎ *690 Newport Center Dr., 92660, ☎ 714/759–0808 or 800/332–3442, FAX 714/760–8073. 285 rooms. 2 restaurants, lounge, pool, massage, sauna, steam room, 2 tennis courts, health club, mountain bikes, concierge, business center. AE, D, DC, MC, V.*

$$$$ Sutton Place Hotel. The eye-catching ziggurat design is the trademark of this ultramodern hotel in Koll Center. The decor is southern Californian, with striking pastel accents. Luxuriously appointed rooms have minibars and built-in hair dryers. This is also the home of Antoine (*see* *above*), one of the best restaurants in Orange County. Special weekend theater and Pageant of the Masters packages are available. ☎ *4500 MacArthur Blvd., 92660,* ☎ *714/476–2001 or 800/810-6888,* 🗚 *714/476–0153. 435 rooms. 2 restaurants, lounge, pool, 2 tennis courts, health club, concierge. AE, D, DC, MC, V.*

$$$ **Newport Beach Marriott Hotel and Tennis Club.** Overlooking Newport Harbor, this Mediterranean-style hotel attracts a large foreign clientele. Arriving guests' first view of the hotel's interior is the distinctive fountain surrounded by a high, plant-filled atrium. Rooms, done in lavender, cream, and teal, are housed in two towers. They each have balconies or patios, and overlook lush gardens or a stunning Pacific view. The hotel is across the street from Fashion Island shopping center. ☎ *900 Newport Center Dr., 92660,* ☎ *714/640–4000 or 800/228–9290,* 🗚 *714/640–5055. 570 rooms. 2 restaurants, lounge, 2 pools, sauna, 8 tennis courts, golf, health club, business services, concierge. AE, D, DC, MC, V.*

$$$ **Sheraton Newport Beach.** Bamboo trees and palms decorate the lobby in this Southern California beach-style hotel. Vibrant teals, mauves, and peaches make up the color scheme. Complimentary morning paper, buffet breakfast, and cocktail parties are offered Monday through Thursday. The hotel is convenient to John Wayne airport. ☎ *4545 MacArthur Blvd., 92660,* ☎ *714/833–0570,* 🗚 *714/833–3927. 335 rooms. 3 restaurants, lounge, pool, fitness center, 2 tennis courts. AE, D, DC, MC, V.*

Orange
DINING

$$ **La Brasserie.** It doesn't *look* like a typical brasserie, but the varied French cuisine befits the name over the door. One dining room in the multilevel house is done as an attractive, cozy library. There's also an inviting bar-lounge. The specialty here is veal chops. ✕ *202 S. Main St.,* ☎ *714/978–6161. Reservations advised. AE, MC, V. No Sat. lunch. Closed Sun.*

$–$$ **City Club.** This restaurant, located in the Doubletree Hotel, specializes in steak and seafood. This dramatic two-story room has floor-to-ceiling windows, which reveal a garden and pond beyond. Service is welcoming. ✕ *100 The City Dr.,* ☎ *714/634–4500. AE, MC, V. Closed weekends.*

LODGING

$$$–$$$$ **Doubletree Hotel Orange County.** This contemporary, 20-story hotel has a dramatic lobby of marble and granite with waterfalls cascading down the walls. Guest rooms are large and come equipped with a small conference table. The hotel is near the shopping center called The City, UCI Medical Center, and Anaheim Stadium. Discount rates are available for summer weekends. ☎ *100 The City Dr., 92668,* ☎ *714/634–4500 or 800/222–8733,* 🗚 *714/978–3839. 435 rooms, 19 suites. 2 restaurants, lounge, pool, 2 tennis courts, health club, concierge floor. AE, D, DC, MC, V.*

San Clemente
DINING

$$$ **Etienne's.** Smack-dab in the center of town, this restaurant is housed in a white stucco historic landmark. There is outdoor seating on a terracotta patio with fountains. Indoors, the decor is French château. Only the freshest fish is served; chateaubriand, frogs' legs, and other French favorites are on the menu, along with flaming desserts. ✕ *215 S. El Camino Real,* ☎ *714/492–7263. Reservations advised. AE, D, DC, MC, V. No lunch. Closed Sun.*

LODGING

$$$ **San Clemente Inn.** This time-share condo resort is in the secluded southern part of San Clemente, adjacent to Calafia State Beach. Studio and one-bedroom units (accommodating as many as six) are equipped with minikitchens and Murphy beds. Limited space is available in summer. Ask about weekly discounts. ⌂ *2600 Avenida del Presidente, 92672,* ☎ *714/492–6103,* ℻ *714/498–3014. 96 units. Pool, sauna, tennis, exercise room, recreation room, playground. AE, D, DC, MC, V.*

San Juan Capistrano

DINING

$$ **El Adobe.** This early California–style eatery serves enormous portions of mildly seasoned Mexican food. Mariachi bands play Friday and Saturday nights and for Sunday brunch. ✕ *31891 Camino Capistrano,* ☎ *714/830–8620. Weekend reservations advised. AE, D, MC, V.*

$$ **L'Hirondelle.** There are only 12 tables at this charming Belgian inn. Duck-
★ ling is the specialty, and it is prepared three different ways. ✕ *31631 Camino Capistrano,* ☎ *714/661–0425. Reservations required. AE, MC, V. No lunch. Closed Mon.*

Santa Ana

DINING

$$$ **Randall's.** Located on the ground floor of an office building with lake-side views, this restaurant specializes in light Louisiana cuisine. Jazz and blues presented nightly. ✕ *3 Hutton Centre Dr., Santa Ana,* ☎ *714/556–7700. Reservations advised. AE, MC, V. No lunch Sun.*

THE ARTS AND NIGHTLIFE

The Arts

The **Orange County Performing Arts Center** (600 Town Center Dr., Costa Mesa, ☎ 714/556–2787) is the hub of the arts circle, hosting a variety of touring companies year-round. Groups that regularly schedule performances here include the New York City Opera, the American Ballet Theater, and the Los Angeles Philharmonic Orchestra, as well as touring companies of popular musicals such as *Les Misérables*. Information about current offerings can be found in the calendar section of the *Los Angeles Times*.

Concerts

The **Irvine Meadows Amphitheater** (8808 Irvine Center Dr., Irvine, ☎ 714/855–4515) is a 15,000-seat open-air venue offering a variety of musical events from May through October.

The **Pacific Amphitheater** (Orange County Fairgrounds, Costa Mesa, ☎ 714/740–2000) offers musical entertainment from April through October.

Theater

South Coast Repertory Theater (655 Town Center Dr., Costa Mesa, ☎ 714/957–4033), near the Orange County Performing Arts Center, is an acclaimed regional theater complex with two stages that present both traditional and new works. A resident group of actors forms the nucleus of this facility's innovative productions.

La Mirada Theater for the Performing Arts (14900 La Mirada Blvd., La Mirada, ☎ 714/994–6310) presents a wide selection of Broadway shows, concerts, and film series.

Nightlife

Bars

Metropolis (4255 Campus Dr., Irvine, ☎ 714/725–0300) is the hottest nightclub ticket in Orange County, with iron-and-gilt decor, pool tables, a sushi bar, restaurant, entertainment, and dancing (you can even take a salsa class); ☛ is $5. The **Cannery** (3010 Lafayette Ave., ☎ 714/675–5777) is a crowded Newport Beach bar that offers live entertainment. The **Studio Cafe** (100 Main St., Balboa Peninsula, ☎ 714/675–7760) presents jazz musicians every night. In Santa Ana, a young crowd gathers at **Roxbury** (2 Hutton Centre Dr., ☎ 714/662–0880) for entertainment and dancing Friday and Saturday evenings. The **Fullerton Hofbrau** (323 N. State College Blvd., ☎ 714/870–7400), a microbrewery, has live music nightly.

In Laguna Beach, the **Sandpiper** (1183 S. Pacific Coast Highway, ☎ 714/494–4694) is a tiny dancing joint that attracts an eclectic crowd. And Laguna's **White House** (340 S. Pacific Coast Hwy., ☎ 714/494–8088) has nightly entertainment that runs the gamut from rock to Motown, reggae to pop.

Comedy

Irvine Improv (4255 Campus Dr., Irvine, ☎ 714/854–5455) and **Brea Improv** (945 E. Birch St., Brea, ☎ 714/529–7878) present up-and-coming and well-known comedians nightly.

Country Music

Cowboy Boogie Co. (1721 S. Manchester, Anaheim, ☎ 714/956–1410) offers a popular country band's tune on Sunday night; music is piped in the rest of the week. The complex comprises three dance floors and four bars.

Dinner Theaters

Several night spots in Orange County serve up entertainment with dinner.

Tibbie's Music Hall (4647 McArthur Blvd., Newport Beach, ☎ 714/252–0834) offers comedy shows along with prime rib, fish, or chicken Thursday through Sunday.

Elizabeth Howard's Curtain Call Theater (690 El Camino Real, Tustin, ☎ 714/838–1540) presents a regular schedule of Broadway musicals. **Medieval Times Dinner and Tournament** (7662 Beach Blvd., Buena Park, ☎ 714/521–4740 or 800/899–6600) takes guests back to the days of knights and ladies. Knights on horseback compete in medieval games, sword fighting, and jousting. Dinner, all of which is eaten with your hands, includes appetizers, whole roasted chicken or spareribs, soup, pastry, and beverages such as mead.

Wild Bill's Wild West Extravaganza (7600 Beach Blvd., Buena Park, ☎ 714/522–6414) is a two-hour action-packed Old West show featuring foot-stomping musical numbers, cowboys, Indians, can-can dancers, trick-rope artists, knife throwers, and audience participation in sing-alongs.

Nightclubs

Coach House (33157 Camino Capistrano, San Juan Capistrano, ☎ 714/496–8930) draws big local crowds for jazz and rock headliners.

ESSENTIAL INFORMATION

Arriving and Departing

By Bus

The **Los Angeles MTA** has limited service to Orange County. You can get the No. 460 to Anaheim from downtown; it goes to Knott's Berry Farm and Disneyland. **Greyhound** (☎ 714/999–1256) has scheduled bus service to Orange County.

By Car

Two major freeways, I–405 (San Diego Freeway) and I–5 (Santa Ana Freeway), run north and south through Orange County. South of Laguna they merge into I–5. Avoid these during rush hours (6–9 AM and 3:30–6 PM), when they can slow to a crawl and back up for miles.

By Plane

Several airports are accessible to Orange County. **John Wayne Orange County Airport** (☎ 714/252–5252), in Santa Ana, is centrally located, and the county's main facility. It is serviced by **Alaska Airlines** (☎ 800/426–0333), **America West Airlines** (☎ 800/235–9292), **American** (☎ 800/433–7300), **Continental** (☎ 800/525–0280), **Delta** (☎ 800/221–1212), **Northwest** (☎ 800/225–2525), **Southwest** (☎ 800/435–9792), **TWA** (☎ 800/221–2000), **United** (☎ 800/241–6522), and several commuter airlines.

Los Angeles International Airport is only 35 miles west of Anaheim; **Ontario International Airport,** just northwest of Riverside, is 30 miles north of Anaheim; and **Long Beach Airport** is about 20 minutes by bus from Anaheim. (*See* Arriving and Departing in Travelers Resources for details on all three airports.)

BETWEEN THE AIRPORTS AND HOTELS

Airport Coach (☎ 800/772–5299), a shuttle service, carries passengers from John Wayne Airport and LAX to Anaheim, Buena Park, and Newport Beach. Fare from John Wayne to Anaheim is $10, from LAX to Anaheim $14.

Prime Time Airport Shuttle (☎ 800/262–7433) offers door-to-door service to LAX and John Wayne airports, hotels near John Wayne, and the San Pedro cruise terminal. The fare is $11 from Anaheim hotels to John Wayne and $12 from Anaheim hotels to LAX. Children under two ride free (but must have a car seat).

Super Shuttle (☎ 714/517–6600) provides 24-hour door-to-door service from all the airports to all points in Orange County. Fare to the Disneyland area is $10 a person from John Wayne, $34 from Ontario, $13 from LAX. Phone for other fares and reservations.

By Train

Amtrak (☎ 800/872–7245) makes several stops in Orange County: Fullerton, Anaheim, Santa Ana, San Juan Capistrano, and San Clemente. There are 11 departures daily, nine on weekends.

Getting Around

By Car

Highways 22, 55, and 91 go west to the ocean and east to the mountains: Take Highway 91 or Highway 22 to inland points (Buena Park, Anaheim) and take Highway 55 to Newport Beach. Caution: Orange County freeways are undergoing major construction; expect delays at odd times. Pacific Coast Highway (Highway 1; also known locally as

PCH) allows easy access to beach communities, and is the most scenic route. It follows the entire Orange County coast, from Huntington Beach to San Clemente.

By Bus

The **Orange County Transportation Authority** (OCTA, ☎ 714/636–7433) will take you virtually anywhere in the county, but it will take time; OCTA buses go from Knott's Berry Farm and Disneyland to Huntington and Newport beaches. Bus 1 travels along the coast.

Scenic Drives

Winding along the seaside edge of Orange County on the **Pacific Coast Highway** is an eye-opening experience. Here, surely, are the contradictions of southern California revealed—the powerful, healing ocean vistas and the scars of commercial exploitation; the appealingly laid-back, simple beach life and the tacky bric-a-brac of the tourist trail. Oil rigs line the road from Long Beach south to Huntington Beach, and then suddenly give way to pristine stretches of water and dramatic hillsides. Stop in beach towns like Laguna Beach, Dana Point, and Corona del Mar along the route.

For a scenic mountain drive, try **Santiago Canyon Road,** which winds through the Cleveland National Forest in the Santa Ana Mountains. Tucked away in these mountains are Modjeska Canyon, Irvine Lake, and Silverado Canyon, of silver-mining lore.

Guided Tours

Boat Tours

At the Cannery in **Newport Beach,** you can take a weekend brunch cruise around the harbor for $31. Cruises last two hours and depart at 10 AM and 1:30 PM. ☎ 714/675–5777 for information.

Catalina Passenger Service (☎ 714/673–5245) at the Balboa Pavilion offers a full selection of sightseeing tours and fishing excursions to Catalina and around Newport Harbor. The 45-minute narrated tour of Newport Harbor, at $6, is the least expensive. Whale-watching cruises (Dec.–Mar.) are especially enjoyable.

Hornblower Yachts (☎ 714/646–0155) offers Saturday dinner cruises with dancing for $56.95; Sunday brunch cruises are $34.05. Reservations are required.

General-Interest Tours

Pacific Coast Sightseeing Tours (☎ 714/978–8855) provides guided tours from Orange County hotels to Disneyland, Knott's Berry Farm, Universal Studios Hollywood, and the San Diego Zoo.

Important Addresses and Numbers

Emergencies

Dial 911 for police and ambulance in an emergency.

DOCTORS
Orange County is so spread out and comprises so many communities that it is best to ask at your hotel for the closest emergency room. Here are a few: **Anaheim Memorial Hospital** (1111 W. La Palma, ☎ 714/774–1450), **Western Medical Center** (1025 S. Anaheim Blvd., Anaheim, ☎ 714/533–6220), **Hoag Memorial Hospital** (301 Newport Blvd., Newport Beach, ☎ 714/645–8600), **South Coast Medical Center** (31872 Pacific Coast Hwy., South Laguna, ☎ 714/499–1311).

Visitor Information

The main source of tourist information is the **Anaheim/Orange County Convention and Visitors Bureau,** located at the Anaheim Convention Center (800 W. Katella Ave., 92802, ☎ 714/999–8999). The **Visitor Information Hot Line** (☎ 714/635–8900) offers recorded information on entertainment, special events, attractions, and amusement parks;information about special events may be outdated.

Other area chambers of commerce and visitors bureaus are generally open weekdays 9–5 and will help with information. These include:

Buena Park Visitors Bureau, 6280 Manchester Blvd., 90261, ☎ 714/562–3560.
Dana Point Chamber of Commerce, 24681 La Plaza, Suite 120, 92629, ☎ 714/496–1555.
Huntington Beach Conference and Visitors Bureau, 2100 Main St., Suite 190, 92648, ☎ 800/729–6232.
Laguna Beach Hospitality, 252 Broadway, 92651, ☎ 714/494–1018.
Newport Beach Conference and Visitors Bureau, 366 San Miguel Dr., Suite 200, 92660, ☎ 800/942–6278.
San Clemente Tourism Bureau, 1100 N. El Camino Real, 92672, ☎ 714/492–1131.
San Juan Capistrano Chamber of Commerce and Visitors Center,26711 Verdugo Blvd., 92675, ☎ 714/493–4700.

10 Los Angeles for Children

By Mary Jane
Horton

Updated by
William P.
Browne

SOME CITIES HAVE ONE FAMOUS ATTRACTION FOR
KIDS; Los Angeles and its sprawling environs has attractions from one end to the other: amusement
parks, children's museums, zoos, train rides, children's theater every
weekend, nature walks, pony rides, art classes, and much more. Add
this to an ideal natural environment—beaches, surrounding mountains,
and warm weather almost year-round—and you have a city tailor-made
for children. Almost tailor-made, that is. A kid will need a willing adult
along, because unlike many big cities, Los Angeles is not a place where
kids can get around on their own.

Curiously, although Los Angeles offers an endless array of options for
children in their own domain, the city does not welcome kids into the
adult domain. Don't go to the trendiest of Beverly Hills restaurants and
ask for a high chair. Do go to the many restaurants that cater to children with high chairs, booster seats, and children's own menus. The
most expensive and poshest of hotels, however, are used to children—
many even offer camps and other programs to help keep them busy.

See Traveling with Children in Chapter 1 or information on planning
your trip to the Los Angeles area.

EXPLORING

Activities for kids are spread throughout the Los Angeles basin, but
there are certain areas where the offerings are concentrated: the city
proper, Anaheim, and the beach towns.

The *Los Angeles Times* provides ideas for the upcoming week in a regular Thursday column, "54 Hours," in the View section. *L.A. Parent,*
a free monthly tabloid found at toy stores and children's clothing
stores, has a monthly calendar.

Los Angeles

Downtown
The **Los Angeles Children's Museum** (*see* Tour 1 in Chapter 2, Exploring
Los Angeles) has lots of hands-on exhibits.

The **Museum of Contemporary Art** (*see* Tour 1 in Chapter 2, Exploring Los Angeles) is great for older kids and for infants in strollers or
carriers; it is not a place to let a two-year-old go crazy. The museum
offers a booklet for kids, *Together at MOCA: A Guide for Families,*
published in several different languages.

Exposition Park
Adjoining the University of California campus, on Figueroa Street at
Exposition Boulevard, this park was built for the 1932 Olympics and
features two major museums. The **California Museum of Science and
Industry,** beloved by preschool and school-age children, has just undergone a $43 million renovation. Interactive exhibits include Molecules
in Motion (where children can make their own rocket fuel) and Urban
Environment Phase II (which explains ecological issues in easy terms).
The chick hatchery has recently reopened, by popular demand. Another
big draw is the Mitsubishi IMAX Theater—five stories and six-chan-
nel stereo. The immense **Natural History Museum of Los Angeles
County** has a lot to fascinate youngsters; be sure to visit the hands-on
exhibits in the Ralph M. Parsons Discovery Center. *See* Sightseeing
Checklists in Chapter 2, Exploring Los Angeles.

Griffith Park

The largest city park in the United States (*see* Sightseeing Checklists in Chapter 2, Exploring Los Angeles), Griffith Park has several prime attractions for kids.

The **Observatory** has loads of exhibits to interest junior astronomers; film buffs may recognize this Art Deco structure from *Rebel Without a Cause*. **Pony rides** (Crystal Springs Dr., entrance near I–5 and Los Feliz Blvd., ☎ 213/664–3266) are safe even for two-year-olds, who are routinely strapped on and paraded around on the slowest of old nags. A ride costs $1.50 for two rounds. To finish up an eventful morning (the lines are long in late afternoon), there are **stagecoach rides** ($1.50) and a **miniature train ride** ($1.75 adults, $1.25 children) that makes a figure eight near the pony rides. ☉ *Summer, weekdays 10– 5:30, weekends and holidays 10–6:30; fall–spring, Tues.–Sun. 10–4, and holidays.*

Just up the road from the pony rides, a 1926-vintage **merry-go-round** offers melodic rides for families.

At **Travel Town,** more than vintage railroad cars welcome onslaughts of climbing and screaming children. The collection includes a narrow-gauge sugar train from Hawaii, a steam engine, and an old Los Angeles trolley; there are also old planes, such as World War II bombers, an old fire engine, a milk wagon, buggies, and classic cars. *5200 Zoo Dr.,* ☎ *213/662–5874.* ☛ *Free.* ☉ *Weekdays 10–4, weekends 10–5.*

Los Angeles Zoo, one of America's major zoos, is noted for its breeding of endangered species, including white tigers. The 113-acre compound holds more than 2,000 mammals, birds, amphibians, and reptiles. Animals are grouped according to the geographic areas where they are naturally found—Africa, Australia, Eurasia, North America, and South America. Don't miss Adventure Island or the interactive exhibits. Seeing the zoo requires a lot of walking, seemingly all uphill, so strollers or backpacks are recommended for families with young children. The Safari Shuttle ($3 adults, $1 children under 12 and senior citizens) takes visitors comfortably to the far corners of the zoo. *Junction of Ventura and Golden State fwys., Griffith Park,* ☎ *213/666– 4090.* ☛ *$8.25 adults, $5.25 senior citizens, $3.25 children 2–12.* ☉ *Daily 10–5.*

Westside

Kitschy as they can be, many **Hollywood** attractions (*see* Tour 2 in Chapter 2, Exploring Los Angeles) are just the ticket for star-struck youngsters. Younger kids, however, may get spooked by the lifelike figures in the Hollywood Wax Museum. If you have dinosaur lovers in your family, go a short distance east on Wilshire Boulevard to visit **La Brea Tar Pits** and **George C. Page Museum of La Brea Discoveries** (*see* Tour 3 in Chapter 2, Exploring Los Angeles).

The **Junior Arts Center** offers refreshingly low-priced arts-and-crafts classes year-round. Every Sunday, the center's patio is set up with worktables and art supplies for a free, two-hour workshop where parents and children work together on projects supervised by local artists. There are also gallery exhibits with strong kid appeal. *Barnsdall Park, 4800 Hollywood Blvd., Hollywood,* ☎ *213/485– 4474.* ☉ *Tues.–Sun. 12:30–5.*

Santa Monica and the Beach Towns

The **Third Street Promenade** in Santa Monica (between Wilshire Blvd. and Broadway) attracts dozens of street performers—magicians, jugglers, 10-year-old violinists; the "cast" changes from day to day. This closed-off street is very stroller-accessible. Near the Broadway end are huge topiary dinosaurs.

The **Museum of Flying** is designed to show kids that there's more to flying than pilots, with interactive exhibits on aircraft design and maintenance, for instance. There are also 40 planes and helicopters on display, and museum workshops help children build model planes and gliders. *2772 Donald Douglas Loop N, Santa Monica,* ☎ *310/392–8822.* ☛ *(donation): $7 adults, $5 senior citizens, $3 children 3–17.* ☼ *Thurs.–Sun. 10–5, extended summer hrs.*

Angel's Attic, a collection of antique dolls and dollhouses in a Queen Anne Victorian, is a popular venue for kids aged about seven years and up; the fact that they can't touch the display makes it a bit difficult for younger children. Tea with cake is served. *516 Colorado Ave., Santa Monica,* ☎ *310/394–8331.* ☛ *$4 adults, $3 senior citizens, $2 children under 12.* ☼ *Thurs.–Sun. 12:30–4:30.*

The **Santa Monica Pier** (*see* Tour 5 in Chapter 2, Exploring Los Angeles) is a great place for kids to mingle with beach-going crowds; younger ones will love a ride on the vintage **merry-go-round.**

The **Venice Boardwalk** (*see* Tour 5 in Chapter 2, Exploring Los Angeles) makes an amusing outing with children: outrageous street performers (fire-eaters, roller skaters, acrobats), cheap souvenirs, and quick food. There's also a playground on the beach. **"Mothers' Beach"** is the local nickname for Marina Beach in Marina del Rey, behind the Jamaica Bay Inn at Admiralty Way and Via Marina. You can see why it's popular with local families: Nestled between the sleek sloops and singles condos and bars, this tiny crescent of man-made beach offers a wonderfully protected environment for very young children.

Palos Verdes, San Pedro, and Long Beach

San Pedro's **Cabrillo Marine Aquarium** lets kids touch live sea creatures in a tidal-pool tank; at nearby **Ports'O Call Village,** you can take harbor cruises. Down in Long Beach you can board the **Queen Mary,** then take a short walk to **Shoreline Village,** which features a vintage carousel. (*See* Tour 6 in Chapter 2, Exploring Los Angeles.)

Long Beach Children's Museum, in a Long Beach mall, has regulation-issue children's-museum hands-on exhibits such as the Art Cafe and Granny's Attic. Go fishing for Velcro marine life. *445 Long Beach Blvd. at Long Beach Plaza, Long Beach,* ☎ *310/495–1163.* ☛ *$3.95, children under 1 free.* ☼ *Thurs.–Sat. 11–4, Sun. noon–4.*

Highland Park, Pasadena, and San Marino

Among the attractions in these towns (*see* Tour 7 in Chapter 2, Exploring Los Angeles), **Kidspace** is a logical stop for families; **Heritage Square** is interesting to school-age children. The **Southwest Museum** brings Native American culture alive for children with real tepees, bear capes, moccasins, etc., plus storytelling, art workshops, and special kids' tours on weekends.

San Fernando Valley

Two entertainment-industry locales here are naturals for families: **NBC Studios,** and the ever-popular **Universal Studios Hollywood** (*see* The San Fernando Valley in Chapter 2, Exploring Los Angeles). Be careful not to bring younger children on the Universal Tour—they may be scared of the very things that their older siblings love: the realistic special-effect simulations of earthquakes and the like. The 45-minute tram ride may be too much for younger kids, but there's plenty else for them to do here.

At **Universal CityWalk,** part of the Universal Studios Hollywood complex, the walkways are packed with things for children to do and see. At The Fountain, kids can run through the unpredictable sprinklers (bring a change of clothes!); Panasonic Pavilion is a free hightech carnival with state-of-the-art games; Cinemania ($4; no one under 42″ admitted) is a cinematic thrill ride in theater-style seats, showing three four-minute shows: Devil's Mine Ride, Cosmic pinball (you actually feel as if you are inside the machine, not operating it), and Stockcar Showdown, a battle with menacing road warriors.

Other Places of Interest

The **Gene Autry Western Heritage Museum** (*see* Other Places of Interest in Chapter 2, Exploring Los Angeles) has a hands-on Children's Discovery Gallery where young visitors (1 year and older) can rummage through a re-created attic with dolls, clothes, and toys.

Lomita Railroad Museum, hidden away in a typical suburban neighborhood, is housed in a replica of a turn-of-the-century Massachusetts train station. Beyond the gate, discover one of the largest collections of railroad memorabilia in the West. *2137 250th St., Lomita,* ☎ *310/326– 6255.* ☛ *$1 adults, 50¢ children under 12.* ☉ *Wed.–Sun. 10–5.*

Paramount Ranch was once wild terrain where grizzly bears ran free; fledgling Paramount Pictures bought the land in 1927 and shot many Westerns here. In 1980 it became part of the Santa Monica Mountains National Recreation Area. Paramount's old Western sets, still used to shoot television shows and movies, are open to the public. The 436-acre site also includes many hiking trails. *Cornell Rd., Agoura Hills (101 Fwy. to Kanan Rd. exit, south on Kanan Rd. to Cornell, turn right, ranch is 2½ mi on right),* ☎ *818/597–9192.* ☛ *Free.* ☉ *Daily sunrise–sunset.*

In Bonelli Regional Park, **Raging Waters,** Los Angeles's major water park, uses 50 acres for swimming pools, lagoons, water slides, and other water-related activities. For nonwater-types there are sunny "beaches" and special pools for the tiniest visitors. Bring your own towels. The park has picnicking spots and fast-food stands. *111 Raging Waters Dr., San Dimas,* ☎ *909/592–6453.* ☛ *$19.95 adults, $11.99 children 42″–48″ tall.* ☉ *June–Sept., weekdays 10–9, weekends 9–10; mid-Apr.–mid-June and mid-Sept.–Oct., weekends only 10–9. Note: Closing times may vary, so check in advance.*

Six Flags Magic Mountain, the only real amusement park actually in Los Angeles County, has 260 acres of rides, shows, and entertainment. The newest thrill ride adventure is Batman, the Ride, at Gotham City Backlot. On Viper, the world's largest looping roller coaster, the first drop is 18 stories high, and three vertical loops turn you upside down seven times. There's also the Roaring Rapids, a simulated white-water wilderness adventure complete with whirlpools, waves, and rapids; the Colossus, the largest dual-track wooden roller coaster ever built, which speeds at more than 62 miles per hour; and the Revolution, a steel coaster with a 360-degree, 90- foot vertical loop. Yosemite Sam Sierra Falls is a two-person raft ride with a 760-foot twisting water slide. Children's World is a minipark with scaled-down rides, such as the Red Baron's Airplane and the Little Sailor Ride. *26101 Magic Mountain Pkwy., off I–5, Valencia,* ☎ *805/255–4111.* ☛ *$29 adults, $18 senior citizens, $15 children 4 ft tall and under.* ☉ *Mid-Apr.–Oct., daily 10–10 (later on weekends); Nov.–mid-Apr., weekends and holidays 10–10. Closing hrs vary so check ahead.*

Orange County

Without a doubt, **Disneyland,** followed by **Knott's Berry Farm,** are the main attractions for children in Orange County (*see* Exploring section in Chapter 9, Orange County), but there's plenty else here to round out a family vacation.

Disneyland

The news at Disneyland is **Mickey's Toontown,** perfect to wind down for kids ages three–eight after a long day. All the Disney characters live in this wonderful play area. Other places in the park for the younger set are **Fantasyland, Tom Sawyer's World,** and **Big Thunder Ranch** in Frontierland. For kids six and older, look for all the mountain rides—**Splash Mountain, Thunder Mountain, Space Mountain,** and the **Matterhorn,** all thrilling roller coasters.

Knott's Berry Farm

This famous theme park has plenty of thrill rides to attract older kids; the littler ones will be happier riding the antique **carousel,** exploring **Ghost Town,** and taking the rides at **Camp Snoopy.**

Inland Orange County

Bowers Museum of Cultural Art (*see* Exploring section in Chapter 9, Orange County), has been in Santa Ana since the 1930s. Children especially like the exhibits on Native Americans, and there is a great interactive video for school-age kids in the Central America Room.

The **International Printing Museum** explains 500 years of printing history. As children watch the presses run, many see their own names set in type and printed. *8469 Kass Dr., Buena Park,* ☎ *714/ 523–2070.* ☛ *$6.50 adults, $4 senior citizens and students.* ☉ *Tues.–Sat., 10–5.*

The **Children's Museum at La Habra** is housed in a 1923-vintage Union Pacific railroad depot, with old railroad cars resting nearby. On Buster the Bus, a retired transit bus, children can climb behind the wheel; Dinosaur Dig is a huge sandbox where visitors "dig up" bones; in Grandma's Attic, children can try on old clothes. *301 S. Euclid St., La Habra,* ☎ *310/905–9793.* ☛ *$4.* ☉ *Mon.–Sat. 10–5, Sun. 1–5.*

Conveniently near Disneyland, **Golf-n-Stuff** offers unusual family golfing fun. Colored lights sparkle on the miniature golf courses' geyser fountains amid windmills, castles, and waterfalls. *1055 E. Firestone Blvd.,* ☎ *714/994–2110.* ☛ *$5 adults and children over 6; special family rates.* ☉ *Daily 10–11.*

Hobby City Doll and Toy Museum houses antique dolls and toys from around the world in a replica of the White House. *1238 S. Beach Blvd., Anaheim,* ☎ *714/527–2323.* ☛ *$1 adults, 50¢ children under 13.* ☉ *Daily 10–6.*

Movieland Wax Museum (*see* Exploring section in Chapter 9, Orange County) is kitschy but fun, although it may frighten younger kids.

Wild Rivers has more than 40 rides and attractions, including a wave pool, several daring slides, a river inner-tube ride, and several places at which to eat and shop. *8800 Irvine Center Dr., Laguna Hills, off I-405 at Irvine Center Dr.,* ☎ *714/768–6014.* ☛ *$16.95 adults, $12.95 children 3–9; discounts after 4.* ☉ *Mid-May–Sept. Call for hrs.*

The Coast

Bolsa Chica Ecological Reserve is great for young nature lovers; the **International Surfing Museum in Huntington Beach** is a good introduction to this quintessential West Coast sport; and the **Balboa Island Fun**

Zone is a charming small set of rides, including a Ferris wheel, near the Balboa Pavilion. (*See* Exploring section in Chapter 9, Orange County.)

Riverside and San Bernardino Counties

Orange Empire Railway Museum is an outdoor museum the size of a town, where children can see—and ride on—many old trains and trolleys: diesel-operated locomotives, electric- and steam-powered locomotives, and cars from Los Angeles's old Red Line. *2201 S. A St., Perris,* ☎ *909/657–2605.* ☛ *Free; to go on rides, all- day ticket costs $5 adults, $3 children under 11.* ◉ *Winter, weekends and holidays (except Christmas and New Year's Day), 11–4; summer, weekends and holidays 11–5.*

A Special Place, Children's Hands On Museum, allows children with or without disabilities to participate side by side. Exhibits include School Days, which helps kids learn history while sitting at old school desks or shoveling coal into a potbellied stove; a Shadow Room; a Drama Area for dress up; and a Disability Awareness area equipped with wheelchairs, crutches, Braille material, and other items used by physically challenged children. *1003 E. Highland Ave., San Bernardino,* ☎ *909/881–1201.* ☛ *$2.* ◉ *Tues.–Fri. 9–1, Sat. 11–3.*

Other attractions in Riverside include the **Castle Park** amusement park and, for older children who enjoy history, the restored Victorian mansion **Heritage House** (*see* Riverside in Chapter 8, Excursions from Los Angeles).

If you're making the trip to Lake Arrowhead, be sure to take your family to **Santa's Village** (*see* Big Bear/Lake Arrowhead in Chapter 8, Excursions from Los Angeles).

SHOPPING

Santa Monica

Montana Avenue in Santa Monica is a treasure trove of colorful clothing and toy stores. If you start at First Street and crisscross, you'll be sure not to miss anything. Look for **And Apple Pie** (1211 Montana Ave., ☎ 310/393–4588), a tiny store with a big selection of the ever-popular Flapdoodles line, Fitigues, and sweaters from Ball of Cotton, all for newborns and toddlers, and **Imagine** (1001 Montana Ave., ☎ 310/395–9553) for custom-designed furniture and bedding as well as a large assortment of European wooden toys and gifts.

Beyond Montana, **Malina's Children's Store** (2654C Main St., ☎ 310/392–2611; 11688 San Vicente Blvd., ☎ 310/820–2806) has the newest of European fashions for boys and girls in sizes newborn–6X, as well as Malina's own custom designs.

Santa Monica Place Mall (315 Broadway, ☎ 310/394–5451) has quite a wide array of children's stores, including **Cotton Kids** for pure cotton clothing; **Gymboree,** for active wear and toys; **Gap Kids,** the junior version of the national clothing chain; **Imaginarium,** one of the area's best chain toy stores; **KCET Store of Knowledge,** sponsored by the L.A.'s public television network; **Toys International,** with toys from around the world; and **Sanrio Surprises,** selling Hello Kitty gifts and stationery.

Fred Segal Baby (500 S. Broadway, ☎ 310/451–5200) sells a great selection of unusual American and European clothing in a corner of the stylish Segal emporium.

Beverly Hills Area

Cotton separates and French designer clothes fill the shelves at **Agnes B** (100 N. Robertson Blvd., ☎ 310/271–9643). **Auntie Barbara's Kids** (245 S. Beverly Dr., ☎ 310/276–2864) is full of unusual American and European clothing. **Baby Guess** (459 N. Rodeo Dr., ☎ 310/274–0515) has a big selection of playwear and lots of denim for children three months and up. An **F.A.O. Schwarz** toy store is at the Beverly Center (8500 Beverly Blvd, at La Cienega Blvd.). **Harry Harris Shoes for Children** (409 N. Canon Dr., ☎ 310/274–8481) offers a wide selection of European leather shoes and sports footwear for kids. **Imaginarium** (Century City Shopping Center, 10250 Santa Monica Blvd., ☎ 310/785– 0227) encourages children to play in the store with its nonviolent and educational playthings. **Oilily** (9520 Brighton Way, ☎ 310/859–9145) stocks women's and children's wear splashed with bright primary colors in designs from the Netherlands. **Pixie Town** (400 N. Beverly Dr., ☎ 213/272–6415) has impeccably designed clothing from newborn to size 14.

Westside Area

Allied Model Trains (4411 S. Sepulveda, Culver City, ☎ 310/313–9353) feels like a huge train museum, with dozens of working train sets toot-tooting around the store.

Children's Book World (10580½ Pico Blvd., West Los Angeles, ☎ 310/559–2665) is a large, airy space with a very tempting selection of children's books.

Hollywood Area

Wacko (7416 Melrose Ave., ☎ 213/651–3811) *is* a crazy place, starting with the fun-house mirrors in the alley entrance. Inside, the shop sells joke items, wild postcards, silly books, and goofy toys. **Hollywood Magic Shop** (6614 Hollywood Blvd., ☎ 213/464–5610) is an institution in Tinsel Town; it sells costumes year-round and has a wide selection of tricks for beginners and experts. **Comic Connection** (1608 N. Hillhurst Ave., Unit C, ☎ 213/665–7715) always has the hottest comic books. **Every Picture Tells a Story** (7525 Beverly Blvd., ☎ 213/932–6070) is an intriguing gallery exhibiting original artwork from children's books. **American Rag Cie Youth** (128 S. La Brea Ave., ☎ 213/965–1404) specializes in vintage and vintage-style clothing for kids; it also has toys and gift items. **Flicka** (204 N. Larchmont Blvd., ☎ 213/466–5822) has cowboy-theme clothing and other unusual items for infants and older children.

Happily Ever After Children's Bookstore (2640 Griffith Park Blvd., ☎ 213/668–1996) has a wide selection of children's books, audio and video cassettes, and parenting books; storytelling is offered on the first Wednesday of each month at 10:30.

Pasadena and the San Fernando Valley

More to Grow On (132 W. Colorado Blvd., No. 7, S. Pasadena, ☎ 818/585–9200) is the place for special-occasion outfits, from christening gowns to party dresses. **Pages Books for Children and Young Adults** (18399 Ventura Blvd., Tarzana, ☎ 818/342–6657) sells books for young children through high schoolers. Almost every shop at **Universal CityWalk** (Universal Studios, Universal City) is intriguing to children. There's **Captain Coconut,** selling stuffed animals, most of them talking;

Golden Showcase for Golden Books and related items; **Wizardz,** a magic shop; **Upper Deck Authenticated,** where fans can buy autographed sports memorabilia; and **Scientific Revolution,** a nature-oriented store.

Orange County

The largest concentration of child-related stores is at **South Coast Plaza,** in Costa Mesa (*see* Shopping in Chapter 9, Orange County), which includes **F.A.O. Schwarz;** the **Disney Store; Warner Bros. Studio Store; Gap Kids; Learningsmith,** jam-packed with books, puzzles, software, and other intriguing learning toys; **Jacadi,** with very stylish clothes; the **Sesame Street General Store; Toys International; Benetton 1–2–3; Gymboree.** The **Polo** and **Armani** boutiques also have children's departments.

PARKS, PLAYGROUNDS, AND BEACHES

Parks

The main park in the city of Los Angeles is undoubtedly 4,000-acre **Griffith Park** (*see* Exploring, *above*), which offers tennis courts, bike lanes, horse trails, and hiking trails as well as the attractions covered above. There are several play areas throughout the park; near the carousel is an especially good one with bars and rings, and bouncy animals for the younger kids.

Will Rogers State Historic Park in Pacific Palisades (*see* Tour 5 in Chapter 2, Exploring Los Angeles) is a wonderful place for children, with broad lawns, walking trails, and even polo games on Saturday and Sunday (call 310/454–8212 for polo information).

El Dorado Regional Park and Nature Center (*see* Tour 6 in Chapter 2, Exploring Los Angeles) has stocked lakes for fishing. Of its two sections, **El Dorado West City Park** has a duck pond, and **El Dorado East** has ducks plus skating and bicycling paths.

William S. Hart Regional County Park (*see* Sightseeing Checklists in Chapter 2, Exploring Los Angeles) is an authentic cowboy ranch, once owned by cowboy actor William S. Hart; there are hiking trails, barbecue pits, picnic tables, and a small museum on the grounds. Guided tours are given of Hart's house, which is filled with Western art and memorabilia.

Eaton Canyon Park and Nature Center (*see* Sightseeing Checklists in Chapter 2, Exploring Los Angeles) offers children tours of the area's natural habitat.

In the **Angeles National Forest,** above Pasadena, you can go to the top of Mount Wilson for spectacular views of Los Angeles. The Chilao Visitors Center, 13 miles north of Mount Wilson, offers nature walks and exhibits about the forest.

At **Vasquez Rocks** (*see* Sightseeing Checklists in Chapter 2, Exploring Los Angeles), in the little town of Agua Dulce in the desert north of Los Angeles, children can scamper around the same rock formations that Fred Flintstone and his cronies called home in the movie *The Flintstones*. The lake at **Huntington Central Park** (Talbert Ave. and Central Park Dr., Huntington Beach) has ducks, friendly fishermen, radio-control-boat enthusiasts, and wonderful hide-and-seek spots along the bank.

Playgrounds

Griffith Park has a small playground near the carousel (*see* Exploring, *above*); there is also one across from the Griffith Park Boulevard entrance, and one just past the golf course. A free map of the park is available at the Visitors Center, 4730 Crystal Drive.

In Beverly Hills, **Roxbury Park** (*see* Sightseeing Checklists in Chapter 2, Exploring Los Angeles) has innovative wooden playing structures— one for younger kids and one for older kids.

Santa Monica's tiny **Douglas Park** (*see* Sightseeing Checklists in Chapter 2, Exploring Los Angeles) has a busy playground at the quiet end of the park. Street parking is only a few feet away. Nearby, an empty cement pond now makes a great rink for young rollerbladers and trike riders.

On the ocean, just below **Palisades Park** in Santa Monica (*see* Tour 5 in Chapter 2, Exploring Los Angeles), is a playground right on the sand, with a view of the Pacific in the background; walk down the stairs at Arizona Avenue.

Lacy Park (1485 Virginia Rd., San Marino, ☎ 818/300–0700) has a fun playground beside a broad lawn with picnic areas; parents can sit under inviting shade trees while their little ones play.

In Laguna Beach, there is a great seaside playground on **Main Beach,** and a more secluded one on **Cress Street.**

Beaches

Young families seem to frequent the beaches in Santa Monica, in South Bay towns such as Redondo Beach, and in Malibu. For write-ups on these beaches, *see* Beaches in Chapter 4, Sports and Fitness. Teenagers flock to Huntington Beach (*see* Beaches in Chapter 9, Orange County), which is the center of Orange County surfing activities.

Best Bets

Santa Monica State Beach is definitely popular with families: a wide expanse of sand with all kinds of facilities including a pier, volleyball courts, and playground equipment.

Mothers' Beach (Marina Beach) in Marina del Rey is good for young kids because there are no waves.

Will Rogers State Beach in Pacific Palisades is a nice family beach with areas for swimming and two separate areas for surfing.

Paradise Cove in Malibu is a secluded family beach with a pier and equipment rentals.

Newport Dunes Aquatic Park (Jamboree Rd. and Pacific Coast Highway, Newport Beach) is a lagoon (with lifeguards) that's perfect for younger children. Different types of boats are available for rent.

In Laguna, **Main Beach,** in the center of town, has the nonstop action; for a more private seaside romp, try **Woods Cove** (*see* Exploring section in Chapter 9, Orange County), which is surrounded by high cliffs and has lots of rocks to climb.

Dana Point (*see* Exploring section in Chapter 9, Orange County) is very popular with kids—there's a sheltered beach for swimming, tidal pools, and a pier with boat rentals and whale-watching tours.

DINING

All but the trendiest Los Angeles restaurants are receptive to families. Most have some booster seats and high chairs, but there often aren't

enough to go around. Certain places welcome children with open
arms, providing special activities and menus; we've listed the best of
them below. For addresses, phone numbers, and other pertinent facts,
see Chapter 5, Dining, and Chapter 9, Orange County.

Los Angeles

The **California Pizza Kitchen** in Beverly Hills really welcomes kids; crayons
on the table keep youngsters busy while they wait for their food.
Teenagers will get a kick out of the unusual types of pizzas. **Ed Debevic's** in Beverly Hills is a raucous place with outrageous DJs, loud music,
and waiters and waitresses in 1950s outfits who sit at your table when
you order. The food is no-nonsense and great for kids. The **Hard Rock
Cafe,** near the Beverly Center, deserves its reputation; it is a great place
to star watch. This haunt for local teenagers will give kids from other
places an inside look at teen culture in Los Angeles. The **Pacific Dining Car** is a downtown Los Angeles landmark, located in a 1920s railroad car, which is a big draw for kids. The prices here are steep, and
it's mostly businesspeople during the week, but on weekends you will
find families here. **R.J.'s the Rib Joint** in Beverly Hills is the epitome of
Beverly Hills casual; younger kids will like all of the activity, and older
kids will have fun filling their plates to the brim at the huge salad bar.

San Fernando Valley

Art's Delicatessen is *the* typical Jewish deli in the valley. Sandwiches
are piled high; after all, Art's corny motto is "Every Sandwich Is a Work
of Art." A children's menu is quite extensive, including breakfast items
and, of course, hamburgers.

Orange County

Inland, a good bet is the boisterous **Angelo's & Vinci's Cafe Ristorante,**
with its cluttered decor, circuslike entertainment, and platefuls of
hearty pasta and pizza. Ocean views are a big pull for children and
adults at the **Beach House** in Laguna Beach, where the waiters are accustomed to serving children. The **Hard Rock Cafe Newport Beach** packages all the rock-and-roll atmosphere for which the chain is known.

LODGING

All hotels in Los Angeles and its environs are happy to welcome children. As a matter of fact, it sometimes seems that the more expensive
the hotel, the more attentive it is to children. Areas near child-oriented
attractions—Disneyland, Universal Studios, the beaches—are especially geared to handle lots of children.

For baby-sitting, try your hotel concierge first; he or she can usually
set something up with at least 24 hours' notice. Rates vary, but run
around $7–$10 per hour. Many hotels use the **Babysitters Guild** (☎
213/658–8792); **Sitters Unlimited** has franchises throughout the area
(Huntington Beach and Long Beach, ☎ 310/596–0550; Orange County,
☎ 714/251–1948; both require a four-hour minimum). All the major
chains—including Sheraton, Hilton, and Marriott—have local hotels
that participate in their corporate children's programs. Many smaller
chains and single properties have programs to entertain your child for
a few hours or an entire day. Most children's programs go full force
only in summer, but the hotels usually continue them during the winter on weekends and during school vacations. The following are some
of the more popular children's programs; *see* Chapters 6, Lodging, and
9, Orange County for addresses and phone numbers.

Los Angeles

The **Ritz-Carlton** hotels in Marina del Rey and Pasadena have some children's activities. **Loews Santa Monica Beach Hotel** has a summer Splash Club with daytime activities for children 2–12. At the **Century Plaza Hotel and Tower,** the "Little Stars" program offers special family rates and surprises for children 3–12: Century Plaza teddy bears, cookies and milk, balloons, and a hotel T-shirt. Free amenities for infants include no-tears shampoo, baby oil, stuffed animals, high chairs, bottles, baby blankets, and even bottle warmers. Mention that there are children in your party when you first make your reservations.

Orange County

At the **Dana Point Resort,** Camp Cowabunga for ages 5–12 (daily in summer; weekends, rest of year; cost: $35 per day, $20 per half day, $15 evenings) lets kids swim, make kites, and handle sea life at nearby tide pools. Watercolors, the resort's restaurant, provides special coloring-book menus and crayons. The **Ritz-Carlton Laguna Niguel** sponsors some children's activities, too.

THE ARTS

Los Angeles has a large selection of arty activities for kids, from children's theater to concerts and great museums. *L.A. Parent,* the free monthly newspaper, is a great guide for up-to-date theater, concert, and movie listings; all listings of performances include a mention of the appropriate ages.

Bob Baker Marionette Theater (1345 W. 1st St., ☎ 213/250–9995) has been a staple on the kid scene in Los Angeles since 1963, with performances at 10:30 every weekday morning and 2:30 on weekend afternoons. Kids sit on a carpeted floor and get a close-up view of the intricate marionettes; ice cream and juice are served afterward. Reservations are required; tickets cost $10 per person, $8 for senior citizens. The **Santa Monica Playhouse** (1211 4th St., ☎ 310/394–9779) offers children's productions of plays such as "Alice and the Wonderful Tea Party" and "Beauty and the Beast." Tickets cost $8; performances are on weekends at 1 and 3.

The **American Cinematheque** (at the Director's Guild Theater, 7920 Sunset Blvd., Hollywood, ☎ 213/466–3456) has a special monthly Saturday Matinees for Children program, performing classic standbys such as "The Adventures of Tom Sawyer."

Storybook Theater (3333 Cahuenga Blvd. W, Hollywood, ☎ 818/761–2203) offers original plays and musical theater for children aged 2–9.

Wonderworld Puppet Theater (☎ 310/532–1741) presents Saturday-morning puppet shows for an audience of short attention spans and curious young minds. After the adventure-filled performance, the curtains come down and children can see how it was done. Call for locations and schedule; tickets are $4–$5.

At **Serendipity** (at Burbank Little Theatre, 1100 Clark Ave., Burbank, ☎ 818/953–8763), performers from the Actor's Company read children's stories and fairy tales, encouraging the audience to supply sound effects and giggles. Free on Saturdays at noon; call for a schedule.

The **Orange County Performing Arts Center** (*see* The Arts and Nightlife in Chapter 9, Orange County) puts on many children's plays.

Laguna Playhouse's Moulton Theater (606 Laguna Canyon Rd., ☎ 714/494–0743), also in Orange County, has a special children's theater with changing fare.

11 Portrait of Los Angeles

THERE MUST BE A THERE HERE SOMEWHERE

By Jane E. Lasky

Hollywood is a town that has to be seen to be disbelieved.—Walter Winchell

WHILE HOSTING A **BRITISH BROADCASTER-FRIEND** on his first trip to Los Angeles, I reluctantly took him to the corner of Hollywood and Vine. Driving toward the renowned street corner, I explained (again) that this part of town isn't the "real" Hollywood. But he wasn't listening. He was on a pilgrimage, too filled with the anticipation of coming upon a sacred place to hear my warning. When we reached the intersection, his reaction was written all over his face: He was, as he later said, "gobsmacked."

As we pulled up to the light, a bedraggled hooker crossed Hollywood Boulevard. Worse, this looked like someplace where nothing noteworthy or memorable ever had, would, or could happen. The area has been called squalid, but that gives it too much credit for being interesting. All there was to see were a few small and struggling businesses, the hulk of a long-defunct department store, a huge neon sign held up by scaffolding, and a couple of unremarkable office buildings.

To rescue the moment from complete disaster, I went into my standard routine: I pointed out that the spot just south of where we stood on the southeast corner is where the illustrious Brown Derby restaurant once thrived, hoping to conjure up an alluring image of movie stars dining in a giant hat. I then recounted historian Richard Alleman's theory about how this unprepossessing street corner became so famous. Alleman, who wrote *The Movie Lover's Guide to Hollywood*, believes that because the radio networks, which maintained studios in the vicinity during the 1930s and 1940s, began their broadcasts with the words "brought to you from the corner of Hollywood and Vine . . . ," the intersection became glamorous by association—at least to radio listeners who'd never seen it.

Pressed to show my British friend the "real" Hollywood, I took him on a tour of the more exuberant architecture along Hollywood Boulevard. He was duly captivated by the lunacy of Hollywood's Art Deco movie palaces, exemplified in the zigzaggy Moderne contours of the Pantages, and by the flamboyant absurdity of such thematically designed theaters as Mann's Chinese, the Egyptian, and the baroque El Capitan. Then we took in some other notable architecture, such as the Capitol Records building, looking—deliberately, mind you—like a 14-story stack of 45s, and an assortment of mock Mayan-, Mission-, Moorish-, Moderne-, and made-up-style structures now housing video stores, fast-food franchises, and offices. The variety of fun and fanciful buildings you'll see throughout Los Angeles reveals, I think, the essence of Hollywood. How else to explain the incongruous jumble of architectural styles sitting side by side in almost any neighborhood? A '50s futuristic house next door to a Queen Anne Victorian, a Craftsman bungalow abutting a French château, a redbrick Georgian across the street from a tile-roof Spanish revival—all on the same block—can be viewed as an extrapolation of a movie-studio back lot, on which a New York street is steps from a Parisian sidewalk café. Yet despite the famous names underfoot and the impressively zany architecture, my friend still felt he'd missed the enchantment, the excitement . . . the movies.

It's hard to fault the intrepid visitor for expecting a more dynamic dream capital. Even seasoned locals, who understand that Hollywood is much more a state of mind than a geographic location, can only just manage to intellectualize the concept. They, too, still secretly hunger for evidence that all the magic and glamour come from an appropriately magical and glamorous place. But, except for the occasional gala premiere, you're not likely to see any movie stars in Hollywood. The workaday world of filmmaking and the off-duty hangouts of the movie crowd have largely moved elsewhere. There is only one major movie studio—Paramount—still operating within Hollywood's city limits. Universal Studios and the Burbank Studios are both in the San Fernando Valley, across the hills to the north, as are most network-television studios. And, although firmly rooted in the spirit of Hollywood, Disneyland is a world away in Anaheim.

EVEN A CURSORY GLANCE at Hollywood's history raises serious doubts that the town was ever as glamorous as we insist it no longer is. Pinning down exactly when its star-studded golden era was is a slippery business. Most people point to the 1930s and 1940s, and the images evoked by those days are irresistible: tan, handsome leading men posed, grinning, with one foot on the running board of a snazzy convertible; heartbreakingly beautiful actresses clad in slinky silk gowns and mink, stepping from long black limousines into the pop of photographers' flashbulbs. The real story, naturally, was a bit different: long hours; the tedium of the filmmaking process; the rarity of achieving and maintaining a successful career, much less stardom; and, for those who did achieve it, the precarious tightrope walk balancing publicity and privacy. Hollywood has never been shy about depicting itself in an unflattering light, and some of the most memorable films ever are grim portrayals of the movie business: *A Star is Born, Sunset Boulevard,* and, most recently, *The Player.* That there is a very seamy side to the movie business is very old news.

The trick to seeing Hollywood is knowing *how* to look at it, as well as where to look for it. The magic of movies is that reality, at least on film, can be made to look any way the filmmakers want it to look. But when you visit Hollywood, your own field of vision isn't as selective as a movie camera's lens, and you're working without a script. It may be helpful to think of Hollywood, the town, as something of a relic, a symbol of past grandeur (both real and imagined), an open-air museum of artifacts and monuments, but hardly the whole story. Tennessee Williams said, "Ravaged radiance is even better than earnest maintenance," and, as regards Hollywood, I couldn't agree more.

It may be that in order to experience Hollywood, you have to go outside it. Only after we'd driven through the canyons, Beverly Hills, and Bel-Air and were rounding the last corner of Sunset that leads to the Pacific Coast Highway and out to Malibu did my British visitor feel truly satisfied. "Yes, well," he said finally, "this is really much more like it, then," and seemed almost physically relieved to have found someplace that matched his expectations of luxurious living. These are lovely places, fitting backdrops for a Hollywood lifestyle; to be sure, successful movie types do, indeed, live here.

Whatever Hollywood is or isn't, I like the place just the way it is: flawed and scarred, full of mysteries and contradictions. Living nearby and seeing it often hasn't taken away any of the enchantment of sitting in a darkened theater and giving myself over to the doings on screen. After all, that's where the real Hollywood lives.

INDEX

✕ = restaurant, 🏠 = hotel

A

Aah's (store), 57
Abbott Kinney (artists' colony), 59
ABS Clothing (store), 59
Adamson House, 33
Adriano's Ristorante, 94
Airport Marina Hotel, 113–114
Air travel, xv–xvi, xxvii
and children, xvii, xxviii
Alan Austin and Company (store), 62
Alexio (store), 57
Alfred Dunhill of London (store), 62
Aliso County Park, 160
AMC Century ✕, 58
American Rag Company (store), 63
Anaheim, 159
hotels, 164–166
restaurants, 161, 164
Anaheim Hilton and Towers 🏠, 164
Anaheim Marriott 🏠, 164
Anaheim Museum, 151
Angeles National Forest, 186
Angelo's & Vinci's Cafe Ristorante, 168
Angel's Attic (antique doll collection), 181
Anita's ✕, 161
Ann Taylor, Beverly Hills (store), 62
Ann Taylor, Century City (store), 58
Antiques, 63
Antoine ✕, 170
Apartment and villa rentals, xxi, xxx
Apples Bed and Breakfast Inn, 136
Argyle, The 🏠, 102–103
Armand Hammer Museum of Art and Cultural Center, 28
Arnie Morton's of Chicago ✕, 84
Arrowhead Queen, 134
Arts, 118–122
children, 189
concerts, 119–120, 173
dance, 120
film, 120–121
television, 121–122
theater, 118–119, 173
Arts & Letters (store), 59
Art's Delicatessen, 91
A. Sulka (boutique), 60
ATMs, xxi, xxx–xxxi
Atrium Marquis Hotel, 169
Avalon Theater, 138

B

Baily Wine Country Cafe, 144
Balboa Island Fun Zone, 183–184
Balboa Pavilion, 154
Balboa Peninsula, 154
Banana Bungalow Hotel and International Hostel, 106
Bangkok IV ✕, 166
Banning House Lodge, 140
Banning Residence Museum and Park, 36
Barami (store), 58
Barnaby's Hotel, 113
Barneys New York (store), 60
Bars, 127–131
Airport/South Bay, 128
Beverly Hills, 128
Century City, 128
Downtown, 128
Hollywood, 128–129
Marina del Rey/Venice, 129
Mid-Wilshire, 130
Orange County, 174
Pasadena, 130
San Fernando Valley, 130
Santa Monica/beaches, 130–131
West Hollywood, 131
Westwood/Westside, 131
Barzac Brasserie ✕, 91
Baseball, 66
Basketball, 66
Battaglia (store), 62
Baylis Park Picnic Ground, 133
Beaches, 73–76
children, 187
Orange County, 160
Beach House ✕, 169
Bear Mountain Ski Resort, 135
Beaurivage ✕, 92
Bernini (store), 62
Best Western Marina Inn, 168
Best Western Royal Palace Inn and Suites, 109–110
Better Business Bureau, xvi
Betsey Johnson (store), 54
Beverly Center, 24, 26, 57–58
Beverly Connection (shopping mall), 57
Beverly Garland's Holiday Inn 🏠, 115–116
Beverly Hills, 26–27
Beverly Hills Hotel, 26–27
Beverly Hills Ritz Hotel, 5, 108
Beverly Hilton 🏠, 106–107
Beverly Prescott Hotel, 108
Bicycling, 68, 158
Big Bear, 133–137
Big Bear Inn, 136
Big Bear Lake Village, 135
Big Bear Queen, 135
Bijan (store), 62
Biltmore Hotel (Los Angeles), 13, 98
Bistro Garden ✕, 86–87
Blue Lantern Inn, 167
Blue Ox Bar and Grill, 135
Boating, 72
Bolsa Chica Ecological Reserve, 153, 158
Bolsa Chica State Beach, 160
Book Star (store), 57
Bootz (store), 59
Border Grill, 95–96
Bowers Museum of Cultural Art, 152, 183
Boxing, 66
Bradbury Building, 13
Brea, 166
Brenda Cain (store), 59
Brenda Himmel (store), 59
Bren Events Center Fine Art Gallery, 152
Brentano's (store), 58
Broadway Deli ✕, 86
Broadway, The, Beverly Center (store), 56, 73
Broadway, The, Santa Monica (store), 59
Bronson Caves, 18–19
Buena Park Hotel, 166
Bullocks (store), 54, 57, 63
Bullocks Wilshire, 19
Burbank, 44
Burbank Airport Hilton 🏠, 115

Burton Chase Park, *31–32*
Bus travel, *xvi–xvii*
By Design (store), *57*

C

Cabaret clubs, *124*
Ca'Brea ✕, *94*
Cabrillo Marine Aquarium, *34, 181*
Cafe Champagne, *144*
Cafe Prego, *140*
Calabasas, *44–45*
California Citrus State Historic Park, Riverside, *142*
California Heritage Museum, *29*
California Museum of Photography, *142*
California Museum of Science and Industry, *45, 49, 179*
California Pizza Club, *57*
California Pizza Kitchen, *87–88, 188*
California Scenario (sculpture garden), *152–153*
Callaway Vineyard & Winery, *143*
Camcorders, *xxviii*
Cameras, *xxvii*
Camp Pendleton, *157*
Camp Snoopy, *150, 183*
Candy Cane Inn, *165*
Cannery, The ✕, *171*
Canter's ✕, *6, 91*
Canter's Restaurant, Deli, and Bakery, *23–24*
Capistrano Depot ✕, *156*
Capitol Records Building, *16*
Card Fever, Century City (store), *58*
Card Fever, Santa Monica (store), *59*
Carlyle Inn, *108*
Carmel Hotel, *110, 112*
Carole & Barry Kaye Museum of Miniatures, *23*
Carousel (Knott's Berry Farm), *150, 183*
Car rentals, *xvii, xxxiii*
Carriage House Bed and Breakfast, *137*
Carroll and Co. (store), *62*
Carroll Avenue, *48*
Cartier (store), *62*
Cash machines, *xxi, xxx–xxxi*
Casino, Catalina Island, *138*
Casinos, *126–127*

Castle Inn and Suites, *165*
Castle Park, *142–143, 184*
Catalina Island, *137–141*
Catalina Island Museum, *138*
Catch, The ✕, *164*
Cava ✕, *96*
C.C. Brown's (soda fountain), *17*
Celine (store), *62*
Cellar, The ✕, *168*
Central Library, *14*
Century City Courtyard by Marriott, *109*
Century City Inn, *109*
Century City Shopping Center & Marketplace, *58*
Century Plaza Hotel and Tower, *108*
Century Wilshire 🖭, *109*
Cha Cha Cha ✕, *5, 89*
Chan Dara ✕, *96*
Chanel (store), *63*
Chanteclair ✕, *168–169*
Charlie's (store), *58*
Chateau Marmont Hotel, *103*
Cheap Frills (store), *58*
Children and travel, *xvii–xviii, xxviii*
  baby sitting, xvii, xxviii
  driving, xxviii
  flying, xvii, xxviii
  local information, xvii–xviii
  lodging, xviii, xxviii
  tour operators, xviii
Children's activities, *179–189*
  arts, 189
  beaches, 187
  hotels, xviii, xxviii, 188–189
  Los Angeles, 179–182
  Orange County, 183–184
  parks, 186
  playgrounds, 186–187
  restaurants, 187–188
  Riverside/San Bernadino County, 184
  shopping, 184–186
Children's Hands On Museum, *184*
Children's Museum at La Habra, *183*
Chinatown, *11*
Chin Chin (café), *26*
Chinois on Main ✕, *92*
Chopstix ✕, *89–90*
Christian Dior (boutique), *60*
Citrus ✕, *88*
City Club ✕, *172*

City Walk, *43–44*
Clearwater Cafe, *92–93*
Climate, *xxxiv*
Clothing, *xxxii*
College basketball, *66*
College football, *66*
Colorado Street Bridge, *41*
Comedy clubs, *126, 174*
Comme des Fous (store), *54*
Computers, *xxvii*
Concerts, *119–120, 173*
Cooper Building, *14, 54*
Copelands Sporting Goods (store), *57*
Corona del Mar, *154–155*
Corona del Mar Beach, *160*
Costa Mesa
  hotels, 166–167
  restaurants, 166
Cottura (store), *54*
Country music, *125, 174*
Country Side Inn and Suites, *167*
Crab Cooker ✕, *171*
Craft and Folk Art Museum, *22–23*
Cranberry House (store), *60*
Cross-Country skiing, *71*
Crown Plaza Redondo Beach and Marina Hotel, *112–113*
Crystal Cathedral, *151*
Crystal Cove State Beach, *155*
Crystal Cove State Park, *160*
Cyril's (store), *62*
Customs, *xviii, xxviii–xxix*

D

Dana Point, *155–156*
  hotels, 167–168
  restaurants, 167
Dana Point Harbor, *160*
Dana Point Resort, *167*
Dance, *120*
Davidoff of Geneva (boutique), *60*
Days Inn, *161*
Delaney's Restaurant, *167*
Del Mano Gallery (store), *64*
Department stores, *63*
Descanso Gardens, *5, 50*
Desert Palm Inn and Suites, *165*
Dining Room (restaurant, Beverly Hills), *87*
Dining Room (restaurant, Dana Point), *167*
Dinner theaters, *174*

Disabilities, hints for travelers with, *xviii–xx, xxix*
travel agencies and tour operators, xix–xx
Discos, *124–125*
Discounts, *xx*
clubs, xxix
senior citizens, xxxiii–xxiv
Disneyland, *146–147, 150, 183*
Disneyland Hotel, *164*
Disney Store, *58*
DIVE! ✕, *80*
Doctors, *xx*
Orange County, 176
Doubletree Hotel LAX, *113*
Dockweiler State Beach, *76*
Dodger Stadium, *45*
Doheny State Park, *160*
Doubletree Hotel Orange County, *172*
Doubletree Marina del Rey L.A. ☷, *112*
Douglas Park, *50*
Downtown, *9, 11–14*
hotels in, 98, 101–102
shopping in, 54
Driving, *xxix*
Duties, *xxviii–xxix*
Dynasty Room ✕, *90*

E

Eaton Canyon Park, *50*
Echo Park, *50–51*
Ed Debevic's ✕, *78, 188*
Eiler's Inn, *170*
El Adobe ✕, *173*
El Alisal, *38*
El Cholo ✕, *6, 95*
El Dorado Regional Park, *37, 186*
El Mercado, *46–47*
El Paseo ✕, *12*
El Pueblo de Los Angeles Historical Monument, *11*
El Rancho Escondido, *138*
El Torito Grill ✕, *171*
Elysian Park, *51*
Emergencies
community service, xx
doctors, xx
Los Angeles, xx
Orange County, 176
pharmacies, xx
Emphasis (store), *54*
Emporio Armani Boutique, *62*

Encino Town Center (shopping mall), *60*
Etienne's ✕, *172*
Exposition Park, *45, 179*

F

Fantasies Come True (store), *56*
Farmer's Market, *23*
Farmer's Market at Atrium Court, *154*
Fashion Island Newport Beach, *154, 157*
Fiesta Marketplace, *152*
Figueroa Hotel, *102*
Fila (store), *60*
Film, *120–121*
travel with, xxii, xxviii
First Congregational Church, Riverside, *142*
Fisherman's Village, *32*
Fishing, *68–69*
Five Feet ✕, *169*
Flower Market, *47*
Folk music clubs, *123–124*
Football, *66*
Forest Lawn Memorial Park, *45*
Forest Lawn Memorial Park-Hollywood Hills, *45–46*
Four Seasons Hotel, *171*
Four Seasons Los Angeles ☷, *107*
Franklin Canyon Ranch, *51*
Frederick's of Hollywood, *17*
Fred Hayman (store), *63*
Fred Segal (store), *56*
Freehand (store), *58*
Fullerton restaurants, *168*

G

Galleria Capistrano, *156*
Gamble House, *40*
Gardens, *50–52*
Garment District, *14*
Gay and Lesbian travelers, *xx–xxi*
G. B. Harb (store), *54*
Gelson's (store), *58*
Gene Autry Western Heritage Museum, *5, 46, 182*
George and Sigi's Knusperhauschen ✕, *135–136*
George C. Page Museum of La Brea Discoveries, *22*
Getty House, *21*
Ghost Town, *150*

Gian Franco Ferre (boutique), *60*
Gianni Versace (store), *60*
Gilliland's ✕, *84, 86*
Gladstone's 4 Fish ✕, *86*
Glendale Galleria, *60*
Gold mine (ride), *150*
Gold Mountain Manor ☷, *136*
Golf, *67, 69, 158*
Golf-n-Stuff, *183*
Grand Central Market, *13*
Granita ✕, *88*
Greystone Mansion, *26*
Griffith Park, *51, 180, 186*
Griffith Park Observatory and Planetarium, *5, 46*
Grill on the Alley ✕, *78*
Guided tours
Catalina Island, 141
Orange County, 176

H

Hale House, *38*
Hammacher-Schlemmer (store), *62*
Hancock Park, *21*
Handball, *71*
Hannah Carter Japanese Garden, *51*
Hard Rock Cafe, The, *24, 57, 84, 188*
Hard Rock Cafe Newport Beach, *171*
Harry's Bar & American Grill, *93*
Health clubs, *69–70*
Hentington Central Park, *186*
Heritage House, Riverside, *142*
Heritage Square, *38, 181*
Highland Park, *4, 38, 40*
Hiking, *70*
Historical buildings and sites, *47–48*
Hobby City Doll and Toy Museum, *183*
Hockey, *67*
Holiday Inn L.A. Downtown, *102*
Holiday Inn-LAX, *114*
Holiday Inn at the Park, *165*
Holiday Inn Maingate, *165*
Hollyhock (store), *56*
Hollyhock House, *46*
Hollywood, *4, 14–19*
Hollywood Farmer's Market, *16*

Hollywood and Vine, *14, 16*
Hollywood Bowl, *18*
Hollywood Guinness World of
  Records Museum, *17*
Hollywood High School, *18*
Hollywood Holiday Inn, *106*
Hollywood Memorial Ceme-
  tery, *18*
Hollywood sign, *14*
Hollywood Studio Museum, *18*
Hollywood Walk of Fame, *16*
Hollywood Wax Museum, *17*
Horseback riding, *70–71*
Horse racing, *67*
Hosteling, *xxiv*
Hotel Bel-Air, *5, 88, 109*
Hotel Inter-Continental Los
  Angeles, *98*
Hotel Laguna, *170*
Hotel Metropole and Market-
  place, *140*
Hotel Nikko, *107*
Hotels
  Airport, 113–114
  *Bel-Air/Westwood/West Los
    Angeles, 109–110*
  Beverly Hills, 106–108
  *Big Bear/Lake Arrowhead,
    136–137*
  Catalina Island, 140
  Century City, 108–109
  *children, xviii, xxviii, 188–
    189*
  downtown, 98, 101–102
  Fodor's choice, 5
  *Hollywood/West Hollywood,
    102–103, 106*
  lounges, 125–126
  Marina del Rey, 112
  Mid-Wilshire, 102
  Orange County, 161–173
  Pasadena, 114
  San Fernando Valley, 114–116
  Santa Monica, 110, 112
  *South Bay Beach Cities, 112–
    113*
  Temecula, 144
Hotel Sofitel Ma Maison, *107*
Hotel Vista del Mar, *140*
Houston's ✕, *58*
Huntington Beach, *153, 159*
hotels, 168
Huntington Beach State Beach,
  160
Huntington Library, Art
  Gallery, and Botanical Gar-
  dens, *5, 42*
Huntington Pier, *153*

Hyatt Hotel-LAX, *113*
Hyatt on Sunset 🖫, *106*
Hyatt Regency, Los Angeles
  🖫 *101*
Hyatt Regency Irvine 🖫, *169*

I

Ice (store), *57*
Ice skating, *71*
Il Fornaio Cucina Italiana ✕,
  93
In-line and roller skating, *71*
Inn at Laguna Beach 🖫, *170*
Inn at 657, *5, 102*
Inn at the Park, *165*
Inn on Mt. Ada, *140*
Inntowne, The 🖫, *102*
Insurance, *xxi, xxix–xxx*
car rental, xxxiii
in the U.K., xxi
International Printing Mu-
  seum, *183*
International Surfing Museum
  in Huntington Beach, *153,
  183*
Iron Squirrel ✕, *136*
Irvine
hotels, 169
restaurants, 168–169
Irvine Marriott 🖫, *169*
Irvine Museum, *152*

J

Jaeger International Shop, *63*
Jazz clubs, *122–123*
Jet skiing, *73*
Jimmy's ✕, *90*
Jogging, *71*
Joss ✕, *89*
J. Paul Getty Museum, *5, 32–
  33*
Junior Arts Center, *180*
J. W. Marriott Hotel at Cen-
  tury City, *108–109*
JW's ✕, *161*

K

Kachina ✕, *170*
Kayaking, *72*
Kanji (store), *56*
Kidspace (museum), *41–42,
  181*
Knott's Berry Farm, *150–151,
  183*
Kokomo ✕, *23*
Koreatown, *19, 21*

L

La Abeja ✕, *40*
La Brasserie ✕, *172*
La Brea Tar Pits, *21, 22*
Lacy Park, *187*
L.A. Eyeworks (store), *56*
La Golondrina ✕, *12*
Laguna Art Museum, *155*
Laguna Beach, *155, 158, 159*
hotels, 170
restaurants, 169–170
Lake Arrowhead, *133–137*
Lake Arrowhead Children's
  Museum, *134*
Lake Arrowhead Resort, *136*
Lake Arrowhead Village, *134*
Lake Gregory, *133*
Lakeview Point, *135*
La Luz del Dia ✕, *12*
Laptop computers, *xxvii*
Larchmont Boulevard, *21, 56*
Las Tunas State Beach, *75*
Laurel and Hardy's Piano
  Stairway, *47*
Lavender & Lace (store), *56*
La Veranda ✕, *87*
LA Vie en Rose ✕, *166*
Le Biarritz ✕, *171*
Le Chardonnay ✕, *92*
Lechter's (store), *59*
Le Dome ✕, *92*
Leo Carillo State Beach, *73, 75*
Leonis Adobe, *44–45*
Le Parc Hotel, *107*
L'Hirondelle ✕, *173*
Lido Isle, *157*
Limousines, *xxi*
Lisa Norman Lingerie (store),
  59
Little Saigon, *157*
Little Tokyo, *13*
Locanda Veneta ✕, *94*
Lodging, *xxi, xxx.* See also
  Hotels
*apartment and villa rentals,
  xxi, xxx*
and children, xviii, xxviii
home exchange, xxi, xxx
Loews Santa Monica Beach
  Hotel, *110*
Loma Vista Bed and Breakfast,
  144
Lomita Railroad Museum, *49,
  182*
Long Beach, *4, 36–37*
Long Beach Children's Mu-
  seum, *49, 181*

Long Beach Water Sports, 37

L'Orangerie ✕, 5, 91

Los Angeles Airport Marriott 🖫, 113

Los Angeles Children's Museum, 12

Los Angeles City Hall, 12–13

Los Angeles County Museum of Art, 22

Los Angeles Department of Parks and Recreation, 50

Los Angeles Hilton Hotel and Towers, 101

Los Angeles Swimming Stadium, 45

Los Angeles *Times complex,* 13

Los Angeles Zoo, 51, 180

Lotus Court ✕, 161

Louise's Trattoria ✕, 5, 93–94

Lower Newport Bay, 160

Luciana's ✕, 167

Luggage, *xxxii–xxxiii*

M

MAC (store), 57

MacArthur Park, 51–52

Magic clubs, 126

Main Beach, 187

Main Beach Park, 160

Main Place (shops), 158

Main Street Riverside, 142

Malibu, 4, 32–33

Malibu Creek State Park, 52

Malibu Lagoon State Park, 33, 75

Malina (store), 59

Mandarin, The ✕, 89

Mandarin Gourmet ✕, 166

Manhattan State Beach, 76

Mann's Chinese Theater, 17–18

Marina del Rey, 31–32

Marina del Rey Hotel, 112

Marina International Hotel, 112

Marina Pacific Hotel & Suites, 112

Marine Life Refuge, 160

Market City Cafe, 41

Marrakesh ✕, 171

Maurice Car'rie Vineyard & Winery, 143

Max Factor Museum, 17

Maxfield (store), 64

May Co. department store, 23

Melrose Avenue, 24, 54–56

Me & Me ✕, 17

Memorial Coliseum, 45

Merry-Go-Round in Griffith Park, 180

Merry-Go-Round in Santa Monica Pier, 181

Mickey's Toontown, 150, 183

Miracle Mile, 21

Miramar Sheraton 🖫, 110

Mission Inn, 141–142

Mission San Fernando Rey de España, 44

Mission San Gabriel Archangel, 48

Mission San Juan Capistrano, 156

Modern Living (store), 56

Mondi (store), 60

Mondrian Hotel, 103

Money, *xxi, xxx–xxxi*

ATMS, xxi, xxx–xxxi

traveler's checks, xxxi

wiring funds, xxi, xxxi

Monica's (catering company), 29

Mon Kee Seafood Restaurant, 89

Montana Avenue, 59

Morgan and Company (store), 57

Morton's ✕, 84

Motel 6, 161

"Mothers' Beach," 181, 187

Movieland Wax Museum, 151, 183

Mr. Gs for Toys (store), 58

Mrs. Knott's Chicken Dinner Restaurant, 151

Mulberry Street Ristorante, 168

Mulholland Drive, 46

Municipal Auditorium, Riverside, 142

Municipal Museum, 142

Murry Feldman Gallery, 26

Museum of Contemporary Art, 5, 9

Museum of Flying, 181

Museum of Tolerance, 5, 27

Museums, 49–50

Anaheim Museum, 151

Armand Hammer Museum of Art and Cultural Center, 28

Banning Residence Museum and Park, 36

Bowers Museum of Cultural Art, 152, 183

California Heritage Museum, 29

California Museum of Photography, 142

California Museum of Science and Industry, 49, 179

Carole & Barry Kaye Museum of Miniatures, 23

Catalina Island Museum, 138

Children's Museum at La Habra, 183

Craft and Folk Art Museum, 22–23

Fodor's choice, 5

Gene Autry Western Heritage Museum, 46, 182

George C. Page Museum of La Brea Discoveries, 22

Hobby City Doll and Toy Museum, 183

Hollywood Guinness World of Records Museum, 17

Hollywood Studio Museum, 18

Hollywood Wax Museum, 17

International Printing Museum, 183

International Surfing Museum in Huntington Beach, 153, 183

Irvine Museum, 152

J. Paul Getty Museum, 32–33

Kidspace, 41–42

Laguna Art Museum, 155

Lake Arrowhead Children's Museum, 134

Lomita Railroad Museum, 49, 182

Long Beach Children's Museum, 49, 181

Los Angeles Children's Museum, 12

Los Angeles County Museum of Art, 22

Max Factor Museum, 17

Movieland Wax Museum, 151, 183

Municipal Museum, 142

Museum of Contemporary Art, 5, 9

Museum of Flying, 181

Museum of Tolerance, 5, 27

Natural History Museum of Los Angeles County, 5, 45, 49–50, 179

Nautical Heritage Museum, 156

Newport Harbor Art Museum, 154

Norton Simon Museum, 40–41
Orange Empire Railway Museum, 184
Pacific Asia Museum, 41
Petersen Automotive Museum, The, 23
Riverside Art Museum, 142
Santa Monica Museum of Art, 29
Southwest Museum, 38, 40, 181
Special Place, Children's Hands-On Museum, A, 184
Temecula Historic Museum, 143
Music Center, 9, 11
Musso & Franks ✕, 17
My Favorite Place (store), 56

N

Naples, 37
Nate 'n Al's ✕, 91
Natural History Museum of Los Angeles County, 5, 45, 49–50, 179
Nautical Heritage Museum, 156
NBC Television Studios, 44
Neighborhoods
Downtown, 9–14
Highland Park, 38, 40
Hollywood, 14–19
Malibu, 32–33
Marina del Rey, 31–32
Pacific Palisades, 32
Palos Verdes, San Pedro, Long Beach, 33–37
Pasadena, 40–42
San Fernando Valley, 43–45
San Marino, 42
Santa Monica, 29, 31
Venice, 31
Westside, 24–28
Wilshire Boulevard, 19–24
New Otani Hotel and Garden, 5, 101–102
Newport Beach, 153, 159,
hotels, 171–172
restaurants, 170–171
Newport Beach Marriott Hotel and Tennis Club, 172
Newport Dunes Aquatic Park, 187
Newport Dunes Resort, 160
Newport Harbor, 153
Newport Harbor Art Museum, 154

Newport Pier, 154
Nicola ✕, 5, 80
Nightclubs, 174
Nightlife, 122–123
bars, 127–131, 174
cabaret, 124
casinos, 126–127
comedy/magic, 126, 174
country, 125, 174
dinner theater, 174
disco/dancing, 124–125
folk/pop/rock, 123–124
hotel lounges/piano bars, 125–126
jazz, 122–123
nightclubs, 174
Nordstrom (store), 58, 63
North Beach Leather (store), 64
Norton Simon Museum, 40–41

O

Ocean Avenue ✕, 86
Off the Wall (store), 56
Oilily (store), 62
Old Navy (store), 57
Old Orange County Courthouse, 152
Old Towne Orange, 157
Old Town Pasadena, 41
Old Town Temecula, 143
Olvera Street, 11–12
Orange
hotels, 172
restaurants, 172
Orange County, 4, 146
arts, 173
beaches, 160
children's activities, 183–184
coastal region, 153–157
emergencies, 176
guided tours, 176
hotels, 161–173
important addresses/numbers, 176–177
inland region, 146–147, 150–153
nightlife, 174
off the beaten track, 157
restaurants, 161–173
shopping, 157–158, 186
sports, 158–160
transportation around, 175–176
transportation to, 175
visitor information, 177

Orange County Marine Institute, 156
Orange County Performing Arts Center, 152, 173
Orange Empire Railway Museum, 184
Orchid Hotel, 102
Orcutt Ranch Horticultural Center, 47
Orleans ✕, 86

P

Pacific Asia Museum, 41
Pacific Design Center, 26
Pacific Dining Car ✕, 80, 188
Pacific Palisades, 4, 32
Pacific Shore ⬚, 110
Pacific Sunwear (store), 59
Packages and tours, *xxxi–xxxii*
Packing for the trip, *xxxii–xxxiii*
Pageant of the Masters, 155
Palace (concert hall), 16
Palisades Park, 29
Palm, The ✕, 84
Palms Depot, 38
Palos Verdes, 4, 34
Pantages Theater, 16
Paradise Cove, 75
Paramount Ranch, 182
Paramount Studios, 18
Parent Tree, 142
Parker's Lighthouse ✕, 36
Parks and gardens, 50–52
children, 186
Fodor's choice, 5
Pasadena, 4, 40–42
Pasadena Historical Society, 40
Pascal ✕, 170
Passports and visas, *xxi–xxii, xxxiii*
Paty's ✕, 80, 84
Pavilion ✕, 169
Pavilion Lodge, 140
Peninsula Beverly Hills, ⬚, 107
Pepperdine University, 33
Personal guides, *xxiii*
Petersen Automotive Museum, The, 23
Peter Strauss Ranch, 52
Pharmacies, *xx*
Philippes's The Original ✕, 80
Phoenix Club ✕, 161

Photography tips, *xxii, xxviii*
Piano bars, *125–126*
Pierside Pavilion, *153*
Pierview ✕, *33*
Pig murals, *47*
Pinot Bistro ✕, *91*
Pirrone's ✕, *140*
Placerita Canyon Nature Center, *52*
Planet Hollywood ✕, *153*
Playa del Rey, *76*
Playgrounds, *186–187*
Plaza de Oro, *60*
Pole (store), *56*
Polo, *67*
Polo/Ralph Lauren (store), *62*
Pony rides, *180*
Pop music clubs, *123–124*
Ports O'Call Village, *36, 181*
Posto ✕, *94*
Pottery Barn(store), *58*
Prego, Beverly Hills ✕, *93*
Prego, Irvine ✕, *169*
Promenade, The (shopping mall), *60*
Psychic Eye Bookstore, *59*

Q

Quality Hotel/Maingate, *165*
Queen Mary, *36, 181*

R

Racquetball, *71*
Radisson Bel-Air 🏨, *109*
Radisson Beverly Pavilion Hotel, *108*
Radisson Hollywood Roosevelt, *106*
Radisson Valley Center Hotel Los Angeles, *116*
Radisson Wilshire Plaza Hotel, *102*
Raging Waters (water park), *182*
Rail travel, *xxii*
Ramada Maingate/Anaheim 🏨, *165*
Rancho Los Alamitos, *37*
Rancho Los Cerritos, *37*
Randall's ✕, *173*
Red Lion Inn, *114*
Redondo State Beach, *76*
Regent Beverly Wilshire 🏨, *5, 27, 107–108*
Remi ✕, *95*
Restaurant Horikawa, *95*
Restaurant Katsu, *5, 95*

Restaurants
    American, 78, 80, 84, 86
    in Big Bear/Lake Arrowhead, 135–136
    Cajun, 86
    California, 86–88
    Caribbean, 89
    on Catalina Island, 140
    children, 187–188
    Chinese, 89–90
    Continental, 90
    deli, 91
    Fodor's choice, 5–6
    French, 91–92
    Greek, 92
    health food, 92–93
    Indian, 161
    Italian, 93–95
    Japanese, 95
    Mexican, 95–96
    in Orange County, 161–173
    Polynesian, 96
    in Temecula, 144
    Spanish, 96
    Thai, 96
Rexall Square Drug (store), *57–58*
Rex II Ristorante, *5, 93*
Richard Nixon Library and Birthplace, *151*
Ripley's Believe It or Not, *17*
Ritz, The ✕, *171*
Ritz-Carlton, Huntington Hotel, *42, 114*
Ritz-Carlton Laguna Niguel 🏨, *155, 168*
Ritz-Carlton, Marina del Ray 🏨, *112*
Riverside, *141–143*
    children's activities, 184
Riverside Art Museum, *142*
Riverside Botanic Gardens, *143*
Riverside County Courthouse, *142*
RJ'S the Rib Joint ✕, *78, 80*
Robert Grounds (store), *56*
Robinhood Inn and Lodge, *136*
Robinson's (store), *59*
Robinson's-May (store), *58, 63*
Rock music clubs, *123–124*
Rodeo Collection (shopping center), *60*
Rodeo Drive, *27, 60, 62–63*
Roller skating, *71*
Roscoe's House of Chicken 'n' Waffles, *84*

Rose Bowl, *40*
Roxbury Park, *52*
Rustica ✕, *90*

S

Safari Inn, *116*
Sagebrush Cantina ✕, *45*
Sailing, *72*
Saks Fifth Avenue (store), *60*
San Clemente, *157, 159*
    hotels, 173
    restaurants, 172
San Clemente Inn, *173*
San Clemente State Beach, *160*
Sand Trap ✕, *140*
San Fernando Valley, *4, 43–45*
    hotels, 114–116
    shopping, 60, 185–186
San Juan Capistrano, *156*
    restaurants, 173
San Juan Capistrano Library, *156*
San Marino, *4, 42*
San Onofre State Beach, *157*
San Pedro, *4, 34, 36*
Santa Ana restaurants, *173*
Santa Monica, *4, 29–31*
    hotels, 110, 112
    shopping, 59, 184–185
Santa Monica Beach, *75*
Santa Monica Museum of Art, *29*
Santa Monica Pier, *29, 181*
Santa Monica Place Mall, *59, 184*
Santa Monica State Beach, *75, 187*
Santa Rosa Plateau Ecological Reserve, *143–144*
Santa's Village, *134*
Schatsi on Main ✕, *90*
Scuba diving, *73*
    alert, xxix
Senior citizens, *xxii, xxxiii–xxxiv*
Senor Fish ✕, *40*
Seventh Street Marketplace, *54*
Shanes Jewelers (store), *57*
Shauna Stein (store), *57*
Sheraton Anaheim, Hotel, *164*
Sheraton Gateway Hotel at LAX, *113*
Sheraton Grande Hotel, *101*
Sheraton Newport Beach 🏨, *172*
Sheraton Universal 🏨, *114*

Sherman Library and Gardens, 154–155
Sherman Oaks Galleria, 60
Shopping
Beverly Center, 57–58
Beverly Hills, 60–63, 185
Century City, 58
children, 184–186
department stores, 63
Downtown, 54
Hollywood area, 185
Larchmont, 56
Melrose Avenue, 54–56
Orange County, 157–158, 186
Pasadena, 185–186
San Fernando and San Gabriel valleys, 60, 105–186
Santa Monica, 59, 184–185
specialty shops, 63–64
West Los Angeles, 58
Westside area, 155
Westwood, 57
Shoreline Aquatic Park, 37
Shoreline Village, 36, 181
Shutters on the Beach 🏨, 110
Sidewalk Cafe, 31
Sightseeing, xxii–xxiv
Sisley Italian Kitchen ✕, 58
Sisterhood Book Store, 57
Sitar Indian Restaurant, 161
Six Flags MagicMountain (amusement park), 182
Skiing, 71–72
Snorkeling, 73, 158
Snow Summit, 135
Snow Valley, 134
Sofi ✕, 92
Song Long ✕, 161
South Bay Beach Cities, 112
South Coast Botanic Garden, 34
South Coast Plaza, 152, 157
South Coast Repertory Theatre, 152
Southwest Museum, 38, 40, 181
Spago ✕, 5, 88
Special Place, Children's Hands-On Museum, A, 184
Spectator sports, 66–67
Sports
baseball, 66
basketball, 66
bicycling, 68, 158
boxing, 66
fishing, 68–69
football, 66

golf, 67, 69, 158
handball, 71
health clubs, 69–70
hiking, 70
horseback riding, 70–71
ice skating, 71
jet skiing, 73
jogging, 71
racquetball, 71
roller skating, 71
running, 158
sailing, 72
scuba diving, 73
skiing, 71–72
snorkeling, 73, 158
spectator sports, 66–67
surfing, 73, 158–159
tennis, 67, 72, 159
theme trips, xxv
water sports, 72–73, 159–160
windsurfing, 73
winter sports, 71–72
wrestling, 66
Sports Chalet (store), 58
Sportsman's Lodge Hotel, 116
Stage Deli, 58
State parks
El Pueblo de Los Angeles Historical Monument, 11
Malibu Creek State Park, 52
Malibu Lagoon State Park, 33, 75
Will Rogers State Historic Park, 5, 32
Stoval's Inn, 166
Strawberry Peak, 133–134
Students, xxiv, xxxiv
Subways, xxiv
Summerfield Suites Hotel, 103
Sunset Marquis Hotel and Villas, 103
Sunset Strip, 26
Surf and Sand Hotel, 170
Surfing, 73, 158–159
Surfrider Beach/Malibu Lagoon State Beach, 75
Sushi Seiha ✕, 161
Sutton Place Hotel, 171–172

T

Tavola Calda ✕, 94
Taxis, xxiv
Telephones, xxxiv
Television, 121–122
Temecula, 143–144
Temecula Creek Inn, 144

Temecula Historic Museum, 143
Tennis, 67, 72, 159
Tesoro (store), 64
Texas Soul (store), 56
Theaters, 118–119, 173
Theodore (store), 63
Third Street Promenade (shopping mall), 59, 180–181
Thornton winery, Temecula, 143
Tiffany and Company (store), 62
Time After Time, (store), 56
Tommy Tang's ✕, 96
Topanga Canyon State Beach, 75
Tortilla Flats ✕, 170
Tour operators, xxiv–xxv
gay and lesbian travel, xx
group tours, xxv
packages, xxv
Trader Vic's ✕, 96
Tra di Noi ✕, 95
Traffic (store), 57
Transportation
Big Bear/Lake Arrowhead, 137
Catalina Island, 141
around Los Angeles, xvi–xvii, xxii
to Los Angeles, xv–xvi, xxii
Orange County, 175–176
Riverside, 143
Temecula, 144
Trashy Lingerie (store), 58
Travel agencies, xxv
gay and lesbian travel, xx–xxi
Traveler's checks, xxxi
Travelodge, 161
Travel Town, 180
Two Harbors (resort), 140
Two Rodeo Drive (shops), 60

U

Underwater Marine Park at Casino Point, 138
Union Station, 12
Universal City, 43–44
Universal City Hilton and Towers 🏨, 115
Universal City Walk, 43–44, 182
Universal Studios Hollywood, 43–55, 181–182
University of California at Irvine, 152

University of California at Los Angeles, *28*
University of Southern California (USC), *46*

V

Valentino ✕, *94–95*
Van Cleef and Arpels (store), *62*
Vasquez Rocks, *52*
Venice, *4, 31*
Venice Boardwalk, *31*
Venice Municipal Beach, *75–76*
Victoria's Secret (store), *58*
Virginia Robinson Gardens, *48*
Visitor information, *xxvi*
  Orange County, 177

W

Wacko (store), *56*
Warner Brothers Studios, *44*
Wasteland (store), *56*
Watercolors ✕, *167*
Waterfront Hilton ▥, *168*
Water parks, *182*
Water sports, *72–73, 159–160*

Watts Towers, *47*
Wayfarers Chapel, *34*
Weather, *xxvi*
Weathervane II (store), *59*
West Beach Cafe, *84*
Westin Bonaventure Hotel and Suites, *9, 101*
Westin South Coast Plaza ▥, *166–167*
West Los Angeles, *58*
Westside, *4, 24–28*
Westside Pavilion, *58*
Westward Beach/Point Dume State Beach, *75*
Westwood, *28, 57*
Westwood Marquis Hotel and Gardens, *109*
Westwood Memorial Park, *28*
Wherehouse Records (store), *59*
White House ✕, *161, 164*
Wild Blue (store), *56*
Wild Pair (store), *58*
Wild Rivers (water park), *183*
Wild Water Wilderness, *150*
Wilger Company (store), *57*
William S. Hart Regional County Park, *52*

Will Rogers State Beach, *75, 186*
Will Rogers State Historic Park, *5, 32*
Wilmington, *36*
Wilshire Boulevard, *5, 19–24*
Wiltern Theater, *21*
Windsurfing, *73*
Winter sports, *71–72*
Wiring funds, *xxi, xxxi*
Wolfe House, *138*
Wolfgang Puck Cafe, *166*
Woods Cove, *155*
Woody's Boathouse ✕, *136*
Wound and Wound (store), *56*
Wrestling, *66*
Wrigley Memorial and Botanical Garden, *138*
Wyndham Bel Age Hotel, *103*
Wyndham Checkers Hotel, *101*

Y

Yujean Kang's Gourmet Chinese Cuisine, *89*

Z

Zuma Beach County Park, *75*

NOTES

Your guide to a picture-perfect vacation

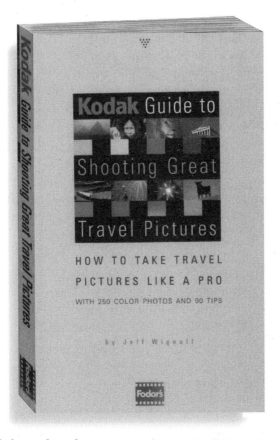

Kodak and Fodor's join together to create the guide that travelers everywhere have been asking for—one that covers the terms and techniques, the equipment and etiquette for taking first-rate travel photographs.

The most authoritative and up-to-date book of its kind, **The Kodak Guide to Shooting Great Travel Pictures** includes over 200 color photographs and spreads on 100 points of photography important to travelers, such as landscape basics, under sea shots, wildlife, city street, close-ups, photographing in museums and more.

$16.50   ($22.95 Canada)

At bookstores everywhere, or call 1-800-533-6478.

Fodor's. The name that means smart travel.™

Fodor's Travel Publications

Available at bookstores everywhere, or call 1–800–533–6478, 24 hours a day.

Gold Guides

U.S.

Alaska

Arizona

Boston

California

Cape Cod, Martha's Vineyard, Nantucket

The Carolinas & the Georgia Coast

Chicago

Colorado

Florida

Hawaii

Las Vegas, Reno, Tahoe

Los Angeles

Maine, Vermont, New Hampshire

Maui

Miami & the Keys

New England

New Orleans

New York City

Pacific North Coast

Philadelphia & the Pennsylvania Dutch Country

The Rockies

San Diego

San Francisco

Santa Fe, Taos, Albuquerque

Seattle & Vancouver

The South

U.S. & British Virgin Islands

USA

Virginia & Maryland

Waikiki

Washington, D.C.

Foreign

Australia & New Zealand

Austria

The Bahamas

Bermuda

Budapest

Canada

Cancún, Cozumel, Yucatán Peninsula

Caribbean

China

Costa Rica, Belize, Guatemala

Cuba

The Czech Republic & Slovakia

Eastern Europe

Egypt

Europe

Florence, Tuscany & Umbria

France

Germany

Great Britain

Greece

Hong Kong

India

Ireland

Israel

Italy

Japan

Kenya & Tanzania

Korea

London

Madrid & Barcelona

Mexico

Montréal & Québec City

Moscow, St. Petersburg, Kiev

The Netherlands, Belgium & Luxembourg

New Zealand

Norway

Nova Scotia, New Brunswick, Prince Edward Island

Paris

Portugal

Provence & the Riviera

Scandinavia

Scotland

Singapore

South America

South Pacific

Southeast Asia

Spain

Sweden

Switzerland

Thailand

Tokyo

Toronto

Turkey

Vienna & the Danube

Fodor's Special-Interest Guides

Branson

Caribbean Ports of Call

The Complete Guide to America's National Parks

Condé Nast Traveler Caribbean Resort and Cruise Ship Finder

Cruises and Ports of Call

Fodor's London Companion

France by Train

Halliday's New England Food Explorer

Healthy Escapes

Italy by Train

Kodak Guide to Shooting Great Travel Pictures

Shadow Traffic's New York Shortcuts and Traffic Tips

Sunday in New York

Sunday in San Francisco

Walt Disney World, Universal Studios and Orlando

Walt Disney World for Adults

Where Should We Take the Kids? California

Where Should We Take the Kids? Northeast

Special Series

Affordables

Caribbean

Europe

Florida

France

Germany

Great Britain

Italy

London

Paris

Fodor's Bed & Breakfasts and Country Inns

America's Best B&Bs

California's Best B&Bs

Canada's Great Country Inns

Cottages, B&Bs and Country Inns of England and Wales

The Mid-Atlantic's Best B&Bs

New England's Best B&Bs

The Pacific Northwest's Best B&Bs

The South's Best B&Bs

The Southwest's Best B&Bs

The Upper Great Lakes' Best B&Bs

The Berkeley Guides

California

Central America

Eastern Europe

Europe

France

Germany & Austria

Great Britain & Ireland

Italy

London

Mexico

Pacific Northwest & Alaska

Paris

San Francisco

Compass American Guides

Arizona

Chicago

Colorado

Hawaii

Hollywood

Las Vegas

Maine

Manhattan

Montana

New Mexico

New Orleans

Oregon

San Francisco

Santa Fe

South Carolina

South Dakota

Southwest

Texas

Utah

Virginia

Washington

Wine Country

Wisconsin

Wyoming

Fodor's Español

California

Caribe Occidental

Caribe Oriental

Gran Bretaña

Londres

Mexico

Nueva York

Paris

Fodor's Exploring Guides

Australia

Boston & New England

Britain

California

Caribbean

China

Egypt

Florence & Tuscany

Florida

France

Germany

Ireland

Israel

Italy

Japan

London

Mexico

Moscow & St. Petersburg

New York City

Paris

Prague

Provence

Rome

San Francisco

Scotland

Singapore & Malaysia

Spain

Thailand

Turkey

Venice

Fodor's Flashmaps

Boston

New York

San Francisco

Washington, D.C.

Fodor's Pocket Guides

Acapulco

Atlanta

Barbados

Jamaica

London

New York City

Paris

Prague

Puerto Rico

Rome

San Francisco

Washington, D.C.

Rivages Guides

Bed and Breakfasts of Character and Charm in France

Hotels and Country Inns of Character and Charm in France

Hotels and Country Inns of Character and Charm in Italy

Short Escapes

Country Getaways in Britain

Country Getaways in France

Country Getaways Near New York City

Fodor's Sports

Golf Digest's Best Places to Play

Skiing USA

USA Today The Complete Four Sport Stadium Guide

Fodor's Vacation Planners

Great American Learning Vacations

Great American Sports & Adventure Vacations

Great American Vacations

National Parks and Seashores of the East

National Parks of the West

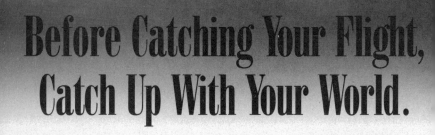

Before Catching Your Flight, Catch Up With Your World.

Fueled by the global resources of CNN and available in major airports across America, CNN Airport Network provides a live source  of current domestic and international news, 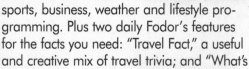 sports, business, weather and lifestyle programming. Plus two daily Fodor's features for the facts you need: "Travel Fact," a useful and creative mix of travel trivia; and "What's

Happening," a comprehensive round-up of upcoming events in major cities around the world.

With CNN Airport Network, you'll never be out of the loop.

Fodor's
TRAVEL FACT
In 1985, 10.7 million Canadians traveled to the United States; by 1994 that number had risen to 17 million.
Source: Fodor's Worldview Travel Update

CNN
Airport Network
A CNN NETWORK

HERE'S YOUR OWN PERSONAL VIEW OF THE WORLD.

Here's the easiest way to get up-to-the-minute, objective, personalized information about what's going on in the city you'll be visiting—before you leave on your trip! Unique information you could get only if you knew someone personally in each of 160 destinations around the world. Everything from special places to dine to local events only a local would know about.

It's all yours—in your Travel Update from Worldview, the leading provider of time-sensitive destination information.

Review the following order form and fill it out by indicating your destination(s)

and travel dates and by checking off up to eight interest categories. Then mail or fax your order form to us, or call your order in. (We're here to help you 24 hours a day.)

Within 48 hours of receiving your order, we'll mail your convenient, pocket-sized custom guide to you, packed with information to make your travel more fun and interesting. And if you're in a hurry, we can even fax it.

Have a great trip with your Fodor's Worldview Travel Update!

Fodor's WORLDVIEW
TRAVEL UPDATE

Customized to your interests and dates of travel

Time-sensitive

Insider perspective

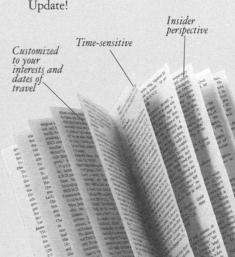

DESTINATIONS

Worldview covers more than 160 destinations worldwide. Choose the destination(s) that match your itinerary from the list below:

Europe
Amsterdam
Athens
Barcelona
Berlin
Brussels
Budapest
Copenhagen
Dublin
Edinburgh
Florence
Frankfurt
French Riviera
Geneva
Glasgow
Lausanne
Lisbon
London
Madrid
Milan
Moscow
Munich
Oslo
Paris
Prague
Provence
Rome
Salzburg
Seville
St. Petersburg
Stockholm
Venice
Vienna
Zurich

**United States
(Mainland)**
Albuquerque
Atlanta
Atlantic City
Baltimore
Boston
Branson, MO
Charleston, SC
Chicago
Cincinnati
Cleveland
Dallas/Ft. Worth
Denver
Detroit
Houston
Indianapolis
Kansas City
Las Vegas
Los Angeles
Memphis
Miami
Milwaukee
Minneapolis/St. Paul
Nashville
New Orleans
New York City
Orlando
Palm Springs
Philadelphia
Phoenix
Pittsburgh

Portland
Reno/Lake Tahoe
St. Louis
Salt Lake City
San Antonio
San Diego
San Francisco
Santa Fe
Seattle
Tampa
Washington, DC

Alaska
Alaskan Destinations

Hawaii
Honolulu
Island of Hawaii
Kauai
Maui

Canada
Quebec City
Montreal
Ottawa
Toronto
Vancouver

Bahamas
Abaco
Eleuthera/
   Harbour Island
Exuma
Freeport
Nassau &
   Paradise Island

Bermuda
Bermuda Countryside
Hamilton

**British Leeward
Islands**
Anguilla
Antigua & Barbuda
St. Kitts & Nevis

British Virgin Islands
Tortola & Virgin
   Gorda

**British Windward
Islands**
Barbados
Dominica
Grenada
St. Lucia
St. Vincent
Trinidad & Tobago

Cayman Islands
The Caymans

Dominican Republic
Santo Domingo

Dutch Leeward Islands
Aruba
Bonaire
Curacao

**Dutch Windward
Island**
St. Maarten/St. Martin

French West Indies
Guadeloupe
Martinique
St. Barthelemy

Jamaica
Kingston
Montego Bay
Negril
Ocho Rios

Puerto Rico
Ponce
San Juan

Turks & Caicos
Grand Turk/
   Providenciales

U.S. Virgin Islands
St. Croix
St. John
St. Thomas

Mexico
Acapulco
Cancun & Isla Mujeres
Cozumel
Guadalajara
Ixtapa & Zihuatanejo
Los Cabos
Mazatlan
Mexico City
Monterrey
Oaxaca
Puerto Vallarta

South/Central America
Buenos Aires
Caracas
Rio de Janeiro
San Jose, Costa Rica
Sao Paulo

Middle East
Istanbul
Jerusalem

**Australia & New
Zealand**
Auckland
Melbourne
South Island
Sydney

China
Beijing
Guangzhou
Shanghai

Japan
Kyoto
Nagoya
Osaka
Tokyo
Yokohama

Pacific Rim/Other
Bali
Bangkok
Hong Kong & Macau
Manila
Seoul
Singapore
Taipei

INTERESTS

For your personalized Travel Update, choose the eight (8) categories you're most interested in from the following list:

1.	**Business Services**	Fax & Overnight Mail, Computer Rentals, Protocol, Secretarial, Messenger, Translation Services
	Dining	
2.	**All-Day Dining**	Breakfast & Brunch, Cafes & Tea Rooms, Late-Night Dining
3.	**Local Cuisine**	Every Price Range — from Budget Restaurants to the Special Splurge
4.	**European Cuisine**	Continental, French, Italian
5.	**Asian Cuisine**	Chinese, Far Eastern, Japanese, Other
6.	**Americas Cuisine**	American, Mexican & Latin
7.	**Nightlife**	Bars, Dance Clubs, Casinos, Comedy Clubs, Ethnic, Pubs & Beer Halls
8.	**Entertainment**	Theater — Comedy, Drama, Musicals, Dance, Ticket Agencies
9.	**Music**	Classical, Opera, Traditional & Ethnic, Jazz & Blues, Pop, Rock
10.	**Children's Activites**	Events, Attractions
11.	**Tours**	Local Tours, Day Trips, Overnight Excursions
12.	**Exhibitions, Festivals & Shows**	Antiques & Flower, History & Cultural, Art Exhibitions, Fairs & Craft Shows, Music & Art Festivals
13.	**Shopping**	Districts & Malls, Markets, Regional Specialties
14.	**Fitness**	Bicycling, Health Clubs, Hiking, Jogging
15.	**Recreational Sports**	Boating/Sailing, Fishing, Golf, Skiing, Snorkeling/Scuba, Tennis/Racket
16.	**Spectator Sports**	Auto Racing, Baseball, Basketball, Golf, Football, Horse Racing, Ice Hockey, Soccer
17.	**Event Highlights**	The best of what's happening during the dates of your trip.
18.	**Sightseeing**	Sights, Buildings, Monuments
19.	**Museums**	Art, Cultural
20.	**Transportation**	Taxis, Car Rentals, Airports, Public Transportation
21.	**General Info**	Overview, Holidays, Currency, Tourist Info

Please note that content will vary by season, destination, and length of stay.

Name

Address

City   **State**   **Country**   **ZIP**

Tel #   (   )   -   **Fax #**   (   )   -

Title of this Fodor's guide:

Store and location where guide was purchased:

INDICATE YOUR DESTINATIONS/DATES: You can order up to three (3) destinations from the previous page. Fill in your arrival and departure dates for each destination. **Your Travel Update itinerary (all destinations selected) cannot exceed 30 days from beginning to end.**

		Month	Day		Month	Day
(Sample) **LONDON**	From:	**6**	/ **21**	To:	**6**	/ **30**
1	From:		/	To:		/
2	From:		/	To:		/
3	From:		/	To:		/

CHOOSE YOUR INTERESTS: Select up to eight (8) categories from the list of interest categories shown on the previous page and circle the numbers below:

1 2 3 4 5 6 7 8 9 10 11 12 13 14 15 16 17 18 19 20 21

CHOOSE WHEN YOU WANT YOUR TRAVEL UPDATE DELIVERED (Check one):
❑ Please send my Travel Update immediately.
❑ Please hold my order until a few weeks before my trip to include the most up-to-date information.
Completed orders will be sent within 48 hours. Allow 7–10 days for U.S. mail delivery.

ADD UP YOUR ORDER HERE. SPECIAL OFFER FOR FODOR'S PURCHASERS ONLY!

	Suggested Retail Price	Your Price	This Order
First destination ordered	$ 9.95	$ 7.95	$ 7.95
Second destination (if applicable)	$ 6.95	$ 4.95	+
Third destination (if applicable)	$ 6.95	$ 4.95	+

DELIVERY CHARGE (Check one and enter amount below)

	Within U.S. & Canada	Outside U.S. & Canada
First Class Mail	❑ $2.50	❑ $5.00
FAX	❑ $5.00	❑ $10.00
Priority Delivery	❑ $15.00	❑ $27.00

ENTER DELIVERY CHARGE FROM ABOVE: + [ ]

TOTAL: $ [ ]

METHOD OF PAYMENT IN U.S. FUNDS ONLY (Check one):
❑ AmEx   ❑ MC   ❑ Visa   ❑ Discover   ❑ Personal Check (U. S. & Canada only)
❑ Money Order/International Money Order

Make check or money order payable to: Fodor's Worldview Travel Update

Credit Card _/_/_/_/_/_/_/_/_/_/_/_/_/_/_/_/ **Expiration Date:**_/_

Authorized Signature

SEND THIS COMPLETED FORM WITH PAYMENT TO:
Fodor's Worldview Travel Update, 114 Sansome Street, Suite 700, San Francisco, CA 94104

OR CALL OR FAX US 24-HOURS A DAY
Telephone **1-800-799-9609** • Fax **1-800-799-9619** (From within the U.S. & Canada)
(Outside the U.S. & Canada: Telephone 415-616-9988 • Fax 415-616-9989)

(Please have this guide in front of you when you call so we can verify purchase.)
Code: FTG   Offer valid until 12/31/97